Sunday, December 7, 1941

The Japanese dropped bombs on an unsuspecting naval base in Honolulu, Hawaii. Pearl Harbor is a name that will always be synonymous with the beginning of WWII. It was 7:55 a.m., a beautiful Sunday morning, when Japanese aircraft appeared in the sky. Through a series of errors and misinformation, they arrived undetected and wreaked havoc and destruction upon the US naval forces stationed here. Three aircraft carriers were out to sea and thus saved from the attack.

The facts: 2,403 were killed
              1,143 were wounded
              18 ships were sunk or run aground

              Yesterday, December 7, 1941—a date which will live in infamy—the United States of America was suddenly and deliberately attacked by naval and air forces of the empire of Japan.
              —President Franklin D. Roosevelt

The United States of America declared war on the Empire of Japan on December 8, 1941. Many young men rushed to join the military.

The USS *Arizona* remains sunken, still commissioned, in the harbor. It is a memorial today. The still leaking oil is called the tears of the fallen soldiers who remain entombed in their final resting place.

The USS *Arizona* Memorial was established on May 30, 1962, to remember the 1,102 sailors and marines killed on the USS *Arizona*. The tour guide at the memorial stated that Elvis Presley played a huge part in donating money to the USS *Arizona* Memorial. He waived his $5,000 appearance fee and wrote a $5,000 check too. He raised and donated $65,000 for the memorial. That was a lot of money in the 1950s. He declined a statue of himself that the organization wanted to build for his donations. He said, "This is not to honor me; these soldiers are the heroes." He didn't want any of the glory. Colonel Parker, his manager, also wrote a $5,000 check, with a nudge from Elvis.

Paul Kennedy—US Navy
Pearl Harbor Survivor

"I was looking up at him, and he was looking down at me. He had his canopy down."

Paul had just finished filming an interview for the History Channel a few weeks prior to my visit, so it was an honor to be able to sit down and visit with him. It was an emotional and humbling experience to listen to all the pain that still remains with Paul after more than seventy-five years. His story is peppered with references to God and how he credits God for looking after him and keeping him safe.

Paul had just turned twenty-one years old on December 2, 1941. He was stationed on the USS *Sacramento*, a gun boat, docked at Pearl Harbor. Paul entered the naval reserves in 1938 at the navy armory on Thirtieth Street in Indianapolis. He was called into active service in 1940.

There were about 275 guys who had all been together in the reserves. The ship sailed down the St. Lawrence River; in Boston, Massachusetts; and in Norfolk, Virginia. There were stops at Guantanamo Bay, Cuba; the Panama Canal; San Diego, California; and ending at Pearl Harbor, Hawaii. They arrived in Pearl Harbor about August 15, 1941. He was at Pearl Harbor from August to December, just enjoying his time in Hawaii.

On the night before the blitz, he was on duty from midnight until four a.m. "I was relieved by a former football player and stayed up and drank coffee with him until about five thirty a.m. His plan was to sleep all day Sunday; however, that plan was not to be. Well, the Japs came in, and the general quarters alarm went off. I thought it was a drill."

His buddy, Brown, threw the covers off of him and said, "Kennedy, come on, the Japs are bombing the hell out of us. Go to your battle station. Get your gas mask and your helmet."

"I knew he was not joking. I didn't even put my pants on. I ran up the ladder to the deck above."

Lester Brown – US Army
"I was lucky enough to survive the battle of Okinawa."

Les went into the army in August 1944, at Ft. Ben in Indianapolis, when he was eighteen years old. "They got our clothes and boxed them up to send them back to our parents," Lester remembered. He took the oath of induction two days later. He went to training camp at Ft. Hood, Texas (IRTC camp). This included seventeen weeks of basic training, which is very strenuous. In December he was given a ten-day leave; he took the train to Indianapolis, then the bus on to Paoli, where he lived.

Lee Allen was one of Lester's best friends. They inducted together and went to high school together. They even stayed together at the same camp. Lee's death would affect Les all his life.

The next stop for Les was Ft. Ord, California, and then Ft. Lawton, Washington, for additional training. As a young man who had not been many places in his life, passing Pearl Harbor in Hawaii was something. He saw the wreckage from the Japanese bombing. He was stationed at Schofield Barracks in the city of Honolulu on Oahu. After passing the pineapple fields, Les said, "I thought it was one of the most beautiful places I'd ever seen."

Les said he remembered K rations—Spam, hash, and pork and beans. Les said, "The pork and beans were a treat."

Leyte, Philippines—January 1945

Les was assigned to the 96th Infantry Division as a replacement. He was in K Company, 383rd Infantry. He spent some time on Leyte shortly before the island was secured. The 96th was nicknamed the "Deadeyes" while in the Philippines. Les said, "They got that name because, well, we were such good shooters…sharp shooters."

Lewis Cowden—US Navy
"…we were hit by a kamikaze, killing forty-two of our guys."

What did you think about Pearl Harbor?

"I didn't think about it. I had an automobile, and that's all I was interested in at that time. I was seventeen years old and very immature. It wasn't until my senior year in high school that I thought about it. I was also running out of gasoline stamps!

"On the first battles of the war, we tried to be soldiers and go out help the [enemy] injured. They would lay there with a hand grenade, and when a soldier would try to help them, they would blow up our people. So, we became animals, too," said Lewis. Fortunately it was not part of what he had to deal with, since he was in the navy. He was glad he wasn't a marine.

Lewis enlisted in the navy in January 1943 under the Minority Cruise program. The Portland Tribune defined the Minority Cruise program as, "a program where people could enlist at seventeen years old and be discharged before their twenty-first birthday." He was seventeen years old at the time and then turned eighteen on February 15, 1943. He completed boot camp at Great Lakes naval base.

December 1943 was the first time he went to sea, on the brand-new destroyer escort ship the USS *Whitehurst DE634*. He described this as his "shakedown cruise" on the ship and was surprised "that the navy sent them out in such rough weather. It was twenty experienced seamen and a hundred and sixty kids."

The shakedown cruise was a time when a new ship was tested and tried out. The *Whitehurst* was named after a sailor who was killed in the Battle of Savo Island, off Guadalcanal, in August 1942. Lewis was onboard this ship for two and a half years. The USS *Whitehurst* was involved in battles during WWII, Korea, and Vietnam

This illustration from James Fenimore Cooper's The Pathfinder *served as the school logo for many years.*

Blaze a Trail

The History
of Pathfinder School 1972-2008

Do not follow where the path may lead.
Go, instead, where there is no path and blaze a trail.

First Edition

ISBN: 978-0-9726273-5-1
Photographs in this book are from the collections of:
Pathfinder School, Reed Zitting, Sharon Rutkowski, Adam Begley, Michelle Johnston, and Arthur and Nancy Baxter.

Hawthorne Publishing 15601 Oak Rd Carmel IN 46033
317-867-5183   www.hawthornepub.comtt

The Pathfinder History book committee: Adam Begley, Sharon Rutkowski, Nancy and Art Baxter, Reed Ziting, Ellen Northway;

This history is dedicated to the thousands of children and their families, teachers, and school personnel who have been enriched by the Pathfinder School experience.

Pathfinder's education has never been confined to the classroom—students and faculty ranged outdoors in the middle of some of the most beautiful scenery in the midwest, including the 1920 original log cabins which are the school's classrooms.

Pathfinder School opened in September 1972 with 64 students.
The tradition of raising the flag and ringing the school bell at the
opening ceremony was begun by Arthur Baxter on the south lawn.
The first flag was presented to the school by Mr. and Mrs. Roger
Watson and had flown over the capitol in Washington, D.C. This
flag-raising photo is from the late 1970s.

There was no day school in Traverse City, no alternative to public education, and the potential was there. Traverse City was already the home of innovative thinking, attracting perceptive and interesting people. Surely there would be enough parents who could support a day school which was set right in the beauty of the scenery near the bays and which would allow for the best in academics and creative, individualized education. At some point, now not remembered, Art and Nancy Baxter decided to found a day school in Traverse City. Discussions evolved gradually around the dinner table. Five of their children were enthusiastic and wanted to be part of founding such a school; they assumed John would continue his studies, taking his junior and senior years at Interlochen.

Six teachers at Leelanau began to join in the talk about the possibility of a day school in Traverse in the fall of 1971. David Waltrip was teaching earth science, Alan Brownlee was a much-loved teacher of history, and Art and Nancy were English teachers. All of these people had experienced success at the school but were ready to leave an insitution that at that time seemed a little conservative in its orientation for them. Mary Lynn Watson was teaching chemistry. Janet Jackson was an art teacher at Leelanau.

The founding group of teachers was operating in the milieu of exploding ideas about the ideal way to educate children—a revolution, really, in educational theory. To explain a little, the book *Summerhill* had come out in 1968, three years before this time, and English classes and intellectual book groups avidly read it. High school students loved the book. Many will remember it to this day. To tell its message in brief form, Summerhill was a school in England which had no rules. Its teaching and learning philosophy was that children had within themselves the potential to learn, that if freed of restrictive curriculum, they would seek their own learning at their own pace. There were no required classes, no attendance taken, no report cards. Kids simply came and learned or didn't learn as they wanted to. It sounded perfect to many teenagers in this Viet Nam War/Green America early 70s.

Free schools were set up across the country and in Michigan.

They had a wide variety of arts and pottery and film-making classes, not much emphasis on math, lots of free-writing opportunities without "restrictive" grammar corrections, and other innovative learning situations. A little less radical was the open classroom movement. In the 1960s public schools across America began asking architects to design schools in the round, with a learning center (library) in the middle and classrooms without doors around the perimeter, like a circle of wagons with the chuck wagon in the center.

EDUCATIONAL PHILOSOPHY BEHIND PATHFINDER'S OPENING

Throughout this section, we'll be presenting excerpts from a round-table discussion held to record the school's founding history in 1984.

From that tape, here is Art Baxter on the founding ideals:

Writers of former times like John Dewey, Maria Montessori, and Jean Piaget were written about in new ways, and books like A.S. Neil's *Summerhill* were discussed in faculty rooms across America. I think Pathfinder certainly has to be considered in that environment. It was an opportunity to sort out some priorities on the part of educators. Pathfinder was set up to focus on the specific needs of each individual student as opposed to what may be administratively convenient, maybe even economically beneficial and certainly not in any way tied to a set pattern. We felt that students had resources within to educate themselves. This would be especially true in class settings of no more than 15 students. A lot more trust, a lot more responsibility could be given to each child for his or her own educational process. That did not mean that the kids did nothing or only what they felt like doing. Far from it; we were not a "free school" or an open school even though those conceps were prevalent at the time.

ANOTHER VIEW FROM THE CO-DIRECTOR-TO-BE

Art and I had a dream while working in other schools of an ideal school, where students were affectionately encouraged and also had an excellent education in a very interesting environment. For us it was a frankly Christian commitment to try to serve others in this way.

We were influenced by these ideas, but they were only one half of the picture. We had good classical educations, Art earning his B.A. in English at Wabash College, M.A. in English at Butler, and I had a B.A. and M.A. from Butler and a half a doctorate in English from the University of Arizona. We admired strong scholarship, ourselves taught high school students the humanities, asked them to memorize the presidents and the English kings in order, and the prologue to the *Canterbury Tales*. We wanted our graduates to be able to read early in first grade, to be the best spellers in the county as fourth graders, to belong to the National Honor Society. And we had been teaching enough to know that ultimate responsibility in a classroom needs to rest in capable, understanding teachers, not students. It was just as simple as that. Still, we wanted to incorporate some of the new ideas for creative learning into our school. How far was the question. I think we had an advantage in starting a school because Art was serving as headmaster at the Leelanau School when these discussions began. He knew where and how far to take us.

The four originally in discussions about starting a school soon parted company. Alan Brownlee went on to other good teaching positions in the South and East and did not open the school with the group, though his good ideas were a part of the way the school was set up. David Waltrip became assistant director and stayed with the school two years before moving on.

That is slightly ahead of the story. We need to discuss how the founders got from the idea to open a school in Traverse City in the late fall of 1971 to that first day, when Mr. Baxter raised the flag at the top of the hill in September 1972 at 11930 W. Bayshore, Traverse City, Michigan.

As soon as the Baxters had determined as a family to try to start a school and talked to teachers about being part of a potential founding group, before any search was made for suitable grounds, the Baxters ran an ad in The *Traverse City Record Eagle,* and a reporter wrote an article about the possibility of a new day school in Traverse City. A meeting would be held at the Holiday Inn on a Sunday afternoon: a new school was forming, with emphasis on individualized learning and strong academics in a beautiful setting.

As they waited for the meeting day to arrive, the potential teachers could talk about what might happen—if the school became a reality (and that wasn't a sure thing. It depended on that meeting). The "maybe we'll be teaching there" teachers: David Waltrip, Art and Nancy Baxter, Jan Jackson, and Mary Lynn Watson, would be speaking at the meeting to make the learning plans concrete—as concrete as they could be when they didn't even know if anybody was interested.

About fifty parents and children assembled to hear the presentation. The message: "School should be different; it should be interesting and rewarding and enjoyable and here's what we plan to do to make it so." When it was over, seventeen parents signed up, including all four children of the Clancey family. It was a start. Art and Nancy were announced as co-directors, Nancy to supervise both Lower and Upper School and teach English and history, Art to be general (business) manager and teach as well.

In 1984 some of the students and teachers present at the founding sat down to reminisce about the early days: From that tape:

> At that Holiday Inn meeting we had a wide representation of parents, a lot of them had kids who for one reason or another weren't fitting into the public schools, either because the schools were going too slow or too fast for them. Others were sort of avant garde people who didn't like all the regimentation and lived on farms and did natural food things, and wanted to

get into what was called at that time "alternative schools." So it was a variety of people. Nancy Baxter

The school was on the first, tentative steps to reality. As preliminary curriculum talks were underway, the group needed, of course, to have grounds for the school. Riding out one snowy day on M-22 just before Thanksgiving, Dave Waltrip, Art, and Nancy saw a winding road leading up a hill. What a nice setting that would be, but there was no indication that it was even being considered for sale. Why should it be? Passing what appeared to be a caretaker's cottage at the foot of the hill, they drove up to see log cabins overlooking two bodies of water: Grand Traverse Bay on the east and Cedar Lake on the west. Pine and birch stood all around; there were trails down to the lake.

Who owned this? Maybe they would consider selling. It seemed about perfect. They stopped at a residence near the road and knocked on the door. The woman who answered listened to the inquiry and nodded her head. "It has just been placed on the market this last weekend. The sign is not up as yet. It is owned by Mr. Meuwenberg who owns the uniform laundry."

An inspection with the owner was the next step. Art and Nancy Baxter avoided the narrow stone stairs going up the hill, covered with ice and snow, and drove to the top, hoping the tires wouldn't slip. Close up they saw the log structure, the central summer house.

"This home was built by the Kier family of American Standard Plumbing," Mr. Meuwenberg told them. That was interesting. Everybody knew their bathroom fixtures. Meuwenberg went on to say the home was built in the early 1920s with tamarack logs shipped in from Canada. "They are some of the largest logs in the area, similar to some in homes on Northport Point."

He added that after the Kiers had left, another family had happily used the house for some years, eventually selling it to him. Now he was ready to sell the entire grounds and building complex complete with furniture inside.

The Baxters paid the asking price, $125,000 for 22 acres fronting Cedar Lake and Lake Michigan. It included the caretaker's house, the guest house down a path from the main cabin, and the boathouse on Cedar Lake.

And the name of the new school? It was at this time, with the grounds secured and lying like a beautiful panorama of the best in Traverse City's inspiring scenery, that the new group began to consider appropriate names. Nancy opted strongly for "Apple Hill" because of the apple trees which grew on the side of the road leading up to the library building. They were old-fashioned snow apples that would in the future be gathered on many autumn days for cooking by various classes. But Dave Waltrip, Art, and other teachers lobbied for a name from James Fenimore Cooper's novel *The Pathfinder*. The early American novel was set in territory which included the Grand Traverse region, and the book emphasized individuality and strength of character. Nancy did not particularly like that name because as a teacher of American literature she believed Fenimore Cooper's writing was outdated and hard to follow. But Pathfinder the school became.

Now the founders were ready to get really serious with the plans for a K-12 school in Traverse City, to open the next fall. The time did not seem extremely short to them, though later it definitely proved to be just that.

The first step in actually setting up an operating school (or reorganizing it in later days) is to have long and detailed talks with the Independent School Association of the Central States, ISACS. This is the midwestern branch of the National Association of Independent Schools in Boston. A really stellar group, ISACS encourages the highest of standards, looking for models to such schools as Cranbrook Academy in Bloomfield Hills and Park Tudor School in Indianapolis. Jim Henderson was head of ISACS at its headquarters in Chicago. He and his wife Ruth made a trip to Traverse City to see what this group of private school teachers were up to. Other schools were planning to start up in Michigan with such names as "Dawn Treader" and the "Japhet School"; Pathfinder was by far the most ambitious. The founding group wished to establish a long-term, viable prep school with many innovative learning techniques, but one able to send students to the finest colleges in the nation.

Jim and Ruth were honest. This would not be Easy Street.

"It will take $500,000 to get this school going," Jim said. "The grounds are beautiful, but these buildings are not fit for students. There are claw-foot bathtubs in these bathrooms—lavender and pink. These need to be boys' and girls' restrooms instead. You will be hiring an architect to redo these buildings? Put in insulation so they are winterized? Central heating? Make these screened-in porches into small classrooms? And not just any remodeling will do. This facility must be brought to code. Local school building codes, state regulations, fire marshal's code—all of that. And you will have to pass state curriculum requirements for public schools in Michigan. All teachers must be certified in this state. Then, if all goes as we say, we would visit you with an ISACS team for preliminary certification."

What was all of this? The founders wanted to have a school with minimum regulations. Nancy Baxter remembers:

> That was not possible, and there were good reasons for it. Schoolchildren cannot live on romantic dreams but must be safe, warm, and well educated. Some months later when the state fire marshal visited our facility to pass it, and when I asked him about all the regulations to close the beautiful fireplaces and so forth, he said, "You wouldn't ask about these regulations if you had seen a school fire like I have."
>
> That was all he needed to say.

Graheck, Bell and Cline became the architects for the total remodeling of the school, a job superlatively done and standing to this very day much as it was done at that time in 1972. They observed all the codes, put siding on the central cabin, now called the library/school, re-roofed all the buildings, built a kitchen for the cooking projects the teachers envisioned, transformed the main bath into a modern-looking, fully equipped chem lab, and closed off the fireplaces in a remarkably short time. Baxters bought the grounds in early winter of 1971 and opened school right after Labor Day 1972.

How and why could the school open so quickly, in what seems to be an almost impossibly short time? First of all, it seemed important once an idea for a school has been presented to have a school ready in the fall. A lot of credit must go to Bob Bell of the architectural firm, who believed in what was going on and thought drawings could be done, codes observed, and work started and completed in two buildings by early September. And of course the other things which needed to be done as prescribed by the goals and dreams of the founding teachers and the master plan of ISACS could go forward simultaneously with the revamping of the buildings.

And after all they were not building a new school. The new kitchen was to be where the old one stood without too much change, the bathroom plumbing was in the right spots, no walls were being changed. It is true that two screened-in porches would be made into small classrooms, but that could be done within the time constraints. Insulating and heating and providing adequate water and new electrical systems, and piping in gas for the former bathroom that would be a small chemistry lab, were, of course, more challenging, and that is where major attention had to go.

While they were accumulating vast piles of building rubbish and trucks were lumbering up the hill and down again as winter ended and spring began, the most obvious things had to happen—students had to sign up and pay and teachers needed to go under contract.

A problem surfaced right away. All teachers needed to be certified to obtain state accreditation, which was a must for the first-class school they were considering. The problem was that Nancy was not certified. She had not needed to be up to this point. She took the couple of classes needed for certification over the summer and did student teaching at Old Mission School in the kindergarten. "I discovered in that process," she said, "that destiny had not decreed that I should directly teach four-year-olds in a school setting."

Faculty who had preliminarily set their courses with us were put under contract. From Leelanau: Mary Lynn Watson, chemistry and math; David Waltrip, earth science; Jan Jackson, art; Art Baxter, seventh grade subjects and sociology; and Nancy Baxter all four years of high school humanities and beginning Spanish. Steve Bowman from the Leelanau staff soon came and "moonlighted" for three days a week for Spanish.

For the Lower School the lineup eventually read: Mary Breu, kindergarten; Patty Olson, 1/2 (which were combined); Tom Terry, 3/4 Alan Middleton, coming from Northport elementary school, 5/6.

Since the group had opted for strong academics to prepare students for any colleges they wished to attend, Latin was even included in the curriculum; Dorothy Lane, a long-time Latin teacher, took on that assignment. Mary Breu's husband Jerry became the faithful, ingenious, and constantly busy maintenance chief.

The founders believed it was important to work with, and keep informed, Traverse City public school people. At frequent intervals they told friends in the administration about what was happening, so they would not feel unnecessary competition from the new school.

Art Baxter goes on with the story:

> Meanwhile, our own children, constantly with us running up and down the hills and helping us put dinghies on Cedar Lake, were getting excited. John Baxter told us he wished to leave Interlochen and come with the rest of the family to the new school. It was a rewarding moment for us personally and his presence as a veteran of a great private school educational program as well as a leader was an asset to the school. Jim would be in seventh grade, Marybeth a sophomore, Janet a freshman, and on the day before school opened Skip (Art Jr.), who had been a holdout for Old Mission where he had friends and was happy, told us he wished to enter Pathfinder's sixth grade. Dan would be in fourth grade with Mr. Terry.
>
> With funds we had come into recently and which were a one-time shot, we funded the renovation of the school, along with those who donated to a capital funds drive conducted

over the summer, goal $40,000. As expenditures mounted and time ran out, we decided to directly work on the guest cottage, which was being refurbished for the kindergarten and first and second grades. My brother and I and the older boys laid carpet and painted the cottage, which had already been fitted for heat, insulation, and new plumbing.

Summer proceeded. The site for the soccer field at the front of the property was surveyed by an engineer, and with some help from the Baxter boys moving rocks out of the field, and others helping, a basic field took shape. The tennis courts got underway, exposing arrowheads from Ojibwa camps of the past. David Waltrip undertook the refurbishing of the caretaker's cottage at the foot of the hill with an allowance of $5,000. He wished to live in it with his family. It stands today basically as he and his on-the-cheap subcontractors built it over that summer. The kitchen was eventually turned into offices.

Students and faculty who had been present at the opening of the school continue their reminiscing. This is the late Mary Lynn Watson, chemistry and math teacher until the mid-1980s:

> The chem. Lab. . . now this was really neat. Looking at other schools around the area, public schools and private ones, I decided what we needed. Some generous individual had provided a $5,000 grant to furnish and stock the lab. We were to locate the chem lab in what was an old dressing room and bathroom, a small space allocated, but we managed to pile a lot in there. The old clawfoot lavender bathroom (remember this was the American Standard Plumbing family) was taken over, the fireplace covered over, and everything stripped to become a lab.

The week before the opening of school there was still a pile of trash about fifteen feet high in the middle of the library building. Parents were coming in for interviews and had to be steered around the pile of trash. They needed to use their imaginations to conceive

Art and Nancy and the other teachers had searching discussions with David Waltrip just before opening, and during the first year, as to how far to go with the open or free school concept. David was sold on the "teacher as facilitator only" concept. He believed schools should only teach students "how to learn," and who could disagree with that concept? The question that followed that statement was "How to learn about WHAT?" It was probably settled the day before school opened, when teachers had a high school planning meeting and without much discussion just allocated rooms to certain subjects and teachers at certain times in the old traditional way. Summerhill notwithstanding, so much for student choice about where and when.

On a clear early autumn morning, September 5, 1972, Art Baxter assembled the children of Pathfinder School and raised the American flag, a flag which had flown over Washington, D.C., given by Polly Watson, one of Mr. Terry's 3/4 students. "You are all pioneers," he told the sixty-four students who formed the first student body.

There was a lot that was "open classroom" and "a good deal of freedom during the academic day," as the founding brochures described it. Jeff Lawson reports:

> Especially the first few years there were animals to care for. Later on that situation became somewhat different, but the first couple of years there were animals in every room, in addition to a fairly large rabbit pen and a flock of guinea hens, some other animals. There were ducks, and a goat just tethered outside the office. There was some trouble with him. A lot of the students would think you could be real friendly with him and then the goat didn't seem to like that. A young student named Beth Nutting was chased by that goat several times.

Both students and teachers seemed to thrive on the informal, home-like atmosphere. Jeff Lawson again:

> Pathfinder was very much a family environment. There

was very little antagonism between the teachers and the students. The teachers were almost like older relatives. You knew that they cared about what was going on with you and you didn't feel as if you were forcing yourself on them as in a traditional school setting—you had to be there. It wasn't the same thing as a job for them. They really cared about what was going on.

One idea from the free-school, open classroom movement was one of the innovations of that first year. Alan Middleton, who had taught in the Northport school system, wished to try a Summerhill-type of experiment with fifth and sixth graders. He served as a resource facilitator, providing books for those who wished to learn, steering lessons. Jeff Lawson and Skip Baxter, working together, began in the eighth grade math book and were done with all the work in it in about three months, then began looking for something else to do.

By the end of the second semester, the totally open classroom idea was abandoned as impractical, and Mr. Middleton began teaching a more standard curriculum. But all the freedom and ingenuity and creativity the open school concepts suggested became integral parts of the school.

First and second grade curriculum in year one was centered around an enriched alphabet learning-to-read program. Each week would bring a different letter into focus, and children would pronounce and understand this letter and its place in reading. Thus during "Mr. M's" week students might bring in objects beginning with M. Students ate candies or other treats which could be identified with Mr. M. A parade through the Upper School brought the ideas to all the students.

The grounds provided many opportunities the first years of Pathfinder, and thereafter for "outdoor learning." Mr. Terry's third and fourth graders planted a garden on the lower level with pumpkins, corn, and green beans, then used the large-jack-o-lanterns carved from their field pumpkins for a contest the whole school enjoyed. Both Upper and Lower School teachers took their students to the woods to tap maple trees in late winter, then boiled the sap for hours until they had maple syrup—and an all-school pancake supper.

Chicks hatched in class, field trips were frequent, and students studied nature in the woods and at the two beaches of Pathfinder School.

A group led by student Tom Kurtz swept snow off Cedar Lake and practiced ice hockey; and the second year an automobile engine provided power for a rope tow on the hill just beyond the upper garden for lunchtime and activity period (potpourri) skiing. Quite soon a path was laid out through the woods for cross-country skiing and eventually a sauna was built, placed midway so everybody could warm up.

Other types of outdoor recreation, these unauthorized, included smoking (banned on the grounds) in the woods. One former student reports, "There were several places where people went out to smoke cigarettes, and Mr. Baxter would promptly go out and catch them. One high schooler had a place called The Pit. It was funny because that place was so close to the school that you could see him from the art building when that was put up the first year."

In general in those days in this closely knit community, with parents often sacrificing to send their children to a private school and a good deal of respect for the situation, as science teacher Mary Lynn Watson reported in the 1980s, "I would say that for the most part students observed pretty closely the strong rules against smoking, drinking, and drugs on that campus. If they felt they had to smoke, it wasn't an obvious thing—going out to the big oak tree or behind that new art building during lunch or something like that."

That reference indicates that construction was continuing at the school. Jerry Breu and Upper School students did significant finishing on the art building, which opened in the fall of '73 and is today Lower School classrooms. George Carr became pottery instructor in that building and added variety to the arts offerings.

Curriculum was rather traditional. It was really the way these typical things were taught. Here is an example of one departure:

The Humanities at Pathfinder

During almost all of the time of the Upper School at Pathfinder, four years of a double-credit class called Humanities was required of all students:

Year One: World History, World Literature:

Text: *The Humanities in Three Cities* (Athens, Renaissance Florence, and New York)

Enrichment activities: Neolithic dinner outdoors, utilizing purchased domestic rabbit for stew; ingredients from Pathfinder garden planted by Lower Schoolers; and apples from the trees on the hillside; Renaissance role-play dinner.

Year Two: American History and American Literature: Texts of both American lit and history, reading of *Huckleberry Finn* and other American literary classics.

Enrichment activities: Trips to Indian burial grounds in Northport and sometimes Gettysburg and Washington, D.C.

Year Three: English History, English Literature Text: *British Literature* with outside sources for history. Enrichment reading of English novels.

Year Four: Government and AP European Literature

In February 1973 Carlotta Schroeder became the first graduate of Pathfinder, her graduation celebrated with a little gathering and cake in the library. Carlotta planned to attend Michigan State.

Both Upper School and Lower School students attended to wish Carlotta well after her one semester study at the school.

HISTORY AFLOAT

The first "History Afloat," in the summer of 1973, took the *Danny B* sailboat from Cape Hatteras to Chesapeake Bay, New York Harbor, the Hudson River, and the Erie Canal, reading books and having classes on the bow of the boat as they went. With Mr. Baxter skippering and tasks divided among all the crew, students earned history and English credit. Students from both Interlochen and Pathfinder participated.

From an article in the ISACS magazine, Spring 1974, on experiential learning:

We were fortunate; to learn about "colonial settlement patterns" we were able to take our students to the Atlantic seaboard, traveling all the way from Spanish Carolina to the Erie Canal by boat.

We drove students over the Annapolis and Albany for two week semester credit sessions combining colonial history, sailing, and oceanography. They stood "deck duty," "galley duty," and stowage duty; they read assignments, had seminar discussions and visited revered spots. Most of all, we tried to get a feel for motivations and atmospheres, the intangibles of American history that would blow the dust from the myths. The project at Jamestown: Evaluate Jamestown as a site for permanent settlement. A student's journal follows.

"We drove over to the original Jamestown and had a tour through there. They sure picked a rotten place to build a fort. It's awful swampy." Next day, 150 years in time and eight miles away in Williamsburg. Another student recorded:
"Jamestown had depressed me, because of the hard times they all had. But Williamsburg didn't bother me even though they were having the troubles of the Revolutionary War. . . To think that in the colonies, in the middle of nowhere, there should be such luxury."

Lasting traditions which began in Year One. . .

Potpourri: This enrichment period was established for the Upper School as a tradition which lasted the whole tenure of the high school. Observed from 1:30-3 pm it reinforced the school's philosophy of excellent academics in an atmosphere of innovation and creativity. Teachers and parents involved themselves in supervising enrichment activities. Ski trips were foremost, to Timberlee ski slopes, with instruction available. Other activities for Potpourri were weaving, art, and sports: the first year an "Everything Team" was organized from grades 6-12, and they began to learn soccer and played tennis on the newly built tennis courts near the property's edge and the Cedar Lake motel. Also available were work internships in the community, in which students would leave school at Potpourri to go to work at some outside interest, for instance a veterinary clinic.

In the Lower School, "time off for a while from the academic schedule for out-of-doors" became known as "Winter Wednesday."

Maple syrup time: Lower Schoolers and some Upper School students and their parents and teachers tapped some of the many maple trees on the property in late winter and began boiling syrup on the stove during school days. Following the lengthy boiling process, a pancake breakfast was held to raise money for school extras.

Mug and spoon lunches: Students brought their lunches, and soup and milk were provided for all students. Upper School scholarship students cooked soup in the school kitchen for students in the central building 3-12 grades. Students in the kindergarten, first, and second grades cooked their own soup.

"Sloppy joe" lunches (or sometimes breakfasts or turkey dinners): They became a firm tradition. Since field trips were planned as a part of the curriculum, sometimes to far-flung places for educational opportunities, money was needed. Sloppy joe lunches every Friday became the norm, with homemade cakes and chips and no board of health regulations governing such activities at that time.

Town Meeting: One of the Summerhill traditions that was used as the rest were rejected was the governance process of the school. The Upper School met once a week to sit as a "committee of the whole" for teachers and students to decide many, even most, of the issues concerning the routine of the school. President, vice president and secretary were elected by the group. All votes could be vetoed by the director and co-director but interestingly, that rarely happened. Issues considered that first year were many including the snitching of lunches, cleanliness of the restrooms, parties and dances, and formation of rules to govern behavior. The school paper explains:

The Town Meeting: Explanation & Opinion

The Town Meeting is a meeting of the citizens of the supper school, like the town meetings in New England during early America.

Mr. Waltrip, the first chairman of the Town Meeting, feels that its goal is to communicate ideas and set some policies of the school, not to discipline. He stresses strongly that all teachers should be present. New officers recently elected by the group are John Baxter, Chairman, Brad Turkin, Secretary, and Marybeth Baxter, Treasurer.

Student opinion is varied about the meetings. Some say they like it, but some say it is dull and boring. Most believe the open atmosphere is a great asset.

We wish continued good luck to the Town Meeting and its officers.

G.J.

TOWN MEETING AND THE GROUP WILL

John Baxter was voted by the student/teacher group as first president of the Town Meeting; Kim Hagerty, as vice president, often chaired the meetings. The Town Meeting, which all teachers and Upper Schools students were required to attend, represented the group will. Robert's Rules of Order were strictly enforced. One of the most beloved objects in the library classroom building was the vending machine. One day it was discovered someone had kicked the vending machine, thus disabling it. The teachers called a Town Meeting to discuss the abhorrent behavior. There was a lively discussion, and one student kept saying, "That was a really bad thing. There are cleat marks on the vending machine. How could anyone possibly kick that machine?" And then all eyes turned towards the person who was protesting so much about what an awful thing it was.

The person, surrounded by all these stern looks, confessed that he had indeed kicked the vending machine. Reparations were suggested and he did them. That was solved—and in the future the group debated and acted on a large variety of subjects: oranges down the john, somebody taking lunches out of the "cubby hole" lockers, the prom, proposed curriculum changes, and Potpourri offerings.

Congenial, close-knit faculty: Lower School teachers met with Upper School teachers in the office upstairs above the animal pens. Later—in a lounge between 4/5 and 5/6.

> Mary Lynn Watson: "We had education courses together at Northwestern Michigan College and when we started the school I saw my classmates Mary Breu and Tom Terry. We met for a Christmas party early in the history, with candlelight, elegant dishes, just excellent food. It was before the fireplace in the library. We'd take out the barrier and have just that one fire per year—until the fire marshall made us stop doing even that.

Advanced Placement courses: Early in the first year AP courses for high schoolers were introduced with French, English, history and math as options for students who wished to take them. Through the years several students obtained enough credit to skip freshman courses in college.

Sports for all students: The J-hi and 5/6 boys triumphed with a 78-0 football win over some poor losing team, now thankfully lost in disgrace in the pages of history. Upper Schooler Josh Wysong led a Potpourri ski team which participated in individual meets, winning trophies. Swimming was added to the activities menu, along with classes in film and radio history.

Lower school students observed physical education in their own classes. High schoolers formed the "All Sports Team," which changed equipment, fields and t-shirts as the year progressed. As a *Pathfinder Trailblazer* newspaper article reported in October 1972:

> The Pathfinder soccer team tied the Buckley Jr. High squad in a scrimmage October 1, and lost to Northport 5-1 and Buckley varsity 2-0 earlier. Some members of the team were Jim, Skip and John Baxter, Tom Young, Tim Force, Jeff Lawson, Glenn Jackson, Matt Sullivan, Dave Stinson, Brian Strong, Tom Kurtz and Duncan Miller.

Pathfinder Upper Schoolers, under Coach Ernie Olson, began

regularly scheduled skiing at Timberlee during Potpourri.

All-sports day: Art Baxter talks about that part of the Pathfinder philosophy:

> It was part of our belief that the school was a community, and that the students learned from each other, and so it was important that the high school seniors know the kindergarteners and first graders by name. We did not want that sense of isolation and separation that happens in schools somewhere along the way. Juniors talk only to juniors and eighth graders to their level friends. One of the best inter-group activities we had was the annual all-sports day, where we had ring toss, kite flying, three-legged races matching Upper and Lower School kids together. There were sufficient prizes and ribbons so that everybody came out a winner. Eventually, when the ski tow rope rotted out and we discontinued downhill skiing, we had rope tugs-of-war with 40 or 50 yelling kids on each side pulling back and forth. Then it was time to eat. In a pig trough that seemed to be left over from the former owners, Jerry Breu set up a charcoal grill with coals and cooked hot dogs on it. Students from the whole school lined up to get hot dogs, chips, and drinks and talk in one of the best mixer events for older and younger students and all teachers.

Work scholarships: Students did the vacuuming, cleaning of bathrooms, and straightening of classrooms every day after school and on some weekends. At regular intervals once a week the school day would also break for another straightening-up time in which all students participated.

Lower School pageant for Thanksgiving: First and second graders dressed as Pilgrims for the Upper School and parents and grandparents visited, the beginning of a tradition which became Grandparents' Day.

Little dinghies on Cedar Lake for learning sailing during Potpourri was popular with Mr. Baxter as teacher.

First-Year innovations which did not becomes traditions:

• Animals on the grounds. Bunnies, guinea hens, chickens, and peacocks strode the grounds of Pathfinder School for the first three years. Gerald Breu attempted to keep them in a pen behind what is now the meeting building, putting them inside in cold weather, but they were often out. A goat, tied up, tried to butt students. Their care and maintenance became too much, and they were paroled to various farm families.

• Trampoline outside the office. Upper School students during study hall times had a good deal of freedom and a few bounced incessantly on the tramp during these times when the danger of trampolines was not yet obvious. It was impossible to supervise them, and the tramp was taken down.

By September, when the beginning of school of the second year rolled around, as has been said, the handsome new art building stood on the campus. Frank Ettawagishik, a tribal leader of the northern Michigan Ojibwa, soon came to teach pottery to students and outsiders who signed up for his courses. He "mined" white marl clay from Grand Traverse Bay for his pottery pieces and fired them in an ancient-style pit kiln he built with students outside the art building. Pottery classes at the new facility were also offered to the community.

By the second year, Fall of '73, Pathfinder School was an established part of the Traverse City area. Sally and Ken Driver came to the school to become two of the all-time best-loved teachers, Sally to teach 5/6 grades, Ken to coach sports and teach business math and other subjects. Interlochen musicians drove in to teach students and a decent music program developed. Other new second-year teachers were Katie Taylor, kindergarten; Trish Woodrow, assisting Patty Olson in first grade; Ruth Bombaugh, ecology; and Steve Bowman, Spanish.

Reed Zitting, who had been teaching drama at Interlochen Academy, had taught photography to Pathfinder students as his daughter Shawn joined the 3/4 grade combination. In the fall of 1973

Drama production in the garden, mid '70s.

Many students who wouldn't normally have given any consideration to participating in a theater production found the touring children's plays that Reed Zitting organized one of their most satisfying high school memories. They brainstorned together about acting Dr. Seuss stories like *Green Eggs and Ham* and cleverly hammed the poems up with interesting props and humorous interpetations.

Mr. Zitting directed serious dramas like *The Effect of Gamma Rays on Man-in-the-Moon Marigold*s for the community, performed in the library.

Soccer became a real sport in the fall of 1973, with our teams competing in a league with teams from Northport, Buckley, and Traverse City, and with new teacher Ken Driver coaching. Pathfinder began edging out other soccer teams, with the *Blazer* reporting, "The Pathfinder Pioneers edged out the Junior High Cross Country team 1-0 in a very exciting game Friday, September 28. The only point scored was by Jimmy Baxter on a free kick. Don Thompson was kept very busy in the goal not with stopping goals but punting the ball after it went out of bounds." Paul Russell and Brad Turkin had been added on defense. Other players were Tom Young, Skip Baxter, Mike Mapes, Mike Fitzgerald, David Stinson, Mike Potter,

Jim Stallard, Glen Jackson and Fred Heslop.

Informality prevailed at lunch time as senior Karl Vandivier played the drums with others in a pick-up band in the sixth grade room.

American History/Lit Humanities students observed the Civil War dinner, with Ron Wiley dressing up like Abraham Lincoln and Wendy Rogers and the Bradford twins, Mary Anne and Mary Alice, doing their stints as southern belles. Seniors traveled to the Detroit Art Institute. The ninth grade took a field trip to Chicago and dined (no blue jeans please) at the top of the Hancock tower after visiting Frank Loyd Wright's contemporary home on the campus of the University of Chicago. and eating at Trader Vic's.

The senior class took a trip to Ft. Lauderdale, Florida, in the school van. As they prepared to graduate, the first real class from Pathfinder, the yearbook said the following things about the seniors who would go on to fine colleges:

Kim Hagerty: "Here she comes, Kim Hagerty-big bright eyes, shiny cheeks, dancing down the halls and stopping to talk to everyone. We'll always remember her work with retarded children."

John Baxter: "A heck of a student type of person. John was somehow stuck with the job of school chauffeur and you could mistake him for a taxi."

Jeff Turkin: "We call him the grouch but we love the way he makes pea soup! Jeff was always busy recruiting people for the Marines and snapping their pictures for the yearbook and the *Blazer*."

Matt Sullivan: "from Sutton Bay, Michigan is notorious for his wrecked cars. Matt took time off to sell oranges and hot dogs for the Earth Science Club."

Cindy Stern: "We'll always remember Cindy for her agonizing diets. . . helping with the little kids and proctoring in the library."

Lisa Hatlem, Ann Morhardt, and Barb Jamrich completed the roster of seniors that year.

Over the summer of 1974 students were reenrolling (always a

good sign) and others were filling out applications, reflecting the region's growth and prosperity. The directors found the school had done very well with students who were of average or above average potential, but was unfortunately not a good place for students with learning disabilities. In the years to come many parents requested places for children with learning disabilities, but Pathfinder advised them to seek more appropriate educational settings.

In 1974 Dr. David and Judy Halsted enrolled their sons, David, a seventh grader, and Mark, a fifth grader. Judith Halsted's speciality in education was the teaching of the gifted and talented, and in addition to serving as librarian, she began to set up and help implement a formal program that had been started for the gifted child at Pathfinder.

IQ and other testing was done as students entered Pathfinder School, and the school in its hiring encouraged teachers who had experience with the gifted.

Lower School students were pulled out of classes for special activities, went on special field trips, and had individualized math, reading and science. A gifted specialist from California visited the school and tested all gifted program candidates with a battery of tests.

The Upper School also evolved a curriculum for gifted and high achieving children, who seemed to thrive in this open and supportive, yet demanding atmosphere. A variety of course options and pull-out opportunities broadened these students' learning opportunities by 1973-74. In the second year of the school seventh graders Skip Baxter and Jeff Lawson were put into a math class of tenth graders; that was one way to provide for their learning level. High school students who were qualified attended Northwestern Michigan College for trigonometry and analytic geometry. Lower schoolers began learning Spanish and eventually French, and their learning was individualized so advanced reading and math levels could be fully put into practice for them.

Hoping to implement an emphasis on the gifted and talented, Pathfinder School instituted the Montessori kindergarten program in its kindergarten with teacher Katie Taylor. Montessori emphasized orderly, highly individualized learning with many hands-on materials. In January 1974 the school was accepted as an affiliate member of the American Montessori Society

History Afloat in its second summer, 1974, saw students journey from Leland to Chicago, where they docked at the marina near the Navy Pier. They proceeded down the Illinois River to the Mississippi as they read Mark Twain's *Tom Sawyer* and then visited Clemens' hometown. Their sailboat with its mast stepped chugged on down the Mississippi, stopping at Vicksburg to reenact the "storming of the Louisiana redoubt" in the Civil War, and eventually ending up driving by van to New Orleans, where they dined at Antoine's.

New staffers joined Pathfinder in the fall of 1974, the third year of the school. Science teacher Dick Parks came from Interlochen to Pathfinder along with his daughter Karen and instituted what became a Pathfinder landmark: the environmental studies program, which included field trips to the Upper Peninsula. Music became important with the arrival of real pro Nancy Brammer, who taught woodwinds, brass, and string instruments as well as vocal music. Widge Powell began to teach art; Donna Stiffler picked up English in the junior high and directed plays for this age group.

Coach Driver led the 1974 fall soccer team in matches with Leelanau, T.C. J-Hi and Buckley, which Pathfinder beat 4-1.

Joan Russell continued her outstanding job as secretary and unofficial manager of the school in the upstairs office. Her son Paul became one of the stars of the Class of '76.

Students "took to the woods" early in the fall semester to go to Innisfree, a weekend camping experience that was to become one of the favorite traditions of the entire school calendar for years to come. Hiking, boating, and getting to know each other in sun or rain were the activities of the day. The camping experience, which has been called by various names, ended with a giant pig roast to which parents were invited.

Joining the Lower School staff in '74-'75 was experienced

teacher Nancy Guy. Nancy moved into the corner "turret" room with her third and fourth grade group.

Classes were now large enough to split in some cases, with class size being held at 15. Katie Taylor was in the newly expanded kindergarten, Trish Woodrow taught first grade, and Sally Driver taught 5/6.

Tennis became a significant sport in the spring of 1975, with the Pioneers team winning all of its matches in April and May. Team members were Fred Heslop, Josh Wysong, Paul Russell, Jeff Lawson, Tom Young, Don Thompson, Jim Baxter, Tami Pronger, Teresa Carboneau, Carla Hammersley, Skip Baxter, Rob Lint, and Tom Shaw.

The Upper School class of '76 was probably the most traveled class group in the history of Pathfinder School. Their sophomore and junior year they raised money to tour Belgium, France, and England. A group of parent chaperones accompanied them, along with Dan Baxter and Peter Young, in April, 1975. Some members of the Class of '75 joined them.

Having studied the battle of Waterloo in humanities class, they journeyed to the battlefield, and as they jumped down from the bus, with all the great scene of Napoleon and Lord Wellington's encounter—rolling hills and fields spread before them—they eagerly began to run towards—the French fry stand. Other highlights were being held as "hostages" on an English channel ferry by the British fishermen's union, standing next to the huge stones of Stonehenge (possible in those days), drinking "milk shakes" (shaken milk and chocolate sauce) and visiting Canterbury Cathedral for Easter services.

The *Reflections* yearbook had this to say about its second graduating class, 1975:

Jim Stallard The class would remember Jim for "music, pottery, backpacking and the card-playing at his apartment."

Marybeth Baxter "Laughing and always jolly, she gave a certain flair to Pathfinder. She plans to major in business management at Michigan Tech."

Wendy Rogers "A deep love of animals, calling them by names like 'Mr. And Mrs. Duck.' She hopes to make a profession of her pottery work."

Robin Goodin: "When she has something to say, people listen. Interests horses, books. She raises roses and hopes to do something with this knowledge."

Mike Potter "Mike had a logical reason for everything he said and did." They remembered his green jeep, the help he gave Mr. Breu, and working at the bakery.

Glen Jackson "Glen always put things into words that nobody else could understand." He hoped to join architect Paolo Soleri, who lectured at Pathfinder on his landmark project Arcosanti, in the fall.

New teachers came to the school in the fall of 1975.

Greg North arrived to teach kindergarten with his wife Carol serving as art teacher for all grades. He continued the Montessori method, helping students organize their things in cubby holes and teaching each student individually. Patti Van Epps began teaching in first and second grades, and Ginny Wolfinger taught 5/6.

An exchange student program was instituted in 1975, with four students coming from Puerto Rico and Janet Baxter, Nikki Cate, Paula Clancey, and Mary Anne Bradford spending time at a private school and living with families in Puerto Rico.

Then several students from Puerto Rico came to Pathfinder and stayed with local school families. Some of the students were trilingual, having mastered Spanish, English, and Chinese.

The soccer team of 1975 played Interlochen, Traverse Christian, Buckley varsity, Traverse City Junior High (twice) and Bible Baptist.

The '76 yearbook lists the team soccer members as "Carmien, Lint, J. Baxter, S. Baxter, Hankes, Force, Ursu, Halsted, Shaw, Carlisle, Smith, Young, D. Miller, Bowen, W. Miller, Livingston and Mapes." Coach Driver instituted a rigorous training program that students eventually came to respect, if not enjoy.

In the Lower School kindergarteners rode on a "real big train." Sixth graders had a three-day campout at Hoffmaster Park near Muskegon, under the direction of parents Bob and Judy Johnson, Ken Neilsen, and Bob Shaw. Music teacher Nancy Brammer directed a "Christmas in Colonial America" holiday program to a packed house in the library and supervised several ensemble groups that met at various times for Lower and Upper Schoolers.

The '75 Humanities I class traveled to Chicago to see the Oriental Institute, Museum of Science and Industry, and as always, Trader Vic's. They raised enough money to stay at the Palmer House in the heart of downtown Chicago.

The freshmen were an active group. From the yearbook: "Humanities I in the winter of '76 had a Roman dinner featuring poor slave Ed Bowen, Cassius Jeff Lawson, and Jupiter Mike Mapes." Each student reenacted the chosen Roman celebrity, telling of his or her life and taking questions from the other patricians and plebians. Many of these history dinners marked the early Pathfinder years and spread to the Lower School, which today still plays roles of famous historical characters.

By the end of this year the school had formed the Pioneer Study Center, accepting and classifying records of the lumber-boom era in the areas around Traverse City. Students helped in this vast work of organizing photos and records. With the aid of the Scott Gamble Memorial Fund, a building was erected to house the center between the kindergarten/first grade building and the new art center, thus completing what would soon be the Lower School complex. Professional historian Donna Stiffler aided in the establishment of the center. It began offering programs in its log-cabin interior, where students from schools all over the region, sitting on birch log benches, saw a slide presentation of past days in the lumber era in Traverse City. Tom Shaw, an avid history buff who would go on to a meaningful career in historical interpretation and costuming, aided in the accessioning and arrangement of the collection and became director.

The senior class of '76, ready for more travel one year after journeying to Europe, traveled for its senior trip in April to Bimini, where they were to explore underwater ruins, that magazines were touting as the lost ruins of Atlantis. A lemon shark almost bit Janet Baxter before she leapt from the water near Bimini.

Snippets from the senior photo section of the *Reflections Year-book*, 1976:

Tim Force "The enthusiastic outdoorsman who is always ready to participate in any activity."

Amy Rengo "One of those jump and go people who is always ready for anything."

Carla Hammersley "President of the Town Meeting, member of Quill and Scroll and National Honor Society, editor of the year-book."

Bob Wentworth "Known as the organizer. He's the editor of the senior section of the yearbook and arranged the senior dance."

Sharon Clancey "Assistant librarian and cross-country skier. Sharon could always be found in corners chomping vegetables."

Don Thompson "He's in Quill and Scroll, a cameraman for WPAT and goalie for the soccer team."

Mary Anne Bradford "Usually found in the art building work-ing on painting, pots or photographs."

Mary Alice Bradford "She loves small children and devoted a lot of time the kindergarteners."

Tom Young "Made front page in the *Free Press* by writing to "Action Line" about haunted castles in England. Member of the Na-tional Honor Society, president of the Town Meeting and in chil-dren's shows."

Janet Baxter "is our actress—she even won the drama award. Quill and Scroll, National Honor Society, editor of the *Blazer* and an environmental person."

New faculty members in fall of '76 included Betsy Nelson, who began teaching 3/4 in the old Pioneer Study room, now a class-room. The caretaker's home at the foot of the stairs for several years served as a home for some school personnel, including Lower School teacher Tom Dayton. The Pioneer Study Center now moved downstairs into the new office in the small house. Wendy Mezelis came to Pathfinder in 1976 to begin her outstanding Spanish program for both Upper and Lower Schoolers.

The soccer team finally broke into the winning side in the fall of '76, with a 3-2-5 record, and skiing seemed to take over the student body after hours, with Pathfinder's ski team posting a 4th in the overall northern Michigan conference.

Pathfinder hosted the world-famous architect Paolo Soleri for the Traverse City community October 18 and 19, 1976. The architect and builder of Arcosanti in Arizona spoke of his futuristic project at the school and at Northwestern Michigan College, which cosponsored the visit.

Patti Van Epps was creatively teaching first grade this year and driving a contingent of students from Kalkaska, one of the far-flung spots that furnished Pathfinder students. Unbelievably and in tribute to the education they were receiving, Pathfinder students in this early period came from as far away as Bear Lake, Honor, Northport, and even Kaleva, sometimes enduring more than an hour of driving each way. Sondra Shaw was director of extracurricular activities and sent students on many good field trips and learning experiences outside the classroom.

Teachers had all decided to name rooms for the "view" out the window. In Betsy Nelson's "Glenview" room 2/3 graders explored amoeba-like formations through microscopes and immersed themselves in the music program.

"Bayview" (the corner room in the library building) had as its teacher Nancy Guy, who began a rigorous program that prepared kids for a spelling bee among other things. Nancy served as head teacher for the Lower School during her tenure at Pathfinder.

Humanities II, American history and literature, traveled East to see Gettysburg and Washington D.C. Tammy Pifer, who was in a wheelchair, was pushed through the White House tour.

They also studied the history of the Pathfinder grounds, eventually discovering that the Markham Brickyards, which produced yellow bricks for many of T.C.'s buildings, stood on the grounds near where the gym stands today.

In the MHSAA all-conference ski meet, Fred Heslop took first place in GS and slalom February 9, 1977, as well as the overall meet victory, making him the first Pathfinder skier to take all three ribbons. Overall that year Pathfinder's ski team took 11th place, with Traverse City High finishing first. Our little school could be proud of this record in competition with so many public high schools.

The Class of 1977 journeyed to the Bahamas for a dream senior trip in Burl Ives' winter home on Elbow Key. They strummed guitars, ventured onto the choppy waters to reach the legendary Hopetown lighthouse and had beach picnics. Later they attended one of Pathfinder's first proms May 21 at the Grand Traverse Country Club. Seniors who graduated in the commencement of 1977, and the colleges they planned to attend were:

Tom Shaw, Carleton College; **Tammy Medell**, Calvin College; **Christy Bowerman,** Michigan Tech; **Lisa Huron,** Michigan State; and **Ron Wiley,** Alma College; **Jim Eichstadt**, no college listed. Commencement speaker was Harlan Hatcher, former president of the University of Michigan. Tragically, after one year of college, Lisa Huron was killed in an automobile accident. The Lisa Huron Memorial Garden is named after her.

Pathfinder began its first summer session under the supervision of Lower School teacher Mary Lammers, with Scot Veenstra and Mary Sawyer as assistants.

In 1977 the school expanded to 125 students and 17 teachers. It joined the Cherryland Conference for its now varied program of athletics. The soccer team, hampered by injuries, lost 9 and won 1 but looked forward to a brighter future in the league placement.

hot dog lunches, and parent parties brightened up the graying land-scape. Meanwhile, Pathfinder students marked the season with good-weather sailing, and fall team sports until winter came and skiing took up, December through early March.

Kay Walter became the school's efficient office manager, with-her daughter Julie joining the freshman class. Pathfinder's ski team had an excellent year in the winter of 1978 with 2 wins, 2 losses, and 3rd place overall. Ski team members were Fred Heslop, Jim Baxter, Skip Baxter, Laurie Shaw, Russ Sims, Dean Templeton, Rob Lint, Scott Lint, Adam Begley, Mike Kibler, Luann Roberts, and Chris Hayes.

The Class of '78 raised its own money and traveled to England, especially enjoying London.

Class of '78 seniors were **Christ Schmaltz** the WPAT TV sta-tion cameraman and goalie for the soccer team; **Scott Lint** yearbook photographer and senior sloppy joe chef (co-winner of the all-sports trophy); **Kathy Spears** WPAT station manger with two years of drama; **Jim Baxter** band leader for Grover Cleveland and co-winner of the All Sports trophy; **Laurie Shaw** town meeting secretary and the first woman Pioneer soccer player; **Mark Lessard** senior section editor and assistant station manager; **Kendall Kuutilla** photogra-pher and WPAT anchorwoman; and **Fred Heslop** Town Meeting president, satirical writer, and avid fan of *Fear and Loathing in Las Vegas.*

Pathfinder students developed serious interest in technology during the 1977-78 year. TV station WPAT took to the airwaves, encouraged by a donation of equipment from Les Biederman at the NBC outlet in Traverse City. New television cameras began filming daily TV shows with student directors and anchors taught in the jounalism classes. WPAT work took students into the community to interview leading citizens. Upper and Lower School students vis-ited the huge mainframe computer in offices by the bay to learn of computer programming, the wave of the future.

But Pathfinder was running out of space. It was time for a ma-jor expansion

Mr. Baxter summarizes the building of the school gym in 1978

The need for a combination gymnasium/classroom building called for action. The gym plans developed, and the facility
was built in the winter of 1977-78. It answered the need to provide space for the educational facilities. The gym building was
planned to have three classrooms facing the athletic field. The
art/pottery room was particularly important because it freed
up what had been the art room in the uphill complex, and that
became a lower school classroom. The gym itself was built to
comply with official basketball court size. It was very tight, but
it worked.

The funding plans were undertaken after much discussion
at various board meetings. Board members willingly pitched
in to take on a substantial commitment: the most expensive
single undertaking in Pathfinder's history. Credit must go to
the board at the time: Fred Heslop, president; Bob Young, Bill
Thomas, Paul Scott, Peter Dendrinos, Frank Hagerty, Bob
Shaw and Jim Preston. They demonstrated the vision, financial
participation, and work characteristic of the best of independent school governing boards. They obtained substantial donations to qualify the school for construction loans from Traverse
City State Bank.

The local bank worked with the school from the beginning and were helpful in the planning stages and in reviewing
the construction specifications, which had to stringently meet
school codes and control future maintenance costs. Michigan
winters were very hard on industrial flat-top roofs, but that approach allowed the school to build a substantial gym on a tight
budget.

Board members under the direction of Fred Heslop,
and some key parents and friends, got the funding underway and convinced the bank to proceed with the loan of over
$100,000.

Construction moved swiftly during the fall, and by spring we were ready for the dedication ceremony attended by parents, friends, bank officials, and board members. The Class of '79 met for a day-long landscaping work bee to complete the woodsy look outside the classrooms. The gym was a major undertaking for a fledgling school, but it allowed the school to offer a full academic and athletic program for all students.

The groundbreaking ceremony for the new gym was held in the fall of '77. Mr. Fred Heslop, chairman of the trustees, turned the first shovel.

Ernie East came to the school in the fall of '78 to teach math and coach tennis and sailing. Karen Frederick began teaching 7/8 grade science, as Nancy Church started a significant tenure teaching art in the new art room in the gymnasium building. Mary Clark taught 1/2 grades, and Pathfinder hired its first first-year teacher, Mary Lammers, who took on 3/4 grades. Jean Coonrod, whose husband was in the piano instruction department at Interlochen, signed on for an expanded Lower School music program. Former grade school principal Ted Johnson came to teach 5/6 and became head of the Lower School.

Parents headed "corporations," which helped students earn money for trips to San Diego, Toronto, and Washington, D.C. They picked apples from orchards, put together a Pathfinder cookbook, and sponsored dinners. Environmental studies students continued to immerse themselves in Dick Parks's trips to northern Michigan wilderness areas, all but mandatory in the Upper School. The class and its off-campus trips exposed students to practical outdoor experience and knowledge of Michigan's state park system in such places as Picture Rocks.

Meanwhile, outside in spring, winter and fall, continuation of sailing, skiing, cross country sking, tennis, and soccer on the Rod Groleau soccer field continued. It was dedicated to honor the grandfather who helped build it and whose grandson was in the Lower School.

Christmas was festive in the Lower School in 1978 with Santa and trees. Upper School and older Lower School students observed Winter Wednesday, a custom that was carried on for several years and included downhill skiing, cross country, swimming at the Easling pool, and bowling. Ski resorts visited were Hickory Hills or Sugar Loaf, with only occasional downhill mishaps.

During this period the school came to be fully certified. Its original certification had been only preliminary. In '76 began the self-examination process that would eventuate in full accreditation. Committees met and groups analyzed the school structure.

ISACS then spent a week at the school in the spring of 1977

and approved it for full certification, replacing its provisional certification. Committees of board members, teachers, and parents began to meet in 1978-79 to continue the ongoing process of school growth, working to implement recommendations from the ISACS committee for improvement. The student *Blazer* editorial page complained that dropoff and pickup time in the driveway at Pathfinder was a mess, a problem that would not be solved until 20 years later.

Cherryland Conference seemed to challenge the Upper School soccer team. The skiing record was better, as the ski team won the first two meets in '79, took a third in the third meet and a second in the season's last meet. Intrepid souls joined students from our sister ISACS school in the Detroit area, Roeper School, at Innisfree for a winter campout.

The "corporation" trips for which everyone had worked so hard finally came about in the spring of 1979.

DIARIES OF OFF-CAMPUS ALL-STUDENT TRIPS

New Orleans Journal *The drum is making a "boom boom" sound and all my senses have been awakened by the powerful music. The group itself is unlikely; with members as different as the music they are playing. . . The trumpet player is wearing an army jacket, brown pants and old black leather shoes. . . . The banjo strings seem ready to break. As the song comes to an end everyone is clapping and throwing money.*—Dean Templeton and Bill Balfour

Washington, D.C. Journal: *The metro arrives and we climb aboard. Looking past the clear window and across the Potomac River I can spot the roof of the Capitol. The bells ring and the doors close; the metro starts and we're off to Arlington Cemetery.*—Dan Baxter

I am standing in the middle of the Washington Cathedral, looking at the stained glass windows and the beautiful wood carvings. The ceiling is a copy of one in the Canterbury Cathedral in England.—Blake Templeton

---

The Class of 1979 had made a junior-year trip east to visit venerable Ivy League schools. They had been interviewed at Hamilton, Colgate, Brown University, Bucknell, Vassar, and Smith, with several students interviewing at more than one school. The following students of the Class of '79 were accepted and found they would be going East: **Eugenie Scott**, Mt. Holyoke; **Skip (Art Jr.) Baxter**, Vassar; **Jeff Lawson**, Brown; **Lisa Rengo**, Smith; David Halsted, **St. John's**. Fine midwestern colleges also drew the Class of '79: **Adam Begley**, Hope College; **Debbie Firestone**, Adrian College; **Dave Thompson**, Michigan Tech.

For those who hadn't made up their mind on college, these were the yearbook editor's comments: **Sherry Clark**: "She was often in the darkroom printing her favorite pictures." **Mark Campell**: "Mark was MVP fullback on the soccer team. He's often seen skiing in a tee-shirt." **Bob Weiss**: "Bob and his hi-jinks on the England trip were worth remembering." **Tami Pifer**: "Tami skipped 9th grade. Everyone remembers her heated debates in Town Meeting."

The fall of 1979 found new coach Mark Fries amassing a good and professional record as coach. Though the soccer team had a 2-10-1 record, their spiffy new uniforms and well disciplined practice sessions did them credit .

The ninth grade again traveled to Chicago. A special destination of these annual Chicago trips was the Oriental Institute at the University of Chicago. Humanities I courses had studied Assyrian and Greek culture, and the group paid special attention to the Robert Braidwood collection of artifacts from these regions. Braidwood was later the model for Indiana Jones in the famous movies.

The ski team had its best year ever in winter of 1980: 7-1. Carloads of spectators went to the Cherryland Conference meet and helped the team return with its trophy: first place. Lower Schoolers observed Patriotic Week and made snow dinosaurs in between challenging art and music classes.

Seniors in the class of 1980 were **Amy Bowen**, who taught in the Lower School; **Paula Clancey**, a member of Honor Society and an eight-year veteran; **Patty Cole**, who was set person for *Romeo and Juliet*; and **Caroline Hardy**, vice president of the Town Meeting. Others were **Art Schuhart**, an all sports performer; **Karen Parks**, who loved camping on Manitou Island; **Chris Hayes**, a member of National Honor Society; and **Rob Lint**, Senior Class President. This large (for Pathfinder) class also included **Bill Seeley**, who spent much of his time in the darkroom; **Russ Sims**, president of the Honor Society; and **Dean Templeton**, also an avid photographer.

Almost ten years had elapsed since the first talks about the school got underway. Much had been accomplished: full classes in the Lower School; an outstanding faculty who came and stayed for the joy of teaching their classes; ISACS approval and the achievement of helping to found AIMS, Association of Independent Michigan Schools. The building of three new buildings, and graduates in many of the leading schools in the nation marked the firest decade.

It was time to take stock, and stock was being taken in 1980. Here is Nancy Baxter's account of that stock-taking in the summer of 1980:

> Scanning the overview of accomplishments and fine classroom experience for students and teachers and determining parents' satisfaction with the program is only one part of finding out how a school is succeeding. It is important in independent schools to honestly look at how financial undergirding is progressing, especially in a relatively new school, how the board and faculty interact; how those at the head of the school can collect and maintain long-term financing and garner community spirit.
>
> Although we had succeeded admirably in all the programs of the school, there were problem areas: faculty salary scales, which were substantially below state standards; the implementing of ongoing financial support such as successful annual funds and capital drives; and the creation of an endowment or large funding operation to retire the mortgage, now owed to us, the Baxters, and to retire the gymnasium loan to

the bank. There were too many unfunded scholarships. Beyond the routine bank loans and mortgage, the school was not seriously in debt, but it would be at some point in the near future.

It was time to turn the school over to the board for management according to standards set by the Independent School Association of the Central States. Finances would need to be directly addressed. The founders could no longer pay bills and assume shortfalls. The board was called upon to assume its full and appropriate role. Pulling and hauling began between us, the founders and the board, who were genuinely interested and committed parents and civic-minded Traverse area people.

And it must be admitted that we, the founders, caught the board by surprise with the news that we would no longer be picking up deficits. Here were loans, and we were not going to pay them. We had not brought these board members along with the rest of the school, probably had not even tried properly. After some twenty-three years in the independent school movement, both at Pathfinder and later at other schools and as a school visitor for both ISACS evaluations and for Art at NAIS in Boston, I can say this: almost without exception, leaders, heads of schools, must choose between two constituencies. Either they bond with the faculty (and by implication with the students), or they bond with the board. From the first day the founders/heads opened the school, we chose the faculty and students. It was natural. We were teachers, first and always. Immersed always in the running of the school, in the interaction with children, in the reinforcement of our teachers, we did not give time to our board, and I believe they were not sufficiently informed or even rewarded for all the service they gave. Long and hard many of them worked, many raising money as they could, presenting us favorably to the community, finding resources. Certainly we had our own reward in a faculty which cared for us, reinforced us in our work, and supported us unilaterally all of our days at Pathfinder. But mutual admiration societies consisting of faculty and heads of schools are not effective for long-term flourishing of a school.

When we informed our Pathfinder board that we wished them to assume financial management and funding, they told us that they wished to run the entire Pathfinder operation. The needs of the next ten years would be different from the necessities of the beginning nine. The founders needed to let their board function. We agreed to step aside, called our parents and said, "Two parties can't be running a school. We need to go."

A new era had begun. Art went to the National Association of Independent Schools in Boston. Dan and I (our only remaining Pathfinder student) went to Daycroft School in Greenwich, Connecticut, he to complete junior and senior years and I to teach. Art joined us on the weekends. It was a new life for us and a new life for the school, and we stayed close to events and cheered from afar.

This first section of the history was written by Art and Nancy Baxter and others present in the early days of the school.

in a new school . . .

Here we all are: teachers, students, chickens, rabbits and lots of visitors in a new school, The Pathfinder to be exact, where sometimes the most important subject seems to be sports and you can't really tell who is in your own grade. The classrooms are friendly and small and they're "too much (which means they're never very quiet) with us in them. And they're all in the woods, which is great.

As we lay down to spell our name, an airplane flew over to take the picture.

Patti Olson with Daryll Steadman.

1972-73 Mr. Terry's class grew a garden at the foot of the hill. Ninth graders used the food for the Neolithic dinner.

Mary Breu and the kindergarten.

Mary Lynn Watson took her students to Dow Chemical.

The "all-sports, everything" team.

(clockwise) Allan Middleton taught 5/6. Jan Jackson was the first art teacher. Tom Terry taught 3/4 in the earliest days of the school. Frank Ettawageshik moved into the newly built pottery building and taught ancient pit-firing techniques.

Nancy Guy and the "turret room" students. (below) Chess in the library during lunch.

Teresa Carboneau is hoping the leaves will stop falling during a fall clean-up afternoon.

The first Senior Class, 1974

January graduates: Barb Jamrich, Lisa Hatlem, Ann Mohrhardt.

(Top to Bottom) John Baxter, Kim Hagerty, Cindy Stern, Matt Sullivan, Jeff Turkin, Carl Vandivier.

Civil War reenactors: 1974.

Eugenie Scott and the sauna.

Dick Parks and students including his daughter, Karen.

Indefatigable Baxter.

Irrepressible Zitting.

Visiting visionary architect Paolo Soleri spoke at Pathfinder and Northwestern Michigan College under the auspices of our school.

Architect Paolo Soleri
To Visit Pathfinder

Patti Van Epps taught first grade and brought a large group from Kalkaska each day.

(top) Jeff Owens, Nathan Vaneps, Rob Johnson; (middle) Kirsten Johnson, Mrs. Guy; (bottom) Jennifer Veeder, Jensen Kurtz, Jenny Paynes and Todd Merchant. (opposite page, from top left)

20

Early Friday, September 29, Pathfinder seniors and art students were on their way to Detroit museums and schools. The above picture is at the Detroit Institute of Art, where students saw the Russian Impressionists collection. *1973*

The Class of 1975 (l-r) Marybeth Baxter, Robin Goodin, Glen Jackson, Mike Potter, Wendy Rogers, Jim Stallard.

Lisa Huron and Skip Baxter enjoy a Winter Wednesday.

Senor Bowman examines los periodicos *with Eugenie Scott, Lisa Vezina, Marcia Firetone.*

Members of the class of 1976 pose in their winter garb.

The Upper School graduation ceremony of 1976 celebrated the first four-year class of the school to be graduated. Janet Baxter, Mary Ann and Mary Alice Bradford, Nikki Cate, and Sharon Clancey lead the class through the garden to the strains of Elgar's "Pomp and Circumstance."

(bottom) The Soccer Team (front row) (l to r) Carmien, Lint, J. Baxter, S. Baxter, Hankes, (middle row) Force, Ursu, Halsted, Shaw, Carlistle, (back row) Smith, Young, Coach Driver, D. Miller, Bowen (missing) W. Miller, Livingston, Mapes.

The Class of 1977 meets in the lower office: Christy Bowerman, Tom Shaw, Tammy Medell, Jim Eichstadt, Lisa Huron, Ron Wiley. Their senior trip was to Elbow Key, the Abacos, in the Bahamas.

The Class of 1978: Jim Baxter and Scott Lint, co-winners of the All Sports Trophy that year, Chris Schmaltz, Kathie Spears; Laurie Shaw, Mark Lessard, Kendall Kutilla, and Fred Heslop.

Laurie Shaw, Lisa Huron, and Kathy Spears plan some new activity for the Upper School in 1976.

Dr. Seuss as performed by Reed Zitting and his troupe took shows to many grade schools in the T.C area. Late '70s.

Chrismas season brought special times at the school. Late '70s.

FOR EACH AND EVERYONE OF US

1978

(Above)
7th Graders (left to right) Eddie Tillitson, Alan Hayes, Jeff Firestone, Sarah Rengo, Geri Peasley, Amy Breyer, Tricia Gilmore, Annie Preston, Shawn Zitting, and Katy Dendrinos.
(Below)
(9th Graders (left to right) Pete Dendrinos, Cindy Bruss, Mark Nielsen, Mike Kibler, Sara Lint, Luann Roberts, Jackie Jones, and Amy Wagner.

Washington trippers Dan Baxter and Hugh Scott present "My Mom's Best Recipes" to Board of Trustees chairman Frank Hagerty.

Dick Parks and the challenge course students. (below) Greg North and kindergarteners about 1979.

Grover Cleveland was a band formed by (l-r) Jim Baxter, Jeff Lawson, Dave Smith, David Halsted, and Skip Baxter. They played at several on-campus dances and traveled as far away as the Kingsley high school prom. The library was never the same.

8th and 10th graders 1978.

8th Graders — (Clockwise)
Frank Peasley, Troy McKinley, Blake Templeton, Kneale
Bronson, Lisa Bruss, Danny Baxter, Phil Clancey, Pete
Young, Jeff Hessler and Hugh Scott.
(Below) 10th Graders (top Row L to R)
Chris Hayes, Chris Holmgren, Art Schuhart, Dean Temple-
ton, Russ Sims
(Bottom Row)
Karen Parks, Paula Clancey, and Patty Cole.

Miss Lammer's class (standing left to right) — Laura McCool, Becky Rodamar, Andrea Slater, Lori Ayers, Andrea Barnes, Betsy Craske, John Sternberg, Randy Lint, Laura Knight, Miss Lammers, (sitting) — Tim Hicks, Miki Firestone, Matt Groleau, Randy Willard, Raquel Walker, Martha Gilmore, Ronnie Hagelstein.

Photos from the prize-winning, small-school Reflections *yearbook tell the classroom story of Lower School '79. Polly Reber & class.*

AND SO
THE DAY
GOES ON ...

... if it's Tuesday of Thursday it must be gym class with Mrs. Zachman ... or music ... little violins squeaky and hopeful, under Mrs. Coonrad's watchful eyes. Sometimes it's trying to get untangled from winter clothes after a recess of cross country skiing or after Frosty Friday.

4

These photos are from the 1979 Reflections Yearbook. (left) Kay Walter served as school administrative assistant.

Humanities class Roman dinner in 1978.

The class of 1979.

Class of 1980

National Honor Society
(Left to right, top; Cheryl Krolik, Sara Lint, Luann Roberts,
bottom; Paula Clancey, Russ Sims, Chris Hayes)

Quill and Scroll
(Left to right; Marcia Firestone, Pete Dendrinos, Luann Roberts)

The infamous vending machine gets serviced by Tim Force.

Class of 1977 trip to the Bahamas. It wasn't all sitting in the sun enjoying the new scenes, but also involved interviewing the Minister of Education.

Tenth Graders, Eleventh Graders 1980.

Tenth grade, (standing) Tony Nesvacil, Blake Templeton, Frank Peasley, Dan Baxter, Phil Clancey, Hugh Scott, Bill Belfour, Jeff Hessler, (sitting) Troy McKinley, Kim Schopieray, Julie Walter; (not pictured) Natalie Kolberg, Beth Bowen, Jackie Jones.

Eleventh graders 1980—(back) Sara Lint, Sara Dillinger, (sitting) Craig Ensfield, Pete Dendrinos, Ali Kenney, Cheryl Krolik, (front) LuAnn Roberts, Marcia Firestone, (not pictured Louise Bolleber) These juniors would go on to be the Class of 1981.

"In an infinite universe plans have have infinite scope, and demand an infinite response."

Blazing New Trails 1980–1985
Reed Zitting

Arthur and Nancy Baxter presented Pathfinder's traditional bronze school bell to Charles Gillies in August 1980 in a ceremony in the gym before parents and faculty. The new headmaster enthusiastically looked forward to his position, and faculty and students were pleased that a strong head for the school had been secured in a relatively short time and was now in place for the beginning of their school year.

The next years were to be challenging. The board, attempting to reconstitute itself into a strong directive body, was also assuming financial responsibility for the school. These were large tasks.

Chuck Gillies believed the school would work best if the headmaster and board had more centralized control than had been typical of Pathfinder before, where the spirit of the Town Meeting ruled classrooms, faculty/director operations, and even board interactions.

Faculty attempted to accept a slightly more structured pattern of operating, and not everyone found the new ways to their liking, but they would need to adjust. Life in the small school on the hill went on, with many happy children as usual.

CHARLES GILLIES 1980-1983
Charles Gillies came from International School of Brussels where he had served as headmaster. Gillies had a B.A. in mathematics from George Washington University, an M.A. in Mathematics from Northwestern University, and a law degree from Harvard University Law School, and many years of experience in private education both as a teacher and an administrator.

Chuck, as he was called by everyone, was a tall man and made a big impression standing at the bottom of the stairs every morning ,greeting students and faculty as they arrived and waving to parents dropping off their children.

The new head quickly established his role with the board as well as with the faculty as a leader who would address the problems of the school head-on and at the same time reinforce the strong programs that had been working well and were flourishing.

One of the programs he felt needed full support was the sports program. It was a showcase of the school for the public in the Traverse City area, as well as a wonderful learning arena for developing young people. Mark Fries had been hired the year before and had been very successful his first year as a teacher and coach. Chuck supported the track and ski program.

TRACK WAS A SPECIAL SPORT AT PATHFINDER

And much of the success of that program, as well as all sports at that time, depended on Coach Mark Fries.

Mark Fries came to Pathfinder in 1980, hired by Art and Nancy Baxter, after having taught physical education for two years at Lahser High School in Bloomfield Hills. His intention was to stay one year, after which he had been assured of his old job back at Lahser, but his success and commitment to Pathfinder grew during the year and he decided to stay. He was hired to teach K-12 physical education and be the athletic director. Pathfinder was a member of the Cherryland Conference in soccer, but because it was a small school, it was not having many successes on the soccer field. Mark's first task was to load up six students in one of the blue vans and drive them to Pennsylvania for a week-long soccer camp. It meant hitting the ground running, and Fries, as everyone called him, never slowed down.

During his first year at Pathfinder Mark Fries assembled a boys' ski team, consisting of Dean Templeton, Jeff Hessler, Phil Clancey and Doug Clancey, that won the Lake Michigan Ski Conference.

That was only the beginning of his list of wins. During the succeeding five years under his guidance Pathfinder students assembled a remarkable list of achievements both on the ski slopes and in track and field. Chuck Gillies supported Fries's program with more funds, and with his support the program flourished over the next years, both under his time as head and under that of his successor.

1980/1985   1st place Boys Lake Michigan Ski Conference
1980-1985   1st Place Girls Division Lake Michigan Ski Conference
1985/86   1st Place–State, Jenny Payne, class D 3200 M Run
1985/86   1st Place–State, Jeanne Stevens Giant Slalom
1985/86   1st Place Jeanne Stevens Midwest Divisionals also went on to Junior Olympic 1984, 8th Place Girls track Class State Final (with a five girl team out of over 100 teams)

1984   State Champion–Jenny Payne track–3200 Meter Run
1984   3rd–Andrea Barnes State 800 Meter Run
1984   3rd–State Girls Track 3200 meter relay (Andrea Barnes, Holly Bowen, Jenny Ladd, Jenny Payne)

A school tradition that continued under Chuck Gillies was a week-long fall camping trip to Innisfree, the camp on Pyramid Point on Lake Michigan with an environmental and outdoor science program. Innisfree's professional staff led workshops, trips, and discussions about the Sleeping Bear area of Lake Michigan and the Great Lakes in general. Each day students would experience a different activity.

As an extension of these experiential learning activities and the general philosophy of getting off the campus grounds, Chuck sought out an archeological hands-on education program at the Center for American Archeology in Kampsville, Illinois. All 64 of the 7-12 grade students and nine faculty members spent a week there in the

First Place Cherryland Conference League Meet, 1981.
(back row) Jennifer Davis, Amy Gosling, Marcia Firestone, Julie Walters, Coach
Mark Fries, (front row) Kim Schopieray, Tricia Gilmore, Beth Bowen, Shaun
Zitting, Cheyrle Krolick, Andy Hammersly, Assistant.

fall of 1981 digging at the Audrey site, which dated back one thousand years.

Students and faculty will always remember this trip, especially for the transportation problems, which included several breakdowns of the bus, missed connections, and almost running out of gas late at night within a couple of hours of getting home.

Under Chuck's leadership the classroom and school environment continued as a college preparatory program, with 85 percent of graduating Upper School students accepted and entering college programs. The Pathfinder approach in both the Upper and Lower School of high academic standards, individual attention, diverse offerings, hands-on experiences, field trips, leadership opportunities, small class sizes, and citizenship continued.

The challenges of maintaining a full and financially sound

program were addressed and sometimes met. Goals for enrollment growth seemed more difficult to meet, although there were several full classrooms as there had always been. Getting, and maintaining, strong teachers for a rather small Upper School added significantly to the budget and the head's and board's challenges.

Native American expert John White conferring with students Mark Halsted and Clint Cameron. Generally two students were assigned to dig in a two-meter square, documenting everything they discovered.

GABOR VOZSONYI 1983-1986

Chuck Gllies left the school in 1983, and the board hired Gabor Vazsonyi, who came from Switzerland and gave Pathfinder a whole new atmosphere of worldliness. Dr. Vozsonyi received his Ph.D. in central-eastern european languages from the University of Budapest. He taught Russian and German at the Interlochen Center for the Arts and Northwestern Michigan Community College in the late '60s and '70s. He was director of the Children's Village in Switzerland, a school for refugee children, before returning to Traverse City to become director of Pathfinder School. Dr. Vazsonyi attracted a number of Upper School students from Switzerland for one year of study in America and began work to incorporate the International Baccalaureate (IB) program at the school. He also took groups of students to Switzerland every summer and taught an Upper School language classes during the academic year.

Faculty and Staff, 1980-86
Since the faculty list did not change radically under both Gillies and Vozsonyi, we can survey the faculty list over the period of two heads.

Upper School
Marcia Bellanger, English
Ernie East, math
Sue East, science
John Grote, humanities
Nancy Crisp, art
Peter Nagy-Farcus, music
Ray Fouch, math
Mary Ann Rivers-Fries, jr. high
Mark Fries, physical education
Judy Halsted, library
Sherri Johnson, jr. high
Marty Trapp, humanities

Joyce MacManus probably has the longest teaching tenure of any one person at the Pathfinder School. She has served under nine directors. She has written a personal chronicle of her years at the school. These short excerpts from one good teacher's viewpoint will help move our story along.

Joyce begins her story. . .

I began working as a substitute teacher at Pathfinder in the early '80s. I noticed how kind and accepting the faculty and staff were. They always talked about the children instead of complaining about their salaries and how hard they worked. I had a child entering third grade and the director, Chuck Gillies, assured me that the tuition would be reasonable if I taught there. Chuck was moving on and the new director, Gabor Vazsonyi, was arriving soon. I applied and was interviewed by Reed Zitting and Robbi Rogers, who were acting as interim directors. I accepted a fourth-grade position and was thrilled with my teaching space with a view of the bay. I had eight children to enjoy and educate.

The school was K-12 and there were no portables. Everything ran smoothly and the students walked past my room laughing and talking among themselves, with overall a sense of happiness and camaraderie. The joy of teaching at Pathfinder came with the realization that I could teach my own way. I have fond memories of those days. I remember lyrics written by Mary Anne Rivers and her students as they put together great plays and musicals. I could drive my class on a field trip in our white Pathfinder school van without asking parents, who gave permission for the trips by signing a letter at the beginning of the year permitting the children to go on instant field trips. The freedom and trust I felt sealed my decision to stay there forever. I'm in my twenty-something year of forever.

One of the lasting traditions of the school established in its founding days began to take on significance and large fundraising results in the period 1980-1986.

As the PathFUNDer fundraising dinner and auction evolved over the coming years it featured a week long radio auction (originally on WCCW) that culminated in an all-day, on-air talent auction with a list of 80 items, a live auction at the dinner offering many high priced items, a silent auction that went on during the dinner, and a dinner with ongoing entertainment and an elimination drawing for the door prize. The event was held at several different locations over the years, including the Grand Traverse Resort, the Traverse City Country Club, and the Embers Restaurant. The door prize was one of the big draws for the evening, with the prizes over the next years including a Corvette (won by Paul Scott in 1978), a his–and–hers compact car, and a pound of gold (1979). The gold was the door prize for several years. PathFUNDer was the first event of this type in the Traverse City area and over the years was successful in helping fund the scholarship program at the school as well as many other projects.

The Pathfinder Summer Program had began in a modest way in the mid-1970s with a day camp format and grew each year under both Gillies and Vozsonyi. It was centered around sailing, hiking, and outdoor sports, with some instruction inside for rainy days.

In the summer of 1981, Chuck Gillies, along with Pat Fulkerson and Greg North, both faculty members of Pathfinder, created a full-fledged summer school program. Pat would become the director and remain in that position through the summer of 1990 seeing the program through many positive transformations and exciting changes.

The Pathfinder Summer Program not only gave students a wonderful day camp experience; it introduced new students and their parents to the school. Several later enrolled.

Dick Parks, science and outdoor education teacher and member of the school's faculty, provided the camp with an innovative and most popular science/outdoor education program. Dick took advantage of the beauty and expanse of the school's 22 acres and waterfront, making it his outdoor classroom. Dick would become an invaluable assistant director of the program.

One of the most popular aspects of the summer program was the overnight campover held every second Thursday of each two-week session. The campers slept in tents on the school property and enjoyed breakfast and a hot dog cookout for lunch the next day.

As time progressed, the Summer Program expanded as did the

Staff member Phil Teleman helps a student with a hot dog lunch after one of the campouts.

summer faculty, with the inclusion of many Pathfinder School faculty members adding their expertise in the areas of music, drama, art, creative movement, languages, science, sailing, tennis, swim lessons, history mystery, academic skill builders, computer classes, and more.

In the summer of 1985 the schedule expanded to include a professionally designed program for "the young child" which was enthusiastically received.

In 1986 a French Camp was added with Madame Sharon Rutkowski as the instructor. The program was planned for beginning French students as well as for children entering the Pathfinder School for the first time in the fall. In 1988 French II was incorporated, as was Spanish I and II.

The summer program provided a professionally staffed extended day for children needing care from 7:30 to 9:00 when the camp program began and from 4:00 to 5:30 p.m. after the camp program ended.

The Pathfinder Summer Program supported and carried on the traditions of the Pathfinder School and extended its outreach into the surrounding community, allowing many more children to experience those things that are so special about Pathfinder.

Contributed by Pat Fulkerson

THE SUMMER SCHOOL FACULTY 1981 THROUGH 1990

Pathfinder School Faculty	Faculty from Other Schools
Susan (Hastings) Anderson	Liz Bannister
Patti Barrons	Nancy Briggs
Nancy Crisp	Dennis Farley
Robin DeWindt	Sue Gross
Mark Fries	Jane LaCourse
Pat Fulkerson	Nancy Landfair
John Grote	Diane Money
Linda Hauser-Mueller	Larry Nykerk
Jack Hood	David Parks
Joyce MacManus	Stan Pasch
Greg North	Therese Povolo
Patti Olson	Carl Scheffler
Dick Parks	Cathleen Sibley
Lynn Pavlov	Toni Stephenson
Mary Anne Rivers-Friese	Black Vance
Robbi Rogers	Diane (Lyons) Walker
Sharon Rutkowski	Linda Winans
Bobbie Stephenson	Nan Worthington
Claire Stevens	
Anita Sommers	
Phil Teleman	
Kate Trainer	
Tracey Westerman	
Phil Teleman	

Open Curriculum also continued in the Upper School 1980—1986. Initiated in the '70s as part of the extensive traveling Upper Schoolers did, Open Curriculum had one primary goal: to provide an extended period of time for exploring an area of study which could include field trips or even out-of-state trips. O.C. was always held between semesters, which meant it took place in late January. Trips to New Orleans, Hearst, Canada on the Algoma Central RR, Toronto, and Jackson Hole, Wyoming, were typical and on-campus experiences included spending five days studying rock and roll with Marty Trapp. The period 1980-1985 saw Open Curriculum develop to its fullest potential.

Pathfinder's Upper School had developed an outstanding reputation, fulfilling its founders' dreams of uniting creative innovation and student-centered education with rigorous academic work and

Open Curriculum trip to Jackson Hole Wyoming. Patty Cole cross-country skiing in Teton National Park

traveling the state, nation, and world to experience it firsthand. Its graduates could be found in colleges all over America, completing work towards medical and law degrees, engineering, teaching, and about fifteen other occupations. They graduated from schools such as Vassar, Smith, Goucher, University of Michigan, University of Chicago, Pepperdine, Michigan State, and many more distinguished and well-recognized schools. They would go on to significant careers owning their own veterinary practices, law firms, and some of the most prosperous corporations in Traverse City and other cities. They would become technical experts, heading up departments of technology for business and industry, they would be tenured university professors, farmers and expert salesmen and women. Pathfinder graduated several teachers; at least one would found her own school. Many grads would marry and establish good families; and some would eventually send their children to Pathfinder School. You can read their own personal experiences in our Upper School in the appendix of this book. But their era was now coming to a close.

It was true that five years after the founders had left, and through two headmasters and a succession of board members, the school had gone forward. An ISACS evaluation in 1985 and 1986 found the school still vital and serving the needs of a good variety of students in creative and innovative ways. But the school community had in the years 1985 and 1986 become divided over leadership, philosophy, and financial security. The ISACS evaluation uncovered feelings of insecurity among faculty and parents.

At the end of three years Gabor Vozsonyi left and the board decided to close the Upper School. It was a financial decision. The school faced increasingly large deficits, and the Lower School's one-teacher, one-classroom structure looked far more fiscally sound than maintaining an Upper School faculty of many disciplines, with its own administrator.

So on Friday, June 6, 1986, with Art Baxter as commencement speaker, the last graduates of the much-respected Pathfinder School Upper School walked up the aisle between seated guests to the playing of the organ to receive their diplomas and close an era of remarkable high school excellence in a small school setting. The commencement ceremonies were typical of those which had been held in the Lisa Huron Memorial Garden for some thirteen years and yet they were probably invested with more of a sense of meaning and significance with the closing of an educational opportunity that had brought much to many

The graduating seniors were Andrea Barnes, Holly Bowen, Cheryl Butler, Jon Cribbs, Daniel Elliott, Carrie Leaureaux, Sherri Leaureaux, Peter Lotscher, Christine Payne, Robert Ream, and Andrew Stireman, Gabriel Vozsonyi. Reverend Gary Hogue of the First Congregational Church gave the Invocation and Benediction.

Dr. Gabor Vozsonyi, in his own valedictory, presented recognitions and awards to students and faculty. Senior responses were given by Holly Bowen, Jon Cribbs, Daniel Elliott, Carrie Leaureaux, and Andrew Stireman. Peter Nagy-Farkus on cello and Katherine Nagy-Farkus on piano played "Andante and Rondo" by Rudolph Mantz.

The following awards were given to Upper School students at the last high school commencement. Achievement Award in Art to Andrea Barnes; Math to Miki Firestone and Vanya Zolikoff; Humanities to Andrea Barnes; Language–German to Amy Peterson and Gabe Hayes; English to Georgia Gloger; Senior Athletic Achievement Award to Andrea Barnes; Sportsmanship to Andrea Barnes; Certificate of Recognition for Outstanding Achievement on the Michigan Competitive Scholarship Test to Andrea Barnes, Jon Cribbs and Andrew Stireman; Presidential Academic Fitness Awards to Andrea Barnes, Holly Bowen, and Andrew Stireman. In addition certificates were presented to Holly Bowen, Andrea Barnes, Jenny Ladd, and Jenny Payne from the Michigan High School Athletic Association for making the All-State Track Team and a plaque to Jenny Payne for first place in her track event at the state level.

Parents understood that the decision to close the much-loved high school had not easily been arrived at. Still, they looked back over the years with nostalgia and wondered if the decision to close really had needed to be made.

The answer can only be yes. The visiting team from ISACS came to Pathfinder in March 1986. One of their recommendations was that the school must objectively and dispassionately reopen its investigation as to the viability of the high school program and document its findings. This recommendation was based on financial viability, not the quality of the high school program.

There were many meetings with parents to discuss the financial problems of not only the school, but also of maintaining the high school program. Finally, Upper School parents and students were asked to commit to the 1986-1987 school year. Teachers were informed that contracts would not be awarded until mid-May, and that process would depend on the number of students re-enrolled. Most of the teachers decided to look elsewhere, but there was a core who would remain. However, there were not enough commitments from parents and students, and the board voted to close the high school and put all their strong efforts into providing an outstanding elementary school.

Graduating Class Lists from 1981-1985

Class of 1981

Luise Bolleber
Peter Dendrinos
Deborah Detwiler
Craig Ensfield
Marcia Firestone
Tricia Gilmore
Jacqueline Jones
Ali Kenney
Mike Kibler
Cheryl Krolick
Sara Lint

Class of 1982

Bill Belfour
Beth Bowen
Jennifer Davis
Mark Feese
Natalie Kolberg
Alex Saratos
Kim Scopieray
Hugh Scott
Blake Templeton
Julie Walter
Pam Wigley

Class of 1983

Jeff Firestone
Lynn Fouts
Bill Greenaway

Sarah Rengo
Lisa Salisbury
Laurie Scherock
Jamie Seeburger
Bob Seward
Chris Waite
Janet Williamson
Shaun Zitting

Class of 1984

Keith Baldwin
Marilee Bishop
Clinton Cameron
Danna Flood
Mark Halsted
Diane Peterson
Matthew Rogers
Becky Taylor
Jenny Taylor
Doug Thorogood
Susie Workman

Class of 1985

Meg Bowen
Elizabeth Fouts
Tommi Lassila
Tim Mauntler
Ed Rutkowski
Fred Schubert
Jeanna Stevens
John Williams
Scott Zenker

A Path Growing Ever Wider 1985–2000

Sharon Rutkowski

The board immediately tackled present financing problems, which would now be easier to solve with reduced salary and Upper School space and activity requirements. The long-term debt at Pathfinder had grown to $650,000. It consisted of two mortgages on the land and improvements and several bank notes covering past operating deficits. Businessmen on the Pathfinder Board of Trustees looked at many different ways of trying to solve this financial problem. In addition to an outstanding debt to Art and Nancy Baxter, who had sold the school facilities to the trustees in 1977, the school had notes at a variety of banks in town secured by personal guarantees in varying amounts by the trustees. Through a combination of generous cash donations, co-signers honoring their promissory bank notes, forgiveness, and other means the school was able to resolve most of these concerns. After a significant contribution by the Baxters, the mortgage on the property that was due to them was paid.

The consolidation of all remaining debt totaled in excess of $1 million, but in reality that daunting sum only seemed to stimulate board determination. The school received revenue-generating properties which helped to service the new restructuring, as well as a cash infusion. The trustees set "a balanced budget in five years" as their goal. This was finally achieved in 1990. Board members should be praised for the achievement of this important goal.

Community leaders were coming on to the Pathfinder board, as well as educators from universities in Michigan. Patrons who believed in the future of the school were consciously recruited and came to bring a degree of "wealth" to the other two "W's" of board duties—work and wisdom.

This wide and successful educational background, especially in lower grades, gave Michelle Johnston special talents for engendering enthusiasm and creativity. The Pathfinder School thrived under her leadership from June 1986 through December 1989. She left to accept the position as Director of the Leadership, Teaching, and Training Institute of Northern Michigan. She is currently the Dean of the College of Education and Human Services at Ferris State University.

The students in nursery through eighth grade, in addition to their core subjects, were able to experience art and art history, physical education, French, and music as an integral part of their education at Pathfinder. The fifth through eighth grade students had designated math and science teachers.

The new elementary school developed its own set of traditions, some based on past years, some entirely new.

Fall Experience continued (and still continues) to be a tradition at the Pathfinder School. Every September students in grades 3 through 8 spend two or three days (depending on the age) getting to know each other and their teachers in a special setting. Activities include a high ropes course, climbing walls, canoeing, arts and crafts, creative dramatics, campfires, hikes, games, story-telling, and just plain fun! On campus the younger students have special activities to fit in the theme of "Fall Experience."

In 1983 two Pathfinder Parents' Association members, Ann Bridges and Chris Fortune, began a most successful project to benefit the library. B.E.A.R. (Be Excited About Reading) Day will celebrate its 25th anniversary in the fall of 2008. This partnership between the school and Horizon Book Store has been mutually beneficial. The school library receives a portion of all sales on that day, and the store gets one of their greatest days of sales for the year.

Also in 1983, the marketing committee of the board (Ron Kimler, Bill Fortune, and Sharon Rutkowski) met to brainstorm ideas to increase awareness of the school and to engage more families on campus. One of the ideas has become a treasured tradition of the school. Grandparents' and Special Friends' Day began simply with special guests visiting the students' classrooms, a hot dog lunch brought to the room, and special programs in the room. The program has now expanded to include a variety of activities including desserts under the tent; visits to the individual classrooms, the art room, the science rooms, and the library; walks around the campus; and sometimes one special program for all guests.

The Town Meeting, the form of student government that was part of the high school, was now continued by fourth through eighth graders as Town Hall. During the weekly meetings students not only voiced their concerns, such as the quality of the pizza served for Friday lunch, but also planned school and community service projects.

In the fall of 1987, the Pathfinder School began an Extended Day Program to serve early morning arrivals and late, after-school departures. Susan Hastings was the first director of this program. A variety of activities were provided, which through the years included 4-H programs, chess club, and board games, among other activities.

Nancy Crisp, Pathfinder's art teacher, added art history to her program. She wanted to add a way of exposing students to the vast visual heritage that we all have. Her goal was to encourage greater depth in the students artwork and to use art history as a means of combating trite visual images. She was pleased that students in pre-kindergarten on loved the subject. They absorbed and retained more than expected and its benefits went far beyond her original intent to improve their art work.

Stone Semi-Circle was also organized by Nancy Crisp. It was modeled after Terry Wooten's Stone Circle, and promoted the oral tradition of our language. Students benefited from monthly meetings with local poets and storytellers. The children were encouraged to read and memorize poems and dramatically retell stories.

Michelle Johnston Reflects on Selecting Pathfinder
and Its Benefits for the Johnston Family . . .A Personal
Recolletion

In 1983, my late husband, Tom, and I wrestled with a question that had the potential of changing our life paths forever. The question was: Should I leave the tenure track and take the mommy track? Actually, after some agonizing, the answer was quite easy, and I decided to take the mommy track, resulting in our move to northern Michigan, specifically, the Grand Traverse region. Every decision, after answering that question and leaving the tenure track, led to the Pathfinder School and a quality of life that continues to enrich our family today.

As is true with everyone who decides to enroll in Pathfinder School, the experience went far beyond the children's education and included the families. The decision set our family on an unchartered course that was true to the life of the original literary Pathfinder, who did not follow paths but made his own. The Pathfinder School helped us make our new and original path.

On one of our many trips to the Traverse City and Leelanau County during the decision-making year before the move, we saw a sign at the edge of a wooded driveway on M-22 that read "Pathfinder Open House." Our eldest, Andrew, who just completed first grade, could read by then and asked to stop at the Pathfinder open house. As soon as Tom, who was driving our old brown Volvo station wagon (eventually a Pathfinder fixture), pulled into the parking lot, Matthew, age five, jumped out of the car and climbed the 56 steps from the parking lot to the top of the hill with the verve of a long-time Pathfinder veteran. Both boys fell immediately in love with Pathfinder School, particularly the science classroom, where everything was alive. For them, the prospect of attending Pathfinder would be like going to school at their grandparents' cottage. The only difference between the Pathfinder science classroom and the cottage kitchen was a resident boa constrictor, Clara Boa.

When we left the open house that summer day, the boys begged to return and attend kindergarten and second grade at Pathfinder in fall semester 1983. Unfortunately, we still had work responsibilities, which kept us in Okemos, Michigan for another year while we organized our lives, moved to Suttons Bay, and enrolled the boys in Pathfinder, where I was lucky enough to work first as a special needs consultant and then as Director.

Andy and Matt entered Pathfinder as third and first graders and thrived within the small classrooms, with the nurturing, creative teachers, and in a natural environment where learning outdoors was as important as learning indoors. Most people do not realize the importance of small classrooms, where children can engage in meaningful instruction, act as co-curriculum developers, be project managers or principal investigators, and have their voices heard in their classrooms. These pedagogical qualities were often associated with graduate school seminars; however, they were everyday occurrences at the Pathfinder School when my children were students.

Additionally, the environmental context of learning is important for your children, especially, in building a foundation for life-long learning. The Pathfinder teachers invited the children to learn in the classrooms, gardens, woods, and beach as well as in the entire region. Just walking through the woods was a natural science lesson because the trees and fauna represented specimens of the northern woodland ecosystem.

In the late '90s the North Central Regional Educational Laboratory (NCREL) presented the concept of engaged learning as a way to promote and improve student achievement. Although the NCREL research reports and papers described learning environments in Illinois, they affirmed the Pathfinder pedagogy of the late-'80s, specifically, the pedagogy experienced by my sons.

However, the transition to Pathfinder was not entirely smooth for the boys. For example, Mrs. Fulkerson, who was the first grade teacher, told us that Matt was having trouble reading. When we asked him what was happening in school and to describe the reading problem, Matt told us in a quite, remorseful voice that he was "fake reading" because, in his perception, the Pathfinder reading was different from the reading which he encountered in Okemos. When Tom and I informed Pat Fulkerson, she did not let his fake reading deter her teaching, took him under her wing, and ensured that he did, in fact, thrive in reading. He did so well that the following year he wrote his seminal paper about the beer which the Pilgrims drank at Plymouth Colony for Mrs. MacManus. We still refer to that memorable paper as it became a standard topic for our Thanksgiving conversations. He read 300 books in the late Alice Waddington's fourth grade classroom. For one assignment, Mrs. Waddington invited her students to select an autobiography or biography for a report. Matthew could not decide between a biography of Albert Schweitzer and *The Art of the Deal* by Donald Trump. After some agonizing contemplation, he finally selected Donald Trump's autobiography, which impacted his future career choice. Pathfinder friends, family, and alumni know the impact of that decision on his life path.

I also believe it was during fourth grade that Janna Dettmer wrote her remarkable and memorable report on the Traverse City State Hospital. To this day, Matt refers to Janna's report every time he declines a dinner invitation for Stella's trendy restaurant within the State Hospital grounds. Within the small classroom settings, the students truly learned a lot about their peers and valued their work which became influential. Pathfinder students often celebrated the accomplishments and expertise of their peers, recognizing personal bests.

Andrew, for whom a school like Pathfinder was designed, also had his adjustment issues. In fourth grade, after reading his favorite rough and tumble poem by Robert Service ("Lipstick Liz") his teacher, not having experienced the classic works of Service, made him stand outside of the classroom as a punishment for using inappropriate, pithy language, even if it was the authentic language of an early twentieth century poet of renown. Since Pathfinder has few hallways, Andy had to stand outside the classroom on a frigid northern Michigan winter morning until the late Mel Meltzer, a custodian and official Pathfinder proofreader, saw him standing in the cold, felt sorry for him, inquired about his dilemma, and rescued him. Because Mel also enjoyed the poetry of Robert Service, Mel gave Andy his first edition copy of the *Ballads of Cheechako* (1909) which he cherished. Usually, Andy always kept the *Ballads of Cheechako* with him at his bedside. However, he is currently traveling light for his work assignments and is keeping his treasures at our family home in Traverse City.

When thinking about their years at the Pathfinder School, I also cherish memories of the sports teams. Pathfinder students participated on every team that school fielded in those years, no matter the skills or gender of the student athletes. Participation, sportsmanship, and fun frequently superseded winning, but that did not matter because their hearts were in the game and their loyalty was for the team. During one memorable away volleyball game, which had a remarkably close score, a player from the opposing team lobbed the volleyball into a baptismal fount, leaving the responsibility of rescuing the ball to a Pathfinder player, T. J. Hamilton. While he dramatically extricated the ball, he displayed his concern for breaking a religious covenant through the absolutely mortified expression on his face; yet, his Pathfinder teammates cheered him on as if he had received a gold medal. When everybody participates in all sports, the young athletes have opportunities to grow physically and develop talents in sports that might be new to them. In the early years, students need balanced diets of food, literature, experience, learning, music, art, and sports to develop into future actualized human beings.

The boys developed broad knowledge bases that emerged at different times. When they were in sixth and fourth grades, we went to New York City for our family vacation. While at the Museum of Modern Art (MOMA), they were overheard by a stranger having a scholarly discussion about Pop Art versus Impressionism. The dumbfounded stranger incredulously asked Tom and me where they learned so thoroughly about the various schools of art. He was even more shocked when we explained about Pathfinder School, its location, and Nancy Crisp, the art teacher.

Because Andy and Matt had opportunities to travel, experiment, solve problems, engage in politics, use their imaginations, and learn a world language throughout elementary and middle school, they are thriving today. Between Mrs. Rutkowski taking Pathfinder students to France, Mr. Parks and Ms. DeWindt leading outdoor adventures, and Mrs. Alfieri teaching them jazz-scat techniques while hosting all-nighters to watch the election returns, they developed an inquisitive, problem-solving foundation that they continued to use in their work. During their Pathfinder years, Andy, who always had a backpack at the ready, could plan anything and everything, and Matt could build unusual devices, like a paddlewheel mounted on plastic piping to measure the current of the Boardman River.

Concomitantly, with the small classrooms and expanded curriculum that goes beyond the basics which are tested so regularly in this culture of over-accountability, Pathfinder students experiment, sample, and explore concepts and disciplines to find their individual talents. Consequently, when Pathfinder students leave the school for their future studies, they tend to be strong, knowledgeable individuals who can endure and succeed and solve problems independently.

After Pathfinder, Andy went to Interlochen Arts Academy where he wrote poetry which was nationally recognized, and Columbia University where he wrote a tribute to the late Mickey Mantle for the New York City Council, graduated *cum laude*, and received Phi Beta Kappa recognition. Matthew went to Phillips Exeter Academy for ninth through twelfth grades, participating in an Exeter internship program with the United States House of Representatives in Washington, D.C. He received his baccalaureate degree from The Stern School at New York University, where he started a business with a friend in New York City as well as having incredible summer jobs and internships at the World Bank and various financial institutions. After graduating from college, in the time period between school and their first jobs, Andy and Matt came home to Traverse City and visited the Pathfinder School to see Bob Prentice to discuss their futures and help him with his work.

Currently, they are following completely different career paths, but they are very close, supporting and celebrating their differences. Andy (32) works for the International Rescue Committee (www. theirc.org) in the Democratic Republic of the Congo, where he is the field coordinator overseeing camps for refugees and internally-displaced persons near Bukavu and North Kivu. Matthew (30) works in New York City for the Fortress Investment Group after having lived in Frankfurt am Main, Germany, for two and a half years. Both live in waterfront residences, which connect them with their years at Pathfinder and reflect their appreciation for the environment. From his window in Bukavu, Andy looks across the water at the countries of Burundi and Rwanda while Matthew sees the Statue of Liberty and Ellis Island from his window.

If we had decided to remain in Okemos, and I stayed on the tenure track, I believe that our lives would be rather staid and not be as enriched, and the boys would not have the broadening life experiences that prepared them for their current life paths. There would have been no backpacks, trips to France, and endurance built up by climbing 56 steps several times a day.

Planting flowers by the Memorial Tree for Thomas Rutkowski.

My Reflection

Because the leadership and fiscal outlook of the Pathfinder School were problematic, my first two academic years and summer inter-sessions at the Pathfinder School, although happy for the children, were turbulent for me and my colleagues. In my memory, the Board of Trustees acted very decisively and made dramatic, corrective decisions in an effort to save the School at the close of the 1985-1986 academic year. Simultaneously, the Board of Trustees decided not to renew the director's contract, close the high school (ninth through twelfth grades), and appointed me director. At my first meeting with the faculty in the fall semester 1986, I said that Pathfinder School was in its teenage years and just went through a turbulent adjustment. That adjustment turned out to be successful for the forthcoming years.

The summer between closing the high school and opening as a K-8 school in the fall semester 1986 was tumultuous. However, Ellen Northway, Sharon Rutkowski, and Bobbi Stevens were always there providing moral support, doing the hard work, and offering humorous antidotes whenever things looked glum. In a humorous coincidence, Weird Al Yankovic had recently released a song entitled "The Check's in the Mail" which became our mantra because we had to worry about paying every bill, including utilities, not to mention salaries and often had to say, "The check is in the mail." Additionally, the word on the street was that Pathfinder School was going under, and the vultures were hovering, almost salivating over the property.

I specifically remember a tall, overbearing developer with huge white gym shoes talking to me about the possibilities of building expensive condos along the ridge where the classrooms were located. In my mind's eye, I can still hear his snarky voice and see his smirking, ornery expression as he disrespectfully propped his huge, size 13-plus foot on a round table in an intimidating posture, trying to frighten me. In an effort not to let him know that I was scared and not sophisticated enough to engage in a financial dialogue with someone whose pitch was so aggressive, I sat up with a very straight, no-nonsense posture and was fairly silent while I stared at him. When he left, Ellen called me Margaret Thatcher—a true compliment. Her insight and humor that summer often saved the day.

Prior to my becoming the director, the salary discrepancy between the director and faculty was excessively large, and the director's office was in the current living room of the Administration Building. I believed then, as I continue to believe, that the difference between administrator, faculty, and staff salaries should be small and reflect equity. That concept is especially important in an independent school that is totally funded by tuition. Therefore, in recognition of the deep and historical financial problems of the school, I accepted a salary which was lower than my predecessor and held my retirement contributions at bay for a year. Additionally, because I believed that the director's office should be relatively functional, not luxurious, I decided to move the director's office out of the living room. Jane Fraser was very helpful in moving offices. She voluntarily decorated the living room in a perfect northern Michigan, country-cottage décor and helped relocate, decorate, and organize my office to the current director's office location. Later, as I toured other independent schools, my decision to move the director's office out of the living room was confirmed because independent schools need special rooms for meetings with visitors, prospective students and their families, and donors. The newly decorated living room provided that special space.

After having been an academic for ten years before moving to northern Michigan and working at Pathfinder School, I was not adequately prepared for the position. I did not know about writing newsletters, developing positive public relationships, designing brochures, attending Rotary Club, Zonta Club, and Chamber of Commerce meetings, fundraising, schmoozing, and a myriad of other skills and strategies that I had to develop and employ during my work at Pathfinder School. While at the school, I wrote my first grants, albeit small, to the Councils of Humanities and Arts. For

authorship. Through town meetings, first the high school students and later the fourth through eighth graders became academically empowered by voicing their concerns, plans, and ideas. During the stone semi-circle events, guests and students recited poetry and told stories. Lastly, the library was open for parent meetings and forums, including one in which Pathfinder School hosted Mr. Po, a Chinese Fulbright Scholar from Ann Arbor.

At that time, we hosted professional development events for area teachers and administrators, seminars for parents, and special community activities. Those special events often brought community members who were unfamiliar with the beautiful campus and contributions of the school.

University faculty and students often visited the Pathfinder School to learn about education in such a unique and beautiful environment. Faculty members from Michigan State University frequently toured the school. Student teachers from Central Michigan University and Aquinas College also were regular visitors. It was actually fun watching the big Central Michigan University buses drive into the parking lot and the students swarm all over the campus. After observing the Pathfinder students and teachers at work, the student teachers and faculty would conduct a debriefing with me in the living room. Years later, I was visiting Central Michigan University and saw a Pathfinder bumper sticker posted on the door of the faculty member who led the excursions to the school. Those adventures were unforgettable for him, his students, and me.

The Pathfunder galas were always interesting and fun with great food and generous donors, except one gala, which followed a dramatic fall of the stock market by a month. Rather than celebrating the school, most people sat around the Grand Traverse Resort ballroom in various states of depression. That was my first dramatic lesson on the impact of the national and global economy on local entities. Watching the organizational skills, energies, and talents of the Pathfunder volunteers always amazed me. Their work was never about them; it was only about the students who were the beneficiaries of the gala. At that time, the Pathfunder volunteers rarely received enough gratitude or kudos.

Pathfinder students always were special. They were bright with talents that emerged because they were free to explore, observe, and hear their own voices in their classes and Town Meeting. Mr. Parks once said that his job was to allow his students to observe, and they did. They observed everything from the constellations and otter slides to the angle of repose at that coal pile on M-22. Through being free to observe from unique and authentic vistas, the students, who were open to learn, developed their curiosity while their enjoyment for learning bubbled to the surface. Often, the students engaged with their teachers in learning and exploring new concepts. At the post-secondary level, that model of instruction is called inquiry-based. Students learn more deeply when they engage in and lead the inquiry.

During my early days at the school, one of the older students told me that the special Pathfinder student personalities came "from the lack of terrazzo." Rather than having to stay cooped indoors, like their counterparts, pounding the hallways with terrazzo floors as in most schools, the Pathfinder students were benefiting from being outside, climbing the stairs, and serving each other pizza on Fridays. "All that stair climbing produced more oxygen in the brain," he said. Who was I to argue with a high school student?

The Pathfinder students, when I was there, also came from special families who lived in many different neighborhoods and circumstances. When our son, Andy, was in third grade, a fellow classmate had parents who chose to live year-round off the grid and in a tent. His parents cooled their food in the Crystal River and sent him to school everyday with healthy fruits and vegetables, like whole zucchinis. Consequently, third grade inadvertently became the healthiest year for Andy and his peers because, at lunch everyday, they traded fruit roll-ups, Twinkies, and chocolate chip cookies for fruits and vegetables. After all, the family cooled their food in the rushing waters of a pure-looking river. What more could a group of third-grade boys want?

Beyond education, Pathfinder students also enjoyed a family

culture because they participated with their families in recognizing their achievements and in social events, including fish boils, spaghetti dinners, square dancing, and Fifties nights, which were fun. The fun was always family-oriented, clean, and wholesome. The students, for example, could dress like the stars of *Grease*, participate in special evenings with their parents, learn pro-social behaviors, and let their imagination take them to different places. Additionally, they learned to participate in activities that promoted sustainability and civic responsibility, such as cleaning up the campus in the spring, delivering holiday food baskets, and having the older students care for the younger students.

Many Pathfinder students often continued attending the school through the summer as Pathfinder campers. Through Pathfinder Summer Camp, they met students from other schools in the region and across the country because some children attended the camp while visiting their grandparents. The Pathfinder Summer Camp offered a plethora of experiences, including swimming in Cedar Lake, computing, tie-dying tee shirts, and spending the night on the Pathfinder campus. The choice of experiences ranged from science camp and sailing to history-oriented field trips in Traverse City and bicycle trips around Leelanau County. There was even a trip to Isle Royale for older campers. I know a Pathfinder student or two who worked at the camp during summers while they were in college. When my children were not at residential camps, they were full participants in Pathfinder Summer Camp which they absolutely enjoyed.

Pathfinder Middle School between 1986 and 1990 always had very low enrollments because the parents frequently transferred their children to junior high school in Traverse City area public schools. At that time, there was only one public junior high school in Traverse City, and it was allegedly the largest east of the Mississippi. I could never understand the rationale for transferring their children, because early adolescents are developmentally most vulnerable and need small, nurturing environments. The junior high school or middle school years are often the years in which the students get lost, personally and academically, right at the time when they need extra support and attention to ensure that they can be successful later. Douglas Heath, emeritus professor and scholar from Haverford College, wrote eloquently about small schools after doing longitudinal studies describing the lives of successful people in all walks of life. All his subjects told him about the nurturing, support, and guidance that they received at critical times of their lives in small schools. Furthermore, my friend and former colleague, Meg Campbell, co-director of the Harvard Outward Bound Project and creator of the School of the Physical City in New York City, often said that successful schools are about being part of a family, not about economies of scale. In the School of the Physical City, small groups of young teens experienced their learning inside and outside of their actual classrooms, just like Pathfinder students. Both Heath and Campbell would agree that middle school students benefit from a Pathfinder-like educational experience, rather than competing with thousands of students who are all trying to figure out who they are.

When I was the director, I opened the school year by ringing a school bell as part of the school tradition. In my current office, I have that bell on a wooden stand, a cherished gift when I left the school. Often, when my job becomes too tense and complex, I look at the bell where I have it in a place of honor and yearn for the Pathfinder days which my mother recalled as the best years of my long and varied career.

Sometimes, I look at the years when my family and I were active at Pathfinder School as the golden years of the school; however, I think that they actually were the golden years for my family because we all grew from the enriching experiences that we had at the school on the hill.

1986-1987 School Year

Faculty

Nancy Crisp–art and art history
Karen Dahman–3/4 grades
Robin DeWindt–phys ed.
Ray Fouch–7/8 math and science
Pat Fulkerson–first grade
Linda Hauser-Mueller–nursery
and pre-kindergarten
Diane Kenel-Truelove–7/8
grade language arts and social
studies
Joyce MacManus–second grade
Dick Parks–5/6 math and science
Sharon Rutkowski–French and
Development Director
Shirley Tweitmeyer–music
Alice Waddington–5/6 grade
language arts and social studies
Susan Vance–kindergarten

Staff:
Dr. Michelle Johnston–Director
Jackie Bowen–Bookkeeper
Deb Matthews–Public Relations
Mel Meltzer–Maintenance
Terri Michael–School Secretary
Bob Prentice–Maintenance
Supervisor

1987-1988 School Year

Faculty

Nancy Crisp–art and art history
Robin DeWindt–phys ed.
Ray Fouch–math grades 4–7
Pat Fulkerson–first grade
Susan Hastings–extended day
program, aide/preschool
Bonnie Hite–aide/pre-kindergarten
Joyce MacManus–2/3 grade
Linda Hauser Mueller–nursery/
pre-kindergarten/preschool
Dick Parks–science 4-7 grades
Lynn Pavlov–kindergarten
Maxine Rideout–music
Sharon Rutkowski–French and
Development Director
Diane Kenel-Truelove–4/5 language arts and social studies
Alice Waddington–4/5 language arts and social studies

Staff:

Dr. Michelle Johnston–Director
Terri Michael–School Secretary
Jackie Bowen–Bookkeeper
Bob Prentice–Maintenance
Supervisor
Dave Salenski–Maintenance
Bobbie Stevens–Adm./Development
Bobbi Ames–Van Driver

1987 Graduates
Jon Buntain
Richard Wunsch

1988-1989 School Year

Faculty

Pam Alfieri–7/8 language
arts and social studies
Ray Fouch–math 5-8 grades and
physical educaion
Pat Fulkerson–first grade
Bonnie Hite–pre-kindergarten aide
Joyce MacManus–second grade
Linda Hauser-Mueller—pre-
kindergarten
Dick Parks–science 5–8 grades
Lynn Pavlov–kindergarten
Sara Rodeck–art and art history
Robbi Rogers–grades 5/6
language arts and social studies
Sharon Rutkowski–French
Susan Hastings-Trahair–Extended
Day Coordinator, aide/nursery
and pre-Kindergarten
Alice Waddington–fourth grade
Claire Stephenson–student
teacher, fourth grade
Tracey Westerman–third grade

Staff:
Dr. Michelle Johnston–Director

Ellen Northway–Bus. Manager
Terri Michael–School Secretary
Bob Prentice–Head of Building
and Grounds
Dave Salenski–Maintenance
Bobbie Stevens–Admissions

1988 Graduates
None

1989-1990 School Year

Faculty

Pam Alfieri–7/8 grade language
arts and social studies and
music
Ray Fouch–6-8 math and
physical education
Pat Fulkerson–first grade
Susan Hastings Trahair–extended
day and nursery school
Linda Hauser-Mueller—pre-
kindergarten
Joyce MacManus–second grade
Dick Parks—5-8 grade science
and fifth grade math
Lynn Pavlov–kindergarten
Sandra Robey–sixth grade
language arts and social studies
and librarian
Sara Rodeck–art and art history
Robbi Rogers–fifth grade language

arts and social studies
Sharon Rutkowski–French
Claire Stephenson–third grade
Alice Waddington–fourth grade
Tracey Westerman–third grade

Staff:

Dr. Michelle Johnston–Director
Jack Hood–Interim Director
beginning January 1990
Ellen Northway–Bus.Manager
Terri Michael–School Secretary
Bob Prentice–Supervisor of
Buildings and Grounds
Jim Hale–Maintenance
Bobbi Stevens–Admissions

1989 Graduating Class
Colin Germaine
Melissa Leuellen
Markelle Smith

1990 Graduating Class
Nat Gray
Andy Johnston
Ryan MacManus

JACK HOOD INTERIM HEAD 1990-1991

Joyce MacManus continues her history. . .

> Jack Hood came out of retirement after having been at
> Interlochen to keep us alive while we looked for a new director.
> He was a kind man with a great sense of humor, who helped
> put children into cars when parents came to get them up in the
> pickup loop. He called the kids "kneebiters" and picked them
> up for hugs, and they loved him. He had no interest in taking
> on the full-time position as head of the school.

Jack Hood received his B.S. and M.S. degrees in biology from
Central Michigan University. His background included teaching in
both public and independent schools and administration. His years
of administrative experience also included serving as headmaster at
White Mountain School in New Hampshire. Jack was serving on
the Pathfinder Board of Trustees when the board asked him to serve
as interim head after Dr. Johnston left.

Jack's goal was to continue and enhance the family atmosphere
of Pathfinder as well as its mission to academic excellence. He firmly
believed in promoting independent schools as a viable option in the
community. Jack's calm demeanor, love of children, and belief in the
mission of the school were the hallmarks of his tenure. The Pathfinder School participated in the Association for French-American
Classes in 1990 and 1991. During this three-week program the
students lived with French families where they learned about, and
adapted to, French life, culture, and schools. They worked on their
American schoolwork in between visiting museums and famous sites.
The other component to this program was French students' visiting
them for three weeks. In 1990 we participated in this program along
with a group of students from Kalkaska. The six students and their
chaperones, Madame Rutkowski and Madame Northway, stayed in

the city of Saint-Prix, a suburb of Paris. In 1991, in addition to a group of Pathfinder students traveling to Limeil-Brevannes, France, 25 Pathfinder families hosted a group of French students and their teachers from this same town.

The decade of the '90s proved to be one of Pathfinder's strongest since its founding. The extraordinary prosperity of the '90s allowed for expanding programs, addressing some physical plant improvements, building an endowment, and raising salaries and benefits. During this time the school enjoyed a period of stability.

To look ahead, by the year 2000, the school would be in excellent financial shape. At the end of the decade, there would be a minimum of debt—a small mortgage balance and a note to a friend–totaling under $100,000. A "sinking fund" had been established from which these two debts were being serviced.

Still, during this last decade of the twentieth century, Pathfinder found itself for the first time experiencing real competition in the market for parents wishing an alternative to public education. In the 1990s more educational choices were offered to the community. In addition to the public schools and Catholic educational system, parents could now choose from charter schools, Montessori programs, gifted and talented programs, and other church-based schools.

Pathfinder School continued to define itself as a school in the "country day" tradition with elements of more free-form alternative education and very strong academics.

Its affiliation with the Independent School Association of Central States and Association of Independent Michigan Schools, which Art Baxter had helped found, aided parents in understanding that this Traverse City school operates out of a tradition which includes such outstanding national landmark schools as Cranbrook, Detroit Country Day, and Roeper School in Michigan. Pathfinder became, and still remains, as the only Independent School Association certified elementary school in the area.

LEONARD KUPERSMITH 1991-1993

Joyce MacManus talks about the early '90s . . .

Jack Hood returned to retirement, and the board hired Leonard Kupersmith. Leonard loved language and proudly used words some of us had to look up on a regular basis. During Leonard's two years the roof was replaced on some of our buildings and two ugly portables were purchased for $1.00 each. It cost a bit more to make them usable. Leonard left after two years to build a new independent school in Kansas.

Dr. Leonard Kupersmith received his B.A. in English from Brooklyn College, City University, New York and his Ph.D. in English from Kansas State University. Prior to his position at Pathfinder he had been at Collegiate School in Wichita, Kansas, from 1974–1991, where he served in a variety of positions, including Chairman of the English Department, Director of Admissions, college counselor, Upper School Head and Headmaster.

Dr. Kupersmith felt that it was important for a head to spend time in the classroom. He taught eighth-grade English and had scheduled "reading" times with classes. Leonard was a wordsmith and imparted a strong sense of intellectual rigor.

1991-1992 School Year
Faculty

Ray Fouch–5-8 grades math
Pat Fulkerson–first grade
Susan Hastings Trahair–extended day and nursery school
Linda Hauser-Mueller–pre-kindergarten
Joyce MacManus–second grade
Patty Leibenguth–physical education

Staff:

Dr. Leonard Kupersmith–
Headmaster
Ellen Northway–Business Manager
ager
Kevin Kalchik–Bookkeeper and
Coach
Bobbie Stevens–Events Co-
ordinator and Summer Camp
Director
Terri Michaels–School Secre-
tary
Marty Korwin-Pawlowski–
Administrative Assistant and
librarian

Bob Prentice–Supervisor of
Buildings and Grounds
Jim Hale–Maintenance

1992 Graduates

David Clark
Michelline Coonrod
Matt Johnston
Ben Maier

New programs and facilities marked Dr. Kupersmith's tenure as head.

A designated Lower School science teacher became part of the school's curriculum offerings. Dawn Iott was hired as the Lower School science teacher, and she soon proved to be an asset to the educational programs in kindergarten through fourth. The importance of science education at all grade levels became a beacon for the school. In addition, computer education became part of the curriculum. A class in logic was added for sixth graders.

Classroom space was in short supply on campus so two new (old) portables were added in the fall of 1992 to house music and six-eigth grade language arts and social studies. They are still being used in 2008.

The third and fourth grade students participated in the Junior Great Books Program as an adjunct to the library program.

DR. MARY QUINN—JUNE 1993-1995

Joyce comments::

Mary Quinn came to us during an ISACS year. Mary was fun and a hard worker and under her leadership we received accreditation from ISACS with delight and great expectations.

Mary Quinn's organizational skills, enthusiasm, and boundless energy in this process resulted in our award. But in Mary's mind it was a validation that the Traverse City community has an exemplary educational progeram available at Pathfinder. Under her administration the school attained the highest enrollment ever as a preschool through eighth grade institution, as well as increased the community's awareness of the quality of the school and the benefits of an independent education.

Beginning in 1993, seventh and eighth grade students traveled every other year to France with Vistas in Education. In addition to seeing the sites of Paris, the students traveled to various regions in France inclding Chartres, the Loire Valley, Brittany, and Normandy. Some years the trip included the eastern borders of France or Provence. An important component of the trip was the "family stay." Each student stayed with a French family, attended school with their host bother or sister, and participated in the family's activities.

New traditions began or evolved during the '90s.

Young Authors' Day

In the spring of the school year the students would share their creative writing with students from other grades. Their books were bound by room parents and included a background sketch of the author.

Enrichment Saturdays at Pathfinder–ESP

On the four Saturdays in March students from the area were invited to participate in a wide range of classes. Most classes were geared to students in grades kindergarten through eighth, but a SAT preparation class was also offered for high school students.

Pathfinder students have always been encouraged to participate in projects which apply academic solutions to practical life projects. Mr. Fouch, middle school math teacher, and one of his classes constructed the large deck outside the art room. They designed the deck, figured the square footage in math class, ordered the material, and cleared the site.

Drama

Kelly Halberg was hired to provide the students with experience in presenting theatrical performances. This was a return to the tradition that was begun in the early years of the school. The students in grades 6 through 8 performed in three Shakespeare plays adapted for young thespians. The plays were *Twelfth Night, Hamlet,* and *A Midsummer Night's Dream.* The students formed a Drama Club.

Other programs the '90s generated were: Friday Pizza Lunch; Toastmasters Club (to teach students public speaking); basketball, volleyball, track and field, and cross country teams; and a canoe skills course.

1993-1994 School Year

Faculty

Susan Anderson–pre-kindergarten
Judy Bucciero–vocal music
Ellen Force–preschool
Suzanne Gindin–instrumental music
Julie Hocking–teacher assistant
Dawn Iott–lower elementary science, computers, logic
Joyce MacManus–second grade
Dick Parks–5-8 grades science
Lynn Pavlov–kindergarten
Sara Rodeck–art and art history

Robbie Rogers–fifth grade language arts and social studies
Sharon Rutkowski–French
Jeff Simpson–math, Phys. Ed.
Duncan Sprattmoran–6-8 grades language arts and social studies
Alice Waddington–fourth grade
Tracey Westerman–third grade

Staff

Dr. Mary Quinn–Director
Ann Anderson–Adm. Assistant
Ellen Northway–Business Manager
Bob Prentice–Supervisor,
Buildings and Grounds
Jim Hale–Maintenance

1994 Graduating Class
None

1994-1995 School Year

Faculty

Susan Anderson–pre-kindergarten
Bonnie Babel—5-8, grades math
Jill Beauchamp–librarian and
all-school aide
Cynthia Cronin–aide in pre-
kindergarten
Ellen Force–pre-school
Pat Fulkerson–first grade
Suzanne Gindin–music
Kelly Halberg–drama
Laurie Hirt–third grade
Dawn Iott—K–4th science,
logic, computers
Joyce MacManus–second grade
Jerry O'Hearn–physical education
Dick Parks—5-8 grades science
Lynn Pavlov–kindergarten
Sara Rodeck—Art and Art History
Robbi Rogers–fifth language

arts and social studies
Sharon Rutkowski–French
Duncan Sprattmoran–6-8
grades language arts and social
studies
Alice Waddington–fourth

Staff

Dr. Mary Quinn–Director
Ellen Northway–Business Manager
Ann Anderson–Administrative
Assistant
Bob Prentice–Supervisor,
Buildings and Grounds
Jim Hale–Maintenance
David Fouch–Bookkeeping As-
sistant
Amy Southwell–Administrative
Assistant–Extended Day

1995 Graduates

Elijah Anderson
Parker Arnold
Shaun Butt
Andrew Calcutt
Katie Cilluffo
Theo Early
Justin Hsu
Breena Johnson
Abbie Pavlov
Zach Pavlov
Stephanie Swatzendruber
Chris Velderman

DEBORAH KARSOE 1995-2000

Joyce continues:

> Deb Karsoe was our next director. Deb stayed with us longer than any other director since I joined the faculty, working hard with board members and the founders of the school to see what Interlochen's approach to Pathfinder School could mean. With board members she negotiated a transfer of the school's assets and programs to the Interlochen Arts Academy, an event which was celebrated at the academy director's home on Interlochen Lake, with expectations for success on the part of both parties.
>
> We moved forward with Deb and all seemed well. Deb left soon after the Interlochen merger.

Deborah Karsoe received her B.S. degree from the University of Michigan and an M.A. degree from Eastern Michigan University. She had experience teaching in independent schools and brought a strong understanding of children's learning abilities and programing.

Pathfinder achieved a sense of stability under the leadership of Deb Karsoe. She was a quiet leader whose love of the uniqueness of every child was evident in all her decisions. Some intriguing opportunities presented themselves.

It was during this time that the charter school program came into the area with its challenges for enrollment at the school. Strong charter school legislation prompted the Pathfinder board to research the chartering process. Parent informational meetings were held and the parental response was overwhelmingly in support of Pathfinder maintaining its independent status. The board voted not to seek charter school status for Pathfinder School.

Programs continued to develop and expand.

The big yellow school bus with THE PATHFINDER SCHOOL on the side was purchased in the spring of 1999. After five years and contributions from hundreds of donors, the goal of $45,000 was finally reached at PathFUNDer 1998. The bus campaign was initiated at PathFUNDer 1993.

Drama continued at Pathfinder with the hiring of Audrey Pittinos. Audrey signed on to teach sixth through eighth grade math and to direct the Pathfinder students' theatrical experience.

During the Karsoe years the Citizen Action Council consisted of a group of students dedicated to working cooperatively to help others. They organized events to benefit the school or greater community.

The Lower School (grades kindergarten through fourth) divided into multi-age groups. Each group studied a particular country, learning about the culture, customs, and foods. After the three-week study there was an all-school program in which the students presented interesting information about their country. This was either preceded or followed by an ethnic pot luck.

Multi-age themes in the Middle School were an innovation. Students in grades five through eight were divided into groups and studied a particular theme across the curriculum. Themes included "The Great Lakes and Endangered-invasive Species" and "Astrology."

1995-1996 School Year

Faculty

Susan Anderson–pre-kindergarten
Bonnie Babel–5th-8th math
Ellen Force–preschool
Pat Fulkerson–first grade
Dawn Iott–K–fourth grade science, logic and computers
Joyce MacManus–second grade
Jerry O'Hearn–physical education
Dick Parks–5th-8th science

Lynn Pavlov–kindergarten
Sara Rodeck–art and art history
Robbi Rogers–fifth grade language arts and social studies
Sharon Rutkowski–French
Becky Sanders–music
Duncan Sprattmoran–6-8 grades language arts and social studies
Alice Waddington–fourth grade
Tracey Westerman–third grade

Staff

Deb Karsoe–Director
Ellen Northway–Bus. Manager
Ann Anderson–Adm. Assistant
Bob Prentice–Supervisor of Buildings and Grounds
Jim Hale–Maintenance
David Fouch–Bookkeeping Assistant
Melissa Elliott–Extended Day Aide
Jean Peltola–Dev. Director
Amy Southwell–Extended Day Business Office Aide

1996-1997 School Year
Carole Beverwyk–5-8 Science
Tom Bourcier–music
Ellen Force–preschool
T. Hanawalt–second grade
Andrea Hornby–preschool
Dawn Iott–K–4th science, logic and computers

Jennifer Lett–kindergarten
Mary Merrill–third grade
Lynn Pavlov–first grade
Sara Rodeck–art and art history
Robbi Rogers–fifth grade language arts and social studies
Sharon Rutkowski–French
Steve Spenceley–math, communications, travel
Duncan Sprattmoran–6-8 grades language arts and social studies
Alice Waddington–fourth grade

Staff

Deb Karsoe–Director
Ellen Northway–Bus. Manager
Clair Crandell–Adm. Assistant
Bob Prentice–Supervisor of Buildings and Grounds
Jim Hale–Maintenance
Melissa Elliott–Extended Day
Stephanie Walters–Aide, Extended Day
David Fouch–Bookkeeping Assistant
Mary Jane Hsu–Development Director
Jennifer Julin–Office Assistant

1996 Graduates

Ryan Fuller
Jesse Iott
Andrew Miller

1997 Graduates

Andrew Bantel
Ashley Christensen
Becca Cilluffo
Michael Clark
Meryl Estes
Lillian Evans
Evan Hsu
Jessica Modrall
Caitlin Prentice
Jordan Semer
Christopher Walter
Josh Willette
Laura Zreliak

1997–1998 School Year

Faculty

Jennifer Abel–kindergarten
Carol Beverwyk–middle school science
Tom Bourcier–music
Melissa Elliott–extended day
Ellen Force–preschool
T Hanawalt–second grade
Andrea Hornby–preschool
Dawn Iott–Lower elementary science, computers and logic
Adrienne Meli–library coordinator/ aide, extended day
Mary Merrill–third grade
Jerry O'Hearn–phys. ed./health

Lynn Pavlov–first grade
Jennifer Petrocelli–aide, language arts and social studies/ special needs
Audrey Pittinos–math
Sara Rodeck–art and art history
Robbi Rogers–fifth grade language arts and social studies
Sharon Rutkowski–French
Duncan Sprattmoran–6th-8th-language arts and social studies
Alice Waddington–fourth grade
Tammy Watt–aide, extended day

Staff

Deb Karsoe–Head of School
Ellen Northway–Bus. Manager
Shane Harrison–Bookkeeper
Mary Jane Hsu–Development Director
Jennifer Julin–Admissions and Marketing Coordinator
Ellen Baxter–Administrative Assistant
Bob Prentice–Supervisor Buildings and GHrounds
Jim Hale–Maintenance

1998-1999 School Year

Faculty

Jennifer Abel–kindergarten
John Beery–music
Carole Beverwyk–Middle School science
Stephanie Burns–aide, extended day
Stacy Claycomb–extended day
Craig Fleuter–art
Ellen Force–preschool
Debra Garver–Phys. Education
Sally Gernflo–fifth grade
Michael Gill–Middle School science
T. Hanawalt–second grade
Andrea Hornby–preschool
Dawn Iott–Lower School science, logic
Joyce MacManus–third grade
Mary Merrill–fourth grade
Merri Oberlin–technology
Lynn Pavlov–first grade
Audrey Pittinos–math
Sandy Robey–librarian
Sharon Rutkowski–French
Duncan Sprattmoran–6-8 grades language arts and social studies

Staff

Deb Karsoe–Head of School
Ellen Northway–Bus. Manager
Bob Prentice–Supervisor–Buildings and Grounds
Jim Hale–Maintenance
Cinda Simmons–Administrative Assistant
Jennifer Julin–Admissions and Marketing Coordinator
Mary Jane Hsu–Development Director
Shane Harrison–Bookkeeper

1998 Graduates

Wynne Calcutt
Erin Fuller
Greg Haugen
Fred Kilbourn
John Newman
Nicholas Nussdorfer
Claire Pomeroy
Ramsey Sprattmoran
Cooper Thoreson
David Walker

1999 Graduates

Meredith Hanson
Betsy Howell
Alice Iott
Katie Miller
Benjamin Schmerl
Colin Smith
Thomas Pezzetti

Edson Sheppard
Richard Skendzel
Tim Wade
Carolyn Weed
Brenin Wertz-Roth
Janet Wolff

1999-2000 School Year

Faculty
Jennifer Abel–Kindergarten
John Beery–Music
Carol Beverwyk–Middle School science
Stacey Claycomb–Extended day
Craig Fleuter–Art
Ellen Force–Preschool
T. Hanawalt –second grade
Shane Harrison–Middle school science
Melissa Heiler–Phys. Education
Andrea Hornby–Preschool
Dawn Iott–Lower School science, logic
Joyce MacManus–third grade
Terri McCarthy–Extended day
Mary Merrill–fourth grade
Lynn Pavlov–first grade
Audrey Pittinos–Math
Sandy Robey–Librarian
Sharon Rutkowski–French
Ruth Smith–fifth grade
Duncan Sprattmoran–Middle school language arts and social studies

Staff

Deb Karsoe–Head of School
Ellen Northway–Bus. Manager
Joyce Odell–Bookkeeper
Cinda Simmons–Adm. Assistant
Bob Prentice–Supervisor, Building and Grounds
Jim Hale–Maintenance
Jennifer Julin–Admissions and Marketing Coordinator
Mary Jane Hsu–Development Director
Janet Coon–Assistant Development Director

2000 Graduates

Charlotte DeKoning
Christina Gray
Caitlin Harrison
Brett Nussdorfer
Alexandra Odell
Andy Rastetter
Brenton Sell
Caitlin Smith

Robbi Rogers provided strong Lower School leadership for several years.

Our Faculty
1995

Seated : Jim Hale, Ann Anderson, Mary Quinn, Ellen Northway, Bob Prentice
Middle Row : Suzanne Gindin, Ellen Force, Pat Fulkerson, Lynn Pavlov, Joyce Mac Manus, Sharon Rutkowski, Dawn Iott, Bonnie Babel
Back Row : Jerry O'Hearn, Duncan Sprattmoran, Laurie Hirt, Sara Rodeck, Robbie Rogers, Alice Waddington, Dick Parks
Not Pictured : Susan Anderson, Jill Beauchamp, Cynthia Cronin, David Fouch, Kelly Halberg, Amy Southwell

Spring 1997. Fifth grade French chefs prepare and serve dinner to parents. Happy girls, below, and great times at the Sock Hop.

(l to r) Olivia Murray, Emily Bantel, Hannah Weber and Cody Sprattmoran work on the literary magazine, The Barking Cat.

Global Studies unit in the early 1990s.

Boys basketball in the 1990s and (below) Chinese ink project. (bottom) an outdoor classroom experience

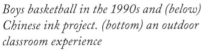

Suzanne Gindin, who taught instrumental music, is with the kindergarten class of 93/94.

Interlochen Pathfinder Years 2000–2007

In the fall of 1999 the Interlochen Center for the Arts expressed an interest in merging with Pathfinder. During the 1999-2000 school year both schools studied the possibilities and ramifications. The Pathfinder School board, parents, faculty, and staff had many questions and concerns. The most important one was potential loss of identity. After a year-long study it was announced in the spring of 2000 that the Pathfinder School and Interlochen Center for the Arts entered an agreement to merge. Everyone felt that the merger was an exciting and timely opportunity offering Pathfinder greater possibilities to realize the objectives and goals outlined in the 1998 Strategic Plan. According to Cary Weed, trustee, these included attracting and keeping good staff, upgrading and improving our physical facilities, attracting and keeping families, strengthening and growing our Middle School, and adding more arts, language, and counseling opportunities for all of our students.

The board, parents, faculty, and staff all felt that the school had a good partner with Interlochen. Their seventy-two year dedication to students and improving their learning environment showed a track record unparalleled in the area. The board was confident that with Interlochen's assistance, Pathfinder would be prepared to meet the ever increasing challenges of educating students in the years to come.

Jon D. Friley 2000-2007

Joyce chronicles the Interlochen Pathfinder Years...

J.D. Friley was hired. J.D. had been an employee at Interlochen and seemed to be the perfect candidate to help us through the transition of the merger. J.D. was large man with a deep voice and a fabulous sense of humor. He arrived early and went home late most evenings. His hard work and the fact that he stayed more than two years helped the school to grow.

J.D. Friley was named director. There was no longer a separate Pathfinder School Board of Trustees. Julie Quinn, president of the Pathfinder board at the time of merger, was named to the Interlochen board. The school name became the Interlochen Pathfinder School. New signage, new bumper stickers, new ways of doing busi-business were adopted, but teachers still were assured of autonomy in their classrooms. September 2000 arrived with great excitement and anticipation.

During the Interlochen-Pathfinder years many improvements were made to the physical plant. Two of the most important ones were the new drive-around entryway, which made arrival and dismissal times safer, and the wiring of the school for technology. Parents were responsible for modernizing and cleaning up the kitchen area in the gym.

J.D. Friley was Head of School from 2000 to 2006. He had come with extensive experience in independent schools, having served in various capacities at Culver Academy and subsequently at Interlochen Arts Academy. He left to accept a position at the Leelanau School as Dean of Students. Mary Sue Wilkinson, who had led an arts focused charter school in the Manistee area, was appointed director for the 2006-2007 school year.

Faculty 2000-2001

Ellen Force–preschool
Andrea Hornby–preschool
Jennifer Abel–kindergarten
Lynn Pavlov–first grade
T. Hanawalt–second grade
Joyce MacManus–third grade
Mary Merrill–fourth grade
Sally Gorenflo–fifth and sixth language arts and social studies
Duncan Sprattmoran–seventh and eighth grades language arts and social studies
Audrey Pittinos–fifth–eighth grades math

Dawn Iott–Lower School science
Shane Harrison–Middle School science
Craig Fleuter–art
Sharon Rutkowski–French
John Beery–music
Susan Sawyer–phys. education
Merri Oberlin–technology
Sandy Robey–library
Stacey Claycomb–extended day
Terri McCarthy–extended day

Staff

Jon D. Friley–Director
Ellen Northway–Coordinator of Adminstrative Services
Jennifer Julin–Admissions Counselor
Mary Jane Hsu–Development Associate
Cinda Simmons–Office Administrator
Bob Prentice–Maintenance Supervisor
Jim Hale–Custodian

2001 Graduates

Emily Bantel
Elizabeth Calcutt
Christopher Campsmith
Ethan Engle
Cory Ferrer

Zara Julin
Michael Kellogg
Melissa Kilbourn
Olivia Murray
Andrew Nance
James Pelizzari
Nicholas Smith
Hannah Weber
Rachel Winn

2001-2002 Faculty

Paula Ward–preschool 3
Andrea Hornby–preschool 4
Jennifer Abel–kindergarten
Lynn Pavlov–first grade
T. Hanawalt–second grade
Joyce Mac Manus–third grade
Mary Merrill–fourth grade
Sally Gorenflo–fifth grade
Mary Hammond–sixth grade language arts and social studies
Duncan Sprattmoran–7/8 grades language arts and social studies
Audrey Pittinos–5-8 grades math
Dawn Iott–Lower School science
Shane Harrison–Middle School science
Craig Fleuter–art
Karen McCarthy–French
John Beery–music
Susie Sawyer–phys. education
Merri Oberlin–technology
Sandy Robey–library

Susan Anderson-Hastings–
extended day

Staff
Jon D. Friley–Director
Ellen Northway–Coordinator of
Adminstrative Services
Jennifer Julin–Admissions
Counselor
Mary Jane Hsu–Development
Associate
Cinda Simmons–Office Ad-
ministrator
Bob Prentice–Maintenance
Supervisor
Jim Hale–Custodian

2002 Graduates

Lindsay Hanson
Tyler Hsu
Brian Karamon
Adam Lockwood
Rachel Neithercut
Lillian Prentice
Cotopaxi Sprattmoran
Nora Stone
Kris Wietrick
Amy Woodward
Kelsey Wright

2002-2003 Faculty

Paula Ward–preschool 3
Andrea Hornby–preschool 4
Jennifer Abel–kindergarten
Lynn Pavlov–first grade
T. Hanawalt–second grade
Joyce Mac Manus–third grade
Mary Merrill–fourth grade
Sally Gorenflo–fifth grade
Sarah Jane Johnson–sixth grade
language arts and social studies
Duncan Sprattmoran–7-8 grades
language arts and social studies
Audrey Pittinos–fifth through
eighth math
Dawn Iott–Lower School sci-
ence
Shane Harrison–Middle School
science
Craig Fleuter–art
Karen McCarthy–French
Lynn Tobin–music
Anne Bara–music
Jennifer Steinorth–dance
Susie Sawyer–physical educa-
tion
Merri Oberlin–technology
Sandy Robey–library
Susan Anderson-Hastings–
extended day

Staff
Jon D. Friley–Director
Ellen Northway–Coordinator of

Adminstrative Services, Associate Director of Development
Jennifer Julin–Admissions Counselor
Molly Bald–Development Associate
Cinda Simmons–Office Administrator
Bob Prentice–Maintenance Supervisor
Jim Hale–Custodian

2003 Graduates

Maria Baker
Keith Davis
Seamus Harrison
Andrew Lang
Thea Prust
Spencer Riebow
Jeremy Thompson
Amelia Walters
Elizabeth Walters
Jessica White
Alexandra Zenn

2003-2004 Faculty

Paula Ward–preschool 3
Andrea Hornby–preschool 4
Jennifer Abel–kindergarten
Lynn Pavlov–first grade
T. Hanawalt–second grade
Joyce MacManus–third grade
Mary Merrill–fourth grade
Sally Gorenflo–fifth grade

Sarah Jane Johnson–sixth grade language arts and social studies
Duncan Sprattmoran–7/8 grades language arts and social studies
Audrey Pittinos–5-8 grades math
Dawn Iott–Lower School science
Shane Harrison–Middle School science
Craig Fleuter–art
Karen McCarthy–French
Lynn Tobin–music
Margaret Bell–choir
Kat Brown–dance
Martin VanMaanen—bands
Susie Sawyer–physical education
Merri Oberlin–technology
Sandy Robey–library
Susan Anderson-Hastings–extended day

Staff

Jon D. Friley–Director
Ellen Northway–Coordinator of Adminstrative Services, Associate Director of Development
Jennifer Jay–Admissions Counselor
Tanya Donahue–Development Intern
Cinda Simmons–Office Administrator
Bob Prentice–Maint. Supervisor
Jim Hale–Custodian

2004 Graduates

Peter Corwin
Catherine Drettman
Taylor Forest
Haley Franklin
Giuliana Hazelwood
Aaron Jaffe
Emily Lundmark
Sarah Malone
Gabrielle Murray
Elise Nagy
Kristen Neithercut
Emma Stone
Nicholas Thomas
Charles Venditto
Caitlin Woods

2004-2005 Faculty

Paula Ward–preschool 3
Andrea Hornby–preSchool 4
Jennifer Abel–kindergarten
Lynn Pavlov–first grade
T. Hanawalt–second grade
Joyce MacManus–third grade
Patty Barrons–fourth grade
Sally Gorenflo–fifth grade
Sarah Jane Johnson–sixth grade
language arts and social studies
Duncan Sprattmoran–7/8 grades
language arts and social studies
Audrey Pittinos–fifth through
eighth math
Dawn Iott–Lower School science

Shane Harrison–Middle School
science
Craig Fleuter–art
Karen McCarthy–French
Lynn Tobin–music
Kat Brown–dance
Martin VanMaanen–bands
Susie Sawyer–physical education
Merri Oberlin–technology
Sandy Robey–library
Susan Anderson-Hastings–
extended day

Staff

Jon D. Friley–Director
Ellen Northway–Coordinator of
Adminstrative Services, Associate Director of Development
Jennifer Jay–Admissions Counselor
Tanya Donahue–Development
Intern
Cinda Simmons–Office Administrator
Bob Prentice–Maint. Supervisor
Jim Hale–Custodian

2005 Graduates

Andrew Ankerman
Tim Coobac
Nell Cunningham
Robert Evans
Linsey Fox

Kimberly Kelderhouse
Erich Kinney
Charlie Master
Charlie Olson
Ashleigh Powell
Clyde Rastetter
Nichlas Skriba
Hannah Stone
Akasha Sutherland
Sam Weber
Amelia Wright

2005-2006 Faculty

Paula Ward–preschool 3
Andrea Hornby–preschool 4
Jennifer Abel–kindergarten
Lynn Pavlov–first grade
T. Hanawalt–second grade
Joyce MacManus–third grade
Patty Barrons–fourth grade
Sally Gorenflo–fifth grade
Sarah Jane Johnson–sixth grade language arts and social studies, library
Duncan Sprattmoran–7/8 grades language arts and social studies
Audrey Pittinos–5-8 grades math
Dawn Iott–Lower School science
Shane Harrison–Middle School science
Craig Fleuter–art
Karen McCarthy–French
Lynn Tobin–music

Kat Brown–dance
Martin VanMaanen–bands
Susie Sawyer–phys. education
Merri Oberlin–technology
Susan Anderson-Hastings–extended Day

Staff

Jon D. Friley–Director
Ellen Northway–Associate Director of Development
Jennifer Jay–Admissions Counselor
Cinda Simmons–Office Admin.
Bob Prentice–Maintenance Supervisor
Jim Hale–Custodian

2006 Graduates

Andrew Bahle
Andrew Campbell
Fiona Carey
Molly Francis
Kiley Harrison
Maddie Johnson
Grant Kennell
Kate Little
Shannon Mahoney
Harry Malone
Chris Newlun
Emily Pittinos
Daniel Prust
Thea Senger

Joyce MacManus completes her chronicle:

By 2007 parents increasingly wanted to be free from Interlochen, and the feeling was mutual. We probably had never been a very good mix in the first place, but those years had served a purpose. J.D, who had grown very fond of the school and defended its independence and interests, perhaps eventually feeling a conflict of interest, left and found employment as Dean of Students at the Leelanau School. We were sent Mary Sue Wilkinson to take us through until the end. Mary Sue would sing with the children, but there was an air of doom and gloom at Pathfinder and Mary Sue had a difficult time leading. It would be a sometimes interesting, often frustrating, few years under the Interlochen umbrella.

The parents got together to discuss the situation and eventually the school was purchased from Interlochen. These hardworking, dedicated parents were not about to let the school die. They worked all summer long, and by the next fall we were back at Pathfinder filled with joy, independence, and a sense of future. It was a wonderful feeling, and our school never looked better. We all worked hard to help Bob Barrett with the transition. Bob was a leader in the parents' struggle to get the school back.

He offered to stay on for the first year to help with the finances and act as head.

The first year of "The New Pathfinder School" was somewhat scattered and difficult. The classrooms still buzzed with enthusiasm, but there were new people in the office and all new forms to get into place. Bob Barrett took the role of Head and with the help of Ellen Northway we made it through the year. The office staff worked hard, but they were looking for paper clips as well as a way to make it all come together. We could not have done it without them and our parents volunteering their time, money, and encouragement.

> As we begin our second year we will be involved in a search for a director of the school. Hopes are high that we will find someone with knowledge of all levels of education who understands independent schools and the mentality of up-north parents. My desire is for him/her to have a great sense of humor and stay for a while.

Though the Baxters had not been actively particpating in the school for some years except as encouraging visitors, it's interesting to read Art Baxter's view on the situation.

> When J.D. Friley asked Nancy and me to visit the new president at Interlochen to get our feel for what the direction might be, it was made very plain that the academy had to consider its own priorities first. Pathfinder must stand on its own without budget subsidies or extravagant growth plans.
>
> There were difficulties in combining two schools with such different interests, geographic locations, and budgetary priorities. Pathfinder had evolved with a strong, independent spirit and independence was a keystone of all its history.
>
> Although Joe Maddy had made an elementary school one of the priorities when he founded Interlochen originally, it was not easy for the larger school to understand the needs of young students—or their parents who would end up having to give support to the school. They could not find strong support, either educationally or financially, without having an independent board of trustees. Being without a separately functioning board was a huge liability to the Traverse City "sister school" of Interlochen.
>
> In the first place, it was impossible to get specifically funded budget priorities for Pathfinder. Our leaders were told we needed to operate in a much larger context, the Interlochen general fund. Many new programs went unfunded. In addition, funds raised by Pathfinder supporters could not always be allocated to the school the supporters wished to support. Interest in giving diminished to a trickle.

135

More important was the feeling that the Pathfinder concerns could not be addressed without a directly active and functioning board of trustees for that school alone.

For their part, Interlochen felt Pathfinder was an increasing drain and distraction. The goals and interests were just too dissimilar. Interlochen faced its own budgetary crunch. In an effort to bring their budget under control in February of 2007 the Interlochen board decided to close the school.

Both Bob Barrett and Curtis Kuttnauer deserve real thanks for their significant leadership. Curtis spearheaded the effort to mobilize the parents and finance the purchase of the grounds. His energy lit the torch and led the way. Bob Barrett has brought strong leadership credentials to the job of head during the transition years. Bob, who was a major in the U.S. Air Force, had served as vice president and chief information officer for Detroit Diesel Allison Division of General Motors. He was later president and CEO of Bank One Services Corporation and was chief officer of other important companies.

The parents rallied to save the school. They made visits and presentations to Interlochen, suggesting new advancement techniques and programs, but it was not to be. The group headed by Bob and Curtis and including many parents decided to take control of the school, re-form it, and run it again. It was a brave and risky strategy, and it is a miracle that it worked. But much of Pathfinder's history has been something of a miracle anyway. This new effort, the re-forming of the school at the hands of amazingly dedicated parents, has to stand as the most glorious chapter of the school's history so far.

The school opened with all licenses in place in September 2007 with 135 students. During that momentous first year, the board embarked upon an ambitious course to create a new strategic plan and to earn ISACS accreditation, both of which were accomplished by 2008.

The Pathfinder School would continue to offer families of the region an independent school option in the tradition that the founders established more than thirty-five years ago.

Curriculum highlights during the 1990s and the Interlochen Pathfinder period are explained by Duncan Sprattmoran. Duncan won the Traverse City Area Chamber of Commerce Outstanding Educator Award.

During the 1990s the Pathfinder faculty, having healthy enrollments in the Lower School yet low enrollment in the Middle School, focused energies on researching Middle School curricula and developing a program that would meet the needs of students in the Grand Traverse area. Seeing that most area Middle Schoolers were enrolled either in public schools that were based on junior high philosophies or were home schooled, we built a challenging academic program that was based on the Pathfinder premise that all children learn when given individual attention and in a program that addresses various learning styles.

With the dissemination of Howard Gardner's conceptual framework of multiple intelligence, the faculty worked to create curricula that provided children multiple approaches—or to use a Project Zero term, entry points—to their academic work. While the Middle School continued to set high academic standards, we recognized that children are visual and kinesthetic learners as well as linguistic and mathematical, and we therefore created a unique blend of assignments that incorporated more visual and dramatic arts, as well as various hands-on projects. Yet at the same time we continued to promote writing across the curriculum and truly nurtured young writers, many of whom went on to high school and college and studied creative writing.

From 1995-1999 Pathfinder was the recipient of several Michigan Council for the Arts and Cultural Affairs mini-grants to bring area artists in to work with our students. Our students worked with Jim Bob and Lucy Stephenson (professor emeritus of theater at Kent State University) for two years creating touring productions of Shakespeare and children's theater, which we performed at area school. Following the Stephensons' residencies, our students and faculty worked with Jane Hawley (currently professor of dance at

Luther College) on two interactive mutlimedia performances of movement and spoken word where the students visited area senior centers and interviewed senior citizens about their childhoods, the Great Depression, and World War II, and developed performances based on what they had heard from the seniors. Most recently, using Rutkoski Grant moneys our students worked with Jenee Rowe on a serious of Andy Goldsworthy-inspired instillation projects using personal writings and found natural materials. During the spring of 2006 our students constructed transitive art exhibitions at the De Young Conservancy property, particularly looking at invasive species and land reclamation.

During our seven-year relationship with Interlochen, the Middle School developed a program of electives—which we called MIADS (Multiple Intelligence Arts Domains)—designed to allow the Middle School student a range of short sampler classes such as cooking, personal finance, fiber arts, eco literacy, etc. In addition to the MIADS, students had a range of longer term arts classes such as theater (in which the students would tour their performances to area schools and nursing homes), readers theater (in which students would collaboratively write and perform radio dramas), dance, production and design, band, and orchestra. While the Interlochen administration expected Pathfinder to add arts programs to the curriculum, what we discovered is that we were already all working with the arts to such an extent that we simply just had to readjust our programming to meet the Interlochen mandate of developing an arts-rich curriculum.

During the early 2000s approximately a third of the school faculty attend Harvard's Project Zero—a week-long symposium at the School of Education that brings educators from around the world together to share and study curricular design and implementation. The Project Zero frameworks provided yet another way for Pathfinder teachers to consider their work with children. As dynamic and innovative as the Project Zero concepts are, what we found was they simply affirmed and extended the educational principles that Pathfinder has always embraced, and so, while they provided us an exciting structure and vocabulary we could all share, we simply incorporated them into the notion children learn given supportive nurturing adults guiding them.

There are so many examples to choose from to illustrate the dynamic learning that happened at Pathfinder over the past years. Here are three revealing the breadth and complexity of our approach.

Every spring we take the entire Middle School on trips to various locations, Chicago, Stratford, Wilderness State Park, and Mackinaw Island. One spring we were all walking the beach at Wilderness when a student found some bones and skin emerging from the surf. Shane Harrison, our science teacher, immediate set to work unburying the find only to discover the sodden remains of a coyote. With the help of many amazed, disgusted, and intrigued students, Shane rolled the carcass into a plastic bag. We brought it back to school on the bus where Shane and the students reburied the coyote, only to disinter it months later when the bones were clean. This was the ultimate in emerging and place-based curriculum. One measure of the success of the project was when a bunch of teenage girls chattered with enthusiastic science vocabulary as they poked and prodded the water logged body.

Each year, the Middle School and cocurricular faculty have designed a two week thematic multi-aged curriculum during which sixth, seventh, and eighth graders all work together on projects. This allows Middle Schoolers the opportunity to really take on different roles than they are accustomed to and to work, learn, and play in different social configurations than they are used to. One year we choose the Renaissance as our focusing theme and students wrote sonnets; painted as groups three foot by four-foot replications of the masters' works; and created a tent village of homemade tents (the math component) on the snowy soccer field, where they took on the characters of minstrels, bards, jugglers, jousters, jesters, and players. The two weeks culminated with a medieval feast of black bread and pickles, drumsticks, and steaming fruit pies.

Another classroom event that typifies our experiential learning style was when Duncan Sprattmoran, hoping by using hands-on kinesthetic project to scaffold conceptual learning, had his eighth grade students engage in an arms race. The students were grouped in teams of two and three, each group representing one of the Great Powers prior to World War I Each group had to acquire their resources (sheets of paper) that were strategically, and not conveniently scattered around the room, and then assemble the resources into paper airplanes. The thirteen students assembled over 570 paper airplanes during the period and certainly remembered the concept of an arms race. Later, to demonstrate the trench warfare of the First World War, Duncan armed the students with gumdrops while he used candy corn and the students had to "go over the top" on whistle command, and cross the no-man's land of chairs and tables, while being bombarded by candy corn. During the attack the room was filled with laughter and hilarity, yet all the students, weeks later, retained the key data about the Western Front. Another example of such learning was when a student made a 3-d model of the western front out of chocolate cake, marshmallows, licorice strands and gumdrops (later to be eaten as a birthday cake). She too retained the key concepts in long-term memory.

While we are charged with covering the curriculum in the published scope and sequence, we all endeavor to make the assignments memorable, relevant, and exciting. So on any given day a visitor may be surprised to find students out of their seats, moving through the classroom, moving through the campus, videotaping, dancing, making things out of found materials, sitting beneath a tree writing, and cooking in the kitchen, always with a teacher who knows them well moving from child to child for the one-on-one discussions wherein the real learning takes place.

2007-2008 Faculty

Trisha Short–preschool 3
Paula Ward–preSchool 4
Stephanie McLean–kindergarten
Lynn Pavlov–first grade
T Hanawalt–second grade
Joyce MacManus–third grade
Patty Barrons–fourth grade
Sally Gorenflo–fifth grade
Sarah Jane Johnson–sixth grade language arts and social studies, library
Duncan Sprattmoran–seventh and eighth grade language arts and social studies
Audrey Pittinos–fifth through eighth math
Dawn Iott–Lower School science
Shane Harrison–Middle School science
Craig Fleuter –art
Karen McCarthy–French
Lynn Tobin–music
Kat Brown–dance
David Warne–percussion
Susie Sawyer–phys ed
Merri Oberlin–technology
Susan Anderson-Hastings–extended day

Staff

Robert Barrett–Head of School
Ellen Northway–Business Manager

Robin Nance–Office Administrator (Sept.–Jan.)
Jules Shellby–Office Administrator
Leisa Hankins–Development and Admissions (started in Jan.)
Bob Prentice–Maintenance Supervisor
Jim Hale–Custodian

The New Pathfinder School Graduating Class 2008

Maxine Burrows
Tatiana Crespo
Jesse Einhorn-Johnson
Phillip Hanawalt
Tate Hanawalt
Phillip Knox
Max Lundmark
Jake Meade
Charlie Pacer
David Pelizzari
Lena Rollenhagen

Eighth grade graduation in the Lisa Huron Memorial Gardens continued in the tradition of the Upper School graduation ceremonies. Each graduating eighth grader offered a special presentation–an original or tradtional script, and so forth.

Students from the 2000s.

2nd grade at Tapestry

Fall Experience at Camp Leelanau,

Devant St. Merri
à côte de la
Centre Pompidou
2001

The annual spring rocket launches were always eagerly anticipated.

6th Grade 2001

Alexander Adams

Jeffrey Byl

Keith Davis

Seamus Harrison

Daniel Kellogg

Patrick Kelly

Jalel Nadji

Jesse Smith

Alexandra Zenn

Keith Davis at the Science Expo

Dan Kellogg in racquet sports

A plant cell big enough to walk through; 6th grade with Shane Harrison and Craig Fleuter.

Dan and Jalel

Patrick Kelly

Jalel, Jesse and Keith

8th Grade 2001

Emily Bantel

Elizabeth Calcutt

Christopher Campsmith

Ethan Engle

Cory Ferrer

Zara Julin

Michael Kellogg

Melissa Kilbourn

Olivia Murray

Andrew Nance

Jimmy Pelizzari

Nicholas Smith

Hannah Weber

Rachel Winn

Olivia making crepes for French Day

Snowshoeing at Cedar Lake

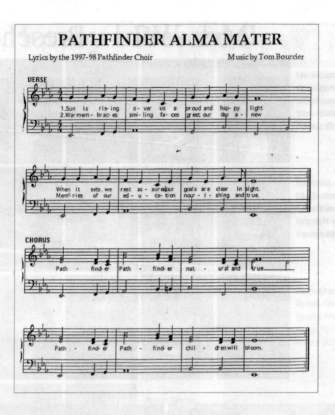

PATHFINDER ALMA MATER

Lyrics by the 1997-98 Pathfinder Choir

Music by Tom Bourcier

VERSE

1. Sun is ris-ing o-ver us a proud and hap-py light
2. Warm em-brac-es smil-ing fa-ces greet our day a-new

When it sets we rest as-sured our goals are clear in sight.
Mem'ries of our ed-u-ca-tion nour-i-shing and true.

CHORUS

Path - find-er Path - find-er nat - ur-al and true.

Path - find-er Path - find-er chil - dren will bloom.

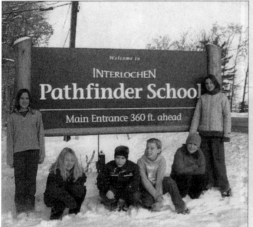

Happy 30th Birthday – Interlochen Pathfinder School!
We thought we would remind you of our past while we look at the events of this school year. Thank you for being an important part of Interlochen Pathfinder's past, present, and future!
Be sure to see the yearbook supplement which will feature more late winter and spring events as well as eighth grade graduation. The second semester yearbook class is hard at work making the supplement to this issue.

First Semester Yearbook Staff: (l to r)
Elizabeth Walters, Lindsey Eldredge-Fox, Nick Skriba, Shawn Barry, Nell Cunningham, Ashleigh Powell

2004 Mrs. Harrison - Eighth Grade

Mrs. Harrison
Peter Corwin
Catharine Drettmann
Taylor Forrest
Haley Franklin

Giuliana Hazelwood
Aaron Jaffe
Emily Lundmark
Sarah Malone
Gabrielle Murray

Elise Nagy
Kristen Neithercut
Emma Stone
Nick Thomas
Charlie Venditto

Caitlin Woods

ON THE RIVER

FIELD TRIP WITH IAA

GROUP PHOTO

HOVER CRAFT

INSECT COLLECTION

Mr. Sprattmoran - Seventh Grade

Mr. Sprattmoran
Laura Adams
Andrew Ankerman
Shawn Barry
Tim Coobac

Nell Cunningham
Robert Evans
Lindsey Fox
Kimberly Kelderhouse
Erich Kinney

Charlie Olson
Ashleigh Powell
Clyde Rastetter
Nicholas Skriba
Hannah Stone

Akasha Sutherland
Sam Weber
Amelia Wright

PROBABILITY

GLAZING

READY FOR THE ROPES COURSE

PathFUNDer 2005

Mr. Sprattmoran - Eighth Grade   2005

Mr. Sprattmoran
Andrew Ankerman
Tim Coobac
Nell Cunningham

Robert Evans
Lindsey Fox
Kimberly Kelderhouse
Erich Kinney

Charlie Master
Hannah McCarthy - Stone
Charlie Olson
Ashleigh Powell

Clyde Rastetter
Nicholas Skriba
Akasha Sutherland
Sam Weber

Amelia Wright

Interlochen Pathfinder School Faculty/Staff
2006

JD Friley

Robin Nance

Jennifer Jay

Ellen Northway

Karen McCarthy

Susan Hastings

Tanya Donahue

Audrey Pittinos

Craig Fleuter

Martin VanMaanen

Dawn Iott

Merri Oberlin

Susie Sawyer

Lynne Tobin

Jim Hale

Kat Brown

Bob Prentice

Not Pictured: Cinda Simmons

Mrs. Pavlov - First Grade

Mrs. Pavlov
Emily Anderson
Jillian Avis
Nicholas Friar

Zachary Hankins
Maxwell Herman
Norah Johnson
Skylar Lensch

Zander Lensch
Erin Makie
Matthew Neumann
Evan Norgaard

Katrina Salon

Mrs. Hanawalt - Second Grade

Mrs. Hanawalt
Ginger Burrows
Calum Conger
Ella Dorman

Sierra Falconer
Maddie Fragel
Cora Kinney
Nicole Kuttnauer

Rowan LaFrance
Emma Nance
Kimberly Snodgrass
Lindsey Weeks

Eve Montie

Mrs. MacManus - Third Grade

Mrs. MacManus
Anna Bahle
Paige Cooley
Jordan Davis

Spencer Firman
Alexandra Friar
Christine Haight
Daniel Hansen

Nicholas Larson
Alexandra Little
Stephanie Long
Amelia Pezzetti

Michael Stypa
Donovan Weeks
Theo Womack

Mrs. Gorenflo - Fifth Grade

Mrs. Gorenflo
Aaron Baker
Stevie Carmien
Callie Chappell

Kelly Conger
Flannery Johnson
Aaron Mahoney
Winton Munch

Trey Pezzetti
Ben Phillips
Hannah Prust
Katie Stanton

Julian VandenBerg
Kendall Young

APPENDIX

The following men and women have served as trustees for Pathfinder School. The list may not be complete.

Robert Andrews, Ed Bantel, Robert Barrett, Charles Bee, Harry Blount, Ken Bovee, James Bruno, Bruce Byl, Betsy Calcutt, Phil Cochran, Leslie Cook, Bob Cornwell, Doug Davis, Peter Dendrinos Sr., Mike Dennos, Chris Dennos, Mike Dettmer, Diane Donley, Tom Drenth, Jim Dutmers, Janet Fleshman, Ellen Force, William Fortune, Jane Frasier, Dr. Don and Barbara Good, David Gray, Rod Groleau, Frank Hagerty, Ward Haggard, David Halsted, David Hanawalt, Leisa Hankins, Ann Hanson, Byron Hanson, David Herr, Fred Heslop Sr., Jeff Hickman, Janet Hodges, Jack Hood, Mecky Howell, Mary Jane Hsu, Stuart Hubbell, Richard Jarvis, Linda Johnson, Johanna Johnson, Ron Jolly, Barbara Kausler, Ken and Sandra Kearney, Ron Kimler, Susan Kuras, Curtis Kuttnauer, Rorie Lewis, David Lint, Larry Linvill, Karen Lundmark, Deb Malone, Jim McIntyre, John McNeil, Jim Merenda, Cass Miller, Kelly Miller, Paul Montie, Susan Nichols, Ellen Northway, Beth Nussdorfer, Harry Oliver, Priscilla Payne, Jean Peltola, Thomas Pezzetti, Stacey Pezzetti, J. R. Preston, Julie Quinn, Steve Riecker, John Rockwood, Terry Rogers, Peter Rush, Sharon Rutkowski, Paul Russell, Paul Scott, Robert Seward, Edson Sheppard, Richard Skendzel, Gregg Smith, Doug Stanton, Dave Stave, Roger Steed, Kate Stevens, Jack Thomas, Tom Turner, Jack Unger, Steve VanZoeren, Tim Wade, Stephanie Walter, David Warm Sr., Roger and Carol Watson, Kevin Weber, Carolyn Weed, Dale Wentzloff, Joe Williamson, Janet Wolff, Maureen Wolin, Bob Young, Gayle Zreliak.

Pathfinder Foundation Board Members—ZsuZsi Danek, Spence Hinds, Emily Killian, Bobbie Stevens, John Stebbins.

MEMORIES FROM THE TRAIL BEHIND US

Sally Driver, Lower School Teacher 1973-1975

Being hired at a school for gifted and talented children was a dream come true to me. The children seemed to thrive on the activities and philosophy at Pathfinder. I remember Chris Oliver not doing well with words on paper, but he would do anything to take apart a typewriter and put it back together. I was allowed to use a system developed in Lansing public schools which allowed children to learn concepts at their own pace. One student of mine in sixth grade was going into the high school for eighth grade math. Lunch was great as we had on occasion the world's greatest pea soup. Winter Wednesdays were amazing with choice of skiing, bowling etc. One day I was to drive the children to the bowling alley in the world's largest van but I backed into a car in the alley and drove back to school with the emergency brake on. I thought that would be my last day, but Art was kind I recall. Reed Zitting working on a hog at the Lake Michigan bluffs along with Jerry Breu staying through the night to be sure it roasted just right. I have continued to teach for thirty-four years, with ten off to be a mom of two kind and accomplished girls and have served most of my time as a special education teacher for preschool kids.

Ken Driver, Upper School Teacher 1973-1975

Most of my memories deal with kids and attempting to put together competitive teams. I always thought we had for our size some good athletes and the kids put forth good effort. I do recall I felt the need for good conditioning as part of practice. That was probably the biggest "sales" job, as most of the kids did not enjoy the running. I recall Jimmy Baxter was a big, big help as he more and more got on board with the running thing and encouraged the others. His attitude was a reason we competed so well in soccer against

Interlochen, Suttons Bay, and Traverse City Christian School. I recall taking our lumps too. I limped off the field one day after a game. I was accidentally kicked in practice. Some of our teams were hot, then cooled. One year we won our first and second games, then we lost a couple of our players to some injuries and we just weren't deep enough to compensate.

I taught basic math concepts to ninth and tenth graders, concepts like buying a car, and taking out a home or car loan when you put so much down and then pay interest. I can still recall the look on some of these kids' faces when the realized how much that car was actually going to cost.

Magic at the Pigeon River
Tom Shaw, Upper School Class of 1977

One of the best classes I took at Pathfinder was Dick Parks' Environmental Studies my sophomore year. Dick was a well seasoned, joyous outdoorsman. He had grown up in the Cable-Seeley area of Wisconsin and had even worked for Outward Bound. In his class we read Aldo Leopold and Edward Abbey. He taught us to be observant in the woods. I was an active Boy Scout and loved nothing more than to hike, ski, and canoe; but some in the class were less experienced and even a little reticent. Dick was a patient teacher of outdoor skills who never let anyone get in over their head and could do everything he taught.

Once a month Mr. Parks took the class on some outing. We hiked through the Kingston Plains to Twelve Mile Beach. We skied around Chapel Lake. Many of us saw our first bald eagles in the Bendon Swamp. In the early spring of 1975 he took us to the Pigeon River State Park near Gaylord. I believe the members of that group were Paul Russell, Janet Baxter, Jim Stallard, Wendy Rogers and Glen Jackson. I distinctly remember that there were still small snow banks in the woods, so it must have been early April. We reached the parking lot before dark on Friday night, shouldered our packs and headed into the woods to find a campsite. The spot we chose was in a small clearing on top of a rounded hill. We pitched our tents and made dinner. Dick tried to drive Leave No Trace ethics into us and recommending that we forget the fire and enjoy the night on its own terms would have been like him. As we were cleaning up and hanging about watching the darkness creep into the clearing, someone heard the strangest whistling noise followed by several obvious birdcalls. Soon another whistling noise, followed by a small thump in between the tents. We all stood trying to figure out what on earth it was. The thump was followed by a peeping sound that traveled down the slope, then birdcalls. Soon one, then another projectile came hurtling into camp. As our eyes became adjusted to the darkness we realized that the projectiles were birds that shot up toward the stars and were descending in spirals. Someone, probably Mr. Parks, realized that the birds were woodcocks and what we were witnessing was the mating dance. We stood stock still in the dark, aware that we were intruders and afraid to cause the wonder to be cut short. Gradually the noises faded as the mating pairs were formed and we were left to wonder about what we had witnessed and drift off to our sleeping bags.

The next morning walking the road, we rounded a right-hand bend with a broad meadow on our left. The Pigeon River State Park was a sanctuary for a herd of elk; and we hoped we would see at least one. The sun had just reached this meadow, and the frost was having its brief moment of sparkling life. We stopped to admire the scene. The frost was sublimating into mist before our eyes, but Mr. Parks noticed that one part of the meadow was steamier than the rest. As if summoned by Walt Disney on a nature film, a sizeable herd of elk stood up from their sleeping spot. I can't remember how many there were but there was at least a bull with several cows and their calves. They stood eyeing us across the sparkling grass. The remarkable thing was they were covered in frost and gleamed like their surroundings.

The class hiked all morning through the soggy, snowbank-dotted woods. We were always slightly wet, but the warm sun and brisk pace made for a very pleasant walk. At noon we stopped at a lightly wooded bend in the Pigeon River. I found a white pine ringed with dry turf and apart from the others. I sat on my sleeping pad with my back against the tree and my face to the sun and began to eat salami and crackers. A jet contrail appeared and thinned above. Everyone was absorbed in their food and the glorious sun. Apart from the spring flow of the Pigeon it was still.

At some point I became aware of a faint noise. Hmm, a mole is tunneling under me, maybe a rodent in the bushes. No, what was it? It was a sort of crackling, pushing noise. I stopped eating and began to listen very carefully. This was starting to bug me. All of a sudden it hit me. I had never actually heard this before, but I knew what it was. Of course I resisted because it was just impossible; my brother and I had said as much many times.

My father had described it every spring. He would come home from the orchard and proudly announce that he had heard the grass growing. This was it, the sound he described. The conditions were perfect. Warm sun, snow melt in the soil. A mat of last year's dead grass below the new grass. New grass pushing through the dead in its reach for the sun. I don't remember if I told anyone. I have never heard the grass grow again, though I am always listening for it in the early spring. I like to think that it is the listening for it and not the actual hearing that is important.

Though my dad and Mr. Parks met a few times, they had no relationship. But they were both ourdoorsmen who knew when to be silent and what to look for. They both were open to the possibility that something remarkable and memorable could happen at any moment. On that spring trip to the Pigeon River it became clear to me that experiences could be great and small in the same instant and were waiting to be stumbled across like a root in the trail. I am sure I have forgotten this more than I have remembered it and passed by some remarkable things because I was too closed or preoccupied to be bothered. On the other hand, I have had similar experiences even now and then and they are few and worth remembering.

Es Bueno!
LuAnn Roberts Kemble, Class of 1980
Teacher, California School System, Murietta

Pathfinder made a difference in my life. I was foolish to leave after my junior year. It was an experience I don't think you could duplicate today. I became a teacher also, after I took a few years off to raise my two children, Brian and Holly. I live in California and have had my credentials for fifteen years When I started teaching there were no jobs to be found in southern California unless you were bilingual. The Pathfinder Spanish classes helped me get a foot in the door and pay my rent! I cannot believe that the thing I hated most—math—I have ended up teaching fifth graders. Mrs. Watson taught us how to follow algebraic solutions step by step. I do the same thing with my students. Murietta, my district, is always focused on state standards, and my students always have the highest scores, one year, ten to twenty-two points higher than the state average. I want Pathfinder to know that it made a difference in my life and consequently, in other children's lives.

Soups, Spoons, and Sponsored Luncheons
Tammy Medell Allen, Class of 1977
Teacher, California

Some of my favorite Pathfinder memories revolve around food. My first field trip with Pathfinder was to New Orleans in January of 1976, with myriad stops in between to visit Civil War battlegrounds and plantations. We picnicked at roadside parks, munching on waxed paper-wrapped sandwiches, and breakfasted on cereal served up with cold milk and juice retrieved from a Coleman cooler. I even recall Mrs. Baxter frying up bacon in an electric skillet plugged into her motel room. If memory serves me correctly, one motel manager paid a visit to the Baxters' room, admonishing them for cooking in their room!

Another food-related memory while on the road is of a frozen turkey riding up the baggage ramp of a plane in a laundry basket. The senior class of 1977 had earned a trip to the Abacos, Bahamas–not coincidentally by way of food, in the form of serving up dozens of sloppy joe lunches throughout the school year. We stayed in a house on Elbow Cay; upon arrival, Mr. Baxter divided us into task-related groups: galley crew, laundry, cooks, etc. We had purchased supplies on the mainland; hence, the turkey-as-baggage.

We didn't always eat on the cheap. I have a fond memory of an elegant meal at the Commander's Palace in New Orleans, where I tried bread pudding for the first time. I don't recall liking the bread pudding too much, but I do remember the graceful surroundings and normally raucous teenagers behaving their best. I turned eighteen on our senior class trip in the spring of 1977 and was delighted by a birthday cake and surprise party given in the motel room. Another poignant food-related memory was of trying papaya for the first time while lounging around the harbor at Man-O-War Cay on that Bahamas trip. A neighboring sailor shared his spread with us, as well as his good humor and conversation.

Whether it was mugs of hot soup sipped at lunchtime, or Mr. Breu's roast pig, food brought us together at Pathfinder. Even oatmeal cooked from a backpacking stove on the coast of Lake Superior seemed like a celebratory meal because it was shared with friends—fond memories of food and friendships!

Team Drama: Starring Dr. Seuss and Adam Begley
Class of 1979
Adam Begley, Property Management Lake Leelanau

At first I thought that being part of Reed Zitting's drama troupe was childish and silly. I seriously felt that I was far too cool to be running around in circles, flapping my arms, pretending to be a crow and rattling off nursery rhymes. After some time and a lot of patience on Reed's part, I began to understand the value of being an integral part of that program. Oh, yeah, everyone knew that I just loved being up on my stage in front of any amount of people in those days, but what I got out of it then and what I continued to filter out of it to this day is that there was more to learn about myself in that class than I ever learned in my entire life up to that point.

The lesson was that of teamwork. I had been on the soccer team, the tennis team at the school, every kind of team, but those teams were largely based on my performance in front of an opponent. Reed Zitting's drama class was not about me, and it was not about my team's competitive agility while combating foes from other school. It was a team effort where my best possible personal performance was absolutely necessary for us all to find success, the most cohesive, meaningful, and pleasing piece of entertainment for our many, discriminating audiences.

One day, many years after our graduation in the Lisa Huron Memorial Garden, I sat up straight in the big, cushy chair as a participant in what Arco Chemical Company (my then employer) referred to as a "Team Building Seminar." They were showing us all how to work together by having us put together popsicle sticks and arrange playing cards and dominos together in a way so they would stand in the shape of a little house. What brilliance money can buy! Again I thought the whole thing was childish and silly, but my mind went back to the time when I didn't want to rush around, flapping my hands like a crow, that is, until I learned what that business was really all about. Teamwork—works!

Thanks all you wonderful teachers and thanks, too, to you Gerald.

Thank you, everybody at the school
Meg Bowen Warm, Northport, Michigan
Class of 1985

I began my adventure at the Pathfinder School as a seventh grader and graduated in 1985. As a teenager, school was the last place I wanted to be, and I didn't understand until years later how fortunate I was to have landed on that campus. Of course, being so young I was convinced that my problems were insurmountable, just like many of the other students round me. Now I'm riding the hormonal roller coaster with my own teens, and my appreciation for the patience and guidance I received over the six years I spent at Pathfinder continues to grow.

My teachers were outstanding, and despite my efforts to be anywhere but in class, I still got a great formal education. Nevertheless, the most indispensable lessons weren't necessarily academic; they were taught by example. It's not easy to summarize this unparalleled school. A small part of the description would include a fundamental balance between self confidence and humility, and the intrinsic conviction that beauty lies within.

Pathfinder endowed me with a lasting gift: the influences of people like Reed Zitting, Ernie East (Reed-n-Ernie as they were called) Marcia Belanger, Marty Trapp, Mark Fries, Mary Lynn Watson, Nancy Crisp, Sue East, John Grote, Brenin Wertz-Roth and of course Bob Prentice, who is still there today, fondly smiling. For those who didn't know them, they are just names. But for those of us who were there, they are earnestly cherished. I think some people have kept the infamous soup cups as mementos. How appropriate, this simple, yet extraordinary keepsake to be admired by those of us who shared the Pathfinder experience. We were the lucky ones.

The Pizza's Late
Bob Barett, Director, the Pathfinder School

One Friday at Pizza Lunch, the pizza was late arriving. In fact, it was very late. As Pathfinder veterans know, the eighth grade students help out by serving the pizza and condiments to the younger students. On this Friday they were all in place with sanitary gloves on, except there was no pizza. The youngest scholars, lined up out the door, were hungry and were becoming slightly unruly waiting for the pizza, which still hadn't arrived.

Suddenly the eighth grade servers came out from behind the tables and began to sing songs they had learned in their early days at Pathfinder. The young ones knew the songs and joined in. They all then came together in a circle and began to dance and sing with the little ones. This went on for fifteen or twenty minutes and certainly until the pizza arrived. The little ones were have such a great time they forgot about being hungry and ornery.

So, tell me another school you know where the eighth grade students would spontaneously engage the younger children in song and dance, in order to pass the time more easily for their younger colleagues.

I don't know of one either. Kindness and civility are not browbeaten into children. They learn by example and the mentoring of their older friends.

Words from Caitlin Prentice, Class of 1997
An author of *Biking the U.S. of Awesomeness*

Since graduating from Pathfinder a decade ago, I have successfully navigated public high school, attended college in Vermont,
won a scholarship to do a master's degree in Scotland, worked as a
climbing instructor, dishwasher, youth worker, sandwich maker, and
classroom assistant, and now find myself at the end of a year-long
postgraduate course in elementary education in Aberdeen, Scotland.
Pathfinder prepared me academically—to excel in the competitive
high school environment, make it into a selective college, and win
the scholarship. But more importantly, Pathfinder prepared me to
be a decent person—to be kind, to work hard, to ask questions, to
live honestly, to have fun, to think critically—the list goes on. I have
experienced many different educational environments in my life, but
it was my time at Pathfinder that inspired me to become a teacher
myself, because I know just what is possible within a school if people
really care about education (and each other).

And from Lily Prentice, Class of 2002

Here is a paragraph from Lily. She was at Pathfinder from
pre-school through eighth grade. After Pathfinder, she spent 4
years at Interlochen for high school. Now she is at Bowdoin
College in Maine. Bowdoin is highly selective and a great opportunity. She plans to spend at least part of next year studying
abroad at a university in Edinburgh, Scotland.

It is difficult to describe Pathfinder in words: for me, it is a
place where so many different kinds of knowledge are instilled.
There I learned about everything from my peers, myself and what I
love to do, how to write a poem inspired by painting, how modern
Americans may have found themselves speaking Mandarin if only
the ancient Chinese sailed east, to how to strategize, from a game

of chess to a game of capture the flag through the woods. To be in a school where more often than not the classroom is the great outdoors, to perform Shakespeare (albeit abbreviated) at the age of 10, to learn how to monitor the health of a local body of water and feel like I was making a difference in the world ecosystem: all of these things and many more combine to create the Pathfinder experience, one that is truly extraordinary.

In the Dark about the English Kings
Marybeth Baxter Fulmer, Class of 1975
Marketing Communications & CRM Coordinator, Trilithic Corp.

What fun we all had in that great classroom environment. It's 1974, and I can see us in the art room, part of it now a classroom, kids on couches and bean bag chairs setting the mood for relaxed learning. We might have been relaxed, but the homework and teaching were preparing us for college and instilling in us a lifetime love of learning. I was on the yearbook and newspaper for all three years. I enjoyed taking pictures all through the year, most of which ended up in the '73-'75 yearbooks.

Looking through those yearbooks, I remember those moments in time and actually snapping the pictures. I recall many times being under deadline and having to develop the pictures during class in the darkroom at the end of that classroom in the art building. I remember listening to my mom teaching my Humanities class.

There I was dipping my photos into all those stinky chemicals listening to the lecture on the Kings of England, getting ready to memorize them all, and in order. The fun activities, the cool buildings, the beautiful environment all made Pathfinder a great experience. But, it was laughing with all my friends, hanging out, running around wild, hitting the slopes, playing soccer, sailing, playing tennis, that balanced the hard school work with fun.

To all my fellow students back then, I would say thanks for the memories and the laughter!!! I love thinking about my best friend Wendy feeding the Turkins, the chickens, and working on her pottery wheel, Mike taking me home after school in his boat across the bay. Jim and Glen always ready to go somewhere and do something, and Robin quietly reminding us about the importance of studying hard and setting the bar higher than it is!

Maybe this book will let me hear from you all about your lives and the families you have built. mb marybethb@yahoo.com

Future School Nurse?
Sarah Williams
Class of 1993

I was lucky enough to spend two school years as a student at Pathfinder, graduating in 1993. My time there, the small class dynamic, creative learning, and progressive teaching—propelled me toward a varied and interesting path. That path began at Interlochen Arts Academy and continued at Brown University, where I graduated with a French language degree in 2001.

Fifteen years after graduating from Pathfinder I came upon the school's ad seeking a French instructor. Despite the fact that I am pursing a nursing degree, I couldn't pass up a chance to apply for the position. The interviews that followed reminded me why I hold this institution in such high regard. While my limited availability kept me from being a serious candidate, perhaps in the future Pathfinder will need a school nurse . . . .

Into the future
Janet Baxter Hale, Class of 1976
President, 3-D Learn Interactive Academy

Appreciation—strong, true and enduring is what I feel for my Pathfinder years. As the daughter of the original founders of Pathfinder School, it wasn't always the easiest thing to live up to or even be a part of with such dynamic, pioneering sprits floating around the blustery wooded hillside in northern Michigan. But the overwhelming love, dedication, and preservation of originality and innovation trumped any insignificant adolescent insecurities I may have had at having school founders as parents. It was an amazing life-changing experience that I think anyone who came in contact with Pathfinder would agree. Some more so than others, but for those of us who it deeply impacted, our lives went on to embrace the Pathfinder ideologue and educational philosophies.

As I look back now on how Pathfinder shaped the creation, founding, and growth of my own immersive education company and school, it's amazing to see just how solidly the Pathfinder ideals are embedded into my own school's educational philosophy. The Pathfinder experience for me meant more than learning from books. It was experiential learning at its best. The visions that are seared into my mind are not images of a student sitting in a classroom staring out the window (although we did have wonderful views of old cedar trees and white birch trees with delicate lake sparkles dancing in the background) but rather they are images of places, events, and feelings while learning about our world. The awe I felt standing on sacred ground at Stonehenge overlooking the misty fields in the morning, trying to imagine what it must have been like to build these giant stones. The wonder of Notre-Dame Cathedral, the curiosity of so many ancient skeletons laid out in rest. As a student on History Afloat, sailing down the Intercostal Waterway and running aground while trying to get to historical sites along its banks. A trip as an exchange student to Puerto Rico where, yes, we had a horrific experience. But good or bad, experiences are how we learn best. Pathfinder allowed its students to have these kinds of experiences and the faculty helped guide, shape and educate by "leading by example."

I would say that roughly 95 per cent of my memories of Path finder have to do with the experiential leaning that went on. Reed Zitting served a very important role during my high school years by encouraging me to participate in the traveling theater troupe. Theater? Me? The dramatics mostly went to my mother. I loved the rush it gave me getting up in front of the cheering crowds (and yes they were just trapped school children in public school gymnasiums), but it was a blast and helped develop self-esteem, confidence and more importantly a sense of self you can not get sitting in a classroom. It tells you who you are as a person and what you can accomplish.

This feeling of self empowerment was intensely carried over into my experiences with Dick Parks' classes through my high school years. Some of the most important events in my development as a person occurred deep within the woods of northern Michigan. One of the most important nights of my life was spent high atop a bluff on South Manitou Island, alone, only my sleeping bag, the stars and no one around but me. Dick had required all participants on this backpacking trip to do a type of 'self awakening'. I viewed it secretly as a type of young girl's vision quest. We were to isolate ourselves apart from each other on this magnificent bluff overlooking Lake Michigan and sleep out under the stars exposed to the elements. This was a scary prospect to me since we had just finished reading *Never Cry Wolf* by Farley Mowat. Would the wolves circle around my sleeping bag sniffing for a tasty morsel of girly flesh? Would the long lost black bears of Manitou awaken to feast on me? What was I doing out here on the top of a bluff all by myself on an island in the middle of Lake Michigan? Growing and changing and finding what I was made of—that's what. I hunkered down inside a small cozy sand dune like a bunny finding a rabbit hole, and feeling more protection from the elements, I was able to lie on my back and see the stars that night. It was truly a life-altering moment and again, one you could not get in a classroom. To this day, we use *Never Cry Wolf* and many of the other Pathfinder resources in the curriculum in the school I went on to found named The 3DLearn Interactive Academy.

I think Pathfinder had an impact on all the students who pass through its doors in those early days, and one thing I have tried to do in my own quest as an educator is to pass on this kind of deeply embedded sense of empowerment, wonder, and excitement about learning. Teaching students that they CAN do it, that they are valued, that their creative ideas are important is a lasting legacy and testament to the Pathfinder School. After college I went on to teach in the public schools for many years but always felt stifled and it was obvious that my non-conforming self and educational ideals did not fit with public education. That's not to say there are not a lot of wonderful things going on with public education. It was just that I had a burning desire to go out and "blaze new trails." At least for me, that's the way it was. I left public education abruptly one day with a desire to start my own school. "Is she crazy?" I heard faculty say. "How can she walk away from a tenured position? What is she thinking? This will never work!" And on and on the negative-naysayers went. What they didn't know was that I was raised with a secret weapon! The Pathfinder upbringing that said, oh yes you can! You can do anything! I knew what I wanted to do and no one was going to stop me. Yes, I couldn't replicate all those experiential educational experiences from Pathfinder but by God, I was going to try to find a way that students would LOVE to come to school and have fun on the way. If education is not fun, then to me, you have not been successful.

Technology in education became a passion for me because it was unknown, evolving, and above all, allowed students to create in ways they could not by using traditional teaching methods. Blaze, blaze, blaze, that was my motto. I would start an "online" school where we would not be limited by physical locations bricks-and-mortar buildings, or held back by old thinking. My school opened its virtual doors in 1998 and we have not looked back since. Today, we are the only

3D online school in the world that offers 3D virtual reality experiential "immersive" education to its students. The pioneering Pathfinder spirit continues. Full-time accredited instruction in a school of the future. Instead of just reading about *Never Cry Wolf*, our students get to create 3D virtual wolf dens, become a 3D wolf, and end up as part of the wolf pack. Instead of just reading about King Arthur, they get to assume an avatar identity of historical characters from King Arthur's court and role play. Students can become immersed in the time period and create their own virtual world to show what they have learned. 3DLearn offers students new ways to experience learning in a 3D virtual campus. Pathfinder alumni can't go back in time, but we can move forward and take with us the experiences that helped shape who we are. So thank you to Pathfinder, to the caring and talented faculty at the time I moved through those woods, and above all, thank you to my parents for providing such a wonderful experience to your child. It made me who I am today.

Janet standing in front of her 3D School, carrying on the Pathfinder philosophy in a new way....www.3dlearn.com

I Always Came Back
A Commencement Address by Shaun Zitting
Class of 1983

I've been attending Pathfinder now for ten years. I came here in the third grade and since then I've been to the junior high for ten days and the senior high school for a semester, and I always came back. I found Pathfinder to be my home and the place I needed to be to grow and become me.

Pathfinder has always had a caring atmosphere where the teachers are your friends not your adversaries. They are sensitive to you and the things that are going on in your life. Pathfinder isn't like a school to me, it's an exciting place to learn, where everyone is supportive of the other. The atmosphere at Pathfinder has always made me feel as if I count and I'm important and I really can achieve my goals.

While the classroom gave me initiative to think, sports taught me discipline. And with the support and guidance of Mr. Fries, I learned that through self-discipline and hard work I could actually do what I set my mind to do. I never truly believed in myself until I achieved a goal in track I never dreamed of. Athletics gave me an outlet for my need to excel and helped me find more out about myself.

Every year for the past ten years, my father and I have been coming to Pathfinder together every morning—we've grown together and watched the school change and grow. This morning was the last morning my dad and I will ever ride to school together. This beautiful campus on top of a hill has become my home away from home. We've all formed a little family up here—we don't compete with each other—we help each other—we work as a team and support one another. The students and teachers work together; they've made learning a challenge, not a task.

On our last trip to Innisfree I tried to make the moments last longer. Our nights by the campfire and signing with the guitar were very special. I can never go back and I won't dwell on my wonderful memories, but I will always treasure them. Pathfinder provided a beautiful place for me to grow and prepare myself for life. It gave me confidence in me. I only wish more people could grow up in this wonderful, positive atmosphere that I've experienced.

Thank you,
Shaun Zitting

The above was Shaun's commencement address. She is the daughter of Reed Zitting. Shaun graduated from Oakland University (Rochester, MI), magna cum laude with a B.S. in human resource development. She has since held a number of roles in leadership training and development for Fortune 500 companies and most recently serves as the vice-president of human resources for a large global conglomerate in Connecticut, where she resides with her spouse Kris and their two kitties.

Behind

An Almanac of Topics
for Public Speaking

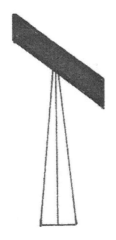

Historically Based, by Date
with Recommended Themes

Volume 1
January-February-March

By

Dr. Jed Griswold
Dr. Frank C. Griswold

ISBN: 978-1-959957-36-2   (Hardcover)
ISBN: 978-1-959957-30-0   (Paperback)
ISBN: 978-1-959957-31-7   (Kindle)

Editor: Elizabeth Hall
History Advisor: Larry Ruark
Format: Jed Griswold

About the Author and Consultant

Dr. Jed Griswold is a published author, a retired college
administrator and Professor of Psychology, a retired
minister, and currently an educational and organizational
consultant living in New England.
He has written novellas, reference books, children's books
and storytelling guides. www.griswoldconsulting.net

Dr. Frank C. Griswold is a retired physician, a Fellow of
the American College of Surgeons, and certified by the
American Board of Surgery. He was the first chair of the
Intensive Care Unit Committee and the first chair of the
Medical Ethics Committee of the local hospital where he
practiced medicine.

NOTES

This is a book for creative speakers, who can adapt or expand the entries for each calendar day of January, February and March.

Some dates have more than one entry, since some days are worthy of more than one notable event.

We have made an effort to be inclusive in our selection of historical and speech-worthy topics in order to offer a wide range of categories, such as language, music, communication, health, literature, science, religion, politics, race, film, culture, sports, business…and more!

To make it easier for readers to find illustrations and topics by date, several are duplicated on appropriate days in this range of January thru March, such as by a date of birth or death, or by a related event.

This is the 1st of four volumes, each covering three months of dates-based entries.

Table of Contents

Prolog

This is a book about Learning to "Speak Illustrations"

by Dr. Frank C. Griswold

When you understand the system, and start to think *the language of illustrations*, you see the world differently.

Once during my attendance at a religious service, a great storm came up with a resultant power failure. All the lights in the room went out. The only light was from the candles on the altar.

There were two ways (at least) to understand the event.

One – "what an inconvenience". With limited light, you could not even read a bulletin or a hymnal.

Two – "this is amazing!" In spite of the miracles of modern electrical engineering, the only light in the room emanated from the candles on an altar. When all else fails, a belief can light the way.

I mentioned the experience to one pastor who "spoke the language" of illustrations and the idea was immediately understood, and then actually appeared in a sermon illustration.

When the same thing happened a few years later, in another state, I mentioned the same interpretation to a different pastor – one who did *not* speak the *language of illustrations*, and the event was only seen a matter of inconvenience, and it never made its way into a sermon illustration.

When you understand illustrations, you see an illustration *everywhere* – in the news or in a routine day-to-day experience. Illustrations are everywhere. You just need to see, hear or read them in the right language.

While this example appeared in a religious setting, illustrations are waiting to be discovered in *any* context.

When we learn to *speak illustration.*

Introduction

Why this book was written, and
how you can use it

by Dr. Jed Griswold

As the Preface suggests, any event observed
first-hand or described in history can be seen as
an illustration which invites reflection.

The entries in this reference book of interesting
events are selected and designed to invite your
thoughts and feelings, which can use used for
preparing a speech, in many contexts, or even for
moments of personal meditation.

To welcome you to this project, here is an
overview of its beginnings and goals:

Its History

The prolog written by my brother reflects the early
history of this book, as we intended to write
meditative illustrations – mental images – which

could foster progressive and inclusive reflection when shared in a religious context.

It all began with a certain speaking style our father used as a minister for over 50 years in the middle of the 1900s. Rev. Dr. Walter H. Griswold had an appreciation for how stories from history could become lessons for the present. Many years before it became a popular idea, he incorporated an "On This Day" illustration in all of his presentations, including sermons, commencement addresses, lectures, classes, communion meditations, family celebrations, and more.

He even used that approach as he prepared for funeral eulogies, noting relevant events which happened on the person's birth or death date. Often times, that connection to history was the most lasting and most positive memory of the funeral.

Its Revisions

Walter's two sons, Frank and Jed, borrowed this approach; Jed in his career as a minister, teacher and writer, and Frank is his own church leadership as an active layperson.

Though our approach to this book has religious roots, our goal here is to offer illustrations encompassing a wide range of interests which invite reflection by all readers, religious or non-religious.

In our *own* use of this style for a half century we would add an observation, depending on the context of the sermon or meditation, fostering a specific focus for reflection.

In this book, however, we have avoided, as much as possible, offering concluding observations. These are open-ended presentations of factual events inviting *your* thoughtful reflections – on the past, the present or the future. This includes asking questions, expressing hopes, and digging deeper into any aspect of the theme.

While there are obviously hundreds of noteworthy events from each calendar day of many years past, we have intentionally selected events by their potential to foster *inclusive* and *progressive* reflection for the present, ideals from our own religious heritage.

Its Goals

- Provide a starting point for preparing a speech, lecture, sermon, etc.
- Recommend illustrations which present a mental image of an important point
- Deliver the ability to catch the attention of listening ears by attaching the date of the speech to a related date in history (if the speaking date and theme are connected)
- Present an idea from history in a form which is also not required to have a specific date attached; most of these entries can be meaningfully presented without mentioning the date
- Offer an introduction, a middle point, or a conclusion for the theme of your speech
- Demonstrate, by providing examples at the end of the book, how any one entry can be expanded into a longer presentation, even in different directions
- Share events from history which could invite a daily meditation

Behind the Podium

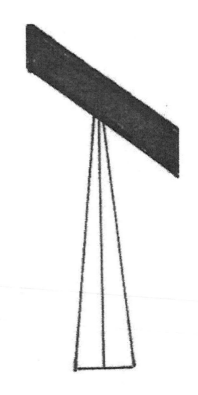

Volume 1
January-February-March

JANUARY

Contributions in the Midst of Failures
Failure, Success, Paul Revere

On January 1, 1735, Paul Revere was born. He is best known from Henry Wadsworth Longfellow's poem for his contribution to America's independence.

But one important fact is often overlooked: Longfellow did not mention the part about Revere's arrest and detainment, right after starting, and well before ending his famous ride.

Paul Revere: 1/1/1735 – 5/10/1818

https://www.paulreverehouse.org/the-real-story/

An Interesting American First
Stamps, Commemoration, Women, Christopher Columbus

On January 2, 1893, the United States issued the first set of commemorative stamps picturing women.

Among those women was Queen Isabella, celebrating the journey of Christopher Columbus to America – a journey with mixed reviews.

https://postalmuseum.si.edu/exhibition/about-us-stamps-classic-period-1847-1893-american-bank-note-company-1879-1893/columbian

A Private Language,
A Global Inspiration
Language, Stories, Personal Gifts, Tolkien

On January 3, 1892, John R. R. Tolkien was born. He was a patient story-teller for his family, creating an entirely new and personal language for the stories he wrote for his children.

That "private language" led to global inspiration through books like *The Lord of The Rings* and *The Hobbit*.

John R. R. Tolkien: 1/3/1892 - 9/2/1973

https://en.wikipedia.org/wiki/Languages_constructed_by_J._R._R._Tolkien

The Legacy of Our Teachings
Legacies, Creation, Misinformation, Bishop Ussher

Bishop James Ussher was born on January 4, 1581. He is best known for his calculation of the date of creation: beginning the night before Sunday, October 23, 4004 BC.

Though first published in English in 1658, the date became etched in modern history when it was published in 1917 in a column of notes, as if it were scientific data, in the *Scofield Reference Bible*.

Bishop James Ussher: 1/4/1581- 3/21/1656

https://en.wikipedia.org/wiki/Ussher_chronology

http://law2.umkc.edu/faculty/projects/ftrials/scopes/ussher.html#:~:text=Bishop%20James%20Ussher%20Sets%20the,Creation%3A%20October%2023%2C%204004%20B.C.

The Legacy of Our Stories
Legacies, Truths, Fairy Tales, Jacob Grimm

January 4, 1785, is the birthday of Jacob Grimm, one the *Brothers Grimm*, whose collection of fairy tales from long ago preserved the view of ancient beliefs and lessons from the past.

Jacob Grimm: 1/4/1785 – 9/20/1863

https://en.wikipedia.org/wiki/Jacob_Grimm

Seeing the Future
Blind, Education, African American

On January 4, 1869, the first school in the United States for African American blind students opened as the "Colored School" in a building rented from the *American Missionary Association* in southeastern Raleigh.

The school continues today as the *Governor Morehead School*, using the motto, *"By Faith, Not By Sight."*

Famous First Facts, *3rd Edition*. Joseph Nathan Kane, page 113.

https://www.ncpedia.org/governor-morehead-school

An Ironic Printing
Irony, Blind, Printing, Braille

Louis Braille was born on January 4, 1809. Blind from early childhood, he invented the *Braille System*. It was a considerable improvement over the most common reading system for the visually impaired at the time, the *Haüy System*. That approach required raised letters of the alphabet, which was cumbersome to process and even more difficult to print.

Braille was an accomplished musician as well, and he later published a musical adaptation of his system, which was, ironically, not published in the *Braille System*, but published using the *Haüy System*.

Louis Braille: 1/4/1809 – 1/6/1852

https://www.perkins.org/first-embossed-book-for-the-blind/

https://www.perkins.org/tactile-books/

A First Step Toward Reconciliation
Roman Catholic, Orthodox, Ecumenism, Conversation, Reconciliation, Pope Paul VI, Athenagoras

When Pope Paul VI met with Athenagoras I, the Ecumenical Patriarch of Constantinople, on January 5, 1964, it was the first meeting between leaders of the Roman Catholic and Orthodox churches since the 1400s.

The first major division within Christianity, known as *The Great Schism*, became an official separation in 1054. It was a consequence of the decreasing power of the Roman Empire and involved social and political differences, not just religious disputes, between the east and the west, still evident in some ways today.

https://www.goarch.org/-/historic-meeting-of-pope-paul-vi-ecumenical-patriarch-athenagoras

https://en.wikipedia.org/wiki/East%E2%80%93West_Schism

https://www.historyforkids.net/the-great-schism-of-1054.html

An Artistic First for Women
Idaho, State Seal, Women, Inclusion, Emma Sarah Edwards

Emma Sarah Edwards, who died on January 6, 1942, became the first and only woman to design a state seal when her artwork was adopted as the official state seal of Idaho.

The inclusive image pictured a woman, a miner, and the state's natural environment.

There is research to indicate that art (and leadership) by women, tends to be more inclusive, when compared to that of men.

Emma Sarah Edwards: ?/?/1856 – 1/6/1942

Famous First Facts, 5th *Edition*. Joseph Nathan Kane, Steven Anzovin, Janet Podell, page 579.

https://en.wikipedia.org/wiki/Emma_Edwards_Green

https://hbr.org/2020/04/7-leadership-lessons-men-can-learn-from-women

https://www.pewresearch.org/social-trends/2018/09/20/2-views-on-leadership-traits-and-competencies-and-how-they-intersect-with-gender/

The First
Federally Mandated Inoculation
Inoculations, Vaccines, Mandates,
Medicine, George Washington

On January 6, 1777, to protect the success of the *American War of Independence*, George Washington ordered that troops entering Philadelphia must be inoculated against smallpox.

A month later, he expanded that order to include *all* troops in the war.

It is interesting to note that Washington himself was a survivor of smallpox as a teenager.

Since Washingtom's time, federal forces have been required to receive vaccines against a number of diseases, including hep A, hep B, measles, mumps, rubella, rabies, pertussis, tetanus, diphtheria, typhoid, pneumococcal pneumonia, and flu.

The list did not appear in one step; it has expanded over many years, back to the smallpox pandemic of George Washington's era.

George Washington: 2/22/1732 – 12/14/1799

https://stlukesmuseum.org/edu-blog/against-all-odds-george-washington-smallpox-and-the-american-revolution/

https://www.snopes.com/fact-check/washington-order-troops-vaccinated/

https://www.newsweek.com/list-vaccines-mandated-us-military-covid-1641228

A First in Electoral Votes
Diversity, Women, Vice President,
Politics, Theodora Nathan

The first electoral vote for a Jewish person *and* for a woman Vice President in the United States, was cast for Theodora Nathan of the Libertarian Party, on January 6, 1973.

Theodora Nathan: 2/9/1923 – 3/20/2014

https://awpc.cattcenter.iastate.edu/directory/theodora-tonie-nathan/

https://www.nytimes.com/1973/01/07/archives/its-official-nixon-won-520-to-17.html

The First African American
State Legislator
Diversity, African American,
American Methodist Episcopal Church (AME),
Politics, Benjamin Arnett

On January 6, 1885, Bishop Benjamin William Arnett, of the *African Methodist Episcopal* (AME) church, became the first African American state legislator to represent a majority white district in the Ohio legislature.

Bishop B. W. Arnett: 3/6/1838 – 10/7/1906

https://en.wikipedia.org/wiki/Benjamin_W._Arnett

Words Are Remembered
Words, Folk Singer, Carl Sandburg

Carl August Sandburg, born on January 6, 1878, was an American poet, biographer, journalist, and editor. He won three Pulitzer Prizes, one for his biography of Abraham Lincoln and two more for his poetry.

Before the 1950's and 60's era of popular folk music, Sandburg gained a reputation as possibly the first *urban folk singer* in America. He would accompany himself with his own guitar when presenting lectures or poetry readings.

Carl A. Sandburg: 1/6/1878 – 7/22/1967

https://en.wikipedia.org/wiki/Carl_Sandburg

An Ironic Printing
Irony, Blind, Printing, Braille

Louis Braille died on January 6, 1852. Blind from early childhood, he invented the *Braille System*. It was a considerable improvement over the most common reading system for the visually impaired at the time, the *Haüy System*. That approach required raised letters of the alphabet, which was cumbersome to process and even more difficult to print.

Braille was an accomplished musician as well, and he later published a musical adaptation of his system, which was, ironically, not published in the *Braille System*, but published using the *Haüy System*.

Louis Braille: 1/4/1809 – 1/6/1852

https://www.perkins.org/first-embossed-book-for-the-blind/

https://www.perkins.org/tactile-books/

Signs of Distress
SOS, CQD, Telegraph, Signals

On January 7, 1904, the Marconi Company established the *CQD* call as the official distress signal to be used by the telegraph.

This has been replaced by the *SOS* signal, and later the contemporary 911 in the United States.

There are many signals of distress around us, of which we should be aware.

https://en.wikipedia.org/wiki/CQD

https://www.webmd.com/mental-health/features/10-signs-ailing-mind

First State Supreme Court
With All Women Judges
Equality. Judges, Courts, Women

On January 8, 1925, Texas became the first and only state to have a Supreme Court with all women judges.

It happened when an all-male organization, *Woodmen of the World*, appealed a case to an all-male Texas State Supreme Court, on which every judge was also a member of the *Woodmen* organization.

The male justices were disqualified from deciding the case, but the Governor, Pat Norris Neff, could not himself find any qualified, non-*Woodmen*-affiliated men to appoint to the court.

So, he appointed three women lawyers to the three-member court.

Famous First Facts, *5th Edition*. Joseph Nathan Kane, Steven Anzovin, Janet Podell, page 153.

https://www.txcourts.gov/supreme/about-the-court/court-history/all-woman-supreme-court/

The Changing Face (and Touch) of Communication
Communication, iPhone, Technology, Connected, Disconnected

The introduction of the first iPhone on January 9, 2007, along with other similar tools of communication, rapidly propelled us to incredible levels of creativity, and also to high degrees of distraction.

We are consequently both more connected *and* more disconnected.

https://www.apple.com/newsroom/2007/01/09Apple-Reinvents-the-Phone-with-iPhone/

https://www.dmu.edu/blog/2010/08/does-technology-connect-or-isolate-us/

Parenting
Parenting, Hugs, Behaviorism, John Watson, Benjamin Spock

John Watson, born on January 9, 1878, was a pioneer of *behaviorism*, and also very influential as his generation's expert on parenting.

His *Psychological Care of Infant and Child* became that topic's most popular book at the time.

An example of his advice on raising children: "Never hug and kiss them...Shake hands with them in the morning…"

It is interesting to note that many famous figures of his era wrote in their autobiographies that they were rarely, if ever, hugged by their fathers.

But just a generation later, the most followed advice came from Benjamin Spock, in *The Common Sense Book of Baby and Child Care*, whose approach was nearly the opposite of Watson's, reflected by his suggestion that a parent cannot hug a child too much.

In about a generation, the approach to raising children changed as much as the dramatic extremes of a pendulum swing.

John Watson: 1/9/1878 - 9/25/1958

https://en.wikipedia.org/wiki/John_B._Watson

https://i.imgur.com/DMtz1.jpg

Standard No Longer
Renewable Energy, Climate Change

The Standard Oil Company of Ohio was established on January 10, 1870, by John D. Rockefeller. Standard Oil played a dominant role in the global approach to energy for over a century, but that influence is changing, as the earth is changing.

Even the *Rockefeller Foundation* has switched its investment portfolio from non-renewable to *renewable* sources of energy, as we reach the former's limits and more fully understand their effect, and as we discover new and limitless renewable sources for our energy needs.

https://www.rockefellerfoundation.org/news/the-rockefeller-foundation-commits-to-divesting-from-fossil-fuels/#:~:text=The%20Rockefeller%20Foundation%20Commits%20to%20Divesting%20from%20Fossil%20Fuels,-12.18.20&text=NEW%20YORK%20%7C%20December%202018%2C%202020,from%20future%20fossil%20fuel%20investments.

The First Elected
Jewish Official in America
Diversity, Jewish American,
Politics, Francis Salvador

On January 11, 1775, Francis Salvador became the first elected Jewish official in South Carolina's Provincial Congress.

He was also the first Jewish person known to die in the Revolutionary War.

Francis Salvador: ?/?/1747 – 8/1/1776

https://en.wikipedia.org/wiki/Francis_Salvador

The First
State Mental Health Hospital in America
Mental Health, Hospitals, Horace Mann

The first state hospital for the mentally ill in the United States opened on January 12, 1833, and was known for a time as the Worcester State Hospital in Massachusetts.

The cause was championed by educator Horace Mann, who advocated humane and equal opportunities in many social aspects of life.

Soon after the facility opened, it became overcrowded. The hospital still operates today.

Horace Mann: 5/4/1796 – 8/2/1859

https://en.wikipedia.org/wiki/Worcester_State_Hospital#:~:text=Worcester%20State%20Hospital%20was%20a,National%20Register%20of%20Historic%20Places.

https://www.britannica.com/biography/Horace-Mann

https://worcesterhistorical.com/the-treatment-of-insanity/

Mystery and Resolution
Mysteries, Trademarks, Agatha Christie

Agatha Christie possessed a masterful ability to use her experience and insight to create and solve mysteries. Though her life ended on January 12, 1976, her legacy lives and will likely live forever.

One of her crime-novel trademarks is the closing scene, in which the detective gathers the characters in a room to summarize what happened, and to solve the crime.

This technique has since been borrowed by many fictional detectives.

Agatha Christie: 9/15/1890 - 1/12/1976

https://www.freelancewriting.com/creative-writing/the-writing-style-of-agatha-christie/#:~:text=Agatha%20preferred%20to%20plot%20her,pull%20readers%20in%20different%20directions.

Two Closings
Broadway, African American,
Best Play Award, Lorraine Hansberry

Lorraine Hansberry, the African American author of the award-winning play, *A Raisin in the Sun,* also wrote a second play which was performed on Broadway, *The Sign in Sidney Brustein's Window.*

It opened in 1964 and ran for over 100 performances. It closed on January 12, 1965, the same day the author died from cancer.

That second play is now revived on Broadway, almost 60 years later.

(See the March 11 entry for a different aspect in her life and work.)

Lorraine Hansberry: 5/19/1930 – 1/12/1965

https://en.wikipedia.org/wiki/Lorraine_Hansberry

The First
Reform Woman Rabbi in Judaism
Women, Rabbi, Paula Ackerman

Paula Ackerman, who died on January 12, 1989, was the first American woman Rabbi in the Reform tradition of Judaism, assuming the position of her late husband.

This occurred long before a woman was ordained in Judaism in her *own* theological career.

Paula Ackerman: 12/7/1893 – 1/12/1989

https://jwa.org/encyclopedia/article/ackerman-paula

The Power of Silence
Silence, Quakers, Religion,
Solitary Confinement, George Fox

George Fox, who died on January 13, 1691, was the founder of the *Society of Friends*, which became known as the *Quakers*. Among their most lasting legacies is understanding the power of reflective silence and progressive social justice.

The Quaker philosophy had an indirect influence on the 1829 construction of the *Eastern Pennsylvania Penitentiary*, in which all prisoners essentially experienced silent isolation, to encourage reflection, penitence, and reform.

This forced silence and isolation actually caused disastrous mental and physical problems, and Quaker leaders soon began to speak out against it.

George Fox: 7/?/1624 – 1/13/1691

https://www.georgefox.edu/about/history/quakers.html

https://www.fcnl.org/updates/2016-09/solitary-confinement-and-quakers

https://en.wikipedia.org/wiki/Eastern_State_Penitentiary

https://www.vera.org/publications/the-impacts-of-solitary-confinement

Predictions
Predictions, Astronomy, Comet, Edmond Halley

Edmond Halley predicted the cyclical return of a comet, now named in his honor. In 1705, he predicted the periodical appearance of what became *Halley's Comet* based on Newton's laws of motion.

He died on January 14, 1742, before he could verify his prediction of the comet's reappearance in 1758.

Edmond Halley: 11/8/1656 – 1/14/1742

https://en.wikipedia.org/wiki/Edmond_Halley

Finding Our Voice
Childhood, Challenges, Deafness, Stammer, Lewis Carroll

On January 14, 1898, Lewis Carroll died.
A childhood fever had left the writer-to-be
deaf in one ear, and he also spoke with a stammer.
But he found and heard a steady voice by
writing stories.

Lewis Carroll: 1/27/1832 – 1/14/1898

https://en.wikipedia.org/wiki/Lewis_Carroll

The Key to Success
Happiness, Success, Albert Schweitzer

Albert Schweitzer, born January 14, 1875, a physician, theologian, organist, and humanitarian, is credited with writing, "Success is not the key to happiness. Happiness is the key to success. If you love what you are doing, you will be successful."

One of the more popular of the current courses taught at Harvard University is a class about *happiness*. Its search is ever-present, even in our age of an ever-present attention to the *self.*

Albert Schweitzer: 1/14/1875 – 9/4/1965

https://www.ipl.org/essay/Albert-Schweitzer-Success-Is-Not-The-Key-FK5U5H74ACFR

https://pll.harvard.edu/course/managing-happiness?delta=1

Picture It
Pictures, Photography, Civil War, Matthew Brady

Matthew Brady, the well-known American photographer, died on January 15, 1896.

If you have ever seen real-time photographs of the American Civil War, or portraits of civilians, or military and political leaders of that era, you have likely seen his work.

His images of war and of mid-19th century America were seared into the public mind.

(See February 9 for an additional entry)

Matthew Brady: ? – 1/15/1896

https://www.loc.gov/collections/civil-war-glass-negatives/articles-and-essays/mathew-brady-biographical-note/

The "I Have a Dream" Speech
Improvisation, Diversity,
Civil Rights, Martin Luther King, Jr.

Rev. Dr. Martin Luther King, Jr., born on January 15, 1928, was known for his civil rights leadership, writings and speeches, and for one distinct event in his life: his powerful speech on the steps of the Lincoln Memorial in Washington, D.C.

When he had progressed through most of his prepared text, he began to *improvise.*

The result was the well-remembered poetry of "I have a dream …"

Martin Luther King, Jr.: 1/15/1929 – 4/4/1968

https://www.nytimes.com/2013/08/28/opinion/mahalia-jackson-and-kings-rhetorical-improvisation.html#:~:text=Martin%20Luther%20King%20Jr.'s,tuning%20it%20earlier%20that%20year.

https://en.wikipedia.org/wiki/Martin_Luther_King_Jr.

https://www.nobelprize.org/prizes/peace/1964/king/biographical/

The First Woman in Space
Women, Diversity, NASA

Sally K. Ride was in the first group of women astronauts introduced by NASA on January 16, 1978, selected from over 8,000 applicants.

She became the first woman in space in 1983.

Sally K. Ride: 5/26/1951 – 7/23/2012

https://en.wikipedia.org/wiki/Sally_Ride

Timing Matters
Timing, Patience,
Statute of limitations, Brinks Robbery

The largest robbery in the United States at the time, was staged at the Brinks Armored Car depot in Boston, MA, on January 17, 1950. There was no trail of the culprits, who had patiently prepared for two years for the burglary.

But after all that patience in the preparation, one of the robbers confessed just days before the statute of limitations was to expire.

https://en.wikipedia.org/wiki/Great_Brink%27s_Robbery

https://www.fbi.gov/history/famous-cases/brinks-robbery

https://www.fbi.gov/history/artifacts/brinks-robbery-cap

Method Acting and Method Living
Method Acting, Systematic, Psychological, Sociological, Behavioral, Stanislavski

Konstantin Stanislavski, born on January 17, 1863, was a Russian character actor who created a systematic approach to developing a role, commonly known as *method acting.*

He explained the ABCs of his method in his books, *An Actor Prepares, Building a Character*, and *Creating a Role.*

He and his followers stressed the need for an actor to identify the psychological, sociological and behavioral aspects of the character being portrayed.

If only we could be that self-aware about our *own* "character".

Konstantin Stanislavski: 1/17/1863 – 8/7/1938

https://en.wikipedia.org/wiki/Konstantin_Stanislavski

Helping Others
Girl Scouts, Helping, Immigrants, Juliette Gordon Low

Juliette Gordon Low (aka, Daisey Gordon), who died on January 17, 1927, established the *Girl Guides* in Savannah, Georgia.

The organization later became known as the *Girl Scouts*, which celebrates her birthday as *Founder's Day*.

She faced a number of obstacles in her personal life, including medical problems as a child, but at an early age, one of her projects was to start the "Helping Hand Club" to make clothes for immigrant children.

Daisey Gordon: 10/31/1860 – 1/17/1927

https://en.wikipedia.org/wiki/Juliette_Gordon_Low

The Inspiration for Stories, and Dreams
Friends, Teddy Bears, Bonding, A.A. Milne

A. A. Milne, born on January 18, 1882, is probably best known for his *Winnie the Pooh* stories.

Many of the characters in those stories were inspired by his very real son, Christopher Robin, and Christopher's equally real stuffed toys, including a teddy bear, a tiger and a donkey.

A.A. Milne: 1/18/1882 – 1/31/1956

https://en.wikipedia.org/wiki/A._A._Milne

Some People Prefer
Being in Charge - *Always*
Control, Death, Abram Hewitt

Abram Hewitt was a politician and businessman who liked to be in charge - *always*.

On his deathbed, on January 18, 1903, lying in the hospital and surrounded by doctors and family, he took the oxygen tube from his mouth, smiled, and said, "And now, I am officially dead."

And he was.

Abram Hewitt: 7/31/1822 – 1/18/1903

Exits: Stories of Dying Moments & Parting Words, by Scott Slater & Alec Solomita

https://en.wikipedia.org/wiki/Abram_Hewitt

https://en.wikipedia.org/wiki/Hardiness_(psychology)

Communication Between Great Divides
Communication, Transatlantic, Radio, King Edward VII, Theodore Roosevelt

The first transatlantic radio broadcast from the United States was sent on January 19, 1903, from Cape Cod, MA to Cornwall, England.

Sent in code, the messages were between King Edward VII and Theodore Roosevelt.

https://guides.loc.gov/chronicling-america-guglielmo-arconi#:~:text=%E2%80%9CWord%20is%20Flashed%20from%20Roosevelt,a%20month%20earlier%20from%20Canada)

A First for Women Bullfighters
Stereotypes, Women, Bullfighting, Arts

On January 20, 1952, Patricia McCormick, an American citizen, became the first North American female professional bullfighter in an appearance in Ciudad Juarez, Mexico.

After retiring from the profession, she became a professional painter, selling line drawings and watercolor scenes of bullfighting. When she died, the New York Times posted an article titled, "Bullfighter Who Defied Convention".

Here lies an interesting example of taking a traditional stereotype "by the horns", and of a blend of very different "arts".

Patricia McCormick: 11/18/1929 – 3/26/2013

https://www.nytimes.com/2013/04/14/us/patricia-mccormick-bullfighter-who-defied-gender-roles-dies-at-83.html

Truth Has a Way of Surviving
Truth, Denial, George Orwell

George Orwell died on January 21, 1950. He was an English novelist and critic, perhaps best known for writing *Animal Farm* and *Nineteen Eighty-Four*.

He is credited with writing about what *lasts*: "However much you deny the truth, the truth goes on existing."

George Orwell: 6/25/1903 – 1/21/1950

https://www.britannica.com/biography/George-Orwell/Animal-Farm-and-Nineteen-Eighty-four

https://www.thecrimson.com/article/1957/5/10/george-orwell-war-of-words-pshortly/

The First American Novel
Novel, Anonymous,
Recognition, William Brown

Considered the first novel by an American author, *The Power of Sympathy* was printed in Boston, MA on January 21, 1789.

It was published anonymously and the author, William Hill Brown, did not receive credit for the work until 1894, over a hundred years later.

William Hill Brown: 11/?/1765 – 9/2/1793

https://www.britannica.com/biography/William-Hill-Brown

Not Picture Perfect
Prejudice, Mistruths, Misrepresentation, *Birth of a Nation*, D.W. Griffith

Born on January 22, 1875, D.W. Griffith became an established figure in a new motion picture industry, yet his legacy is forever tarnished by the distorted and racist representation of the Civil War era in America, in his movie *The Birth of a Nation.*

The film premiered in Los Angeles, CA, and fostered stereotypes of African Americans that continue into the present, over a century later.

Ironically, the *D.W. Griffith Middle School* in Los Angeles had a 99% minority enrollment in 2016, with similar numbers persistent in data collected from 2018-2021.

D.W. Griffith: 1/22/1875 – 7/23/1948

https://www.usnews.com/education/k12/california/griffith-middle-263348

https://en.wikipedia.org/wiki/D._W._Griffith

A Political "Glass Ceiling"
African American, Arts,
Civil Rights, Blacklist, Paul Robeson

Paul Robeson, who died on January 23, 1976, earned 15 varsity letters in college - in four different sports - and was his class valedictorian. But his remarkable career did not end there.

He earned a law degree from Columbia Law School while playing for the NFL, spoke over 20 languages, and is recognized for his scholarly work on the structure of language.

An actor and singer during the Harlem Renaissance, he later received recognition for performances in *Show Boat* and *Othello*, in spite of government efforts to limit his career because of his civil rights activism.

Paul Robeson: 4/9/1898 – 1/23/1976

https://en.wikipedia.org/wiki/Paul_Robeson

https://www.archives.gov/education/lessons/robeson

Patience, While in a Hurry
Patience, Urgency, Phillips Brooks

Phillips Brooks, who died on January 23, 1893, was an American Episcopal clergyman, author, long-time Rector of Boston's *Trinity Church*, and briefly Bishop of Massachusetts.

He is also well-known for writing the lyrics of the Christmas hymn, *O Little Town of Bethlehem.*

He is credited as saying, "The trouble is that I'm in a hurry, but God isn't."

Phillips Brooks: 12/13/1835 – 1/23/1893

https://en.wikipedia.org/wiki/Phillips_Brooks

https://cathedral.org/sermons/dean-lloyd-patience/

Successes in Spite of Failures
Success, Failure, A Roller Coaster Life,
Sir Winston Churchill

Sir Winston Churchill died on January 24, 1965. He is remembered for his successful leadership in WWII, but his political career was actually a roller coaster of success and failure:

- removed as First Lord of the Admiralty after poor decisions in a deadly WWI maneuver
- selected as Prime Minister for WWII
- turned out of office in 1945
- return to office from 1951-1955.

Sir Winston Churchill: 11/30/1874 – 1/24/1965

https://www.britannica.com/biography/Winston-Churchill

Conspiracy Theories, Old and New
Conspiracies, Fluoridation, Evidence, Dental Health

The first water system to introduce fluoridation was in Grand Rapids, MI on January 25, 1945.

Even though scientific research had validated at the time (and continues to validate today) that its use results in a significant improvement in dental health, its introduction was accompanied by conspiracy theories.

https://www.cdc.gov/fluoridation/basics/anniversary.htm#:~:text=Grand%20Rapids%2C%20Michigan%20became%20the,public%20water%20supply%20in%201945

The First
Reform Woman Rabbi in Judaism
Women, Rabbi, Paula Ackerman

On January 26, 1951, Paula Ackerman became the first American woman Rabbi in the Reform tradition of Judaism, assuming the position of her late husband.

This occurred long before a woman was ordained in Judaism in her *own* theological career.

Paula Ackerman: 12/7/1893 – 1/12/1989

Famous First Facts, 5*th* *Edition*. Joseph Nathan Kane, Steven Anzovin, Janet Podell, page 476.

https://jwa.org/encyclopedia/article/ackerman-paula

Building Blocks
Vaccines, Inoculations, Smallpox, Pandemic, Misinformation, Edward Jenner

Edward Jenner created the first vaccination, which was for smallpox, an age-old and deadly pandemic, still virulent in his day.

His innovation was built upon centuries of inoculations, traced back to early African cultures. Though the vaccination was successful, he was not universally popular because of misinformation about the vaccine printed in many newspapers of the day. In fact, he received death threats.

Shortly before his death on January 26, 1823, he shared that he was not surprised that some were not grateful for his vaccine, but he wondered if they might be grateful to God for "the good which he has made me the instrument of...for my fellow creatures."

Edward Jenner: 5/17/1749 – 1/26/1823

https://www.ncbi.nlm.nih.gov/pmc/articles/PMC1200696/

https://en.wikipedia.org/wiki/Edward_Jenner

Our *Words* Can Influence Our *Thinking*
Words, Thinking, Behavior, Sapir-Whorf, Edward Sapir

Edward Sapir, born January 26, 1884, was an anthropologist and linguist known for the study of indigenous North and South American languages, and a major contributor to The *Sapir-Whorf Hypothesis*, which proposed that *how we speak* influences *how we think*, not just the reverse.

For example, using inclusive *language* can foster inclusive *thinking*, and using *exclusive* language can result in *exclusive* thinking.

And, naturally, our *thinking* influences our *actions*.

Words really *do* matter.

Edward Sapir: 1/26/1884 – 2/4/1939

https://www.britannica.com/biography/Edward-Sapir

Finding Our Voice
Childhood, Challenges, Deafness, Stammer, Lewis Carroll

Lewis Carroll was born January 27, 1832.
A childhood fever had left the writer-to-be deaf in one ear, and he also spoke with a stammer.
But he found and heard a steady voice by writing stories.

Lewis Carroll: 1/27/1832 – 1/14/1898

https://en.wikipedia.org/wiki/Lewis_Carroll

The Complexity of Prejudice
Prejudice, Complexity, Diversity, Jewish American, Supreme Court, Louis Brandeis

Louis Brandeis was nominated to the U.S. Supreme Court on January 28, 1916, to become the first Jewish Supreme Court Justice.

The progressive supporter of civil rights was appointed by Woodrow Wilson, who ironically endorsed racial segregation and received the support of the voting base of the Ku Klux Klan, an antisemitic, anti-Catholic, anti-Black, anti-immigrant organization.

Louis Brandeis: 11/13/1856 – 10/5/1941

https://en.wikipedia.org/wiki/Woodrow_Wilson

https://www.brandeis.edu/about/louis-brandeis.html

https://en.wikipedia.org/wiki/Louis_Brandeis

https://woodrowwilsonhouse.org/wilson-topics/wilson-and-race/

A First Among Lawyers
Diversity, Women, African American, Law, Violette Anderson

On January 29, 1926, Violette Neatley Anderson became the first African American woman to be admitted to practice law before the US Supreme Court.

She was also the first female African American law school graduate in the state of Illinois.

Violette Anderson: 7/16/1882 – 12/24/1937

https://www.blackpast.org/african-american-history/anderson-violette-neatley-1882-1937/

https://en.wikipedia.org/wiki/Violette_Neatley_Anderson

A Life for Peace
Thoughts, Words, Actions,
Habits, Values, Mahatma Gandhi

Mahatma Gandhi was a lawyer, an advocate for non-violent protests for civil rights, and a major activist for India's independence. His death by assassination on January 30, 1948, was an unjust price for a life which advocated for peace and justice.

Yet his global legacy has lived on, through the lives of Martin Luther King, Nelson Mandela, John Lewis, and others to come.

At a young age, he accepted a job in South Africa to work as a lawyer. Upon his arrival, he was immediately met with discrimination: he was not allowed to sit near Europeans on a stagecoach (and required to sit on the floor next to the driver), and he was removed from a train because he had a first-class ticket.

His experiences in South Africa greatly influenced his later civil rights activism.

It is interesting to note the similarity with Rosa Parks' experience of not being able to take a seat properly paid for.

Mahatma Gandhi: 10/2/1869 – 1/30/1948

https://en.wikipedia.org/wiki/Mahatma_Gandhi

An Inspiration for Stories
Friends, Teddy Bears, Bonding, A.A. Milne

A. A. Milne, who died on January 31, 1956, is probably best known for his *Winnie the Pooh* stories.

Many of the characters in those stories were inspired by his very real son, Christopher Robin, and Christopher's equally real stuffed toys, including a teddy bear, a tiger and a donkey.

A.A. Milne: 1/18/1882 – 1/31/1956

https://en.wikipedia.org/wiki/A._A._Milne

NOTES

FEBRUARY

Illustrating the Words
Artist, Illustrator, Charles Dickens, Grimm's Fairy Tales, George Cruikshank

George Cruikshank, who died on February 1, 1878, was a British artist who illustrated several of Charles Dickens' books as well as the first English translation of *Grimm's Fairy Tales*.

In addition to those respectful illustrations, he was also known for his racist caricatures of non-western and non-British citizens, including Irish and Chinese.

George Cruikshank: 9/27/1792 – 2/1/1878

https://www.illustrationhistory.org/artists/george-cruikshank

https://brierhillgallery.com/george-cruikshank-1792-1878 (scroll down on that gallery site)

The Great Stone Face
Actor, Director, Producer, Screenwriter, Deadpan, Stunt Performer, Silent Films, Buster Keaton

Joseph Frank Keaton, known professionally as Buster Keaton, died on February 1, 1966.

He was an American actor with many additional talents: he was a director, producer, screenwriter and stunt performer.

He is probably best known for his performances in silent films, in which his trademark physical comedy is almost always played with a steady, stoic, deadpan expression.

An expression-*less* face can, at the same time, be an expression-*full* face.

Buster Keaton: 10/4/1895 – 2/1/1966

https://www.britannica.com/biography/Buster-Keaton

https://en.wikipedia.org/wiki/Buster_Keaton

The First Use of "Black is Beautiful"
**Diversity, African American,
Lawyer, Abolitionist, John Rock,**

John S. Rock was one of the first African Americans to graduate from medical school. His career and activism have a long list:
- he was an abolitionist
- he was a dentist
- on February 1, 1865, he became the first African American to be admitted to practice law before the US Supreme Court.
- he is also credited with the first use of the expression, "Black is beautiful."

John S. Rock: 10/13/1825 – 12/3/1866

Famous First Facts, 5th Edition. Joseph Nathan Kane, Steven Anzovin, Janet Podell, page 316.

https://www.loc.gov/exhibits/civil-war-in-america/biographies/john-s-rock.html

An African American Court First
Diversity, African American, Law, Jonathan Wright

Jonathan Jasper Wright became the first African American state Supreme Court Justice in America, in South Carolina, on February 2, 1870.

This event was one of many short-lived advances during the Reconstruction era in US history, an era brought to a premature end.

It took nearly a century for the next Black state Supreme Court Justice to be appointed.

Though a legal review of Wright's court decisions reflects a mixed political gain for freed slaves, advances *often* exist along a continuum.

Jonathan J. Wright: 2/11/1840 – 2/18/1885

Famous First Facts, 5*th* *Edition*. Joseph Nathan Kane, Steven Anzovin, Janet Podell, page 152.

https://ballotpedia.org/First_Black_justices_on_the_state_s
upreme_courts

https://www.brennancenter.org/our-work/analysis-
opinion/jonathan-jasper-wright-americas-first-black-state-
supreme-court-justice

The Power of "Typecasting"
Typecasting, Frankenstein, Dracula, Boris Karloff, Bela Lugosi

Boris Karloff, who died on February 2, 1969, has 206 acting credits, but he is probably best remembered for only *3* performances as the monster created by Dr. Frankenstein.

Bela Lugosi has 114 acting credits, but he is probably best remembered for only *one* iconic performance as *Count Dracula* (setting aside his only other, and less serious portrayal of that role, in a comedy with Bud Abbot and Lou Costello).

Boris Karloff: 11/23/1887 – 2/2/1969

https://www.imdb.com/find/?q=boris%20karloff&ref_=nv_sr_sm

Bela Lugosi: 10/20/1882 – 8/16/1956

https://www.imdb.com/find/?q=bela%20lagosi&ref_=nv_sr_sm

A Systemic Perspective
Chemistry, Systemic,
Periodic Table, Dmitri Mendeleev

Dmitri Ivanovich Mendeleev, who died on February 2, 1907, was a Russian chemist who created the *Periodic Table of Elements*, which demonstrates, in one full view, how the elements are interconnected and part of a system.

This systemic perspective has also influenced disciplines beyond chemistry.

Dmitri Mendeleev: 2/8/1834 – 2/2/1907

https://www.britannica.com/biography/Dmitri-Mendeleev

Understanding the *Whole* Concept
Novelist, Feminist, Harvard, Radical Empiricism, William James, Gertrude Stein

Gertrude Stein, born on February 3, 1874, was an influential American novelist, art dealer, and feminist. While a student at Radcliffe, which was at that time a part of Harvard University, she studied under William James, the first American educator to offer a college level psychology course.

James had introduced the perspective of *radical empiricism*, which presented a then-new argument that any understanding of human behavior is incomplete without considering the interaction of a person's values, philosophy and motivation along with their physical responses.

This view influenced the field of psychology *and* his student, Gertrude Stein.

Gertrude Stein: 2/3/1874 – 7/27/1946

https://en.wikipedia.org/wiki/William_James

https://www.britannica.com/biography/Gertrude-Stein

A Brave Message
Actor, American Cancer Society, Cancer, Facing Death, Education, William Talman

William Talman, born February 4, 1915, was an accomplished American actor best known for his role as *Hamilton Burger*, Raymond Burr's perpetual opponent in the TV series, *Perry Mason*.

In that role, week after week, Hamilton Burger would lose his case against Perry Mason. He was once asked how he felt about always losing, and the response was, "How can a district attorney lose when he fails to convict an innocent person?"

After many years of cigarette smoking, Talman developed lung cancer, and when he learned about his terminal prognosis, a certain death, he agreed to do a short film, the first of its kind, for the American Cancer Society, to be shown nationally on TV *after* his death.

He explained in that film, as he cautioned viewers against smoking, "Before I die, I want to do what I can to leave a world free of cancer for my six children,"

The *real* Hamilton Burger argued his last case in the court of public opinion.

William Talman: 2/4/1915 – 8/30/1968

https://historynewsnetwork.org/article/473

https://en.wikipedia.org/wiki/William_Talman_(actor)

A First Under the 15th Amendment
Elections, African American, Voting, Thomas Peterson-Mundy

Thomas Peterson-Mundy made history long before he died on February 4, 1904.

He lived in New Jersey which had, in 1807, abolished the previously existing voting rights for free Blacks. But the *Fifteenth Amendment* granted a *nationwide* right for male Black citizens to vote.

That Amendment became legal on March 30, 1870, and the very next day, on March 31, Peterson-Mundy may have become the first African American to vote under that new law, ironically, in an election in New Jersey.

After waiting so long for a right to be restored, one does not want to wait to exercise it.

Thomas Peterson-Mundy: 10/6/1824 – 2/4/1904

Famous First Facts, *3rd Edition*. Joseph Nathan Kane.

https://www.archives.gov/milestone-documents/15th-amendment#:~:text=Passed%20by%20Congress%20February%2026,men%20the%20right%20to%20vote.

https://en.wikipedia.org/wiki/Thomas_Mundy_Peterson

https://nj.gov/state/historical/assets/pdf/it-happened-here/ihhnj-er-peterson.pdf

https://www.nps.gov/articles/voting-rights-in-nj-before-the-15th-and-19th.htm

We Are Our History
Historian, Writer, Philosopher, White Supremacy, Antisemitism, The Everlasting Yea/No, Charles Dickens, Thomas Carlyle

Thomas Carlyle, who died on February 5, 1881, was an influential British historian, writer, philosopher and mathematician. He coined the phrases, "The Everlasting No" and "Yea" to refer to an adamant disbelief or belief in God. And his historical account of the French Revolution inspired the Dickens' novel, *A Tale of Two Cities.*

Carlyle himself was racist, and his observation that "the history of the world is but the biography of great men", could explain both the strengths and weaknesses of our historical story, given that mostly white men have shaped and written western history, unfortunately influenced by beliefs in stereotypes of many forms.

Thomas Carlyle: 12/4/1795 – 2/5/1881

https://en.wikipedia.org/wiki/Great_man_theory

https://en.wikipedia.org/wiki/Philosophy_of_Thomas_Carlyle

https://glasgowmuseumsslavery.co.uk/2020/11/18/thomas-carlyle-historian-writer-racist/

The First
Federally Mandated Inoculation
Inoculations, Vaccines, Mandates,
Medicine, George Washington

On February 5, 1777, to protect the success of the *American War of Independence*, George Washington ordered that all troops fighting the war must be inoculated against smallpox. This was an expansion of an earlier mandate.

It is interesting to note that Washington himself was a survivor of smallpox as a teenager.

Washington wrote at the time that this requirement might cause "some inconvenience", but warned that without this action, we might have more to dread from the disease "than from the swords of the enemy."

George Washington: 2/22/1732 – 12/14/1799

https://founders.archives.gov/documents/Washington/03-08-02-0281

https://stlukesmuseum.org/edu-blog/against-all-odds-george-washington-smallpox-and-the-american-revolution/

https://www.snopes.com/fact-check/washington-order-troops-vaccinated/

https://www.newsweek.com/list-vaccines-mandated-us-military-covid-1641228

Preparing for Today's Challenges
Sports, Baseball, Baseball Hall of Fame, Winning, Babe Ruth

Babe Ruth, born on February 6, 1895, was one of the most skilled and famous of baseball players in its long history. He played 22 seasons and was one of the first 5 inaugural players to be named to the *Baseball Hall of Fame*.

This icon of baseball is credited with saying, "Every strike brings me closer to the next home run."

Babe Ruth: 2/6/1895 – 8/16/1948

https://www.baberuth.com/quotes/

A Japanese American Legal First
Lawyer, Japanese American, K. Elizabeth Ohi

On February 6, 1937, K. Elizabeth Ohi became the first female Japanese American to receive a law degree in the United States.

Not many years after that achievement, WWII made such advances difficult for the next generation.

And in spite of her contributions, she was arrested, along with other Japanese Americans, after the attack on Pearl Harbor.

K. Elizabeth Ohi: 2/9/1911 – 8/14/1976

Famous First Facts, *3rd Edition*. Joseph Nathan Kane, page 338.

https://en.wikipedia.org/wiki/Elizabeth_K._Ohi

A Sound of Music
Saxophone, Music, Near Death Experiences, Inner Voice, Adolphe Sax

Adolphe Sax invented the saxophone, and also the saxotromba, the saxtuba and the sax-horn. He also played the flute and the clarinet.

He nearly died at least seven times from childhood to adulthood, including a three-story fall (where he was presumed dead), falling into a river and almost drowning, falling onto a hot cast-iron frying pan, drinking acidic water thinking it was milk, almost suffocating from sleeping in a room where newly varnished furniture was not yet dry, and more.

In spite of his near-deaths (and his actual death on February 7, 1894), his gift to music lives on.

Musical inventions can bring life to inner voices, and perhaps even *extend* life.

Adolphe Sax: 11/6/1814 – 2/7/1894

https://en.wikipedia.org/wiki/Adolphe_Sax

Managing Challenges and Change
Novels, Social Reforms, Bending,
Charles Dickens

Charles Dickens, born February 7, 1812, was an exceptional novelist and social critic.

He was a tireless advocate for children's rights and other social reforms, while editing a weekly journal for twenty years, writing five novellas and fifteen novels, including the iconic *A Christmas Carol*, an annual tradition around the world.

Perhaps a reflection of his own life, he wrote this line in *Great Expectations*: "I have been bent and broken, but – I hope – into a better shape."

Charles Dickens: 2/7/1812 – 6/9/1870

https://www.britannica.com/biography/Charles-Dickens-British-novelist

http://www.literaturepage.com/read/greatexpectations-542.html

A Systemic Perspective
Chemistry, Systemic,
Periodic Table, Dmitri Mendeleev

Dmitri Ivanovich Mendeleev, born on February 8, 1834, was a Russian chemist who created the *Periodic Table of Elements*, which demonstrates, in one full view, how the elements are interconnected, and part of a system.

This systemic perspective has also influenced disciplines beyond chemistry.

Dmitri Mendeleev: 2/8/1834 – 2/2/1907

https://www.britannica.com/biography/Dmitri-Mendeleev

Not Picture Perfect
Prejudice, Mistruths, Misrepresentation,
Birth of a Nation, D.W. Griffith

On February 8, 1915, the film *The Birth of a Nation* premiered in Los Angeles, CA.

Its director, D.W. Griffith, became an established figure in a new motion picture industry, yet his legacy is forever tarnished by the distorted and racist representation of the Civil War era in America in this movie.

The film fostered stereotypes of African Americans that continue into the present, over a century later.

Ironically, the *D.W. Griffith Middle School* in Los Angeles had a 99% minority enrollment in 2016, with similar numbers persistent in data collected from 2018-2021.

D.W. Griffith: 1/22/1875 – 7/23/1948

https://www.usnews.com/education/k12/california/griffith-middle-263348

https://en.wikipedia.org/wiki/D._W._Griffith

A Landmark in Medicine
Medicine, Women, African American, Rebecca Lee Crumpler

Rebecca Lee Crumpler, born on February 8, 1831, received an M.D. from New England Female Medical College, which merged in 1873 with the Boston University School of Medicine. She was the first African American woman physician.

After a career in medicine, she published *A Book of Medical Discourses,* which was one of the first medical publications written by an African American.

Dr. Crumpler once referred to her academic credential as "doctress of medicine," perhaps a commentary on her generation's view of female doctors.

Rebecca Lee Crumpler: 2/8/1831 – 3/9/1895

https://cfmedicine.nlm.nih.gov/physicians/biography_73.html

The Present Shapes the Future
Novels, Short Stories,
Constructing the Future, Alice Walker

Alice Walker, born February 9, 1944, is perhaps best known for her short stories and her novel (and later movie), *The Color Purple.*

She is credited with writing, "Look closely at the present you are constructing: it should look like the future you are *dreaming*."

Alice Walker: 2/9/1944 –

https://laidlawscholars.network/posts/the-present-you-are-constructing-should-look-like-the-future-you-are-dreaming

https://alicewalkersgarden.com/about/

https://en.wikipedia.org/wiki/Alice_Walker

A First in Electoral Ballots
Diversity, Women, Vice President, Politics, Theodora Nathan

Theodora Nathan, born February 9, 1923, became the first Jewish person *and* the first woman to receive an electoral ballot for Vice President in the United States in 1973.

Theodora Nathan: 2/9/1923 – 3/20/2014

https://awpc.cattcenter.iastate.edu/directory/theodora-tonie-nathan/

A Japanese American Legal First
Lawyer, Japanese American, K. Elizabeth Ohi

K. Elizabeth Ohi, born February 9, 1911, became the first female Japanese American to be admitted to the bar in the United States, in 1937.

Not many years after that achievement, WWII made such advances difficult for the next generation.

And in spite of her contributions, she was arrested, along with other Japanese Americans, after the attack on Pearl Harbor.

K. Elizabeth Ohi: 2/9/1911 – 8/14/1976

https://en.wikipedia.org/wiki/Elizabeth_K._Ohi

A Match Remembered,
and a Future Predicted
Computer, Chess, Predictions, Gary Kasparov

On February 10, 1996, a computer defeated Gary Kasparov, the world's ranking grandmaster of chess.

Over several games and rematches, Kasparov eventually conceded.

Did the future of AI arrive that long ago?

Gary Kasparov: 4/13/1963 –

Famous First Facts, *5th Edition*. Joseph Nathan Kane, Steven Anzovin, Janet Podell, page 267.

https://en.wikipedia.org/wiki/Garry_Kasparov

An African American Court First
Diversity, African American, Law, Jonathan Wright

Jonathan Jasper Wright, born February 11, 1840, became the first African American state Supreme Court Justice in America, in South Carolina.

This event was one of many short-lived advances during the Reconstruction era in US history, an era brought to a premature end.

It took nearly a century for the next Black state Supreme Court Justice to be appointed.

Though a legal review of Wright's court decisions reflects a mixed political gain for freed slaves, advances *often* exist along a continuum.

Jonathan J. Wright: 2/11/1840 – 2/18/1885

https://www.brennancenter.org/our-work/analysis-opinion/jonathan-jasper-wright-americas-first-black-state-supreme-court-justice

United -- Occasionally
Disaster Support, Ohio River Floods, Unity, Divisions

On February 11, 1937, a radio broadcast was made from Radio City Hall on all three networks of the time (CBS, NBC and Mutual), to benefit a Red Cross relief fund for the Ohio River floods that were affecting several states.

It was the first time all radio networks made a simultaneous broadcast.

The increased number of media platforms today have brought advantages (such as increased cooperation, with more information) *and* disadvantages (such as increased division, with more *mis*information).

Famous First Facts, 5th *Edition*. Joseph Nathan Kane, Steven Anzovin, Janet Podell, page 456.

https://www.dmu.edu/blog/2010/08/does-technology-connect-or-isolate-us/

Not the Only Mask for Safety
Masks, Safety, Baseball,
Frederick Thayer

On February 12, 1878, Frederick W. Thayer received a patent for the first baseball catcher's mask.

Thayer was a team manager who developed and tested the mask for a catcher who had been frequently injured by pitched balls.

Protective masks have been successfully, and gratefully, used for safety for many years and in many contexts.

Frederick W. Thayer: 8/14/1854 – 9/17/1913

Famous First Facts, 5th edition. Joseph Nathan Kane, Steven Anzovin, Janet Podell, page 536.

https://history.nebraska.gov/frederick-w-thayers-invention/

Once Owned, Never Free?
Slavery, The Fugitive Slave Act,
Human Rights, George Washington

On February 12, 1793, the *Fugitive Slave Act* was passed by the Second Congress of the United States. It was supported by America's first President, George Washington, a slave owner himself.

This act was reaffirmed and in some ways strengthened by the *Fugitive Salve Act of 1850.*

Both laws were repealed in 1864.

George Washington: 2/22/1732 – 12/14/1799

https://www.britannica.com/event/Fugitive-Slave-Acts

https://www.battlefields.org/learn/primary-sources/fugitive-slave-act#:~:text=Passed%20on%20September%2018%2C%201850,returning%2C%20and%20trying%20escaped%20slaves.

Recognition, At Last
Baseball, National Negro League,
Acknowledgment, Rube Foster

The original *Negro National League* was established on February 13, 1920, by Rube Foster, the owner/manager of the *Chicago American Giants*.

It consisted of 22 major league teams, with some black baseball players whose statistics outperformed the best of the all-white leagues.

The league dissolved in 1931, mainly because of the economic effects of the Great Depression.

A second *Negro National League* started in 1933, and another short-lived *American Negro League* was established in 1937.

Recently, these statistics are being recognized in a shared major league database.

Rube Foster: 9/17/1879 – 12/9/1930

https://baseballhall.org/hall-of-famers/foster-rube

https://en.wikipedia.org/wiki/Negro_National_League_(19 20%E2%80%931931)

https://en.wikipedia.org/wiki/American_Negro_League

Then, and Now
McCarthyism, Conspiracy Theories,
Anti-Communist, Joseph McCarthy

On February 13, 1950, Senator Joseph McCarthy, best known as the public face of anti-communist conspiracy theories of the cold war era (aka, *McCarthyism*), held up a piece of paper during a speech, claiming it was a list of 205 "card carrying" communists working in the US State Department.

When later asked at a hearing before the *Senate Committee of Foreign Relations*, he was not able to provide any list,

Apparently, the card was blank.

Joseph McCarthy: 11/14/1908 – 5/2/1957

https://en.wikipedia.org/wiki/Joseph_McCarthy#:~:text=McCarthy%20is%20usually%20quoted%20to,policy%20in%20the%20State%20Department.%22

https://www.ushistory.org/us/53a.asp

The Value of an Assist
Hockey, NHL Records, Assists, Wayne Gretzky

On February 14, 1975, Wayne Gretzky set a National Hockey League record for seven assists in one game.

He repeated this record three times.

Now retired, he still holds the NHL lead for goal scorer *and* assists.

Wayne Gretzky: 1/26/1961 –

https://en.wikipedia.org/wiki/Wayne_Gretzky

Beauty as Harmony
Beauty, Harmony, Architect, Artist, Poet, Priest, Linguist, Cryptographer, Leon Alberti

Leon Alberti, born on February 14, 1404, was an Italian architect, artist, poet, priest, linguist, philosopher, and cryptographer, who represented the essence of the Renaissance.

He is credited with writing that beauty was "the harmony of all parts in relation to one another."

Leon Alberti: 2/14/1404 – 4/25/1472

https://www.britannica.com/biography/Leon-Battista-Alberti

https://exhibits.stanford.edu/leonardo/feature/the-architectural-treatise-reading-like-an-architect

How We Treat Others
Reform, Equal Rights, Susan B, Anthony

Susan B. Anthony, born on February 15, 1820, left a lasting legacy as an American social reformer and activist, including her persistent efforts for women's rights, both white and African American.

She once wrote, "Men who fail to be just to their mothers cannot be expected to be just to each other."

How we treat others in one context can be a measure of how we treat others in another context.

Susan B. Anthony: 2/15/1820 – 3/13/1906

https://susanb.org/susan-b-anthony-quotes/

https://susanb.org/her-life/

https://ajournaljourney.com/2022/03/07/heres-to-women/

Educational (and Athletic) Firsts
Deaf, Education, Football Huddle, Gallaudet College

The first college for the deaf was established on February 16, 1857, in Washington, DC. It was called the *Columbia Institution for the Deaf, Dumb and Blind* and later became *Gallaudet College*.

The evolution of the name (avoiding the misunderstood term "dumb" which was previously used to mean "mute") indicates the progressive arc of the school's history.

Though a significant event at the time for the deaf community, it wasn't until 1988 that the college chose its first deaf president.

Football enthusiasts may know another first related to the school: that the "huddle" originated at Gallaudet to prevent opposing teams from reading their sign-language play calls.

https://en.wikipedia.org/wiki/Gallaudet_University

https://gallaudet.edu/museum/history/when-gallaudet-university-football-invented-the-huddle/

The Stethoscope ... Version 1
Stethoscope, Interpreting Sounds, René Laennec

René Laennec, born on February 17, 1781, invented the stethoscope, a significant advance in medicine.

It allowed a doctor or nurse to listen in an entirely new way to a patient's lungs and heart, leading to a better diagnosis of a medical problem.

While the stethoscope was an advance, a drawback is that it only allows a single person to listen. What was heard by one had to be interpreted to others.

When we are inspired by a new insight or a new discovery about life, our inner voice is heard by just one person.

René Laennec: 2/17/1781 – 8/13/1826

https://www.ncbi.nlm.nih.gov/pmc/articles/PMC157049
1/

The Stethoscope ... Version 2
Stethoscope, Transferable Skills, René Laennec

René Laennec, born on February 17, 1781, was a physician, musician, and inventor of the stethoscope.

That invention was a result of a transferable skill, from the art of making wood-carved flutes.

René Laennec: 2/17/1781 – 8/13/1826

https://en.wikipedia.org/wiki/Ren%C3%A9_Laennec#:~:text=Ren%C3%A9%2DTh%C3%A9ophile%2DHyacinthe%20Laennec%20(,working%20at%20the%20H%C3%B4pital%20Necker.

In a League of its Own
Baseball, Women Athletes, Women Athletes, the AAGPBL, Sophie Kurys

Sophie Kurys, who died on February 17, 2013, played professional baseball as a second basewoman for the *All-American Girls Professional Baseball League*, from 1943 to 1952.

She was a co-founder of that organization, which was fictionalized in the movie, *A League of Their Own.*

She recorded 1,114 stolen bases in her career, even better than Ty Cobb's record of 892. In 1946, she stole 201 bases in 203 attempts.

The League sponsored ads promoting their games with a purposeful inclusion of phrases such as, "Community Welfare", "Femininity" and "Family Entertainment."

If only women's sports – and other accomplishments – could be seen in the same light.

Sophie Kurys: 5/14/1925 -- 2/17/2013

https://en.wikipedia.org/wiki/Sophie_Kurys

https://en.wikipedia.org/wiki/All-American_Girls_Professional_Baseball_League

Three is an Important Number
Education, Land Grant College. Ohio University

On February 18, 1804, Ohio University in Athens, OH, was founded as the actual first land grant college in the United States.

The University opened with only *three* students in its first class.

Ohio University obviously succeeded, grew, and continues a legacy of education -- well beyond its first three students.

Famous First Facts, *5th Edition*. Joseph Nathan Kane, Steven Anzovin, Janet Podell, page 173.

https://en.wikipedia.org/wiki/Ohio_University

An African American Court First
Diversity, African American, Law, Jonathan Wright

Jonathan Jasper Wright, who died on February 18, 1885, became the first African American state Supreme Court Justice in America, in South Carolina.

This event was one of many short-lived advances during the Reconstruction era in US history, an era brought to a premature end. And it took nearly a century for the next Black state Supreme Court Justice to be appointed.

Though a legal review of Wright's court decisions reflects a mixed political gain for freed slaves, advances *often* exist along a continuum.

Jonathan J. Wright: 2/11/1840 – 2/18/1885

https://www.brennancenter.org/our-work/analysis-opinion/jonathan-jasper-wright-americas-first-black-state-supreme-court-justice

Evidence-Based Perspectives
of the Universe
Heliocentric Theory, Galileo, Evidence-Based Theories, Religious Theories, Nicolaus Copernicus

Nicolaus Copernicus, born February 19, 1473, was not the first person to propose a heliocentric theory of the universe; a Greek astronomer beat him to that record by 18 centuries.

But his explanation is probably the best known and the most influential upon Galileo's later support of heliocentrism.

The evidence-based Copernican explanation was opposed by the less scientific theories of the Church, which at the time, determined both scientific *and* religious matters.

Nicolaus Copernicus: 2/19/1473 – 5/24/1543

https://www.britannica.com/biography/Nicolaus-Copernicus

https://en.wikipedia.org/wiki/Galileo_Galilei

A Repetitive Cycle of Exclusion
Prejudice, Asian, Japanese, Immigration Act of 1907

On February 20, the Immigration Act of 1907 restricted the entry of Japanese workers into the United States.

https://en.wikipedia.org/wiki/Immigration_Act_of_1907#:~:text=The%20Act%20was%20part%20of,ones%20regarding%20disability%20and%20disease.

A Monument with Lessons
to a Person and to the Times
Know-Nothing Party, Pope Pius IX,
Prejudice, Washington Monument

The Washington Monument was completed and dedicated on February 21, 1885, though the construction had begun 37 years earlier.

Evidence of a pause in 1854 can be seen in the different color of the exterior about halfway up.

During that pause, a stone contributed by Pope Pius IX was destroyed by the anti-Catholic, nativist American Party, known as the "Know-Nothing Party".

Although a minority party in Congress, it had considerable influence during this era.

While the obelisk was a monument to one of the nation's most prominent founders, progress of the project was slowed during a period of a lack of governmental financial support, prejudice, and a civil war.

(The destruction of the Pope's stone: 3/6/1854)

https://en.wikipedia.org/wiki/Washington_Monument

https://www.nps.gov/wamo/faqs.htm#:~:text=When%20the%20monument%20was%20under,marble%20from%20a%20different%20quarry.

Personalized Perceptions of Now and of the Future
Painting, Landscapes, Perspective, Last Words, Jean Corot

The accomplished French landscape painter, Jean Corot, died on February 22, 1875.

His last words were, "How beautiful it is! I have never seen such beautiful landscapes."

Jean Corot: 7/16/1796 – 2/22/1875

Exits: Stories of Dying Moments & Parting Words, by Scott Slater & Alec Solomita

https://www.nationalgallery.org.uk/artists/jean-baptiste-camille-corot

A Significant Vaccine
Inoculation, Polio, Vaccine Resistance, Vaccine Access, Jonas Salk

The first mass inoculation against polio, using the Jonas Salk vaccine, took place on February 23, 1954, at an elementary school in Pittsburgh.

In spite of the availability of the vaccine today, polio cases are increasing worldwide.

Jonas Salk: 10/28/1914 – 6/23/1995

On this Day in America, John Wagman,

https://www.salk.edu/about/history-of-salk/jonas-salk/

There are Tears, and There are Tears
Funerals, Tears, Stan Laurel

Stan Laurel, who died on February 23, 1965, was the sad-faced half of the *Laurel and Hardy* comedy team of stage and screen, both silent and 'talkies.'

With his trademark half-blank look and half-smile, he is credited with saying -- with a straight face -- "If any of you cry at my funeral, I'll never speak to you again."

Just like Stan Laurel's blank look could express a range of feelings, tears can also express a range of emotions.

Stan Laurel: 6/16/1890 – 2/23/1965

https://en.wikipedia.org/wiki/Stan_Laurel

https://m.imdb.com/name/nm0491048/quotes/

Words Are Important
Anthropologist, Folk Tales, Dictionary,
Brothers Grimm. Wilhelm Grimm

Wilhelm Grimm, who was born on February 24, 1786, was one of the *Brothers Grimm*.

As an anthropologist, he collected and preserved old folk tales.

He and his brother also worked together to compile the largest German dictionary ever published.

Words are important, whether alone, or in a collection with other words.

Wilhelm Grimm: 2/24/1786 – 12/16/1859

https://en.wikipedia.org/wiki/Jacob_Grimm

Picture This
Artist, Illustrator, Alice in Wonderland, Punch, Creative/Destructive, Sir John Tenniel

Sir John Tenniel, who died on February 25, 1914, was an accomplished artist, perhaps best known for the memorable illustrations in the first publication of *Alice's Adventures in Wonderland*, including those of Alice, the Queen of Hearts, and the Cheshire cat, shaping creative imaginations for generations.

The power of graphic art can also be used to shape *destructive* imaginations by drawing distorted caricatures of minorities.

One example of destructive images appeared in a British magazine of the 1860s, called *Punch*. The magazine had a clear political position of anti-Irish Nationalism, with political cartoons picturing the Irish as sub-human, ape-like figures.

The political cartoonist for *Punch* and the illustrator for *Alice's Adventures in Wonderland* were one and the *same*: Sir John Tenniel.

Sir John Tenniel: 2/28/1820 – 2/25/1914

https://en.wikipedia.org/wiki/John_Tenniel

Long-Lasting Stories
The Hunchback of Notre Dame, Les Misérables,
Long-Lasting, Victor Hugo

Victor Hugo, born February 26, 1802, was a French writer whose career spanned more than six decades. And his popularity extended even further.

His works are perhaps best known in the film world for the epic 1923 silent screen version of *The Hunchback of Notre Dame*, starring the talented Lon Chaney, Sr., and the 1939 speaking version, starring Charles Laughton.

And his reputation was further solidified by the epic stage production of *Les Misérables*, which had a record-setting run of over 30 years in London.

Victor Hugo: 2/26/1802 – 5/22/1885

https://en.wikipedia.org/wiki/Victor_Hugo

The Source of Innovation
Playwright, Financial Need, Inventions, Lithography, Alois Senefelder

Alois Senefelder died on February 26, 1834.

He was a law student when his father died, and he had to drop out of school to support his mother and siblings by becoming an actor, like his father.

He ventured into writing plays and even producing a successful first script. But he couldn't afford to have a second one published …

So, he invented an affordable method of printing, now known as *lithography*.

Alois Senefelder: 11/6/1771 - 2/26/1834

https://en.wikipedia.org/wiki/Alois_Senefelder

A Recipe for Writing
Writing Environment, Historical Environment, Henry Wadsworth Longfellow

Henry Wadsworth Longfellow, born on February 27, 1807, was an influential American writer whose poems based on events in American history, reflected the political trends of his day.

After retiring from teaching, he spent the rest of his life living and writing in the house where George Washington established his headquarters in Cambridge, MA, during the American War of Independence.

A writer's historical and residential environment is a part of the recipe for inspiration.

Henry Wadsworth Longfellow: 2/27/1807- 3/24/1882

https://en.wikipedia.org/wiki/Henry_Wadsworth_Longfellow

https://www.nps.gov/long/index.htm

Narrow Focus, Wide View
Entomology, Silk Production, Paper Production, The Strength of Rope, René Antoine de Réaumur

René Antoine de Réaumur, born on February 28, 1683, was a French entomologist, whose 1710 paper on using spiders to produce silk was translated into Chinese.

He also observed wasps making paper from wood fibers, and while it took more than a century before wood pulp was used in large scale paper production, he is credited with that significant step in the history of paper-making.

He even verified experimentally that the strength of a rope is more than the sum of the strengths of its separate strands.

Starting with a very *narrow* focus, even on something as small as insects, can lead to very *wide* discoveries.

René de Réaumur: 2/28/1683 – 10/17/1757

https://en.wikipedia.org/wiki/Ren%C3%A9_Antoine_Ferch ault_de_R%C3%A9aumur

Picture This
Artist, Illustrator, Alice in Wonderland, Punch, Creative/Destructive, Sir John Tenniel

Sir John Tenniel, born on February 28, 1820, was an accomplished artist, perhaps best known for the memorable illustrations in the first publication of *Alice's Adventures in Wonderland*, including those of Alice, the Queen of Hearts, and the Cheshire cat, shaping creative imaginations for generations.

The power of graphic art can also be used to shape *destructive* imaginations by drawing distorted caricatures of minorities.

One example of destructive images appeared in a British magazine of the 1860s, called *Punch*. The magazine had a clear political position of anti-Irish Nationalism, with political cartoons picturing the Irish as sub-human, ape-like figures.

The political cartoonist for *Punch* and the illustrator for *Alice's Adventures in Wonderland* were *one* and the *same*: Sir John Tenniel.

Sir John Tenniel: 2/28/1820 – 2/25/1914

https://en.wikipedia.org/wiki/John_Tenniel

A Good Award Given in a Bad Way
Segregation, Academy Award, Best Supporting Actress, *Gone With the Wind*, African American, Hattie McDaniel

Hattie McDaniel received an Academy Award Oscar for *Best Supporting Actress* on February 29, 1940, for the 1939 film, *Gone With the Wind*.

She was the first African American (either male or female) to receive an Oscar.

That night, she was required to sit in a side room of the Ambassador Hotel, segregated from her fellow nominees and performers.

And when she died in 1952, she was not allowed to receive a final award for her life and career -- an opportunity to be buried in *Hollywood Cemetery*, because the cemetery was segregated, for "whites bodies only".

It took nearly a quarter of a century before the next Oscar was awarded to a Black actor - Sidney Poitier, for *Lilies of the Field*.

Hattie McDaniel: 6/10/1893 – 10/26/1952

https://en.wikipedia.org/wiki/Hattie_McDaniel#:~:text=At%20the%20Oscars%20ceremony%20in,whites%2Donly%20at%20the%20time.

A Rare Voice is Heard
Shakers, Pacifist, Ann Lee

Ann Lee, born on February 29, 1736, was the founder of the *United Society of Believers in Christ's Second Appearing*, better known as the *Shakers*.

Born in England, she moved to America in 1774 and maintained neutrality during the War of Independence, taking a pacifist position.

Ann Lee: 2/29/1736 – 9/8/1784

https://en.wikipedia.org/wiki/Ann_Lee

MARCH

A Landmark in Medicine
Medicine, Women, African American
Rebecca Lee Crumpler

On March 1, 1864, Rebecca Lee Crumpler received an M.D. from New England Female Medical College, in Boston MA. On that day she became the first African American woman physician.

After a career in medicine, she published *A Book of Medical Discourses,* which was one of the first medical publications written by an African American.

Dr. Crumpler once referred to her academic credential as "doctress of medicine," perhaps reflecting her generation's view of female doctors.

Rebecca Lee Crumpler: 2/8/1831 – 3/9/1895

https://cfmedicine.nlm.nih.gov/physicians/biography_73.html

An Individual Play by a Team-Member
Baseball, Triple Play, Unassisted, Paul Hines

Paul Hines, born on March 1, 1855, was a centerfielder for the *Providence Grays* who accomplished the first unassisted triple play in organized baseball, in a game between Providence and Boston.

Providence won, 3 to 2.

Even unassisted plays can happen on a team, but teamwork is still a factor.

Paul Hines: 3/1/1855 – 7/10/1935

https://en.wikipedia.org/wiki/Paul_Hines

A Step Forward and a Missed Step
Slavery, Slave Importation,
Legislation

On March 2, 1807, the US Congress passed a law prohibiting slave importation, two centuries after the beginning of slavery in America...

...but two centuries before many changes.

On This Day in America, John Wagman

International Rescue Cat Day
A.S.P.C.A, Stress, Meditation, Yoga,
Deep Breathing, Positive Thinking, Stress Relief

Each year, March 2nd is observed as *International Rescue Cat Day.*

When we think of cats, we think of their purring sound. Much thought and some recent research has gone into the question of "why do cats purr?"

The obvious *first* answer is that purring is a sign of feeling secure and comfortable.

But cats *also* purr when they feel just the *opposite* -- *in*secure and *un*comfortable -- in an effort to *self-calm.*

Perhaps we can learn a valuable lesson from cats in finding ways to "purr" in human ways, by deep breathing, positive thinking, meditation, or yoga.

Research supports the awareness that these are effective ways to reduce stress, and they are actions under our own control, even when we encounter stress that is *not* under our control.

https://pets.webmd.com/cats/why-do-cats-purr

https://nationaltoday.com/international-rescue-cat-day/

King Tut's "Wishing Cup"
Archaeology, King Tut,
Wishing Cup, Howard Carter

Howard Carter was the archeologist best known for discovering the pristinely preserved tomb of King Tutankhamen, aka, *King Tut*.

When Carter died on March 2, 1939, his tombstone bore a phrase taken from a chalice which Carter called the "Wishing Cup", found with King Tut --

May your spirit live,
may you spend millions of years,
sitting with your face to the north wind,
your eyes beholding happiness.

Howard Carter: 5/9/1874 – 3/2/1939

https://en.wikipedia.org/wiki/Howard_Carter#:~:text=His%20love%20for%20Egypt%20remained,thy%20wings%20over%20me%20as

The Original *Fiddler* Story
**Writer, Russian, Yiddish, Triskaidekaphobia, *Tevye*,
Fiddler on the Roof, Solomon Rabinovich**

Solomon Rabinovich, born March 2, 1859, was a Russian writer of Yiddish stories, who published his tales of *Tevye the Dairyman,* which served as the basis for the award-winning stage and movie productions of *Fiddler on the Roof.*

He was known to have a life-long mortal fear of the number 13, and his writing drafts never had a page 13, but had a "12a" in its place.

Ironically, the date of his death was May 13th. His tombstone avoided the number 13 by using dates from the Hebrew calendar.

Solomon Rabinovich: 3/2/1859 – 5/13/1916

https://en.wikipedia.org/wiki/Sholem_Aleichem

From Literature to Science
Interdisciplinary, Fiction, Diagnosis, Munchausen Syndrome, Baron Munchausen, Erich Raspe, Richard Asher,

Richard Asher, born on March 3, 1912, was an eminent British medical doctor and researcher, who identified a then-new disorder called the *Munchausen Syndrome*.

The journey of this diagnosis began with Baron Karl Munchausen, known for his embellished tales of world travels, and for being the inspiration of a book by Erich Raspe, a contemporary of the Baron.

Raspe's book described a fictional version of Munchausen, who was self-abusive in order to receive the attention of care-givers.

Over a century later, Asher's description of the syndrome was partly based on Raspe's character.

From an actual figure in history, to a fictional character in literature, to a medical discovery – sometimes new insights develop through many interdisciplinary links.

Karl Munchausen: 5/11/1720 – 2/22/1797
https://en.wikipedia.org/wiki/Baron_Munchausen

Erich Raspe: 3/?/1720 – 11/1/1784
https://en.wikipedia.org/wiki/Rudolf_Erich_Raspe

Richard Asher: 4/3/1912 – 4/25/1969
https://en.wikipedia.org/wiki/Richard_Asher

Changes Are Constant
Congressional Law,
Supreme Court, Number of Justices

On March 3, 1837, Congress increased the number of U.S. Supreme Court justices from seven to nine.

The number of justices has changed 6 times before settling on the current number.

On This Day in America, John Wagman

https://www.supremecourt.gov/about/institution.aspx#:~:text=The%20number%20of%20Justices%20on,an%20average%20of%2016%20years.

https://en.wikipedia.org/wiki/Supreme_Court_of_the_United_States

A Name is an Identity
U.S. Cabinet member, Women, Social Security, Birth Name, Francis Perkins

On March 4, 1933, Francis Perkins became the first woman to serve in the U.S. Cabinet.

She served as Secretary of Labor for a record term of 12 years, and was instrumental in creating the *Social Security* program.

Though married, she kept her birth name, having to defend that decision in court. That apparently caused the Senate to delay her cabinet approval.

Francis Perkins: 4/10/1880 – 5/14/1965

https://en.wikipedia.org/wiki/Frances_Perkins

https://francesperkinscenter.org/learn/her-life/

https://www.ssa.gov/history/fpbiossa.html

A Stone Holds a Key
Egyptology, Language, *Rosetta Stone*,
Jean-François Champollion

Jean-François Champollion, who died on March 4, 1832, was a French scholar and an expert in Egyptian hieroglyphs.

He is recognized as a founder of *Egyptology* and was one of the first scholars to realize the value of the *Rosetta Stone*, a significant key to understanding ancient languages.

A single key can open many doors.

Jean-François Champollion: 12/23/1790 – 3/4/1832

https://en.wikipedia.org/wiki/Jean-Fran%C3%A7ois_Champollion

Pandemics Past and Present
Inoculation, Mandate, Smallpox, Massachusetts, Supreme Court

The first state law requiring every citizen to be infected with Cow-Pox, and hence inoculated against smallpox, was enacted in Massachusetts on March 6, 1810, during the pandemic of that century.

The law was upheld by the U.S. Supreme court in *Jacobson v. Massachusetts* in 1905.

Famous First Facts, 5*th* *Edition*. Joseph Nathan Kane, Steven Anzovin, Janet Podell, page 339.

https://supreme.justia.com/cases/federal/us/197/11/

A First in Representation
Diversity, African American,
American Methodist Episcopal (AME),
Politics, Benjamin Arnett

Bishop Benjamin William Arnett, born on March 6, 1838, was an educator, minister and Bishop in the *African Methodist Episcopal* (AME) church.

He was once the foreman of an all-white jury (except for him); probably a first.

In 1885, he became the first African American state legislator to represent a majority white district in the Ohio legislature.

Bishop B. W. Arnett: 3/6/1838 – 10/7/1906

https://en.wikipedia.org/wiki/Benjamin_W._Arnett

A Monument with Lessons
to a Person and to the Times
Know-Nothing Party, Pope Pius IX,
Prejudice, Washington Monument

On March 6, 1854, during a pause in the construction of the Washington Monument, a stone contributed by Pope Pius IX was destroyed by the anti-Catholic, nativist American Party, known as the "Know-Nothing Party".

Although a minority party in Congress, it had considerable influence during this era.

Evidence of that pause can be seen in the different color of the exterior about half way up.

Construction of the monument began in 1848 but was not completed until 1885.

Though the obelisk was a monument to one of the nation's most prominent founders, progress of the project was slowed during a period of a lack of governmental financial support, prejudice, and a civil war.

(The monument's dedication: 2/21/1885)

https://en.wikipedia.org/wiki/Washington_Monument

Early Restrictions in American Voting
Massachusetts, Voter Registration

On March 7, 1801, Massachusetts became the first state to require voter registration.

With immigration increasing, this might have been a way to decrease their participation in politics.

The state later introduced literacy tests and poll taxes.

Famous First Facts, *5ᵗʰ Edition*. Joseph Nathan Kane, Steven Anzovin, Janet Podell, page 215.

https://www.wgbh.org/news/post/blame-bay-state-voter-registration

https://en.wikipedia.org/wiki/Voter_registration_in_the_United_States#:~:text=During%20the%2019th%20century%2C%20and,voting%20by%20immigrants%20in%20cities.

Filling a Need
Great London Fire, Architect, Physicist, Astronomer, Transferable Skills, Christopher Wren

Christopher Wren, who died on March 8, 1723, was a well-known British mathematician, physicist, and astronomer.

He had no formal training as an architect.

But after the *Great London Fire* of 1666, which eventually destroyed 80% of the city, with no prominent architects in England at the time, he saw a need and stepped up to the task.

By the time Christopher Wren died, he had helped build or rebuild no less than 52 churches in London, including his masterpiece, *Saint Paul's Cathedral.*

Christopher Wren: 10/30/1632 – 3/8/1723

https://en.wikipedia.org/wiki/Christopher_Wren

https://en.wikipedia.org/wiki/List_of_works_by_Christopher_Wren

Adapting is Growing
Silent Films, Acting, 3D Photographs, Adapting, Harold Lloyd

Harold Lloyd, who died on March 8, 1971, is best known for his silent film roles, and less known for his experiments with color film and 3D photography. Some of the earliest tests of 2-color Technicolor were filmed at his Beverly Hills home.

Many silent film actors could not make a successful transition to the modern world of *talkies,* and slowly faded away.

Lloyd's personal and professional growth from silent film to a modern era was certainly a creative and giant leap forward.

Harold Lloyd: 4/20/1893 – 3/8/1971

https://en.wikipedia.org/wiki/Harold_Lloyd

A Landmark in Medicine
Medicine, Women, African American
Rebecca Lee Crumpler

Rebecca Lee Crumpler, who died on March 9, 1895, had received an M.D. from New England Female Medical College, in Boston MA.

She was the first African American woman physician.

After a career in medicine, she published *A Book of Medical Discourses,* which was one of the first medical publications written by an African American.

Dr. Crumpler once referred to her academic credential as "doctress of medicine," perhaps a commentary on her generation's view of female doctors.

Rebecca Lee Crumpler: 2/8/1831 – 3/9/1895

https://cfmedicine.nlm.nih.gov/physicians/biography_73.html

Eugenics in America
Before the Holocaust
Indiana State Legislature, Eugenics

On March 9, 1907, the Indiana state legislature passed what is considered the first modern eugenics law, which allowed for the involuntary sterilization of "confirmed criminals, idiots, imbeciles and rapists."

Other states implemented similar laws during the 20th century, some of which were still in place and sometimes used in the 21st century, often for racial reasons.

A study by the University of Vermont estimated that over 60,000 forced sterilizations have occurred in 30 American states since 1907.

https://www.genome.gov/about-genomics/fact-sheets/Eugenics-and-Scientific-Racism#:~:text=Eugenicists%20worldwide%20believed%20that%20they,by%20them%20to%20be%20unfit.

https://www.in.gov/history/state-historical-markers/find-a-marker/1907-indiana-eugenics-law/#:~:text=Governor%20Hanly%20approved%20the%20first,Thomas%20Riley%20Marshall%20halted%20sterilizations.

https://www.uvm.edu/~lkaelber/eugenics/IN/IN.html

https://www.uvm.edu/~lkaelber/eugenics/

The Art of Mailing a Letter
Letters, Mail, Letter Box, Albert Potts

On March 9, 1858, Albert Potts invented a "New and Improved combination of Letter-Box and Lamp-Post for Municipalities."

Its purpose was to make it easier to mail letters, without having to visit a post office.

https://postalmuseum.si.edu/happy-albert-potts-day

One Person's Footprint
Slavery, Underground Railroad, National Park, Harriet Tubman

Araminta Ross was born a slave in 1822; she died as Harriet Tubman, on March 10, 1913.

This one person managed to free at least 70 slaves by way of the *Underground Railroad*, and over 700 slaves as a regiment leader in one battle of the Civil War.

And she didn't stop there.

She became an active suffragette, willed her house to become a home for the elderly and sick, *and* has *two* national parks named for her.

Harriet Tubman: c. 3/1822 – 3/10/1913

https://www.npca.org/articles/2314-5-facts-you-might-not-know-about-harriet-tubman?gclid=CjwKCAjw36GjBhAkEiwAKwIWyZFNrltl Y3ei0Qcve8Ni_BGmP5FNiayplxer99zNB8ZNDRjfjONO WRoC3-kQAvD_BwE

https://en.wikipedia.org/wiki/Harriet_Tubman

The First State Mental Health Hospital in America
Hospitals, Mental Health, Horace Mann

The first state hospital for the mentally ill in the United States was authorized by the Massachusetts legislature on March 10, 1830.

The hospital in Worcester, MA, has been known by different names over the years.

The cause was championed by educator Horace Mann, who advocated humane and equal opportunities in many social aspects of life.

Soon after the facility opened, it became overcrowded. The hospital still operates today.

Horace Mann: 5/4/1796 – 8/2/1859

https://en.wikipedia.org/wiki/Worcester_State_Hospital#:~:text=Worcester%20State%20Hospital%20was%20a,National%20Register%20of%20Historic%20Places.

https://www.britannica.com/biography/Horace-Mann

https://worcesterhistorical.com/the-treatment-of-insanity/

Helping Others
Helping Hand Club, Girl Scouts,
Struggles, Juliette Gordon Low

On March 12, 1912, Juliette Gordon Low (aka, Daisey Gordon), established the *Girl Guides* in Savannah GA.

The organization later became known as the *Girl Scouts*, which celebrates her birthday as its *Founder's Day*.

She faced a number of obstacles in her personal life, including medical problems as a child, but at an early age, one of her projects was to start the "Helping Hand Club" to make clothes for immigrant children.

Daisey Gordon: 10/31/1860 – 1/17/1927

https://en.wikipedia.org/wiki/Juliette_Gordon_Low

How We Treat Others
Reform, Equal Rights, Susan B, Anthony

Susan B. Anthony, who died on March 13, 1906, left a lasting legacy as an American social reformer and activist, including her persistent efforts for women's rights, both white and African American.

She once wrote, "Men who fail to be just to their mothers cannot be expected to be just to each other."

How we treat others in one context can be a measure of how we treat others in another context.

Susan B. Anthony: 2/15/1820 – 3/13/1906

https://susanb.org/susan-b-anthony-quotes/

https://susanb.org/her-life/

https://ajournaljourney.com/2022/03/07/heres-to-women/

Pluto is Pluto, by Any Name -- or Classification
Planet, Classification, Percival Lowell, Pluto

The verifiable discovery of the celestial body known as *Pluto*, actually occurred in stages, some of which were not initially recognized.

Percival Lowell, the founder of *The Lowell Observatory* in Arizona, had apparently captured two images of the planet in 1915, though he did not realize it for over a decade. There were as many as fourteen previous potential observations dating back to 1909.

Long after its official discovery was announced on March 13, 1930 (Lowell's birthday), its classification eventually came into question, and was changed from "planet" to "dwarf planet".

Any existence, either a celestial body or a human body, does not depend on any "classification" or date of discovery, for it has a value of its own.

Percival Lowell: 3/13/1855 – 11/12/1916

https://en.wikipedia.org/wiki/Percival_Lowell

An Artistic First for Women
Idaho, State Seal, Women, Emma Sarah Edwards

On March 14, 1891, the state of Idaho officially adopted its state seal. It was created by Emma Sarah Edwards, the first and only woman to design a state seal.

The inclusive image pictured a woman, a miner, and the state's natural environment.

There is research to indicate that art (and leadership) by women tends to be more inclusive when compared to that of men.

Emma Sarah Edwards: ?/?/1856 – 1/6/1942

Famous First Facts, *5th Edition*. Joseph Nathan Kane, Steven Anzovin, Janet Podell, page 579.

https://en.wikipedia.org/wiki/Emma_Edwards_Green

https://hbr.org/2020/04/7-leadership-lessons-men-can-learn-from-women

https://www.pewresearch.org/social-trends/2018/09/20/2-views-on-leadership-traits-and-competencies-and-how-they-intersect-with-gender/

Parenting
Parenting, Hugs, Behaviorism,
John Watson, Benjamin Spock

Benjamin Spock, who died on March 15, 1998, was the author of his generation's most popular book on parenting, *The Common Sense Book of Baby and Child Care.*

In that book, he suggested that a parent cannot hug a child too much.

Only a generation earlier, the most popular authority on parenting at *that* time was John Watson, a pioneer of *behaviorism.*

His then-widely-read book, *Psychological Care of Infant and Child*, took a very different approach: "Never hug and kiss them; shake hands with them in the morning…"

It is interesting to note that many famous figures of Watson's era wrote in their autobiographies that they were rarely, if ever, hugged by their fathers.

In about a generation, the approach to raising children changed as much as the dramatic extremes of a pendulum swing.

Benjamin Spock: 5/2/1903 – 3/15/1998

https://en.wikipedia.org/wiki/The_Common_Sense_Book_of_Baby_and_Child_Care

A First Step -- Literally
Journey, Racewalking, Edward Payson Weston

On March 15, 1909, Edward Payson Weston started, on his 70th birthday, a 104-day hike from New York City to San Francisco.

It wasn't his first nor was it his last effort to encourage the sport of racewalking, a sport for which he advocated all of his life.

As the proverb suggests, a journey of 3,795 miles always begins with one step.

Edward P. Weston: 3/15/1839 – 5/12/1929

https://ultrarunninghistory.com/edward-payson-weston/

https://en.wikipedia.org/wiki/Edward_Payson_Weston

Greetings
Abenaki, Indigenous, Pilgrims, Welcome, Samoset

Samoset was a chief (a *sagamore*) of the Abenaki indigenous tribe of North America, and the first Native American to address the newly arrived Pilgrims, on March 16, 1621.

He had learned some English from earlier New England fishermen, and spoke briefly: "Welcome, Englishmen."

One wonders what he was thinking at the time, or what he would be thinking today.

Samoset: c. 1590 - c. 1653

Famous First Facts, 5*th* *Edition.* Joseph Nathan Kane, Steven Anzovin, Janet Podell, page 424.

https://www.worldhistory.org/Samoset/

https://www.heritage-history.com/index.php?c=resources&s=char-dir&f=samoset

https://www.notablebiographies.com/supp/Supplement-Mi-So/Samoset.html

Leadership Reaches Beyond Borders
Tibet, Tibetan Buddhism, Exile, Dalai Lama

The history of the *Dalai Lama* dates back to the first monk ordained to that position, in 1391. For centuries, the one bearing that name has been the leader of Tibet's people and of Tibetan Buddhism.

Born in 1935 as Lhamo Dhondup, the 14th Dalai Lama was eventually tutored in poetry, drama, composition, synonyms and Buddhist religious teachings, to prepare him to be a global teacher of wisdom.

On March 17, 1959, after China suppressed an effort for independence, the Dalai Lama began his exile from Tibet in an escape to Dharamsala, in northern India.

This was not the first religious exodus, for spiritual leaders and wisdom have no boundaries.

The Dalai Lama: 7/6/1935 --

https://www.dalailama.com/

https://www.dalailama.com/the-dalai-lama/biography-and-daily-life/brief-biography

Music Belongs to All Cultures
Opera, The MET,
Frederick Stephen Converse

On this day, March 18, 1910, the Metropolitan Opera House in New York City produced its first American-composed opera.

It took 27 years before this first happened at the MET, perhaps because of a popular stereotype and misperception that "proper opera" was the domain only of Italian or European composers.

The opera was *The Pipe of Desire*, by Frederick Stephen Converse.

He would later teach at Harvard and the New England Conservatory of Music.

Music, like any art, has no boundaries.

Frederick S. Converse: 1/5/1871 – 6/8/1940

https://en.wikipedia.org/wiki/Frederick_Converse

The Influence of Alignments
Ptolemy, Celestial, Alignment, Lunar Eclipse

According to the early Greek scientist, Ptolemy, the first recorded lunar eclipse was documented on March 19, 721 BCE, by Babylonians.

A lunar eclipse requires an alignment of all three significant celestial players: the earth, moon and sun.

Perhaps human events are also influenced by the alignment of significant players orbiting around *us*, including social, religious, environmental, historical, psychological, political, and more important players.

https://en.wikipedia.org/wiki/Ptolemy

https://www.weather.gov/fsd/suneclipse#:~:text=A%20Lunar%20eclipse%20occurs%20when,a%20portion%20of%20Earth's%20shadow.

Science *Fiction*
Can Sometimes Predict Science *Reality*
Futuristic, Science Fiction,
2001: A Space Odyssey, Arthur C. Clarke

Sir Arthur C. Clarke, who died on March 19, 2008, was a British science writer, and one of the "big three" science-*fiction* writers of his time, alongside Isaac Asimov and Robert Heinlein.

Clarke co-wrote the 1968 screenplay for *2001: A Space Odyssey*, a futuristic and yet realistic prediction of our current experiences in space and science. The film earned a long list of theatrical nominations and awards.

While it is important to know the difference between *science* and *fiction*, perhaps without science *fiction*, we might have less *science reality*.

Sir Arthur C. Clarke: 12/16/1917 – 3/19/2008

https://en.wikipedia.org/wiki/Arthur_C._Clarke

https://en.wikipedia.org/wiki/2001:_A_Space_Odyssey_(film)

https://www.imdb.com/title/tt0062622/

The Legacy of Our Teachings
Legacies, Creation, Misinformation, Bishop Ussher

Bishop James Ussher died on March 21, 1656. He is best known for his calculation of the date of creation: the evening before Sunday, October 23, 4004 BC.

Though first published in English in 1658, the date became etched in modern history when it was published in 1917, in a column of notes, as if it were scientific data, in the *Scofield Reference Bible*.

Bishop James Ussher: 1/4/1581- 3/21/1656

https://en.wikipedia.org/wiki/Ussher_chronology

http://law2.umkc.edu/faculty/projects/ftrials/scopes/ussher.html#:~:text=Bishop%20James%20Ussher%20Sets%20the,Creation%3A%20October%2023%2C%204004%20B.C.

Timing is Everything
Time, Timing, *Faust*, Johann Wolfgang von Goethe

Johann Wolfgang von Goethe died on March 22, 1832.

He is best known for writing *Faust*.

It took him 58 years to complete it, and sadly, he died only a few months later.

Johann von Goethe: 8/28/1749 – 3/22/1832

https://en.wikipedia.org/wiki/Johann_Wolfgang_von_Goethe

https://en.wikipedia.org/wiki/Faust

Caught in the Middle
Evolution, *A Civic Biology,* John Thomas Scopes

On March 23, 1925, the Governor of Tennessee signed a law forbidding any public schools or universities from teaching "any theory that denies the story of the Divine creation of man as taught in the Bible."

Later that year, John Thomas Scopes was convicted of violating that law.

But teachers in those public schools were *also* required by state law to use a biology textbook which *endorsed* evolution.

The situation was further complicated because that text, *A Civic Biology*, used evolution as a reason to support white supremacy and eugenics.

John Thomas Scopes: 8/3/1900 – 10/21/1970

Famous First Facts, 5th *Edition*. Joseph Nathan Kane, Steven Anzovin, Janet Podell, page 185.

https://www.mtsu.edu/first-amendment/article/1100/scopes-monkey-trial

All in a Family
Oscars, Awards, Family, Winners

At the same ceremony on March 24, 1949, a father and son each won Oscars.

And more interesting, they were for the same film, *The Treasure of Sierra Madre*.

Walter Huston won for Best Supporting Actor and John Huston won for Best Director.

https://www.imdb.com/title/tt0040897/

https://en.wikipedia.org/wiki/The_Treasure_of_the_Sierra_Madre_(film)

The Consequences of a Disaster
Fire, Safety, Triangle Shirtwaist Company

The *Triangle Shirtwaist Company Fire* of March 25, 1911, was one of the worst industrial disasters in American history, killing 123 women and 23 men, mostly Italian immigrants.

Their escape was hampered by locked doors to the stairways, a common practice in that era, to prevent employees from taking unofficial breaks.

The disaster fostered increased safety laws.

https://en.wikipedia.org/wiki/Triangle_Shirtwaist_Factory_fire

To Self-Publish or Not to Self-Publish
Self-Publishing, Leaves of Grass, Walt Whitman

Walt Whitman, who died on March 26, 1892, was a prolific and famous American writer.

Perhaps his most famous work, *Leaves of Grass*, was published at his own expense, printed by a local print shop, in between its commercial projects.

No author was indicated on the title page of the first printing.

"Self-publishing" today is much debated, and sometimes avoided, for fear of a negative stigma, but it appears to have been a successful strategy for Whitman.

Leaves of Grass was one of his best-selling books.

Perhaps *your* self-published book could become a best-seller…

Walt Whitman: 5/31/1819 – 3/26/1892

https://www.loc.gov/exhibits/whitman/leavesofgrass.html

https://www.baumanrarebooks.com/blog/the-story-behind-the-first-edition-of-walt-whitmans-leaves-of-grass/

Grateful in Spite of Problems
Polio Vaccine, Grateful Response, Jonas Salk

When Jonas Salk announced the successful testing of a polio vaccine on March 26, 1953, it marked the end of a terrible disease, and the beginning of a grateful nation.

He was quickly called a *miracle worker,* in spite of problems during the vaccine's development and first application.

Jonas Salk: 10/28/1914 – 6/23/1995

Jonas Salk - Wikipedia

https://www.ncbi.nlm.nih.gov/pmc/articles/PMC1383764/#:~:text=In%20April%201955%20more%20than,polio%20had%20to%20be%20abandoned.

https://www.cdc.gov/vaccines/vpd/polio/hcp/effectiveness-duration-protection.html#:~:text=Two%20doses%20of%20inactivated%20polio,polio%20vaccine%20(tOPV)%2C%20or

Science and/or Religion
Geology, Evolution, James Hutton

James Hutton, who died on March 26, 1797, was a Scottish naturalist, physician and manufacturer. But he is probably best known as the "father of modern geology".

He was an early proponent of the theory that the earth's geological history can be determined from studying present-day rocks. He argued that geological features were subject to continual changes over long periods of time.

From this evidence, he argued against conventional religious beliefs of his day, concluding that Earth was not young, but very old, having endured changes over many centuries.

Influenced by deism, his proposed theory foreshadowed Darwin's theory of evolution.

James Hutton: 6/3/1726 – 3/26/1797

https://www.amnh.org/learn-teach/curriculum-collections/earth-inside-and-out/james-hutton

A First for Women Bullfighters
Stereotypes, Women, Bullfighting, Arts
Patricia McCormick

Patricia McCormick, who died on March 26, 2013, was an American citizen, who became the first North American female professional bullfighter in an appearance in Ciudad Juarez, Mexico.

After retiring from the profession, she became a professional painter, selling line drawings and watercolor scenes of bullfighting.

Here lies an interesting example of taking a traditional stereotype "by the horns", and of a blend of very different "arts".

Patricia McCormick: 11/18/1929 – 3/26/2013

https://www.nytimes.com/2013/04/14/us/patricia-mccormick-bullfighter-who-defied-gender-roles-dies-at-83.html

Stability Supported by *Mobility*
Radio, Synagogue, Computer

On this day, March 27, history rhymes with the theme of *mobility in communication* in these examples:

- The first radio broadcast from a moving train, in 1932, on a B&O Railroad
- The first mobile synagogue, the *Riding Rabbi Bus*, was dedicated in Charlotte, NC, in 1955
- The first mobile computer station, in 1961, in a motor van operated by the Sperry Rand Corporation.

Stability is not the same as being stationary.

Famous First Facts, 5th Edition. Joseph Nathan Kane, Steven Anzovin, Janet Podell, pages (in the order listed 476, 456, 136

Tenure, Under Any Name
American Literature, Mrs. Claus,
America the Beautiful, Katherine Lee Bates

Katherine Lee Bates, who died on March 28, 1929, was a professor of English literature at Wellesley College, and probably best known for writing *America the Beautiful*, during a severe American economic depression in 1893.

She also wrote children's books and essays promoting social reform, and one of the first college textbooks on American literature.

She is credited with popularizing the role of Mrs. Santa Claus, whom she described, in a collection of children's stories, as the *organizer* of Christmas Eve.

Though she achieved a rare success for women educators of her time, she never married, perhaps because she would have lost tenure if she had.

Katherine Lee Bates: 8/12/1859 – 3/28/1929

https://en.wikipedia.org/wiki/Katharine_Lee_Bates

Easter, a.k.a. Christmas
Hymns, Christmas, Easter, Charles Wesley

Charles Wesley, who died on March 29, 1788, wrote the words for over 6,000 hymns.

He originally selected the same tune for the Christmas carol *Hark! The Herald Angels Sing* and the Easter hymn *Christ the Lord Is Risen Today*.

Though the contemporary tunes have changed, his choice at the time was intentional: to musically link the two holiest days of Christianity.

Charles Wesley: 12/18/1707 – 3/29/1788

https://en.wikipedia.org/wiki/Hark!_The_Herald_Angels_Sing

Our Path in Life
Art, Normal, Vincent van Gogh

Vincent van Gogh, born on March 30, 1853, was an accomplished painter of both landscape and still life.

By most biographical descriptions, he apparently did not have a "normal" life, nor did his journey follow a comfortable path.

He once wrote, "Normality is a paved road: it's comfortable to walk, but no flowers grow on it."

Sometimes, diversions along life's path are of our own choosing; sometimes they are the choice of fate.

But walk it, we must.

Vincent van Gogh: 3/30/1853 – 7/29/1890

https://en.wikipedia.org/wiki/Vincent_van_Gogh

https://www.oxfordstudent.com/2015/01/22/review-the-van-gogh-museum-amsterdam/

Sources of Light
Lighthouses, Illumination

On March 31, 1791, the first lighthouse to be built after America became an independent country, was contracted to be located at Cape Henry, VA.

The first source for illumination was fish oil, then the source changed through the years, to whale oil, colza oil, lard oil, kerosene, gas, and electricity.

There are many sources of any illumination, whether physical, cognitive, spiritual, emotional, creative, and more.

Whatever enlightens us is of value.

Famous First Facts, *3*rd *Edition*. Joseph Nathan Kane, page 346.

A First Under the 15th Amendment
Elections, African American, Voting
Thomas Peterson-Mundy

On March 31, 1870, Thomas Peterson-Mundy made history – by acting quickly.

Just one day after the *Fifteenth Amendment* was passed, granting a nationwide ability for African American male citizens to vote, he was apparently the first to exercise that right, by casting a ballot in a special election in Perth Amboy, New Jersey.

In 1807, that state had restricted the previously legal voting rights of Black citizens.

After waiting so long for a right to be returned, one does not want to wait further to exercise it.

Thomas Peterson-Mundy: 10/6/1824 – 2/4/1904

Famous First Facts, *3rd Edition*. Joseph Nathan Kane, page 226.

https://www.archives.gov/milestone-documents/15th-amendment#:~:text=Passed%20by%20Congress%20February%2026,men%20the%20right%20to%20vote.

https://en.wikipedia.org/wiki/Thomas_Mundy_Peterson

https://nj.gov/state/historical/assets/pdf/it-happened-here/ihhnj-er-peterson.pdf

https://www.nps.gov/articles/voting-rights-in-nj-before-the-15th-and-19th.htm

9 EXAMPLES

OF

TOPIC-TO-SPEECH

This section offers examples of how any topic
from this book could be expanded.

Three different illustrations are used here,
with three different expansions for each.

The Legacy of Our Teachings

Sample 1 of 3

Bishop James Ussher is best known for his calculation of the date of creation: beginning the night before Sunday, October 23, 4004 BC.

Though first published in English in 1658, the date became etched in modern history when it was published in 1917 in a column of notes, as if it were scientific data, in the *Scofield Reference Bible*.

Many religious persons think science and religion are in opposition when explaining our beginnings. This misperception is likely caused by the different primary questions science and religion ask, not by a difference in a common search for truths.

One major difference between the two is that science is primarily designed to address the ***how*** questions of life, while religion is primarily designed to answer the ***why*** questions of life.

For example, science's ***how*** questions include:

- How was earth created?
- How is earth affected by the systemic nature of the cosmos?
- How do humans differ from other earthlings?

Examples of religion's ***why*** questions include:

- Why did God create earth?
- Why did God create *me*?
- Why am I alive *now*, rather than in the past or future?

These two categories of questions are just that – *categories*. Both categories are in search of truth, and truth has many dimensions.

Asking questions is a beginning step of knowledge, and it is valuable to keep in mind that asking an important question in the *appropriate* category is a "best practice" and will yield more helpful answers.

For example …

"*How* was earth created?" is a better question for a scientist, not a theologian.

"*Why* did God create *me*?" is a better question for a theologian, not a scientist.

And yet, if these questions are asked with *both* a scientist and a theologian in the same room, we could learn even more.

As we understand that knowledge is not restricted to science *or* religion, and is meant to be discovered through science *and* religion, we will be more open to finding comprehensive answers to difficult, but important questions.

Our journey of learning follows many pathways…

NOTES

The Legacy of Our Teachings

Sample 2 of 3

Bishop James Ussher is best known for his calculation of the date of creation: beginning the night before Sunday, October 23, 4004 BC.

Though first published in English in 1658, the date became etched in modern history when it was published in 1917 in a column of notes, as if it were scientific data, in the *Scofield Reference Bible.*

Many religious persons think science and religion are in opposition when explaining our beginnings. Perhaps one reason for misunderstanding sacred texts is in the misunderstanding of two meaningful words commonly used – and *misused*:

Myth and Truth

One common definition of myth is "a false belief or idea", equal to a misconception, misbelief or fallacy.

Myths, by the second definition, can be presented with narrowly focused themes or with much broader themes intended to offer a wider understanding of more significant questions about life, and how to live it.

These more *global* myths are found in sacred texts, and the story of creation is one of those.

Science properly focuses on the evidence-based mechanics of creation, discovering that creation never happened in just six days, and exploring how it likely (and realistically) happened over eons.

Religion properly focuses on discovering the *global* message of the sacred text, including the repeated observation in the story of creation in Genesis -- that each step of creation was *good*.

The details of the story never really happened, but one of the *always happening* goals of creating is to nurture *good*.

And that observation from a true myth is just the beginning…

NOTES

The Legacy of Our Teachings

Sample 3 of 3

On this day, January 4, 1581, Bishop James Ussher was born. Probably not a household name you would immediately recognize, but a calculation he made about creation is one you have likely heard. He claimed that creation occurred on the evening before October 23, 4004, BC.

He had calculated that date by using only Biblical sources; he did not use any scientific research.

Though first published in English in1658, the proposed date of creation found a place in modern history when it was included in a column of notes in an early edition of the *Scofield Reference Bible,* over a century ago.

That inclusion in the *Scofield Bible* has been misinterpreted by many Christians as a part of the Bible itself, and not just a footnote lacking verification.

Many religious people have unquestioningly accepted Ussher's date, which became popular enough to appear in the stage play and movie, *Inherit the Wind*. It has been a part of arguments by very conservative Christians that creation happened literally in only 6 days, while ecological, astronomical, archaeological, biological, and other scientific evidence, would find that date quite unrealistic.

Science and religion share a common goal in wanting to reach conclusions about important questions, though their approach is different. At the core of a comparison of science and religion are these two questions:

- What is the standard approach that scientists use before reaching conclusions?
- What is a common approach that religious persons use in reaching conclusions?

These are key factors in their different approaches:

Science is based on observable and measurable facts, researched by using the scientific method. It is very important to note that the first stage of the scientific method is *neutral* observation, *not* forming a hypothesis. The second is shaped by the first, not the reverse.

From an observation, then to a hypothesis, then to research (best done when controlling for all influential factors) and then – only then – arriving at a verifiable conclusion.

The temptation for a religious person may be to begin, not with neutral observation, but with a conclusion, aka, a belief (i.e., 'creation happened literally in just six days'), and then work in reverse to find evidence to confirm the conclusion. In the realm of logic, this is referred to as *confirmation bias* -- looking for evidence to confirm a belief.

While science and religion begin with different first steps, religion *can* apply the same neutral observation before arriving at a theological insight.

And continuing the comparison, another difference arises in a common confusion about "facts."

Since science is shaped by the scientific method, new observations of a previously studied topic may reveal new data, which can shape a new hypothesis, new research and new conclusions.

That is how "facts can change."

The field of science understands this as enriched knowledge; some religious persons may view this as evidence that "facts can lie" – especially if facts do not support a *set-in-stone* belief, even before investigating a theological question.

Based on the degree of neutral observation and open questions, both facts and beliefs can change.

Neither science nor religion is stagnant, and both can foster knowledge, insights and direction for our lives.

Mystery and Resolution

Sample 1 of 3

(This example is for a Eulogy connected to this date)

Agatha Christie possessed a masterful ability to use her experience and insight to create and solve mysteries.

One of her crime-novel trademarks is the closing scene, in which the detective gathers the characters in a room to summarize what happened, and to solve the crime. This technique has since been borrowed by many fictional detectives.

If only we could borrow that technique in our own lives, and especially in a time when we are facing a real mystery about life and death, and *remembering* a life.

We clearly experience many, many mysteries about *both* life *and* death, with many unexplained questions, including …

Understanding the mystery of life and death…

- The mystery of "If only…."
- The mystery of "What if …"
- The mystery of "What about…"
- The mystery of "When will we…"
- The mystery of "How will we…"

We are all quite naturally asking -- quietly to ourselves, or out loud to our family and friends – these and more questions, as we face the mystery of loss in our life.

In the face of these yet-unsolved mysteries, if we only had a gathering like Agatha Christie's "here's what happened…" to resolve all of our questions.

But – perhaps we *are* in that gathering right *now* – to focus not so much on "here's what *did* happen" but on "here's what *will* happen."

As we find the support we need, here among family and friends, some old and some new – all drawn together by our shared loss – we may not have all the answers to the mystery of death, but we *will* have a resolution to one mystery – we are experiencing a loss of a loved one only *physically*, but not *spiritually*.

Because we are gathered here to keep a special life *alive* in our hearts, to remember, to celebrate, to hope together, to care for each other, as we face the mysteries of life, lived in our here-and-now, and living in the eternity.

Though one life has ended, one mystery is solved: a legacy lives forever.

NOTES

Mystery and Resolution

Sample 2 of 3

Agatha Christie possessed a masterful ability to use her experience and insight to create and solve mysteries.

One of her crime-novel trademarks is the closing scene, in which the detective gathers the characters in a room to summarize what happened, and to solve the crime. This technique has since been borrowed by many fictional detectives.

We all experience mysteries in our lives, and for some situations and for some persons, a wrap-up or de-mystification *may* or *may not* be welcomed.

For example …

Imagine a storyteller who has just shared a tale about a mysterious and magical spirit who helped guide a lost soul to safety. Every child in the audience – and many adults – could relate to the theme of the story.

Imagine that there is definitive scientific evidence to de-mystify a spiritual event in your own life?

Would you welcome that explanation, or bypass it?

Some mysteries are meant to be solved, and some are meant to remain unsolved.

Where do you fit on that continuum of experiences?

NOTES

Mystery and Resolution

Sample 3 of 3

Agatha Christie possessed a masterful ability to use her experience and insight to create and solve mysteries.

One of her crime-novel trademarks is the closing scene, in which the detective gathers the characters in a room to summarize what happened, and to solve the crime. This technique has since been borrowed by many fictional detectives.

Imagine that someone tries to explain what happened in a past experience which you could *never* have influenced to *any* degree. You might say, "I don't want to focus on a *why* from a matter I *could not* control; I prefer to focus on what I *can* control."

A constant struggle in our lives is trying to distinguish between what we *can* control and what we *cannot* control.

As with most things, the answer to this question falls along a continuum. Rarely is there a matter over which we have 100% control, or over which we lack *any* control. Every decision and factor in our lives exists somewhere along a 0-100% spectrum of *can* or *cannot*.

Consequently, at any given moment, the context of control is a blend, leaving us with choices to make about where to focus our attention and actions. Thus, finding that degree of control is a critical factor.

There is considerable research in medical and social sciences related to the mystery about factors which contribute to a *resilient personality* (sometimes referred to as a *hardy personality*), one which both survives and thrives through our challenges. One of those factors is when a person focuses on *what, when* and *how* we can control our circumstances, rather than dwelling on what we cannot control.

A first strategy in dealing with any difficult situation could be to make a list of factors influencing your decisions, including the *what, when* and *how* with a scale of "I have control" at one end and "I have no control" at the other.

Then focus on the list of factors you **do** have control over. A friend or an objective counselor could guide your steps.

This approach could apply to any range of decisions – from narrowly focused decisions which apply to everyday actions, or decisions which have a more global impact, such as political or social actions.

It all depends on *what, when, how* -- and to *what degree* -- you do have appropriate control.

We *are* in control of deciding that first question.

NOTES

Finding Our Voice

Sample 1 of 3

Lewis Carroll had a childhood fever which left him deaf in one ear, and he spoke with a stammer. But he found and heard a steady voice by writing stories.

Finding our own voice is one way of finding a sense of self.

Some may be *literally* deaf and some may be *figuratively* deaf, but, with effort, we are all truly able to *listen* to the thoughts and emotions of others.

Some may *literally* stammer while speaking and some may *figuratively* stammer, but, with effort, we are all truly able to be heard.

Some may be *literally* mute and some may be *figuratively* mute, but, with effort, we are all truly able to speak from our mind and heart.

Some may have *literal* physical disabilities and some may have *figurative* physical disabilities, but, with effort and assistance, we are all truly able to walk the extra mile.

Some may have *literal* learning challenges and some may have *figurative* learning challenges, but, with effort, we are all truly able to learn.

Some may be *literally* unable to sleep and some may be *figuratively* unable to sleep, but, with effort, we are all truly able to dream.

Some may be *literally* blind and some may be *figuratively* blind, but, with effort, we are all truly able to have a vision.

Some may have *literal* doubts and some may have *figurative* doubts, but, with effort, we are all truly able to continue.

Some may have *literal* fears and some may have *figurative* fears, but, with effort, we are all truly able to overcome.

Some may have *literal* limits and some may have *figurative* limits, but, with effort, we are all truly able to grow.

May we all find our voice, find our calling, find our abilities, find our dreams…and find our way.

Finding Our Voice

Sample 2 of 3

Lewis Carroll had a childhood fever which left him deaf in one ear, and he spoke with a stammer. But he found and heard a steady voice by writing stories.

Finding our own voice is one way of finding a sense of self.

But what if we hear *opposing* voices from within our hearts?

We are constantly challenged, especially in our current environment, by opposing *external* voices, which may lead to a confusing struggle of *internal* voices.

Two areas of research in social psychology are relevant to understanding this task of listening and reality-checking our external and internal voices.

One is called the *Hardy Personality.* Research in that topic indicates that those who are strongly connected to a community, such as family, a faith community, a neighborhood, social organizations, etc., are more resilient when facing stress.

Being strongly connected to others increases the presence of a *listening board*, a useful tool for sorting out the voices around and within us.

The function of the *listening board* is enhanced if it comes from a community with some diverse voices to listen to. So, another relevant topic in social psychology is called *Group Think.*

Research in that topic indicates that being surrounded *only* by persons who are *mirror images* of ourselves -- philosophically, politically, religiously, sociologically, etc., -- leads to a belief that the mirror image is the only valid reality. It's like looking into a mirror and asking advice – and we would only hear one voice.

Additional research in social psychology indicates that we tend to find persons who are more similar to us for friendships, dating, marriage, etc. And when that applies to serving on a committee or a board or a council – or even to hiring employees --the mirror image becomes even more influential.

The *Group Think* research indicates that our decision-making process then becomes, in effect, seeking advice from a *one*-person "mirror voice" with only *one* perspective, rather than a process of sorting out the pros and cons of a proposal by listening to not just one common voice, but to diverse voices, offering more options in a given decision.

And even further, *Group Think* research indicates that gathering people around us who are just like us will foster the belief that "I'm hearing everyone agree with me, so my own perspective is confirmed and any different voice must not be valid."

Relating to people with different views will expand our understanding of different perspectives and will contribute to more open listening, to the voices of others and to our *own* inner voice.

One related teaching handed down from Buddhism is to "look within; be still [and] free from fear and attachment [to] know the sweet joy of [truth]."

Finding Our Voice

Sample 3 of 3

Lewis Carroll had a childhood fever which left him deaf in one ear, and he spoke with a stammer. But he found and heard a steady voice by writing stories.

Finding our own voice is one way of finding a sense of self.

But a voice without action is *voiceless*.

Whether from politicians or preachers, even a poetic voice without action is not real leadership.

And no matter how many voices are lifted, if there is no action, they are voiceless sounds.

There are four core steps from *finding* our voice to *forming* the best action.

First, *listening* to that inner voice which speaks from our heart and soul.

Second, *speaking* that voice.

Third, *acting* to express that inner voice.

And fourth, assuring that our actions are *consistent* with that inner voice.

It is worth noting that the first four of Buddhism's *Eight-Fold Path* includes –

1. Right Understanding
2. Right Thought
3. Right Speech
4. **Right Action**

And a saying from Sufi wisdom is, "Look to what you *do*, for *that* is what you are worth."

And the *Golden Rule* (which appears in all religions, including Christianity) is "Do to others what you would have them do to you."

Whether our actions are local and specifically focused, or global with a wide-ranging goal, they are best if the inner voice behind them is hearable.

And even better if the voice and its action both express caring and respect.

3 TIPS

FOR SUCCESSFUL PUBLIC SPEAKING

One of the first rules in medicine is to "do no harm." That rule is also useful in public speaking. Considerable research supports these three tips.

One example is related to *word choice*. When you know that a word or phrase is hurtful, or if it has the possibility of making someone uncomfortable, why go out of your way to impose it on ears that may, consciously or unconsciously, hear only the *hurt*, and miss your *main point*?

So here are three suggestions:

1. Avoid the phrase, "I'd give an arm and leg for that" because, unknown to you, there might be a military veteran in the audience with an artificial limb, or someone with a close friend or relative in the same situation. Be creative – think of another way to make that point.
2. Avoid the phrase "black or white" when describing a topic involving an "either/or" decision, or a concept that exits on a continuum. Again, why go out of your way to trigger a stereotype that one color is perceived as *good* and the other is perceived as *bad*?
3. And for the same reason, avoid phrases which could mock or stereotype mental illness, such as "looney", "a screw loose", or "retard".

Be kind to your audience.

Epilog

This project began about 75 years ago, with illustrations used by our father, Rev. Dr. Walter H. Griswold, in sermons, communion meditations, graduation speeches, eulogies, family celebrations, and more.

It has gone through a number of changes over those years, including different formats and goals, in order to be as relevant as possible for as wide a readership as possible.

And it had taken three retirements (from each of the contributors) to find the time to bring it to its present form.

We offer our best wishes as you use these topics for any occasion, for speaking or for moments of personal reflection, *and* as you consider *writing your own.*

Dr. Jed Griswold

Dr. Frank C. Griswold

And on behalf of our father, who started this retirement dream, generations ago -

Dr. Walter H. Griswold

NOTES

Index of Topic Titles

Index of Themes

NOTES

Index of Names

Made in the USA
Middletown, DE
15 October 2023

40641665R00144

WWII Heroes

We Were Just Doing Our Jobs

Linda E. Minton

To Marilyn,
Enjoy the stories!
Linda E. Minton

As Americans, we love our country and seek ways to serve our country. As a young Hoosier, I volunteered to serve in the United States Navy, a decision which led to much deeper insight into the challenges and dangers that faced the United States. I came to have special admiration for those with whom I served who had faced wartime combat, had watched comrades lose their lives, frequently had suffered serious wounds, and yet continued to serve and prepare others to meet life-threatening days ahead.

My admiration for those veterans who trained and guided me was unbounded. I will always salute, remember, and tell the stories of how much their service meant to me, my family, and my country.

—Richard G. Lugar
United States Senator (Ret.)

List of All WWII Veterans Interviewed

Max Bates	US Navy
Vernon Bothwell	US Army Air Corps
Thomas Boyd	US Army
Lester Brown	US Army
Scott Brown	US Navy
Robert Buchert	US Army
Albert R. Clark *	US Army Air Corp
Gilbert E. Coleman *	US Army
Ralph Cooley	US Army
Lewis Cowden	US Navy
James Crabb	US Navy
Robert Crouch	US Navy, Pearl Harbor survivor
Clell Downey	US Navy
Elmer Eakle *	US Army
Glen Eakle	US Navy
Henry Eakle *	US Army
Melvin Eakle *	US Army
Paul Ross Feeney *	US Navy, USS *Indianapolis*
William Fischer	US Army
Eunice Walter Francis *	US Army
Frank Milton Francis *	US Army
John R. Geilker *	US Army
Halbert Gillette	US Navy
Richard Greenfield	US Navy
Wayne Guerin	US Navy
Edgar Harrell	US Marines, USS *Indianapolis* survivor
Lester Hartley	US Navy, Pearl Harbor survivor
Irvin Herman	US Navy

William Hill	US Army
Robert C. Hlavacek *	US Army
Paul Kennedy *	US Navy, Pearl Harbor survivor
William Kincheloe	US Army
Richard Kolodey	US Marines
Donald Kuhlenschmidt	US Air Corps
Earl Lautzenheiser	US Army
Gene Leffler *	US Army
Harry Lyons *	US Army Air Corp
Cleatus Lebow	US Navy, USS *Indianapolis* survivor
Evanula Ledbetter *	US Army
Charles McDonald *	US Army
Herman McGregor	US Army Air Corps
Arlin McRae	US Marines
Wilbur Meyer *	US Navy
John R. Miller	US Army
Robert Miller	US Army
Jerry Moser	US Navy
William Muller	US Army Air Corps
Ralph Myers	US Army
Richard Negus	US Navy
Harold Norlin	US Navy
Albert (Bud) Oliver *	US Army
Harold (Pete) Palmer *	US Army
Robert Pedigo	US Army Air Corps
Harold Pettus	US Army
James Pike	US Marines
Paul Pitcher	US Navy
Robert Poole *	US Army Air Corps

Robert Reed	US Army
Richard Robinson	US Army
Allen Sanderson	US Army Air Corps
Dr. William Schmidt	US Army
Robert Sisk	US Army
Robert Swift	US Army
Harold Weber	US Navy
Bob W.	US Army

* Deceased

TABLE OF CONTENTS

Author's Note

WWII has been depicted in movies, books, magazines, and newspapers. The stories in this book are told through a series of interviews. These men and women have presented their personal experiences of the war. They have shared sad and often painful moments of their past.

Where did I find over sixty-five WWII stories?

Cruise ships seem to attract WWII veterans. There were three veterans enjoying the open seas. Several of my friends knew many of these vets. Six of my uncles served in the military during WWII. Two WWII vets have spoken to elementary children at my school. By telling their story, they are teaching history to a new generation.

Survivors of the USS *Indianapolis* and the families of the men lost at sea have reunions in Indianapolis. I attended a public presentation at a recent reunion. A survivor spoke of his harrowing experiences in the ocean following the sinking of the ship. Another survivor was willing to talk about his time aboard the USS *Indianapolis*, before it sank.

There are three interviews from Pearl Harbor survivors. They saw the attack on December 7, 1941 first hand. Like all the WWII veterans, these stories will never be forgotten.

Many interviews were obtained in Evansville Indiana. The Evansville area has many WWII vets and women who were important to the war effort. Several of the women interviewed worked in the factories making airplane wings or weapons.

Some WWII veterans wear their gold and black military service hats. Whenever one appears in a nursing home, airport, restaurant, or a military air show reunion, I have asked to hear their story. The veterans' stories are in their own words, or told posthumously by family members, and edited as needed.

— Linda Minton
Indianapolis, Indiana

Pearl Harbor—December 7, 1941

The Beginning

"A lot of the guys went down with their ships. Then a lot of torpedo planes came in dropping torpedoes."

—Paul Kennedy
Pearl Harbor survivor, US *Sacramento*

Part 1
Pearl Harbor Quotes

Scott Brown: Scott was fourteen years old when the Japanese bombed Pearl Harbor. "Everyone was glued to the radio, listening to FDR."

Lewis Cowden: "I didn't think about it. I had an automobile, and that's all I was interested in at that time. I was seventeen years old and very immature. I was also running out of gasoline stamps!"

Bob Crouch (Pearl Harbor survivor): "First thing they hit were the airfields...They destroyed them totally! We never got a plane in the air. A bomb went down the turret of the *Arizona*. The Japanese targeted the battleships in the harbor. The submarine dock was full, but they never touched it. They never touched any oilfields. They were after the six battleships."

Clell Downey: Clell was fifteen years old when he went into the navy. "I was just a kid and had not learned to be afraid yet."

Bobbie Downey: "It was on a Sunday in Columbia, Tennessee. We were going to a Sunday afternoon movie. I was waiting on my parents, and they were upstairs. I called up to them and asked, 'What's the holdup?' My parents said, 'I think we are at war.' I asked if we were still going to the movies. Being a fourteen-year-old child, I went to pieces and started to cry."

Irvin Herman: "I didn't think too much about it then. It was so far away and so remote."

Paul Kennedy (Pearl Harbor survivor): Lt. Fuchida was the Japanese pilot leading the raid. "I was looking up at him, and he was looking down at me. He had his canopy down. As soon as it cleared our ship, he dropped that torpedo in the water, and it went across the harbor...It hit the battleship *Oklahoma*...and it went down in twenty minutes."

Dick Negus: "I was thirteen years old at the time of the bombing of Pearl Harbor. That evening my dad was called up to go to the coast to look for Japanese ships. They didn't see any enemy ships or subs."

James Pike: He heard about the bombing of Pearl Harbor on the radio. "I just took it as it came. Roosevelt was making a speech, and he said we will just go over and whup their ass for them."

Turret from the USS Arizona

We were downhearted and blue because we knew we had taken a beating, and to see that flag!

—Paul Kennedy
WWII veteran

Lester Hartley—US Navy
Pearl Harbor Survivor

"I saw two torpedo planes come down and drop their torpedoes."

Lester is a Pearl Harbor survivor. On September 6, 1940, eighteen years old, Lester joined the navy in San Francisco. Lester was assigned to the USS *Jarvis*, a ship that his brother, Charles, had previously been assigned to as well. They were on the *Jarvis* at the same time. Lester boarded the *Jarvis* on November 11, 1940. "We came into the navy yard at Pearl Harbor on Thursday evening, December 4, for a ten-day upkeep."

What happened on Sunday, December 7, 1941?

Lester was a fireman first class at that point. "I was asleep on a cot in the Repair Shop on the main deck, as there was not any air-conditioning on the ship. The only air-conditioning you would have was to open up everything. It was enclosed, but the doors and portholes were open. Where I was sleeping, I could see out over Ford Island. All the battleships were all lined up side by side. This was where the attack started. My station for general quarters was on number four gun, on the fantail." They had to cut the awning down before they could start firing their guns.

"I was the hot shell man that day," Lester continued. "That meant you caught this hot shell and laid it down on the deck some place. I was busy there, and I didn't see a lot of things that other people said they saw."

Did you see the pilot?

"I saw two torpedo planes, that were 150 feet out from our stern, drop their torpedoes. I did not see them hit the battleships. There were more than that, but the two planes are all I saw up close. They were about fifty feet or less off the water. They were down real low and had their canopies open. Lot of them did, when they were flying real low. You could see the pilots real clear, almost as clear as I can see you. That's the way it was. I didn't have enough sense to be scared! Nothing scared me that day. Everything was busy that day…everything that we had been trained to do for a year. It was automatic. The Japanese pilots had their jobs to do, and they did it."

Lester remembered seeing "boats in the water and oil in the water. They were picking up bodies; some of them were dead, and some were alive.

"It wasn't long before I got my orders to go down below in the fire room and start the high-pressure compressors. There were sixteen torpedoes on the main deck that had to be charged with air to make them work right. I got those air compressors going, and it took until six thirty or seven o'clock that night. So I stayed down there all day. Our lunch, or whatever we had to eat, was brought to us. Cooks were scattered around all over the ship, and they brought us sandwiches or whatever."

"At approximately ten thirty a.m., we got underway. We backed away from where we were moored and went out to sea. From then on, for the next four days, we were at sea looking for the enemy. The sea was very rough, and we were either on watch or battle stations most of the time. We had very little sleep."

"Wednesday evening we were running low on fuel and had to come in. We fueled up and tied up to a buoy in the harbor. All night, we provisioned the ship [supplied it with food and water], and we even changed some of our ammunition. We found out that some it wasn't any good anymore.

"There was an enemy sub in the harbor, so we were on guard. We didn't sink it; one of the other ships did. USS *Jarvis* went out the next morning looking for submarines. There were eight ships of our class, and four of us went out submarine hunting. I don't know where all we went. We dropped all our depth charges, but don't know if we ever sunk anything or not!

"In October 1941 the *Jarvis* was in a convoy taking supplies to Wake Island. The supply ships unloaded everything. We left Wake Island and headed back to Hawaii. There were two evenings when it was calm and beautiful. Back when I was a kid, at the movies they showed this luxury liner out at sea with a few scattered white clouds. I saw that for two nights." This was a pleasant memory. "For guys like me who were on the night watches, we didn't want to go to bed. It was real nice."

"It's about the middle of December, Wake Island is being attacked. On the way to Wake Island with a task force, the *Jarvis* was fueling ship. I got my arm mashed in an airtight door. We were lucky to have a division doctor on our ship, and he put a splint on it. When I got back to Pearl, I went over to the hospital ship, and they x-rayed it. They said it was perfect, so I just left the splint on it for a couple weeks."

"While we were fueling our ship, Wake Island fell, and they had to give it up. So our task force was dispersed. Part of us went up toward Midway. Tankers go until they run out of fuel, and we escorted one ship back to Pearl Harbor. The *Jarvis* was a convoy ship used for everything. It had four five-inch, thirty-eight caliber guns on it and torpedoes.

"In January they were planning an attack on some islands south of Hawaii. One of the first big drives. We got a dispatch to go back and pick up a tanker. So we wanted to rendezvous with the tanker. They always wanted ships to have full tanks of fuel before they attacked. The lookouts before daylight spotted gunfire—splashes of light on the horizon. When we got up there, our tanker had been sunk. We pick up approximately 175 men off the tanker. Some of the men had gone down with the ship. We didn't stop because the submarine was still in the area. We picked up everybody by just cruising around. We shot holes in the little boats there, so they would sink, and headed to Pearl. I don't know what happened to the attack that was going to occur.

"It's getting late in January, about the last week of January, and we were sent with another destroyer over to Hawaii. They said there was a submarine off the coast of Hilo. So we went flying out there!" Lester went on to say, "We spent several hours there. Occasionally we would drop depth charges. The second day we got a good contact, and one destroyer went one way and the other one went the other way to drop our depth charges. Then in a little while, you could see the debris coming to the surface and the dirty water. Well, later on in the war, Japanese submarines would release junk to make you think they had been hit. Apparently we sunk this one, because we never heard any more about it."

"We went back to Pearl Harbor, and from there I got transferred to Norfolk, Virginia, for diesel engine school. I had been transferred previously on— December 6, 1941, but that didn't happen because the war started. There were PT boats being loaded on the transport headed to the Philippines, so that's why they wouldn't take us onboard for transportation."

You almost missed the big show?

"Yes, but I saw enough of it."

"I always felt sorry for the ones in the Pacific after Pearl Harbor because the navy was in bad shape for the first year. People didn't realize they were giving most of the supplies to Europe. Everything was going to Europe, and the Pacific had to do with what they had.

"After diesel engine school, I was assigned to a mine sweeper. It operated in the Atlantic Ocean until July 1944. After that, they sent us back to the US mainland and took all the sweep gear off to make us a patrol craft. The hull was already a patrol craft. We were sent to the Strait of Gibraltar. We went to Africa for a week, then to Naples, Italy, on August 14, 1944.

"We left Italy and went on to southern France. On August 15, 1944, we got in position to make the invasion on southern France. There were about three different beachheads. We were up there for about three days, and we ran out of food. We finally found an LST (Landing Ship Tank) that would let us have some supplies. We were operating up and down the coast of Italy, and our base was in Sicily. It was spring 1945, we were in Leghorn, Italy. A German sub and cruiser were in a base in northern Italy, and we wanted to keep those ships there. We did this for three or four nights. The war in Europe ended May 8, 1945."

"In July 1945 we were sent to Jacksonville, Florida, for a major overhaul. We were getting ready to fire up the engines when the war in Japan ended, August of 1945. I still had a little over a year left in the service and was transferred to the west coast of the United States. The rest of my career in the navy was spent on the west coast."

What did you think about the United States dropping the bomb on Japan?

"I didn't think too much about it—anything to end the war. If they hadn't done it, and an invasion occurred, there would have been a whole lot of people die. Japan was fortified to fight back. They had airplanes and civilians lined up for defense. They never expected what they got. If there had been an invasion, many people would have died. They wouldn't give up. I see no wrong with it. That's the way it went, and there's nothing you can do about it. Japan attacked the United States, and they had no sympathy. That's war."

What happened to the USS Jarvis?

USS *Jarvis* was sunk on August 9, 1942, off Guadalcanal, and all the crew were lost. There was no debris or anything left in the area. It was a couple of days overdue before anyone investigated. Lester knew many of the men on that ship. It wasn't known what happened to the ship until after the war, when Japanese records were searched, and what had taken place was pieced together. Lester never returned to the *Jarvis* after his diesel training class. Another sailor who left for training when Lester did returned to the *Jarvis* but died when the ship went down. Sometimes God has other plans for you.

Lester was stationed on the *LST 838* from January 1945 to March 1945, until it was decommissioned in Portland, Oregon. The *LST 838*, renamed the USS *Hunterdon County*, went on to serve and earn awards in the Vietnam War.

"I don't regret one minute of my time in the navy." This quote summed up Lester's thoughts: "The only way you can preserve history is in black and white—things happen to computers."

Robert Crouch—US Navy
USS *Sacramento*, Pearl Harbor Survivor
"The harbor was a mess because of all the oil."

Bob, twenty-two years old, joined the navy on September 30, 1940. He had been working at Diamond Chain in Indianapolis and going to night school at Butler University. He thought he would join the navy, get his two-year commitment over with, and go home. The Empire of Japan changed Bob's plans.

Bob began his navy career in Michigan City and the Great Lakes, going through the St. Lawrence River. Their first stop was the Boston Navy Yard, where the ship was to be painted and overhauled. Early in 1941 they went to West Virginia; Guantanamo Bay, Cuba; Jamaica; and the Panama Canal to San Diego. "We then went over to Pearl Harbor. It took us a long time to get there because the ship, or gun boat, could only do fifteen knots." In May 1941 Bob arrived in Pearl Harbor.

December 7, 1941

The day began about eight o'clock in the morning, and Bob was still down below. Then they sounded general quarters, and he went to his station. There was an awning on the front of their ship that had to be removed, so Robert was up there with a butcher knife trying to cut it down before they could fire their guns. He finally got it down.

"So this guy and I went to the machine gun. Next we were in the harbor trying to pick up the dead. The harbor was a mess because of all the oil. We burned up the motors in the motorboats because of all the oil in the water."

Robert went on to explain, "First thing they hit were the airfields…They destroyed them totally. We never got a plane in the air! A bomb went down the turret of the *Arizona*.

"The carrier *Enterprise* came into Pearl Harbor to give the island a little protection. Unfortunately none of the ships were warned, and as they flew over the center of the bay, we shot all of them down in less than a few minutes. By nightfall we all had a firing course that covered the sky. The minute they went inside the pattern, the sky lit up like a light. Later we were told that most of the pilots ejected, but I don't know how true that was."

How did you feel when all this was happening?

"Scared. We had general quarters, and I was a machine gunner. We think we were credited one time with one plane, and we got lots of shots off in the harbor. The Japanese targeted the battleships in the harbor. The submarine dock was full, but they never touched it. They never touched any oil fields. They were after the six battleships."

Bob credits the installation of a big crane on the dock beside the *Sacramento* with saving their ship, possibly their lives. "The dock we were tied up to, directly across from Battleship Row, was very, very large. As a matter of fact, we could play limited softball on the dock in the evenings. At four thirty on Friday night, when the shipyard workers went home, they parked this enormous crane, about thirty to forty feet high and about twenty feet wide, on the rail tracks of the dock right next to our ship, the USS *Sacramento*. Actually it was within a few feet of our gangplank. We were mad as hell because it interfered with our playing softball or passing the football in the evenings and on the weekends. It saved our butts because the Japanese torpedo planes could not get in to us."

December 8–10, 1941

"Beginning December eighth we started to lay out bodies, identify them, put them in white sheets, and put them into wooden built caskets. We then dug graves up in the hills by Pearl Harbor and started to bury the dead. The graves were mostly dug by hand. We dug the graves with picks and shovels. They were forty inches wide, ninety inches long, and three feet deep. I am not sure whether or not they have ever reburied the people; I have never asked or been back there to see them. The fuel oil spilled in the harbor was a great health hazard. A lot of fires, and the stink was very bad, and our eyes would burn like they were on fire.

"Starting at noon, and for the next two to three days, we were busy picking up the injured and the dead, which was a horrible scene. The oil from the hit ships had all leaked into the water, coagulated like lard to about a foot and a half deep, which made it next to impossible to get our motorboats through it." He went on to say, "There were eleven or twelve of us digging with shovels and picks. The next day the city brought some diggers, so we didn't have to use shovels and picks. It was sandy soil up in the mountains." Bob said he dug eleven graves by hand.

December 17, 1941

"We then stayed in Pearl for about another week, getting fueled up, taking on supplies, and getting ready to go to sea. We were dispatched to the island of Hawaii, with the main town being Hilo. Our duty was to try to protect that part of the Hawaiian Islands and serve as a lookout ship for Pearl Harbor. We stayed there for some time and helped them build a fighter plane landing strip. When we left there, we were sent to a southern island, Palmyra. Lucky for me, our ship was too slow to work with the Pacific Fleet. In Palmyra we took care of six torpedo boats for about two months. Then they sent us back to the US, San Diego, to train merchant marine sailors in the use of artillery. They were used to protect the merchant ships carrying supplies to our men."

Bob told the story of when President Franklin Roosevelt had a secret meeting with Stalin and Chiang Kai-Shek after dark. "We were docked in San Diego, where they were working on this ship, the USS *Baltimore*, and we didn't know what was happening until a day or so later. When we get underway, maybe fifty miles out, all of a sudden there are all these ships. One ship throws a cable to another ship, and here comes President Roosevelt."

One funny story was when they thought they saw a torpedo in the water, which turned out to be a whale! Another time they saw what looked like a torpedo, and the general alarm was sounded. This time it turned out to be porpoises.

Should we have dropped the atomic bomb on Japan?

"I thought it was perfect—the best way to save thousands of lives. It was a way to show them [the Japanese] that we could destroy them."

Celebrities and Golfing experiences

He met the Andrew Sisters, Sammy Davis Jr., Carol Lombard, Hedy Lamar, Peter Lawford, Tommy Dorsey, Harry James, and Frank Sinatra at various clubs. Bob was quite a golfer and played golf with many 1940s celebrities— Elvis Presley, Gary Player, Buddy Hackett, Andy Williams and Paul Anka. In the military he played golf with Admiral Chester Nimitz. Also Bob played golf with then President George H. W. Bush and Vice President Dan Quayle at Andrews Air Force Base. President Bush gave him a commemorative crystal glass golf club and golf ball.

Return to Pearl Harbor—

In 1974 Bob and his granddaughter returned to Pearl Harbor, but he does not care to go back again. He still has bad memories of what happened that day. Bob knows a fellow crew member, Paul Kennedy, also on the *USS Sacramento* that terrible December day. Bob said, "I saw some of the Japanese pilots that day who were flying just above the water." He just kept shooting at them.

Just as he was going up the ladder, there appeared a large plane with a big torpedo. It was the first torpedo that was dropped that morning. Lieutenant Mitsuo Fuchida was the one leading the raid. Paul saw him in the cockpit of that plane. It was coming in low and slow. "I was looking up at him, and he was looking down at me. He had his canopy down. As soon as it cleared our ship, he dropped that torpedo in the water, and it went across the harbor. I watched it, as I had never seen anything like that before. It hit the battleship *Oklahoma*, and that battleship was on its side in twenty minutes. Fellows were scrambling for their lives and trying to get out before they drowned. Lot of them started swimming across the harbor toward us. We sent boats out there to pick them up. We took them aboard and took care of them until later." Later in life, Mitsuo Fuchida became a Christian evangelist and moved to the United States.

"A lot of the guys went down with their ships. Then a lot of torpedo planes came in dropping torpedoes. The Japs were after the battleships—any big ships. There were forty-four torpedoes dropped. Every time a torpedo would hit a ship, it would open up a hole, and the oil would run out into the harbor. Eventually the oil in the harbor was six inches thick on top of the water. There were some dead men lying on top of the oil, and our ship, as well as other ships, sent boats out to get them, and a Jap plane came strafing the men in the lifeboats. The boats were unprotected, but these guys would strafe them.

"As soon as I saw that torpedo drop into the water, I went to my battle station. My job was to use the flags and run them up the pole. All this time there are planes dropping bombs on ships. So there are Japanese zeros all around. One of these planes dropped a five-hundred-pound bomb on the battleship USS *Pennsylvania*. The *Pennsylvania* was in dry dock. We were sitting at dry dock a week prior to where it was sitting now. So they had moved us out and moved us closer to the dock, so they could move the *Pennsylvania* in.

"The pilot did a good job because he killed some guys that were in the gun turret. As soon as he did that he turned the plane around and headed for us and started strafing us." Paul went on to say, "I am up there without any protection, and I think I am going to die." He said, "I could hear the bullets hitting the bulkhead all around me. You can't see them, but you can hear them. "So help me, God put a shield around me. I know that I had a shield in front of me. Since I was sixteen years old, I have been a child of His. He saved my life about four or five times."

The plane missed everybody aboard Paul's ship. He was shot down by the *Sacramento*'s gunners as he went over. "So, he paid the price," said Paul.

As soon as that happened, the USS *Mugford* and the USS *Jarvis* were to get underway. "The skipper on the *Mugford* called over to us and asked if we could spare any fifty-caliber ammunition. Our skipper said, 'Sure.'" He ordered Brown, Kennedy, and Benefield to move the ammunition over to the *Mugford*.

At that time Paul weighed about 125 pounds. The cases of ammo weighed about seventy pounds each. He carried cases two at a time over to the ship three times. "The adrenaline was flowing freely in my body," said Paul. While he was doing this, the ship pulled up the gangplank and started to move out. He asked permission to stay aboard, which was denied. The skipper told him to jump, so he did, and the fellows aboard the *Sacramento* caught him by the arms. He bumped his nose and knees but was OK. He didn't break anything.

"By this time, the battleship *Nevada* was underway and trying to get out of the harbor. All those airplanes concentrated on sinking that ship. They would have done it too, if the *Nevada* hadn't beached itself." Paul remembered, "It beached itself on Hospital Point.

"Things were not going good at all. People were getting shot up. In an hour and forty-five minutes, we lost twenty ships, 2,335 killed, and another 1,143 wounded. There were some things that happened…" Paul trailed off on that thought.

That night three planes from the aircraft carrier *Enterprise* flew over Pearl Harbor. "They were told not to fly over Pearl Harbor, but they did. You can't tell a flyboy anything! So help me, it was the most beautiful pyrotechnic display you will ever see in your life."

The planes were shot down. Paul said, "The pilot who survived said if he could have gotten out of his plane, you could have walked to earth on the lead that was coming up, and I believe it."

The USS *Baltimore* was tied up next to us. "I told one of the guys to get a rifle and patrol back and forth over on the *Baltimore*. He said, 'What for?' And I said, 'I don't know, just keep your eyes open.'" Paul continued, "About three thirty in the afternoon, he hollered over to me that he just saw a periscope come up and go down." Paul got in touch with the officer of the day, Lieutenant Adrian Marks from Frankfort, Indiana. Lt. Marks called the base, and they sent three PT boats over there. Paul continued, "They started dropping depth charges. The Japanese midget submarine beached itself, and the Jap surrendered. It was on display at Pearl Harbor for a while until Japan wanted it back. So they gave it back to Japan."

As a side note, Paul said, "Adrian Marks was a private pilot and had a pilot's license before he entered the service. He wanted to join the navy air force, so he got permission to be transferred to Pensacola, Florida. He went down there and got his wings, and he wound up flying a PDY on patrol duty. He was the pilot of the plane that rescued many of the survivors of the *USS Indianapolis*. He asked for permission to set the plane down in the water, and they said no." He went on to do it anyway, and many of the survivors who had been in the water for four days were saved. "He saved a lot of lives." Paul did the eulogy for Adrian's funeral.

A day or two after the war started, "There was a Japanese submarine that lobbed three torpedoes into Hilo, Hawaii," said Paul. "There was no navy down there to protect Hilo, so we went down there. By golly, it was like going on a vacation. There wasn't nothing going on down there. The war was going on in the Pacific and in Europe, but we are sitting down there going on liberty every three days. I got so bored; I wanted to kill Japanese, and I couldn't get to them."

Well, it so happened that a yeoman from Paul's ship fell and broke his arm, so they sent him to the hospital. The yeoman wrote Paul a letter saying he was in the transfer division. Paul wrote back, "Get me off this ship." Brown, Benefield, and Paul were sent to San Francisco. Paul said, "It was just like sending a letter to Santa Claus! We were packed and off that ship in thirty minutes, after we got our new orders."

What are your feelings about what happened at Pearl Harbor?

During the attack everybody acted very normal; no one got out of control. "I wasn't afraid of anything, and I wasn't afraid of getting hit. I was very concerned about what was going on, naturally. You just have to accept it. There isn't anything you can do about it. I was under attack many times after that, and it never did bother me. I always thought if I was going to get it, then it's God's will.

"My feelings now are I don't hate anyone. I got over that hatred when I was forty years old. I was an executive vice president of a large company in San Francisco, and I dealt with slant eyes all the time. Every time I would see a Japanese, it would hurt me inside, and I had the feeling that I wanted to kill him. I prayed to God to take the hatred away from me, and he did. I don't hate anybody now. I have accepted the fact I am getting old and on the precipice of leaving this world, which is OK with me." Paul was ninety-five years old at the time of this writing.

He has been back to Pearl Harbor eleven times. The last time he stayed on the launch. He just couldn't see the *Arizona* memorial again. He saw it all happen the first time.

He remembered sights that will always be with him: "Looking out about ten thirty that night and seeing no lights, just the smoke and fire from the *Arizona*. The flag from the *West Virginia*, which was sunk in front of the *Arizona*, was waving through the smoke. It really boosted our feelings. We were downhearted and blue because we knew we had taken a beating, and to see that flag! Today, when I hear 'The Star Spangled Banner,' I get cold chills down my back. So it's just a memory that I just don't forget."

He still has a friend from the USS *Jarvis* who lives locally, and he still talks to him. Most of the others have died.

Paul's wife dies

Paul's first wife, Ruth, died on his birthday, December 2, 1944. She died from complications of appendicitis, leaving him with a small baby boy. He received a telegram upon arriving in England informing him of her death. "That was a rough day," said Paul. "I buried her on December twenty-sixth." Paul went on to marry three more times— Juanita, Charlotte, and Marie. "I have buried four wives."

Paul and Ruth Kennedy

What happened to you after Pearl Harbor?

Pearl Harbor wasn't the end for Paul. He went on to serve in the Atlantic in 1942. He was on a sub chaser, #715, for eighteen months. The German subs were sinking our ships. "That's no good." He discussed one time during a terrible storm the engine stopped off Cape Hatteras, and the ship started to shake. Paul said, "Our ship was like a cork in the water." The ship was leaning and shaking. The skipper was afraid the ship was going to capsize. He sent an SOS for help. It was a dark, cold morning and the water was cold and rough. "It is the roughest water in the world. I had my leg around the stanchion pole and was holding on to the light with one hand. With the other hand, I sent the SOS. I was able to hold on, but remember crying out 'God help me.'"

After eighteen months he was assigned to the USS *Poole*, a destroyer escort. There were six destroyer escorts in his unit. He was the signal man for the ship. The USS *Poole* sunk ten German subs. "There was one German sub that was unhappy because we put a hole in the bottom of their sub. The German sailor came up and was about ten feet from us when he came out of the water. The first guy out of the sub had a submachine gun and started strafing us. He didn't live very long before they shot him."

Paul received a Purple Heart for an injury to his hand during this attack by the German submarine. They took seventeen German sailors and two officers from the sub as prisoners. "There was one German in the water that was cussing us in German, a real troublemaker, and they didn't want to take him aboard, so they shot him." They took the rest of the Germans aboard and had them onboard for two days, until they arrived in Ireland.

Did you talk to any of the German prisoners?

"Yes, but most of them couldn't speak English. They slept in our beds and ate with us. We didn't put them in the brig or anything."

In April 1944, "we were escorting a merchant ship to Glasgow, Scotland. It was loaded with fuel." The *Pan-Pennsylvania* was blown up by a German U-boat waiting for them. The captain of the *Pan-Pennsylvania* waved Paul's ship off, telling them they had it from there, as they were near the coast. Paul looked back, and there was a terrible explosion and fire from all the fuel that the ship was carrying. We picked up three bodies; two were dead and one died aboard ship. There were no other survivors.

"There was another time when we were heading back to the States with a bunch of merchant ships, and I was in charge of the quartermaster and signal gang." A small voice made him feel uneasy, so he went to check on subs in the area during a time when the subs got active. He went up the ladder to the bridge, but as soon as he was halfway up he "saw the torpedo in the water coming at us! You could see the propeller on the torpedo, the wake. I hollered out, 'Torpedo ho.' I told them, 'Ten points off starboard.'"

The captain immediately said, "Full speed ahead, full right rudder." Paul said, "That ship moved ahead like it had been goosed! It turned right, and we watched that torpedo go right beside us. God was looking out for us."

Over two and half years, Paul made eighteen trips from New York to different places in Europe. "Another time we were trying to get into New York before a hurricane came in, but we didn't quite make it. It was so rough that night that everyone was ordered below decks except two lookouts. The ship really jumped around that night. That was a rough night!"

Where were you when you found out the war was over?

"Well, my wife died on December 2, 1944, and I was no good to the navy after that. I was a physical and mental wreck. They shipped me to Great Lakes training station to be an instructor. I was in charge of some kids from Kentucky, and they were finishing up on their training course. They got their first liberty, and I told everyone they had to be back by midnight—that was their curfew. That meant inside by midnight. I was tough!

"There were three guys missing out of the whole group. About one o'clock, here they came down the street just singing, and they were drunk! They came aboard, and I was standing there mad as hell. I told them to go to bed, and I would see them in the morning. One kid said, 'Who is going to make me?' I hit him in the mouth and knocked his teeth out! I called the MPs and told them to come and get this guy and take care of him. They sent two MPs over—one for him and one for me.

They put me in a padded cell. I wouldn't talk to anyone, not even the doctors. After about a month, they gave me twenty-eight dollars—the bus fare to Indianapolis—and my medical honorable discharge. They said go home, and don't talk about it."

What did you think about the bombing of Japan?

Paul had just gotten home a couple of days before the bombing of Hiroshima. He said, "Absolutely, no question. There would've been millions of dead bodies if we had invaded Japan. Plus the fact that it was retribution. It ended the war!"

Pacific Theater

I was lucky enough to survive the Battle of Okinawa...war is a horrible thing!

—Lester Brown
US Army, Pacific Theater

Pacific Theater Veterans

Lester Brown	Paul Kennedy
Scott Brown	Richard Kolodey
Robert Buchert	Earl Lautzenheiser
Lewis Cowden	Cleatus Lebow
James Crabb	Charles McDonald
Robert Crouch	Arlin McRae
Clell Downey	Wilbur Meyer
Glen Eakle	John Miller
Paul Feeney	Richard Negus
Halbert Gillette	Howard Norlin
Wayne Guerin	Harold (Pete) Palmer
Edgar Harrell	James Pike
Lester Hartley	Paul Pitcher
Irvin Herman	Robert Poole
William Hill	Robert Sisk
Robert Hlavacek	Bob W.
	Harold Weber

Part 2
The Pacific Theater

The Pacific Theater refers to the fighting in the Pacific after the sneak attack on Pearl Harbor. Many of the major sea and land battles occurred on the many islands and areas of the Pacific Ocean. Some of the South Pacific Islands included Corregidor, Guadalcanal, Guam, Iwo Jima, Midway, New Guinea, Philippines, Saipan, Tinian, and Wake Island.

Corregidor, located near the entrance of Manila Bay, is on the archipelago of the Luzon Island, Philippines. The Battle of Corregidor took place on May 5–6, 1942. It was a victory for the Japanese and the fall of the Philippines. The Japanese wanted to control Manila Bay. There were thirteen thousand US troops versus seventy-five thousand Japanese troops. The American troops were led by General Jonathan M. Wainwright. General Wainwright was a prisoner of war and sent to Manchuria.

Guadalcanal, located in the Solomon Islands, was the turning point of the war in the Pacific. The Battle of Guadalcanal, or Operation Watchtower, took place from August 7, 1942 to February 9, 1943. Guadalcanal is positioned northeast of Australia. The Allies, six thousand US marines, took control of the island and the airfield that the two thousand Japanese were building on the island. The Japanese were unsuccessful in retaking the airfield.

Guam is an island in Micronesia in the Western Pacific and the largest of the Mariana Islands. The Japanese captured the island and occupied it following the attack on Pearl Harbor. American forces freed the people of Guam on July 21, 1944. Guam has a Liberation Day to celebrate this victory.

Iwo Jima is located 750 miles south of mainland Tokyo. The Battle of Iwo Jima, or Operation Detachment, was fought from February 19 to March 26, 1945. The battle, a famous and important fight, has been made more recognizable by the famous picture of soldiers hoisting the American flag on Mount Suribachi. It was an American victory that was not without loss; more than six thousand US lives were lost. It was one of the bloodiest battles of the Pacific warfare.

Midway is an atoll located about halfway between North America and Asia. Six months after the attack on Pearl Harbor, the Battle of Midway took place, on June 4–6, 1942. The leaders of the offensives were American Admiral Chester W. Nimitz and Japanese leader Isoroku Yamamoto. The United States lost a carrier, a destroyer, and 150 aircraft versus the Japanese loss of four carriers, a heavy cruiser, and 248 aircraft. It was also an important naval battle of the Pacific Theater.

New Guinea is the second largest island in the world and is located in the Southwest Pacific, in the Malay Archipelago. It is north of Australia. New Guinea was occupied by the Japanese for a time but was freed later in the war. The New Guinea Campaign was from January 23, 1942–August 1945. The Australians and American forces were responsible for starving the Japanese by way of naval blockades that prevented food and medical supplies from getting to them.

Warfare in the Philippines included the Battle of Bataan, December 1941–May 8, 1942; the Battle of Leyte Gulf, October 23–26, 1944; the Battle of Luzon, January 9–15, 1945; and the Battle of Manila, February 3–March 3, 1945. By 1944 Allied force had freed the Philippine islands from Japanese domination. The Filipino people were fierce fighters and aided the Allied forces. General Douglas MacArthur made his famous promise: "I shall return." He returned in October 1944 to liberate the Philippines and said, "I have returned. By the grace of almighty God, our forces stand again on Philippine soil."

Saipan is part of the Mariana chain and the scene of the Battle of Saipan, Operation Forager, which took place June 9–June 15, 1944, and resulted in an American victory. The US Navy Fifth Fleet was led by Admiral Spruance, who had lost some friends at Pearl Harbor and was going to get even. Saipan was commanded by Admiral Nagumo, who had directed the air raids on December 7, 1941. American troops boarded assault LSTs for this invasion, and there was fierce fighting on the beaches. LSTs were ships used for transporting troops, tanks, and jeeps from one area to another.

Tinian Island, located in the Mariana Islands, is an important name in WWII history because the USS *Indianapolis* delivered atomic bomb parts there. The Battle of Tinian was fought July 24–August 1944. Many American and Japanese lives were lost while Allies secured the island to be a base during the Pacific Campaign. The *Enola Gay* took off from Tinian to make history by dropping the first atomic bomb on Hiroshima. *Bockscar* also took off from Tinian and dropped Fat Boy on Nagasaki, Japan which ended WWII.

Wake is an atoll of three islets—Peale, Wake, and Wilkes—and belongs to the Marshall Islands. This area is about two thousand miles west of Hawaii. The Battle of Wake Island took place December 8–23, 1941. The Allies were overrun by the Japanese forces, fresh off the attack on Pearl Harbor. The Japanese army held the island for the remainder of the war.

The Battle of Okinawa—April 1, 1945–June 1945

Okinawa is seventy miles long and eighteen miles wide. It is three hundred miles from Japan. "We knew that there was an invasion coming up," said Lester. "There was a beachhead landing. We were loaded on LSTs and hit the beachhead. Some LSTs had gates, but luckily ours drove all the way up on the beach. The first day a man yelled to get in this ditch and stay there to keep safe. We felt fire and resistance coming our way."

The navy bombarded the Japanese with heavy artillery. After four days the Japanese pulled back. The Japanese caught the American soldiers in a trap going up a hill. They were surrounded on three sides. They lost a hundred and fifty men, with only thirty men surviving. Fortunately, Les was one of the latter. He fought in the battle of "Hacksaw Ridge," then called "The Big Encarpment."

On the fourth day, a sniper wounded Les. He was treated with sulfa drugs and put in the back of the group. He stayed in the back for one day. The division was short on men, so he went to the front lines again. The American troops would break the Japanese line of resistance, penetrate it, and move forward, then hit another hill. The battle lasted for eighty-two days.

Les was wounded again. He and the company medic remained friends until Doc's death. During the invasion he and his fellow soldiers dug into foxholes. They carried spades on their backs. A foxhole was a place to sleep, and there were three men in each. One would stand guard, and the other two would try to sleep.

Okinawa was full of caves and tombs. The GIs would take cover in the caves when shelling began. Sometimes there would be dead Japanese soldiers in the caves. Later in life Les had scars on his back from a fungus that was in the cave environment.

"The officers got right up front with the fighting." Les remembered Colonel May, who was looking through field glasses and was killed by enemy fire. Sadly, on day four, Les' friend Lee was hit with shrapnel and died at age nineteen. Les went over to see Lee, but he was already dead. Les would never forget Lee and the sacrifice he made for his country.

"I was lucky enough to survive the Battle of Okinawa." Les described kamikaze pilots, one-man planes loaded with explosives, hitting the ships in the water. He said the US forces lost thirty ships to these kamikaze planes. He saw many of the hits on the ships.

Prior to America's capture of Okinawa, many of the Okinawan people dove off cliffs and killed themselves. After the battle, when Okinawa was secured, engineers came in and laid tracks for airplanes and fighter planes to land and fight from Okinawa.

Les recalled graveyards and trucks loaded with bodies stacked like cords of wood. The trucks were bringing the bodies back from the battle.

What were your feelings about the war?

"I was young and hardly realized how quickly things would be happening. It was something you had to do. War is a horrible thing!"

After the battle Les was sent to Mindoro, a rest camp; he was there when he learned the war was over. Harry Truman "saved my life by dropping the bomb. I was on the list and the ships were in the harbor to start the invasion of Japan," said Les. The division was deactivated, and many of the soldiers were sent back to the States. Les did not have enough points to come home, so he was sent to Corregidor, a scene of fierce fighting during the war. He worked as a duty guard at a Japanese stockade for about thirty days, until he had enough points to go home.

Les was awarded two Purple Hearts, since he was wounded twice during the Battle of Okinawa, and a Bronze Star. On the way home, he recalled, he saw the Golden Gate Bridge and Alcatraz Island in San Francisco. He was discharged in April 1946 and took a train from San Francisco to Camp Atterbury in Indianapolis.

Lee's funeral

Les was a pallbearer at Lee's funeral after the war. "Lee was a big, strapping farm boy, so he was given a Browning automatic rifle. He was a target. It was hard to face his family…"

Erelene, Les's wife, said, "It is the one thing that has bothered Les throughout his life. He hasn't gotten over it." They still visit Lee's grave at Liberty Church Cemetery near Patoka Lake in Southern Indiana.

After the war Erelene Gilliatt and Les Brown were married, in July 1954. After he was discharged, he wrote her a letter and went back to Paoli. They dated and decided to get married after her graduation from college. They had two children—Brad and Beth. Les went on the Dayton, Ohio Honor Flight to

Washington, DC. Les went to IUPUI (Indiana University Purdue University in Indianapolis) on the GI Bill for two years.

Erelene Gilliatt Brown

Erelene said, "when Les and I were first married, one night it was thundering, and I awoke with Les's hands around my neck." Also, Les's mother said if there were bad thunderstorms, Les would walk around the yard because he couldn't stand the thunder. It reminded him of the war.

Erelene remembered D-Day, June 6, 1944, "sitting in the swing on our porch and everyone listening to the radio reports". Also she recalled the death of FDR. She was hanging clothes on the clothesline. Her aunt came to the house, and was crying. When her dad came home, he cried about FDR's death. People didn't know how the war would go on. They went to church for a prayer session.

"There was a peddling wagon that had grocery items that would come by on Friday afternoon. You would use your ration stamps to buy items. She remembered eating Spam for the first time. She liked it. Erelene remembered her youth, "as an idyllic time in life. We didn't know we were poor."

Milkweed pods for life jackets

"The children in my school picked milkweed pods for the war effort. The children would go out into the field to pick the milkweed pods; then put them in sacks. The school superintendent would come by the one room school and collect the sacks. He would fill his trunk with the sacks. In return for the efforts of the children, he would give them a book for their school library. Also, so many of the sacks of pods would equal a stamp for their ration books. The milkweed pods were used in the life jackets for the military.

Scott Brown—US Navy
"People were driving down from the hills to go to Honolulu to celebrate."

Scott, a very quiet, thoughtful man, began the interview with this thought: "The United States was a country that wasn't out of the Depression but turned into a warring nation after Pearl Harbor." He was quick to point out that the home front sacrificed a lot to help the United States. "The home front was very important to the war effort." We discussed how many of the Indianapolis factories retooled and were converted to making items for the war effort. "For example, the Naval Ordnance Plant, now Raytheon Technologies, manufactured the highly secret Norden bombsights which were considered one of the most important technological advances in WWII."

Scott was fourteen years old when the Japanese bombed Pearl Harbor. He said, "Everyone was glued to the radio, listening to FDR." Three years later Scott enlisted in the navy at seventeen. His high school diploma would have to wait until he returned from the war.

Military Life

He did his boot camp training at Great Lakes station, which was very large in those days, housing thousands of men in 1945. From Great Lakes Scott was sent to Camp Shoemaker in Pleasanton, California. It was a facility that funneled personnel out to the Pacific. It also had a huge hospital, Shoemaker Naval Hospital, where people were brought back for treatment. He spent some time waiting to be shipped out. He was moved to Treasure Island near the Bay Bridge in San Francisco. This was a staging area where the navy brought five thousand soldiers on a transport ship with a final destination of the Philippine Islands.

Along the way the transport crossed the international date line where it intersects the Equator. All aboard received the Golden Dragon card followed by a great celebration. Everyone on the ship was inducted into the Order of the Golden Dragons as part of the celebration. The Gold Dragon card is given to a sailor when he crosses the international dateline on a ship.

The first personnel dropped off were navy fliers at Admiralty Island. Then it was on to Guam, where more troops departed the ship. From there the ship sailed to the island of Samar and the Philippines. Following that, Scott was placed in a receiving station awaiting assignment to a ship. Scott explained that the Seabees were building "real wide" roads and the base was being developed as a staging area for the invasion of Japan. The mess hall was operational, but they slept in tents on wood platforms with no plumbing and a fifty-five-gallon drum for a shower. The water was heated by the sun during the day. When the warm water was gone, there was no more.

Pearl Harbor

While at Samar, Scott was assigned to the *USS Neshoba* APA 216, which is named for a county in Mississippi. The ship was damaged in the Battle of Okinawa and was headed to Seattle for repairs with a stop at Pearl Harbor. Scott and about seventy other sailors were put on another ship and sent to Pearl Harbor to meet up with the USS *Neshoba*. While Scott was on the ship returning to Pearl, he learned that Germany had surrendered on May 7, 1945.

Upon arrival at Pearl Harbor, the group of seventy sailors found that the USS *Neshoba* had already departed Pearl Harbor. Thus, Scott had to remain in Pearl Harbor for three months awaiting its return. While at Pearl Harbor, from May to September 1945, Scott had the job being a store keeper for the mess hall.

Japan Surrendered—August 14, 1945

Scott was at Pearl Harbor when the Japanese surrendered. Prior to the surrender, total blackouts were enforced at night. "When it was announced that the Japanese had surrendered, every searchlight in the area was suddenly turned on. The crossing of each beam created a huge spider web in the sky. People were driving down from the hills to go to Honolulu to celebrate."

What did you do to celebrate?

"The chapel was open, so I went to the chapel." This was an eighteen-year-old man; he would become a minster when the war was over.

Yokohama, Japan

In September 1945 *APA 216 Neshoba* returned to Pearl Harbor. The ship was enroute to Yokohama, Japan transporting equipment and 2,500 soldiers who would join other personnel in occupying Japan. While there, they were given three hours to go into Yokohama.

In Yokohama, "there were bombed out places, and the people were not hostile," said Scott. "They wanted to buy cigarettes from the soldiers. There were about twenty kids on the dock begging for candy. I imagine they were glad it was over."

China—Early October 1945

Along with other transport ships, USS *Neshoba* APA 216 dropped anchor at the mouth of the Teinsin River. [The name of the river and city were changed when the Communists took over.] Their task was to get the last group of marines out of China before the Communists took over. Since their ship was too large to navigate the river, they were put on smaller naval vessels to travel the river. The journey took Scott past boat people, who were very poor. As an eighteen-year-old, it was difficult to see so much poverty. "Children surrounded you begging," said Scott. American sailors were required to stay in an American hotel and eat their meals there.

On the return trip to the ship, they found they could not board their ship because of choppy waters. They remained on the small craft overnight. The sailors were fed one slice of bread, one slice of pineapple, and one piece of Spam. In order to board their ship, the soldiers climbed up the cargo nets. Then the ship sailed back to San Francisco with a stop at Pearl Harbor to pick up mail and supplies.

On the last night at sea, the men couldn't sleep. Many of them polished their shoes to a very shiny spit shine. Sailing under the Golden Gate Bridge was quite a sight! Scott likened it to what the Statue of Liberty would mean to people arriving in New York.

They anchored in Sausalito, California, in the North Bay area. That night, half of the ship had overnight liberty in San Francisco. When you were on leave, there were "taxi ships" that would run back and forth from shore to the ship. Scott and his fellow soldiers waited and waited for a "taxi" to come by and take them back. None arrived that night. A lot of the guys stayed in one hotel room. They were on the floor and lying across the bed. The next morning, when his buddy checked out, the hotel staff was not very happy with them!

When the sailors returned to await the shuttle back to the ship, no shuttles arrived. Thus, at eight o'clock a.m., there were considered AWOL. The next morning, they found out the ship had moved during their leave and was located at the south end of the San Francisco Bay, which is many miles from its original spot in the North Bay. Navy buses were sent to transport them to Hunter's Point. AWOL status was never entered on the records perhaps due to the kindness of the captain or consideration of the amount of work it would create for the yeoman.

Next Scott was sent to Stockton, California Naval Supply Depot on the Sacramento River. The USS *Neshoba* APA 216 was decommissioned, "mothballed," and later scrapped. Scott had served for nineteen months and could go home. He was discharged in mid-August 1946 as a storekeeper third class. Following his discharge, Scott returned home to Indianapolis where he completed his interrupted high school education at Emerich Manual Training High School.

After the War

Scott married Ruth Layton in 1948, and they raised six children—four girls and two boys. He graduated from Indiana Central College and took his graduate work at Christian Theological Seminary. Scott ministered at both Hansing Park Christian Church and Buck Creek Christian Church.

Scott has read several books about the sinking of the USS *Indianapolis*. The USS *Indianapolis* means a lot to him for the following three reasons:

1. The ship was named after our city, Indianapolis.
2. Two months prior, [Guam to Philippines] Scott and the men aboard his ship sailed the same route as the USS *Indianapolis*. It could have been me.
3. The ship carried atomic bomb parts.

What did you think about the atomic bombs?

"I don't know if Truman could have done something else. It [the atomic bombing] probably saved my life and millions of others. [At] Pearl Harbor [the Japanese] killed many of our people. Had we invaded Japan, they would have lost many more Japanese and American lives. Again, it was not the first bombing of Japan. In some areas, the living quarters were very fragile—thus large living areas were destroyed by fires as a result of the bombing."

How did the American government handle the Japanese after their surrender?

"They helped establish government and assisted in restoring what was destroyed during the war. This kind of effort on the part of the country that prevailed in a war was unusual and set America apart."

In 2016, Scott was undergoing chemo and radiation for prostate cancer. His candid account of his WWII experiences on a day when he was fighting another battle—this time with cancer—was characteristically humble.

Robert Buchert—US Army
"I saw lots of desolation, and the Japanese people were frightened because they had been told a lot of things about us."

Bob was drafted into the army in about 1943 then joined the Airborne unit. He was assigned to the 152 Anti-Aircraft Battalion, 11th Airborne Division. After starting out doing qualitative jumps, he was assigned to the South Pacific Theater, to the Marshall and Gilbert Islands area.

The war ended before he had to jump into enemy territory. However, he did make other jumps while serving in Japan after the war's end.

After the surrender of Japan, "we moved up to Manila in the Philippines," said Bob. "We were there until we were sent to Japan as occupational troops."

Jumping in Japan

Bob explained that he got fifty dollars extra pay, or "jump pay," for making jumps. For the jump pay to continue, you had to make jumps every three months. He remembered making a jump in Sendai, Japan. Sendai is a city located on Honshu Island, northeast of Tokyo.

He also remembered being stationed in Akita, Japan. Akita is a city located on the northeastern part of the island of Honshu. "I saw lots of desolation, and the Japanese people were frightened because they had been told a lot of things about us." He went on to say, "We were strange to them." As it was recorded, "our bombers came over and bombed the [Japanese] cities." It would not be unusual for a conquered nation to be afraid of the former enemy arriving in their cities. Bob completed his military service with the US Army paratroopers and was discharged in 1946.

Should the United States have dropped the atomic bomb on Japan?

"Yes. It could have saved my life because we were going to invade Japan." He was scheduled to invade Japan, but thankfully the war ended. Later he went into Japan during the occupation, not jumping into battle.

Do you still jump?

"I made enough jumps. I don't have to jump anymore." Bob thought it was funny that Max Bates jumped out of a plane on his ninetieth birthday.

In my search to include as many WWII stories in this book as possible, I spotted one of those beloved black and gold WWII veteran hats in the Orlando International Airport. Bob was travelling from Orlando, Florida, with his daughter, Karen, back home to Indiana and graciously agreed to an impromptu WWII interview while waiting for the plane to arrive.

During this flight Bob didn't have to worry about jumping out of the plane. So many years ago, this would have been a very different kind of trip. There may have been enemy gunfire below him instead of white, fluffy clouds.

The flight attendant told everyone to turn off their portable phones and electronic devices. These particular items were not even dreamed about seventy-plus years ago. Today nearly everyone on the plane had one in their bag or pocket. Bob is one of a rapidly dying breed of brave soldiers of another generation.

As we began to talk, Bob said, "This all happened a long time ago." We don't want people of today and in the future to forget what so many soldiers gave up for us, this present generation. Perhaps all Americans should feel like singer Norah Jones when she said at a recent concert that she was thankful to America for the freedom "to have a song that I can sing on Election Day."

We should all be grateful, Norah!

During the war years, the USS *Whitehurst* was involved in several invasions in New Guinea, Leyte in the Philippines, and Okinawa. Lewis's job aboard the ship was on the evaporator, a distillery that converted sea water into drinking water aboard the ship. He had training for a month from the Carrier Corporation on refrigeration. He was the ice machine man as well and the only one aboard who knew anything about refrigeration. There were about five sailors in the auxiliary gang. Lewis took care of maintenance. He was responsible for making sure the evaporator was working and cleaning up the coils whenever it became clogged. "Every once in a while," he said, "we would have to tear it apart and clean it."

"Being sailors," Lewis noted, "we didn't have any idea what was going on." They escorted tankers, navy transports, and ammo ships. Some of the time the USS *Whitehurst* escorted supply ships between the islands. Lewis recalled, "We took part in several invasions over the years. They called us MacArthur's Navy."

Why were you called MacArthur's Navy?

"MacArthur was involved in taking back New Guinea from the Japanese, and we were there. We were shot at once; also we were shot at by artillery. We were in Leyte harbor on the night of the invasion. We shot down a Japanese airplane while protecting our convoy. We sank a Japanese sub that sank a ship like ours fifteen or twenty miles ahead of us. We tried to protect the USS

Bull that was picking up survivors. The ship that was sunk was the USS *Eversole DE 404*. The *Whitehurst* arrived on the scene and saved the USS *Bull*."

In November 1944, at Palau, during the invasion of the Philippines, the USS *Whitehurst* was taking on stores when the USS *Mt. Hood*, an ammunitions ship, blew up. Lewis was going up a ladder when he was blown backward. The *Whitehurst* was just going by the ship when it blew up. This is part of the reason Lewis wears hearing aids today. Only a few sailors from the *Mt. Hood* who were on leave were safe; the rest of the crew were killed by the blast. There was a fire onboard that ignited the ammo on the ship.

Lewis's ship made it to Brisbane, Australia, but they were there only three days before being called back to help with the Battle of Okinawa. Lewis was unhappy not to be able to see more of Australia and not to have leave there.

They escorted the USS *New York* at Okinawa. The USS *New York* fired on the island to clear out the Japanese before the troops landed.

"Okinawa, the last battle that we were involved in, when we were hit by a kamikaze, killing forty-two of our guys. It happened April 12, 1945, the same day that FDR died. The crew spent two whole days plugging holes. There was a convoy leaving Okinawa, so we joined it and left. They didn't want lights to be seen by Japanese ships or subs. We left Okinawa and stopped in Saipan, where we took all the ammo off the ship—no use to carry it back home."

How did you feel after you got hit?

"I was never afraid until we got hit. Then I was afraid. When that clanging started for battle stations, well, I was afraid. But you still do what you have to do; it's your job. I was still immature." Lewis was only twenty years old.

"We arrived in Pearl Harbor the middle of May 1945. We were all disappointed that they repaired our ship. They welded a new bridge onto the ship. They converted it to a power supply ship. It was repaired and ready to go back to sea by the Fourth of July. They took fifteen of us who had some special training home for a thirty-day leave. We went home on the USS *Intrepid*, which took us to San Francisco." Lewis got an extra seven days for travel time because he was going to Ohio. The war was far from being over at that point. The United States was looking at invading Japan.

"Our ship was powered by turbo electric drive. It would make electricity like we have at our homes. Our job was a power supply ship instead of a destroyer. We arrived in Manila and supplied electricity to the city of Manila until November 1945."

What did you think about dropping the atomic bomb?

"Didn't think anything about it. It ended the war, that's all we thought about it. I think people who think we shouldn't have dropped the bomb are idiots. It took their emperor to end the war. There were some idiots in Japan who wanted to fight to the death."

They were engaged in seven battles. His medals include seven battle stars, a Good Conduct Medal, an American Campaign Medal, the Asiatic Pacific Campaign Medal, and the Philippine Liberation Medal.

The USS *Whitehurst* was used in the movie The Enemy Below. The movie starred Robert Mitchum, and several of the original sailors were given bit parts. The USS *Whitehurst* was sunk on April 28, 1971, off the coast of Washington state. Lewis is computer savvy and used the DE634 website to trigger some long-forgotten memories of his WWII days.

James Crabb – US Navy
"The GI Bill was the biggest thing that made us what we are today."

In January 1945 Jim graduated from Tech High School in Indianapolis. He had taken some ROTC classes while he was in high school.

Jim was on the USS *General Burner* in the Pacific Theater. His job was on a troop ship transporting troops to Okinawa, preparing for the invasion of Japan.

How do you feel when strangers come up to you?

"Wonderful feeling! Keep on thanking us. It's great the way people treat us." Jim has also been on the Indy Honor Flight to Washington, DC.

He was asked about his feelings concerning the book *Unbroken*, by Laura Hillenbrand. He replied, "I don't know how he got through it and the brutality of the Japanese."

He said, "The GI Bill was the biggest thing that made us what we are today." The GI Bill was a program that provided educational assistance to military personnel.

What did you think about the United States dropping the atomic bomb on Japan?

"I didn't know what it was. I didn't know there was that kind of technology." He was on the ship going to Japan when he heard the news. They were glad.

Jim was friends with Colonel Paul Tibbets, pilot of the *Enola Gay*, who was responsible for dropping the atomic bomb on Hiroshima, Japan, on August 6, 1945. Later in Paul's life, "people would stop him and ask if it was really necessary to have dropped the atomic bombs on Japan." Paul Tibbets said, "Yes, it was; it saved many lives."

Japan

Tokyo, the capital city of Japan, is located on the island of Honshu. The city was bombed by Lieutenant Colonel Jimmie Doolittle on April 18, 1942, in the first attack on the homeland of Japan, also known as the Tokyo Raid. The city was bombed by sixteen US B-25 bombers. The bombers had to take off from an aircraft carrier, drop their bombs on Tokyo, then fly on to China, as they didn't have enough gas to return to United States soil.

Osaka, the second largest city in Japan, is located on the south coast of the island of Honshu. The first air raid there was on March 13–14, 1945. The second air raid was on June 1, 1945, and the last air raid was on August 14, 1945, the day before the Japanese surrendered. Unfortunately a train had just arrived at the train station when the US bombs were dropped, killing over seven hundred people. Osaka was an important center for industry and war supplies, making it an important target for the Allies.

Hiroshima is located on the southwestern part of the island of Honshu. It was the site of the first atomic bomb explosion, dropped by the US airplane *Enola Gay*, piloted by Paul Tibbets Jr. on August 6, 1945. The bomb was named Little Boy. Hiroshima sustained a loss of more than eighty thousand Japanese lives, and thousands more were wounded. Tibbets said openly he had no regrets about dropping the atomic bomb, as it saved lives. The Allies were planning an invasion of Japan that would have taken many Japanese and Allied lives.

Nagasaki is located on the island of Kyushu in Japan. The second atomic bomb, Fat Man, was dropped three days after the first bomb, after the Japanese government refused to surrender. The pilot, Frederick C. Bock, flew the B-29 Superfortress *Bockscar* over Japan, looking for Kokura. However, the city was fogged in. The plane then went to the secondary target, Nagasaki, which was targeted because of the war plants and industry in the city. Over 50,000 people were killed in this attack. On August 15, 1945, the Japanese surrendered; they formally signed the surrender agreement aboard the USS *Missouri* in Tokyo Bay on September 2, 1945.

General Douglas MacArthur was preparing for an invasion of Japan, which was set for the fall of 1945. After the Japanese surrendered, MacArthur was put in charge of the formal surrender ceremony aboard the USS *Missouri* battleship.

Clell Downey—US Navy
"I was in more danger on an aircraft carrier than Guadalcanal."

In 1942 Clell joined the navy, when he was fifteen years old. The recruiter asked him if he had a birth certificate. He said no, but he had a Bible record back in Tennessee, where he was from. The navy recruiter said, "as long as you have it, it's OK. You don't have to go get it." So Clell joined in Florence, Alabama, and took the train to Birmingham to pick up another train. He remembered it was a Pullman, and he slept in the upper bunk. When the train had to cross a river, it was put on a barge. "We got out on the other side instead of going across a bridge. We took the southern route through El Paso, Texas," Clell said.

"Mostly they fed us on the train, but sometimes we got out at a restaurant to eat. While eating at one restaurant, some guy said, 'Throw me the salt. So I picked up the salt shaker and threw it. The salt shaker hit the big guy in the forehead! He shook his head, as though he couldn't believe I'd done that. He was a big redheaded guy."

When he arrived in San Diego, he got his navy uniform. Because he was dirt poor, these were the "best newest clothes I'd ever owned. I thought I was rich." The Depression had hit, and Clell's family was very poor. He made fifty dollars a month in the service. He kept fifteen dollars and sent his mom thirty-five dollars; with the government matching it, his mom got seventy dollars altogether. According to Rights and Privileges of American Servicemen, servicemen were allowed to make a voluntary allotment to either his wife or dependent parent or other family members. The Government provided a designated amount according to the amount of money the soldier was making.

Boot camp

Boot camp was not too hard for Clell, since he had worked as a delivery boy. He had gotten exercise delivering groceries at home in the hills of Tennessee. He was in good shape. There were several guys at the start of this one exercise they were doing—running up and down a field. At the end of the exercise, there were only five left, and he was one of them.

In 1942 the military needed lots of soldiers overseas. Some of the boys had been in boot camp only two weeks, and they were sent overseas. However, Clell had twenty-six weeks of boot camp. He was sent to radio school, where he had an attack of appendicitis. He spent twenty-one days in the hospital, until he could return to duty. So he flunked out of radio school.

Next he was sent to North Island Naval Base, San Diego, California. His job was to work on huge wheels, filling them with air and attaching them to seaplanes. His next assignment was in Estonia, Oregon, at the Naval Air Station. His job there was putting ammo into aircraft. He then moved to Sheldon, Washington, for six months, then was sent overseas. The first stop was Ford Island in Pearl Harbor.

Pearl Harbor

He said there is a little known and little reported incident where twenty-two LSTs loaded with ammo blew up. The LSTs were tied together, and there was a chain reaction explosion. The men on the ship spent several weeks afterward picking up body parts. The military kept it out of the news, as it was not good for morale. Clell saw the USS *Arizona* before the December 7th bombing. It is still commissioned; it has never been taken it out of service. His impression of Pearl Harbor in 1942 was that there was lots of asphalt, as it was paved for an airstrip. He stated, "I was just a kid and had not learned to be afraid yet."

Clell was on a world cruise. One of the ports of call on this cruise was Honolulu, Hawaii. His wife, Bobbie and he returned to Pearl Harbor during this cruise.

How did you feel about returning to Pearl Harbor after so many years?

He didn't say how he felt about returning after more than sixty years. He did say he had mentioned the above incident with the LSTs to someone at the base while he was there. He was told the navy was going to recognize it at a later date with a celebration to let people know about the disaster.

Clell remarked several times about how kids are not able to recognize fear. He gave this example: Two officers were drinking, and one said, "I can do a slow roll on takeoff." The other one said, "No, you can't, and I bet five dollars you can't!" So they went out to a plane to settle the bet. The pilot didn't make it and crashed into the head, killing the guy going to the restroom in there as well. Two people died over a silly bet!

Guadalcanal

Guadalcanal, located in the Solomon Islands, was code-named Operation Watchtower. Fighting occurred there between August 7, 1942 and February 9, 1943. It was the first major battle, and a very important victory, against the Japanese army. Japan was trying to stop the supply and communication routes that ran between Australia, New Zealand, and the United States. The Allies wanted Guadalcanal as a base. There were 7,100 deaths and more than seven thousand wounded; twenty-nine ships were lost, and 615 aircraft were lost.

Clell was sent to Guadalcanal, and it took the ship two months to arrive. They were going very slowly, four knots an hour, with no escort, on a Dutch merchant ship. They were zigzagging to avoid subs. There was a sub alert, but nothing happened. The island was tropical and very hot. He found a smooth place on the deck to sleep at night. Breakfast, lunch, and dinner consisted of bread and meat sandwiches, maybe bologna and cheese.

When Clell arrived in Guadalcanal, the marines had already secured the island. He was stationed there for one year. One night, while he was sleeping in a Quonset hut, he woke up, and his bunk was shaking. "I thought we were being invaded again. The sky was red!" he recalled. An ammo ship had blown up. Only one man survived; he was blown off the ship but lived.

"Even though it wasn't a war zone, it was a dangerous time and place to be," said Clell. He had a buddy who was hit by a plane and killed because the pilot couldn't see him. Planes had to go one way or the other because they couldn't see what was in front of them. The plane was tipped up in front. When his buddy was hit, Clell ran over to see if he could help, but his buddy died immediately.

After returning to the States, Clell had some time left in the service. He had a choice of duty stations. He chose Astoria, Oregon. It was 1945, and the war was over. He was assigned to Treasure Island for two months, with very little duty, so he basically played the whole time. He was on a seagoing tugboat for a while before he was discharged on August 23, 1946. He returned to Tennessee and was just nineteen years old.

Korean War

Clell's time in the military was not over. In 1950 he was called up again for the Korean War. He was assigned to the carrier USS *Franklin D. Roosevelt*, doing Mediterranean Sea duty. He said, "We lost seven men the last day I was on the ship—just accidents, not enemy fire. I was the eighth accident on the ship. I was working on the flight deck when I was blown almost over the length of the ship by the jet blast. I wore the seat off my pants and some skin. There was material on the deck to help keep the planes from skidding; however, it was like sandpaper on me! I was in more danger on an aircraft carrier than [on] Guadalcanal."

What did you think about the United States using the atomic bomb against the Japanese cities of Nagasaki and Hiroshima?

"Best thing that happened. It saved more lives than it took. We would have killed more of them. They [the Japanese] wouldn't give up."

Family life

When Clell was forty-six years old, he went to college at Tennessee State University. He majored in industrial arts and became a teacher. In his junior year, he was named Outstanding Student of the Year.

Clell had met a girl named Bobbie when they were twelve years old in Columbia, Tennessee. Later in life they were reunited. They have been married since 2015 and have been on five world cruises.

Bobbie and Clell Downey

What do you remember about the bombing of Pearl Harbor?

Bobbie replied, "It was on a Sunday in Columbia, Tennessee. We were going to a Sunday afternoon movie. I was waiting on my parents, and they were upstairs. I called up to them, 'What's the hold up?"

"'I think we are at war!' said my parents. I asked if we were still going to the movies. As a fourteen-year-old child, I went to pieces and started to cry."

Bobbie started to cry remembering Pearl Harbor, which she and Clell had just recently visited. "I had friends whose fathers were in the war," she said, "and one friend's father was a POW. It was hard on him. "FDR was the first president she remembered. She said, "He has always been my hero."

After returning to Great Lakes, Glen was sent to Boston and assigned to the USS *Sanctuary*, one of the newest hospital ships built during that time. Glen was an electrician in charge of replacing lightbulbs on the ship. It was important to keep it lit up at night, so the Japanese would know it was a hospital ship. "Here is where we trained on two ships to learn how to shoot the big guns. We had to sleep down in the hole, where the bunks were stacked five high. I simply cannot tell you how uncomfortable this was...like sleeping in an oven! On the USS *Sanctuary*, the bunks were one and two high and much wider. Also, we had real showers with both hot and cold water, and the ship was air-conditioned.

"In Norfolk we loaded supplies and headed for the canal. This was interesting to see those little machines called mules pull our big ship through the canal. We got liberty in Colon, a small town in the canal zone.

Hawaii and Guam

"Next stop, Hawaii. We were there for three days, and everyone got liberty at least once. The enemy had made a mess of our navy there. Next was Guam. Our purpose in being there was to pick up the wounded and transport them to Hawaii. We were there long enough for some of the crew to get liberty. I was among that group. In Guam some of us went to play on the sandy beach. The Japanese living in caves fired some shots at us."

Asia

Then Glen went on to Asia. "The next stop was a long ride, and we had some bad weather. I think we were out there for thirty days without seeing land. More wounded servicemen were collected in Saipan. From Saipan we went to Iwo Jima to pick up any servicemen fighting for the Allied group.

Japan

"The next stop was on to Nagasaki, Japan. What I saw was unbelievable! The atomic bomb was very small compared to what we have today. It completely destroyed one city and killing many people. Many of these bodies were still on the ground five weeks after the explosion of August 9, 1945.

"The smell was awful...dead, burnt flesh. There were over 50,000 people killed. The only ones that survived were the people hidden in caves underground when they heard the planes approach." Later, he added, "many things were incinerated, except the valleys were green. Whenever the captain went on land, he had his own big black four-door sedan.

"The marines were there before us, so our captain wired Admiral Halsey and told him that his men had not had liberty since Pearl Harbor. We had just come from Pearl about two months ago, but the admiral thought the captain was referring to the bombings in 1941. Anyway, the whole ship's crew, except those on duty, were given a party! The marines supplied the trucks for us to ride in and gave us a tour. Each sailor was given two case of beer." Glen didn't drink, so he had a lot of friends.

"I remember seeing a bomb factory that had rows of empty bomb cylinders all lined up. Also, there was a bombed out submarine factory where subs stood upright instead of the way you think about seeing them. I was told that there were ninety Americans there; they were not servicemen and women but were missionaries and people of that caliber. I did see the detail carrying boxes twelve inches by twelve inches by twelve inches. [the remains of the Americans that were killed] This was after we had returned to the ship from our party. I never want to see what I saw on the tour again.

Hawaii

"The next morning we set sail for Hawaii. We made a stop in the China Sea for the night; then, the next morning, one of the anchors was stuck. The anchor windlass would not work, so the captain ordered the chief machinist mate to cut the chain with a torch. The chain was cut and permitted to drop to the bottom of the China Sea, about five miles deep. The next day we hit the worst typhoon we had ever encountered! I had learned to walk on the deck, but I felt very sorry for the soldiers we were carrying to Hawaii. Hundreds of these guys, hanging over the deck rail trying to vomit.

"The ship was being tossed about so badly that the cooks could not prepare hot meals. So the cooks got out the peanut butter and bread. We were permitted to make our own sandwiches. The weather was so bad that for four days our ship stayed in the same spot.

"Now we are headed back to Hawaii to unload the human cargo. Also, we had a lot of Australians. We were there for two days, and two days of liberty again. September 10, 1945—we are in the Panama Canal again and up the East Coast to Norfolk. The war is over, and we want to go home."

Were you ever shot at while you were in the military?

"Last trip before we came home, somewhere in the China Sea or the Pacific, we were shot at for three days. We didn't take it seriously. We joked that they didn't get us! They were using six-inch shells. We could see red streaks of shots.

"My commander pleaded with me to re-up, but I had enough. I was homesick for Louisville, Gamaliel and Tompkinsville, so I signed up to come home, July 1946."

Should the United States have used nuclear bombs to end the war?

"They [the Japanese] were going to kill that many more of us. Yes, they should have done it. Stop this silly war!"

Dr. Halbert Gillette—US Navy

The military is "a feeling of belonging to something special. I still miss it today."

In 1944, at age seventeen, Hal enlisted in the navy in Galesburg, Illinois. He had attended Galesburg High School. Coming from a large family of ten children, he was the oldest child, with eight of his siblings still living. He participated in the first helicopter development squad—VX3 development.

Hal spent his time in the military in Miami; Kingsville, Texas; and Key West. He had prepared to go to the Pacific but found out the war was over; he didn't have to go. He participated in the seaman to admiral program and made lieutenant commander by the time he left the military.

He is hard of hearing today due to the firing of the five-inch guns on the carrier and destroyer. The only protection was wads of cotton.

One interesting story was about the time he spent in Key West, Florida. In the late 1960s, he guarded President Nixon in Guam. He was in charge of a security detail. Hal said of Nixon, "He was great!"

When Hal and Dotty were first married, they lived in Key West. Dotty said they went to ten-cent movies while they lived there. Dotty walked around looking for a place for them to live. She found a place that was over a bar and located next door to Margaret Truman's laundry. On their first night, the bed was full of termites, and there were scorpions on the floor. Needless to say, the next day she looked for a new place to live! Hal got to shake Truman's hand when he was visiting the Truman Little White House in Key West. The Truman Little White House, built in 1890, was the presidential getaway for many presidents.

Later in Hal's military career, he was in Japan, where he met with senior officers from other countries on a destroyer in the Mediterranean. During this time, he was teaching at a mine warfare school.

After spending thirty years in the navy, Hal left and taught school for thirty years. Hal was able to attend the University of Nebraska and went on to get his doctorate later in life. He and Dotty had four children—three sons and one daughter. One of his sons was killed while climbing a mountain in Switzerland.

Hal ended with this joke: "The marines are part of the navy? Yes, the men's department!"

Should the United States have dropped the atomic bomb on Japan?

"Absolutely, glad for it. Thank goodness for it."

Hal said the military was, for him, "a feeling of belonging to something special. I still miss it today."

Wayne Guerin—US Navy Seabees
"There wasn't anything that Seabees couldn't do. They built roads, and they built buildings."

"There are three things that I never learned to do—never tasted wine, whiskey, or beer or any alcohol in my life; never smoked a cigarette in my life; and never learned to curse. Just some things that my mother and dad told me not to do." Wayne grew up in the hills of Stewart County, Tennessee, with four brothers, all of who were in the military.

Pearl Harbor

"I was a freshman or in eighth grade at that time. I registered on February 11, 1944. I was called to be examined a month later in Georgia. There were two busloads of us. By November I was ready to go overseas."

"In June 1944 I went into the navy in Nashville, Tennessee. I took my boot training at Camp Peary, Virginia. I was eighteen years old, and a few of the boys were even younger.

I was aboard ship in San Francisco in November 1944. "I was assigned to the Seabees and went overseas to Hollandia Bay, New Guinea. We gathered up about a thousand marines. There wasn't any place for them to sleep, but they just laid down on the deck. They were getting ready to invade Luzon and Manila. We transported them as far as the island of Leyte, where they went ashore.

"We stayed there for several days because the army would not let us go ashore. They didn't have time or personnel enough to guard us, because we were a noncombat outfit. We were there to prepare and repair the airstrips. The bombers were taking off every day, and quite frequently got torn up by landings, take-offs, and bombs and what have you.

Leyte

"They moved us over to another island sixty miles away—Leyte. That was the first island invaded by MacArthur and his army. This was in the last week of October, and I had arrived much later. We did carry carbine rifles, that was all. So we went over to Samar in December."

One event Wayne described involved his ship, the HMS *Sommelsdyk*, which was owned and managed by the Netherlands. The *Sommelsdyk*, built in Rotterdam around 1941, was used during WWII. At the end of the war, it was returned to the Netherlands. The ship was repaired enough to sail, and it returned to Pearl Harbor to be further repaired.

Ship is torpedoed at Samar

"I had worked KP all day and was on deck. The ship was torpedoed in our number one hold, in the front of the ship, and we took on water. The hold on the ship was about the size of a boxcar. This ship was huge, about six hundred feet long. We were anchored out in the bay about a mile and started taking on a lot of water. So the only thing they could do was crank up the engine and run [the ship] aground as far as it would go. The bow hit the ground, and we were about a half mile from shore. It was leaning to one side, and we were given orders to abandon ship."

Wayne got a little upset when he recalled the rest of the story. "It was Christmas night, and some of the men were sitting up on the rails talking to one another. When the torpedo hit, some of the men went into the sea. Well, the first thing we did was throw out the life preservers. A lot of the men were thrown overboard. The plane went down in the water. The sad thing was the Jap that dropped the torpedo was fished out of the water wearing a US life preserver! One of the Filipino guards on the shore got him. I saw him dead, lying in the back of a dump truck. We lost a few men; I don't think it was more than eight or ten people. One guy broke his leg going down a ladder, but most of us got ashore OK." This was at Samar, a much larger place than Leyte.

Wayne went on to explain, "We had four LSTs. Many of the LSTs were built in Evansville or Pittsburgh, pulled alongside the ship, and we had these rope ladders, or cargo nets, over the side of our ship. It didn't take long to get a bunch of young men off the ship. The LSTs transported us into the harbor."

He recalled driving a truck out the front of an LST, where the door dropped down in the front of the LST. After that "we went ashore with nothing besides what we had on. It took a few days for them to get our things out of the ship.

Tacloban, Philippines

"The Filipino people were nice to us, and we tried to be nice to them. There was this old Catholic priest that came down to the shore where all these men, probably about twelve hundred of us, were standing. [The priest said,] 'Men, this church behind me is mine, and you are welcome to come up and use it to spend the night.' Some of the men were half dressed, and some with clothes on." Wayne chuckled. "Well, I was right behind him and spent the night in one of the pews!

"The first night that I got there, I slept at the church. I don't know how many of them got in there, but they were in the pews and on the floors. It took them a while get quiet and go to sleep. The next day we went up into the mountains, begged, borrowed, and stole what we could from the army, to live for about three months. The army had captured some Japanese food, such as canned wieners and tons of rice, so we ate rice three times a day." His wife, Gail, said he won't eat rice now.

"Then we put up tents to sleep in. The next night we slept on the ground. Eventually we got some cots. We worked then, which was important to do. I always appreciated the old priest coming down and making that offer. Since then I have gone into the computer and found quite a bit about this particular ship and the huge stone church. Apparently he had done this many times before. This church had been used by sailors on nights like this when they came in. This area was in Tacloban, Philippines.

"Much of the equipment was underwater and had to be redone. We were on the island of Samar for two and half or three months. Then they moved us to Leyte, where we were scheduled to do our work. From then on I spent the rest of my time on Leyte." He was there until February 1946.

"Seabees stands for construction battalion. We were all navy, but we did manual work repairing the airstrips and pumping fresh water out of the rivers and the mountains out to the tankers. I know when they invaded Iwo Jima and Okinawa, we learned that we had to furnish water for several days into the tankers. Fresh water was pretty scarce up there. That was our biggest job. We built roads and buildings and repaired everything. Our biggest problem was air raids. They continued to have air raids for clear up to the middle of 1945. They were aiming at the airstrip but missed their target sometimes by about half a mile or more. I worked for the army as well as the navy.

"I was on was a troop ship with about twenty-five hundred men, plus officers. The officers running the ship were from the Netherlands. Some of the other men were Javanese. I remember them saying…gibberish, which we finally figured out was 'the boatswain mate to report to the steam room.' We were on the ship from November 17 to December 25, 1944."

Wayne summed up the Seabees by saying, "There wasn't anything that Seabees couldn't do. They built roads, and they built buildings."

Brothers Finding Each Other

Wayne's brother, Ray, was also in WWII and in the army. He was stationed nearby and would come up to Leyte to visit Wayne.

"My brother came up to eat with us on weekends, because the food was better in the navy," Wayne explained. "He was about my size, and I would slip him a pair of dungarees and a shirt, and he would go through the chow line with us. We managed to get away with it." His brother has since passed away.

Wayne said that he heard "the largest naval battle that was ever conducted was in Leyte Gulf. It was an unpleasant time. The Japs came down from the big island of Luzon and made bombing runs. They were not very successful. Any airstrip that they could tear up, we had to repair. The airstrips are made of coral. We furnished this machine that used the coral that they would dig out of the sea. It is like the limestone rock that we would crush. They would roll it out as firmly as they could, and then we had a steel mesh that fit together and hooked. They covered the strip and sometimes planes would hit too hard and had to be repaired. The big problem was when you had an explosion when the plane failed to get into the air properly and the bombs would explode.

"We had planes that guarded the airstrips from the Japanese bombing raids. We had the Mustangs, the main fighting planes, and the B-24 Liberators. It is a four-engine plane with twin tails, and they would leave in the morning and fly to Formosa or Taiwan."

Japanese prisoners

They captured many Japanese who were hiding in the hills. "We would find them half-starved and bring them back to camp. At one time there were about five hundred Japanese prisoners in camp. There were about fifty soldiers guarding them day and night. We fed them and took care of them. Doctors took care of their injuries, and if one of them died, we buried them. We weren't mean like the Japanese were. It is hard for me to forgive what the Japanese did. Then they would ship them out to other places."

Wayne reminisced, "It was an interesting time for an eighteen-year-old person who had never been anywhere to speak of, except in the hills of Tennessee. I don't recall any sailor griping about anything. I never heard anything like that. I am really proud to say that." However, he said, "Now, there were arguments or fist fights, but that's what happens with a bunch of young men." Like many men who enlisted during WWII, two or three would decide to join the military together. Wayne had a picture of himself and three other guys from his area.

What did you think of dropping the bomb on Japan?

"I think it was the best thing that they ever did. I could give you a reason, if you want. I don't see any difference, if you had a brother and he was going to be killed. Shooting him with a rifle and getting it done at one time. I don't hold anything against President Truman or anyone that made the decision. Because there is no doubt in my mind that it saved a lot of lives. The Japanese intended to use all civilian people that were able to walk and carry a gun to protect those four big islands. I think we saved more Japanese lives than we did American. I really do. If we had invaded each of those islands with rifles, bazookas, and cannons bombs, I think we would have killed a lot more people than we did in Nagasaki and Hiroshima! I think it did end the war. Every one of my buddies was happy, because we had seen so many terrible things that the Japanese had done. So I am for it. I hope it is never used again."

Did you see any shows or movie stars?

"I saw the all-soldier show, *This Is the Army*, written by Irving Berlin, who, dressed in his WWI uniform, attended the show."

Fortunately we got to stay on the beach, since our job was to set up communications with the ships to bring in supplies.

"The troops made their way onto the island and toward the cliffs. We had landed on the eighth wave at approximately eight thirty a.m. on Orange Beach. There was so much confusion and turmoil on landing that it was after noon [when] we finally got our radio in service for shore-to-ship communications. They dug foxholes in the sand on the beaches. In about three weeks, the majority of the Japanese had been annihilated, and Peleliu was essentially secured. After a month on the island, we left on troop transports for our return to Pavuvu."

Irvin said when they had some breaks from their training, they made some shell necklaces that he brought home for his wife, Dolores. They picked the shells off the coral reefs. "If we had time, we would bury them and let the worms eat the living parts out of them," he said. "If we didn't, we would use gasoline to clean the guts out." This was a pastime for the sailors.

Okinawa

Upon returning to Pavuvu, Irvin's team prepared for Okinawa. They experienced a mock landing on Guadalcanal when they were getting ready for the landing on Okinawa. "On April 1, 1945, Easter Sunday, we landed on the island of Okinawa," said Irvin. "Unlike Peleliu, there was no opposition on the beaches. The Japanese were hiding away from the beaches on the island."

"We were still on Okinawa on V-J Day, August 6, 1945. However, Japanese planes were still conducting kamikaze hits against our ships in the harbor," Irvin said. "About four o'clock one afternoon, a plane hit the battleship *New Mexico*." He heard later that about thirty-four sailors were killed in that attack.

The 4th JASCO was disbanded on August 31, 1945, and the naval personnel were assigned to other naval vessels. Irvin was assigned to the troop transport *APA-150*. As a side note, one of his buddies was assigned to the ship that also had Ernie Pyle onboard. He has several pictures of Ernie Pyle on the ship.

While Irvin was working in the radio shack aboard *APA-150*, there was a typhoon on Okinawa. "So our ship moved out to sea for a couple of days until the typhoon subsided," he said. "Then we returned to Okinawa and picked up marines and took them up to Tientsin, North China, for occupational duty. From here we set sail in the South China Sea for the Philippines. The second day out, we ran into another typhoon. Our ship reversed course and rode with the typhoon, instead of bucking it for two days, until it subsided." After this excitement they resumed the trip to the Philippines. The ship anchored in Subic Bay, Philippines, and they had one day liberty in Manila. Irving said this was the only time he wore his white dress uniform.

Going back home

"Then we received army personnel aboard ship to take them back to the United States for discharge," he said. "On November 16, 1945, we sailed under the Golden Gate Bridge and arrived at Treasure Island naval base near San Francisco. It was good to be back home.

"On December 19, 1945, I hitchhiked out of Treasure Island on a thirty-day leave. I stopped in Indianapolis for a couple of days before I continued my trip back home to Pennsylvania." Irvin stopped in Indianapolis to visit his future bride, Dolores, whom he had met when he was seventeen and she was fifteen. They wrote many letters during the war, which Dolores still has.

"After my leave," said Irvin, "I reported to the Philadelphia Navy Yard. Shortly, I left by train for Camp Shoemaker in California. I was here at the US Naval Personnel Separation Center until April 3, 1946, when I received my honorable discharge, having served thirty-two months in service."

Dolores and Irvin Herman

Dolores said, "We were the only class that began high school in 1941, at the beginning of the war and graduated at the end of the war in 1945." She attended Shortridge High School in Indianapolis, Indiana. She and Irvin met in Indianapolis when he was in radio school. It was a blind date at a skating rink. Dolores and Irwin have been married for seventy years.

Pearl Harbor Memories

Irvin was fifteen when the attack on Pearl Harbor occurred. He said, "I didn't think too much about it then. It was so far away and so remote."

China

He went to Taku, China, after V-J Day, and there was a dragon parade in honor of the American troops when they arrived there. The first night there, they couldn't get their radio working, so they had to return to the ship the next day.

Bob Hope Show

"In early 1944 Bob Hope came to Pavuvu, along with Frances Langford. They flew in separate planes onto our island and did a show for us."

In conclusion, "Our outfit was not scheduled for any other invasions and dissolved after the war ended. They did not need our skill anymore. We were glad that the bombing ended the war."

William Hill – US Army

"War affects everyone…the suffering of wives, mothers, and children. There were so many that didn't come back."

What was it like on December 7, 1941, the day Pearl Harbor was bombed, when you were fourteen or fifteen years old?

Living in Edgewood, south of Indianapolis, he said, "Everything changed—tires, sugar, food was rationed. Many people were drafted—twelve to sixteen million."

Bill attended Tech High School and took classes in Morse code training. In 1944, at age eighteen, he enlisted in the US Army at the armory in downtown Indianapolis. Later he went to Camp Atterbury. He tried to enlist in the navy, but he was color blind, and they would not take him. In 1945 he was sent overseas to Okinawa.

What was an interesting event while you were in the military?

Bill related this story: "We were in Saipan for a month's training. The next step was Okinawa. The last evening, it was rec time. One of the guys received a telegram informing him his brother was killed in Italy. He asked if the fellows would sing the song 'My Buddy.' He said, 'Would you all sing this song?' All the guys sang the song two times for him. In that same spirit, 'My Buddy' was sung by the audience at the Indiana State Museum with him."

Bill said, "War affects everyone…the suffering of wives, mothers, and children. There were so many that didn't come back." He wears his veteran's hat to connect with other WWII vets. They can relate to each other like no one else can. They are comrades; there is a bond between them. Bill is the last man standing—he is the last one of his division left.

Indy Honor Flight

Bill went on the Indy Honor Flight, like many other veterans in Indianapolis. On the way home from Washington, DC, the veterans got mail call on the plane. They never had this honor, of being made to feel so special, when they came home after the war. Mail call during the war meant perfumed letters from Bill's girlfriend. He would smell them first. He gave her an engagement ring while he was in the service and married her when he came home.

What did you think about dropping the atomic bombs on Japan?

Bill said, "It saved thousands and thousands of people. It was unfortunate, but it saved Japanese, US, and Russian lives too. After the second bomb was dropped, we were elated because we knew the war was going to be over."

Bill wanted readers to remember all the men and women who were killed and didn't return from the war. Currently Bill is in a wheelchair but is very eager to talk about his experiences and explain to children about the war. He has a website that he developed with his daughter. He has talked to children at some local schools in Indianapolis.

S/Sgt. Robert C. Hlavacek—US Army
by Deborah Hlavacek Ledbetter
"I was just doing what I was supposed to do or should do."

Bob Hlavacek enlisted in the army before Pearl Harbor with some of his buddies, because he couldn't find a job in the war days of the 1940s. He did mechanic training at Chanute Field. In the military he dropped the *H*, sometimes going by Lavacek, which means "head man" or "large head" or "boss man." He married his wife, Arlene Nigg, and they had seven children, five girls and two boys. Bob was born on August 2, 1921, and died on March 15, 2005, at eighty-four.

Bob was training as a pilot, but while he was flying he chased the cattle in the area. After he was warned not to do it again, he chased the cows and was pulled off pilot training. So he trained to be a navigator on the planes.

The Superfortress left Grand Island Army Airfield, Nebraska, and headed for the West Indies. During one of the missions of search and rescue, his Superfortress army bomber caught fire. At that time he had been married only a short time. Debbie said he remembered thinking, "Please, God, do not let me die. I've only been married two weeks!"

Since the plane was on fire, the pilot dove the plane into the water to try to put the fire out. There was a six-man crew and six observers onboard. Bob squeezed through a little window, as he was a very thin man. Bob saved two people's lives by pulling them out, but the plane was engulfed in flames. He couldn't do anymore. Refusing to take the medals and honors offered to him, he said, "I was just doing what I was supposed to do, or should do." Five members of the crew were lost in the crash.

The crew, lost on a raft floating around Puerto Rico, spent three days without food or water. The guys on the plane had eaten the food and drank the water, so there wasn't anything left on the plane. Deb said, "My dad was always hungry. He was a very hyper, super nervous kind of guy."

After the men were rescued, they spent two weeks in the hospital recovering from dehydration and sunburn. Bob hurt his knee, but he was not really sunburned, since he kept his jumpsuit on in the plane. Most of the others had taken their flight suits off because the plane was so hot.

Since Bob was involved in a plane crash, he could request ground duty, and he did. After the crash he repaired and maintained planes. Planes would come in 24/7, at all times and on all days. The guys needed to be there and available, so they would take naps or maybe get an hour's sleep lying on the hangar floor.

After V-E Day, Bob started training for the invasion of Japan. Many of the veterans interviewed in this book described thinking the invasion would happen soon. All the soldiers were dreading the invasion of Japan. Historical accounts stated one million American soldiers and five or six million Japanese people may have died. Of course only a few people were in the know about the impending development of the atomic bomb.

After the War

After the war Bob returned to the Chicago area. He worked in a factory for a while but didn't like it. Then he was a teaching golf professional. He was a very good golfer. In fact when he was sixteen, Joe Lewis would come pick him up to be his caddy. Some golf courses in that area allowed blacks. Debbie stated, "He trusted Dad so much that he gave Dad the keys to his car." He told Bob to go pick up his wife, Marva, and take her to get groceries. Joe Lewis called him Bobby.

Joe Lewis, professional boxer, entertaining the troops

During the war Joe Lewis would go around to the military bases to entertain the troops with boxing matches. When he was coming to Bob's base, Bob told the guys, "I know Joe Lewis!" They mocked him and said, "Sure you do!" When Joe Lewis did come, he saw Bob and went over to talk with him. Lewis said, "Bobby, come here. Come stand in my corner." So Bob stood behind Joe Lewis while he was fighting.

Debbie described her dad as "a very smart man and a cutup kind of guy!" It would have been a pleasure to meet Bob. He was a hero who didn't want the honors or medals because he was just doing what was expected of him—his duty.

Richard Kolodey—US Marines
"Over a third of the squadron was shot down and killed."

Richard enlisted in Dallas, Texas, on October 17, 1942, when he was seventeen years old. He was born in Brady, Texas, on Valentine's Day 1925. Later his family moved to St. Antonio and Dallas. His father was wounded in Germany during World War I and later died at fifty-nine years old, when Richard was a young man of twenty-one or twenty-two.

Richard participated in three major campaigns in the Solomon Islands from July 1943 to August 1944. According to his discharge papers, he participated in Bismarck Archipelago Operations, the Bougainville Campaign, and the consolidation of the Northern Solomons. He earned a Presidential Citation for meritorious performance of duty in action and a Navy Commendation Medal. He was honorably discharged in November 1945.

Richard qualified for flight air training after boot camp. He was put in the First Marine Air Wing. He was sent to North Island in San Diego for three weeks. "The marines were still part of the navy, and we were flying navy airplanes," Richard explained. Next he was sent to a marine air base in Norman, Oklahoma, for radio, radar, and gunnery training. He had to learn sixteen words in Morse code and how to manipulate the radio. There was a little radar screen. In Pursell, Oklahoma, Richard went to gunnery school, where he learned to shoot fifty-caliber guns out of turrets.

What was your job in the marines?

Richard's job in the marines was belly gunner and turret gunner. "We would take turns flying in the turret and the belly of the plane," he said. "We had a gun out the back. Whoever was in the bottom took care of the radar and radio."

"When I got there, I rode an LST from New Caledonia to New Hebrides, where the airplanes were." Many of the LSTs were made in Evansville, Indiana, just a few miles north of where he lives now in Kentucky. "New Hebrides was the main marine air base in the South Pacific.

"The Solomon Islands consist of over six hundred islands, with Bougainville being the largest and Guadalcanal being second largest. I have landed on fourteen of these islands and have flown over all of them." Richard went on to say, "The marines were doing all the flying, and the navy was bringing all the ships, food, and fuel. The army was down in New Guinea. The Japs had half of the island tied up."

Richard has some information from the archives in Maryland that outlined all the flights, or sorties, they flew during his time in the Solomons. He has a letter from relatives in Ohio who wanted some information on their deceased relatives. He has been researching the background of the flights.

What kind of losses did your squadron suffer?

Richard was in two squadrons—232 and 233. "About a third of the squadron was shot down and killed," he said. "They would check the radar, such as it was in those days. Out in the Solomons, I don't know about the rest of it. If you got shot down in the ocean, they didn't see you again—you were gone."

They lost six planes and eighteen guys on one mine laying mission in Rabaul. He cannot find any living pilots or gunners from those days when he was in the Solomons. He feels like they have all died now.

How many flights were made in a day?

"We flew one hundred sorties a day. They dropped millions of tons of bombs over the islands. The marines were left to take care of the Solomon Islands because of battles in Tarawa and the Marshall Islands. I started at Guadalcanal and ended at Emirau. Emirau, which is near the equator, is 120 degrees in the shade," said Richard.

"At Emirau the airstrips went off both sides of the island. We were bombing at Rabaul, which was the Japanese stronghold in the Pacific. Our planes had a one-thousand-mile range. They put a two-thousand-pound bomb or four five-hundred-pound bombs in them. We could not reach Rabaul. We had to move up to Bougainville in order to get in range of Rabaul. At Bougainville we were about 350 miles from Rabaul. The whole chain of islands runs eight hundred or nine hundred miles. Up to Emirau is 1,400 or 1,500 miles."

How did you get many of the pictures that you have from the war?

Some guys and the Marine Corps had cameras, so Richard was able to have some pictures to keep and to show others seventy-three years later. His sea bag was misplaced, and he lost many of the pictures he had. He has pictures of his class, and there have been twenty or thirty men who were killed from the original class,

Where did you go for furloughs?

Richard went to Brisbane and Sydney for furloughs, to get out of the combat area. He saw Sydney Bay and the Harbor Bridge. "There were kangaroo in the park in Sydney," he said. "They would take half of us at a time, and the others would continue fighting. We got a little room near King's Cross."

He went on to say, "The mess hall was open twenty-four hours a day because we flew twenty-four hours a day."

There is a song that went with the Red Devil Squadron:

> Hush, little Nippo! Stop caterwauling.
> Jump in your foxhole and turn out the light.
> Hark! From the east wind your fathers are calling:
> The Red Devil Squadron is flying tonight.
> Hear in the heavens the drone of their engines;
> Over the palm trees they swing to the right.
> Pray to your honorable ancestors, Nippo.
> The Red Devil Squadron is flying tonight.
> Fast the Avengers slide down on your bivouac.
> The scram of their bombs turns your yellow face white.
> When you clasp the hands of your honorable fathers,
> Say, "The Red Devils were flying tonight!"
>
> Mtsgt. Andy Heaton, Pacific

They destroyed thirty-five enemy ships and ten enemy planes.

Back in the United States-

He returned home on a ship that was carrying P-47s. He said, "Some of them may have been made in Evansville. I don't know. They had them strapped down on the deck."

On returning to the States from the Solomons, Richard went to Cherry Point, North Carolina. Later he applied for flight training and passed the tests. He was assigned to a B-25 squadron. He went to Murray State Teachers College for four months of training classes in navigation, orientation, and everything

Glen Eakle - US Navy
"I never want to see what I saw on the tour again."

"I was drafted at seventeen, in October 1943; they gave us our high school diplomas, even though we weren't there to graduate," Glen said. "No one in my family owned a car, but I hitched a ride from my best buddy's father to the county seat. A school bus picked up all the inductees from Monroe County, Kentucky, and drove us to Louisville, to the army hospital in downtown Shively." Since it was determined that Glen had flat feet, he was assigned to the navy. "Apparently flat feet made me a better swimmer!"

He continued, "The first night in the Great Lakes training center, our group from Louisville was asked for volunteers to drive trucks. I had been cautioned earlier not to fall for that scheme. They wanted people to push wheelbarrows!

"We got in some marching the next day, along with pictures of how to identify Japanese airplanes and warships. We had thirteen weeks of training to change us from the kids some of us were to fighting sailors. All this was going on in February. Hiking and marching was no fun in this kind of weather. The worst activity we had to do in this weather was two days of firefighting. We were practicing with fire hoses and had icicles on our chins, noses, and eyebrows.

"At the end of our training period, we were given a two-week vacation to go home. This was good and bad...I visited with friends and relatives. All this was good. Then, two days before returning to Great Lakes, I contracted the mumps. I called Dr. Smith, and he said that I should stay in bed for ten days. So he called the Red Cross to extend my vacation ten days. Now I know that this illness may have saved my life. When I got back to Great Lakes, I was given light duty for a short time. During that four weeks, all the sailors that I trained with had been assigned to ships and were gone from the training center. A student from my high school who had left with an earlier group was killed."

Irvin Herman – US Navy
"The Japanese were hiding away from the beaches on the island."

Irvin, born and raised in Pennsylvania, graduated from high school in May 1943. On August 9, at age seventeen, he joined the US Navy and reported to the US naval training station at Great Lakes, Illinois, for eight weeks of boot camp. Next, on November 1, 1943, naval training radio school followed in Indianapolis, Indiana, for five months of schooling to become a radio operator.

By March 15, 1944, Irvin was on his way to Oceanside, California, by train. He joined the JASCO, or Fourth Joint Assault Signal Company. The 4th JASCO consisted of navy radiomen and signalmen and marine communications and supporting personnel. They trained on the sandy beaches of Alyso Canyon outside of Oceanside, digging foxholes and setting up radio equipment.

On July 2, 1944, he sailed from San Diego, California, on the *Poelau Laut*, an old Dutch liner that had been converted into a troop ship. The ship had a Dutch captain. Irvin tried to use some of his Pennsylvania Dutch to communicate with the staff, but it didn't work too well. Irvin's grandfather had come from Germany at an early age. The *Poelau Laut* was the ship Irvin was assigned to as a troop to go overseas.

He arrived at the island of Pavuvu about a month later, located in the Solomon Islands. On Pavuvu the 4th JASCO joined the First Marine Division. At that point they were divided into communication teams and different battalions. Irvin's mission was to engage in training maneuvers in preparation for the invasion of Peleliu.

They left Pavuvu on September 4, 1944, on LST troop ships for Peleliu, a two-mile-wide by six-mile-long island in the Palau Islands. On Peleliu, they landed on the beaches after several days of intense shelling and bombing of the island by the navy and air force. "Approximately ten thousand Japanese soldiers were dug in the cliffs and caves," said Irvin. "At night they would slide open some doors in the cliff and throw mortar shells down on the beach. They were shelling the beach as we were coming in for the landing.

pertaining to flying. He met his future wife at Murray State. They dated and were married for over fifty years. In 1996 she died of cancer.

Giving back today

Today he speaks at local schools about his WWII experiences and has had several write-ups in the local newspapers. He still drives and has coffee with his buddies at the local café in town.

Richard has not missed going to Sunday school for over sixty-eight years. He has an attendance pin for each year. His goal is to get to seventy years of perfect attendance. God bless him!

Earl Lautzenheiser – US Army
"The Japanese tried to find us and dig us out."

Earl was drafted into the US Army on April 4, 1942, when he was twenty-two years old. He was first sent to Ft. Wayne, Indiana, with about a hundred other men to be sworn in and get their shots (lots of them, he said) and physicals. He had worked in a gas station with his brother before being drafted.

Earl took the bus to Indianapolis. He was sick and was sent to the hospital for five days. When he was released from the hospital, all the other GIs in his group were gone. He was sent to Drew Field, which was a tent city, in Tampa, Florida, on the troop train. There were no buildings. He was there for about three weeks.

From Florida he took the troop train to San Francisco, California. It took five days. There were about a thousand men on the train. No one knew where they were going at that point. "Orders were when the train made a stop, there was to be one soldier on one side and one soldier on the other side of the train to guard the exits. The orders were to shoot anyone that tried to get away," said Earl.

Was anyone ever shot?

Earl said, "No."

Earl didn't officially go through basic training. He had a small amount of training on five guns, including the Tommy gun, the '03 rifle, and handguns. Earl grew up with a rifle and shotgun, so he had no trouble with shooting.

After five days they arrived in San Francisco, California. "They don't tell you anything," said Earl. Many of the men had never seen the Pacific Ocean before, so as they were going under the Golden Gate Bridge there was quite a lot of excitement. They would be returning to San Francisco in two and half years.

Earl's job was in the signal corps working with the radar unit assigned to the air corps. He said, "During roll call they asked if anyone wanted to go to radio training, so I said I did. The officers in charge said I couldn't go because I hadn't gone through basic yet." He had missed basic training when he was ill and in the hospital. Making a joke and being silly, he said, "I won't go overseas because I haven't had basic training." Earl said, "At the end of the day, I was told that I would be going overseas!"

Brisbane, Australia

While on the troop ship, Earl and his fellow soldiers docked in Auckland, New Zealand to pick up some civilians who had escaped from the Japanese. These people were from some islands nearby. Earl didn't talk to them, as they were on another part of the ship. When the ship docked in Australia, there was an airplane flying above the ship with a tail sign reading

"WELCOME YANKS." Earl got a little choked up while telling this part of the story.

"The Australians were so nice and grateful that we were there," he said. During this time in Australia, the American troops got in groups and marched. "It was too hard to exercise on the ship, so they had to toughen you up." They were in Brisbane for approximately six weeks. They spent the time training and assembling equipment.

New Guinea

New Guinea, north of Australia, was still overrun with Japanese during this time in the war. Another soldier asked Earl, "Do you have your foxhole dug yet? You will!" It was important to be protected if there was an attack.

Earl's unit was stationed fifty miles down the coast from Port Moresby, the capital city. The Japanese had control of the east coast of New Guinea and the tip of the island. "We were driving them back up the coast," said Earl. "There were other platoons of radar groups set up too. Each platoon was self-sufficient, with a cook, radar operator, et cetera. Their job was to pick up enemy activity fifty miles away. That gave our guys time to get our fighters in the air. That ten to twelve minutes before the enemy got there was often enough time to keep people safe. Many times fighters on duty would sleep in their planes."

Part of Earl's job was to tell our people the enemy was on the way by phoning or using the telegraph. "The Japanese tried to find us and dig us out." Earl used the decoding machine and sent coded messages.

"The worst time I had was during an air raid, when the signal went off, and I didn't have a foxhole! Japanese planes flew right over me, just above the trees, and dropped bombs a few feet away from me." All soldiers had their own foxholes just by their tents. Then they could roll out of bed into the foxholes.

Earl was not involved in hand-to-hand combat, but he saw some of the captured Japanese prisoners in camp and some dead Japanese soldiers. He never got close to them or tried to talk to them. However, one of the GIs who was guarding the prisoners said, "They don't want to escape. They have been taken prisoner, and they are happy about it. The Japanese prisoners seemed perfectly happy."

Coming Home

Earl was relieved of duty on October 15, 1944, after two and a half years in New Guinea. He went back to San Francisco and then home for leave. The troops saw the Golden Gate Bridge again, except this time they were going home, so there was quite an uproar of whooping and hollering.

After being home for a while, Earl was so cold, he didn't want to be stationed near home in Indiana. He was assigned to a desk job in Santa Ana, California. He was sent to New York for a month for schooling, to learn to "process out" soldiers who were discharged and returning to civilian life. At that time, he achieved the rank of sergeant and was working in personal affairs.

Family

Earl met Su on the Super Chief train when he was returning from his grandfather's funeral in 1945. They exchanged addresses and wrote to each other. He was discharged from the Army on October 23, 1945, and they were married on December 3, 1945. After his captain talked him into it, he was in the air force reserves for thirty years.

A Couple of Funny Stories

During roll call it was asked, "Who can type?" Earl said he could. Out of a thousand men, he was the only one who could type, so he got a job as a clerk. Earl had taken typing in high school. He wasn't sure if he was the only one who could type out of all the men or just the only one who would admit it!

Another story was that he was nicknamed Effie by the other men in his group because he was bowlegged. Effie was in a comic strip or cartoon series during the 1930's. The lieutenant where he worked said, "Who is Lautzenheiser?" Earl thought he was joking, but the lieutenant thought Earl's real name was Heffie [or Effie], not Lautzenheiser.

Charles McDonald – US Army
By Kew Bee McDonald and Robin McDonald

Charlie's wife, Kew Bee said, "I was a freshman, and Charlie was a sophomore. It was a terrible four years in high school. Times were tough for Evansville because of the Depression and the 1937 flood." Then Kew Bee said, "When Charlie turned eighteen, he was drafted. It didn't matter that he had not graduated from high school. He had to go anyway." Charlie was in the army from September 1943 to March 1946. "He wanted to be in the navy, being a river man, but he was just three people away from the desk when they said they were full. He had to join the army infantry unit.

"Charlie was assigned to New Guinea, Luzon, Philippines, and Japan. He spent eighteen months overseas." Kew Bee has saved many commendations and letters from Charlie's time in the army.

When asked about dropping the atomic bombs on Japan, she said, "It was terrible what they did at Pearl Harbor. It was terrible what they did to the Japanese children. The Japanese would not have given up without the bomb being dropped on them."

Charlie McDonald, as Reported by His Son, Robin McDonald

Charlie was on guard duty, and his replacement came to relieve him. When the fellow soldier asked if he had seen anything, Charlie said, "There were some Japanese soldiers over there, with white gloves and white hoods." The replacement said, "Stay here, and I'll be back." He knew what that meant. He came back with a crank radio and radioed the ships. The ship's guns blew up the ammo dump. It went off for three days and three nights. He felt like he had saved some US soldiers' lives by helping to get rid of the ammo dump. Charlie said the shells fired by the ships looked like Volkswagens flying through the air.

Robin also mentioned this story, which his father told to another veteran:

Charlie was scared to death all the time he was overseas. He was just a country boy. He showed other soldiers how to shoot guns. He never wanted to know people very well, as you never knew if they would make it or not.

Charlie got to know and respect his drill sergeant. The drill sergeant was a short guy, and he liked to box. So Charlie and the sergeant had a boxing match. The sergeant beat him well. When they landed on what they thought was a secure beach, the sergeant was standing on the beach giving orders. Suddenly he was shot in the head by a Japanese sniper and died. Charlie was scared!

Arlin McRae—US Marines
"K rations are the nastiest things in the world."

"I was one of the strangest marines you would ever encounter. My mother was a strict Methodist. She didn't believe in any sinning at all. No sinning! I made a vow that I would do nothing that my parents would disapprove. No drinking. No gambling. No cursing. I kept that vow." Being the youngest of 150 marines, Arlin was nicknamed "Chick"; the oldest was called 'Pop."

He graduated from high school in Griffin, Indiana, one of only six graduates. He received his draft notice in 1943, on his birthday. He then explained how he became a marine. There were three desks during the physicals, and when he sat down beside the desk he asked to go into the navy, but they had reached their quota for the day. So the marine sergeant said he should go into the marines. Arlin said, "I only weigh a hundred and twenty-six pounds." The marine officer said, "That's OK. You will make a smaller target."

Arlin described himself as "a green country boy." He was sent to a marine base in San Diego. He was told by an officer that he was in the Marine Corps now—he wasn't supposed to be tired.

He told of a time he was with some drunk friends near Oceanside, California, and all the problems he had getting them back to camp without getting caught by the MPs. He wouldn't go out with them again. However, one of guys, who had a brown belt, later told him how to do some tae kwon do moves he could use to protect himself.

He spent an extra week in basic training so he could learn to swim. To qualify, he had to swim three times the width of the pool, which he couldn't do because his mother hadn't believed in letting him swim at home. So when he got liberty in Los Angeles, he went to the YMCA and taught himself to swim.

"There were eighty to a company, and I was the smallest. I hated boot camp, and I didn't make any friends."

Camp Pendleton, California

On to Camp Pendleton, where he found he was really good at throwing antitank grenades. "It fitted down over the end of your rifle, and you would fire the rifle," he said. "It was used to destroy tanks or pillboxes." Arlin explained that pillboxes "are like igloos—instead of being make of ice, they are made of steel-enforced concrete, and it has slits on four sides that you fire machine guns out of."

At Camp Pendleton, "we marched five miles morning, noon, and night. We trained on rafts and how to exit a ship and how to use netting, et cetera." His worst experience in California was on a twenty-nine-mile hike up a mountain. Many of the guys were sick and passing out. He passed out and was sick much of the next day.

"My regiment, the 26th division, left the States and went to help Guam. We left early, and when we got out to sea almost everybody got over their seasickness.

Hawaii

"We learned that Guam had been secured, and they didn't need us. We stopped in Hawaii; between two mountains you could see the lava. We arrived at Parker Ranch, the second largest ranch in the country, with the King Ranch in Texas being the largest," said Arlin. "The Parker Ranch leased the ranch to the United States for one dollar a year. So that is where we trained. You would think training in Hawaii would be great, but it was hot. It could be blowing red dust, drizzling rain, and the sun shining all at the same time. It was not a very pleasant place at all. If you bivouacked all night, they would bring you breakfast in the morning, and it would have a layer of red dust on top of it."

They trained there until Tokyo Rose said on the radio the marines were going to leave on January 1, 1945. "Tokyo Rose said, 'We don't know where they are going and what place they are attacking, but the 5th Marine Division is leaving January first.' So we were afraid they would destroy our ships with our equipment ammunition on them. There were Japanese submarines around there.

"Well, a few months prior to this we were ordered to build ammo dumps in the hills behind Hilo, Hawaii. It rained every day in the afternoon, so every day in the morning we would work building the ammo dumps and go into town in the afternoon. We would go to a movie, take a nap, or go to this little café in town. There was this cute little waitress who had long black hair. She was of Hawaiian and Chinese descent. The guys used to kid me about dating her, but she said, 'My mother won't let me date marines.' I think she had a very smart mother!

"She was a cashier and would leave her place and come over and talk with us. We were there for two weeks, and the last week she said, 'Do you read shorthand?' She wrote a lot of things on the napkin and said, 'Take this back to camp and find someone that reads shorthand.'" After laughing, he said, "Now, where am I going to find someone who read shorthand?"

"They got [us] up at four in the morning and put us on flat cars, and no one was supposed to know we were leaving, but everybody knew. When [we] passed the fields, the workers in the pineapple fields were tossing things down. You just never knew what you were going to catch. We left on January second instead of the first."

"The whole time I was in the service, I never got a furlough. My family had never seen me in a uniform, so I had this taken in Hilo and had a bunch of pictures taken before we left Hilo. They were sent to my family."

Why didn't you get a furlough?

"I got mess duty instead. I got mess duty for a whole month. So when I went to apply for a furlough, the sergeant said, 'You are going on a trip, but you are going west instead of east.'"

He went on to say, "You couldn't get anything from the quartermaster. Then this lieutenant came around and said, 'We need six volunteers to go help at the quartermaster's shack for the navy. We are going to load some boxes onto trucks to go a navy ship.' We said, 'Why don't those damn swabbies load their own ship?'

"You know the marines are part of the navy. They can command us to do it, and we have to do it. So I was one of the six people to load the ship. The lieutenant said, 'There is this box of socks, and we need socks to fight with more than the navy does to swab decks. I want you to steal socks. Not just enough for yourself—I want you to steal enough for the whole company, two hundred and fifty men. I'll tell you the boxes are long and narrow and high.

I'll tell you where they are located. This is what you are to do: Throw a box or two, and then wait awhile. Then throw another box or two, and I will go around in the jeep and pick them up.'"

Arlin said, "We stole enough socks for everyone in the company. I also saw some fur-lined vests and a navy sweater that I stole too." He laughed as he said his mother would have died. This was his first experience with stealing. When someone stole his bayonet after mess duty. The lieutenant said, "Doesn't anyone else have one on mess duty? Son, I don't want someone in my company that can't take care of themselves. A good marine is never caught short, but he's never caught stealing." Enough said, I guess.

Iwo Jima

"So we were told on ship that we were going to attack a little island called Iwo Jima. None of us had ever heard of it before. Iwo Jima was an island that was shaped like a kidney. It was a volcanic island, and Mt. Suribachi was on it. We were told we were going to land at the base of it. My regiment, the 5th marine outfit, was to attack at the base of the volcano.

"The night before the ship landed was total blackout. The Japanese were bombarding it from several different directions. We got up the next morning at four o'clock and ate an early breakfast. I went back and patched my clothes, because I kept getting letters from Mom saying, 'We can't buy clothes because it's all going overseas.' I thought, well who the hell is getting it? I had holes in my trousers, holes in the knees and seat, and holes in my socks. I patched and patched because I lived on the farm during the Depression, so I knew how to patch.

"At eight in the morning, we left our ship and went down the netting to the landing barge, or Higgins boat. We waited and waited until everyone was ready to go, so at nine o'clock we went in and attacked Iwo Jima. We went in with the second wave. Boats were being hit with artillery all around us. The sand on the beach was so deep, you would sink down to your knees in it. It was slow going."

Was there anyone killed from your group?

"Oh my, yes. Going in, we survived pretty well. The first guy that got killed going in was shot between the eyes. He was our first death. I foxholed with him the first night. He was a really good guy to foxhole with.

"Our first really bad experience on Iwo Jima came on the nineteenth of February. It wasn't too bad until about the twenty-third. That morning there was cold drizzle, and I was running along with Richard Hall, my buddy from California. He was blond and had a big smile. He got more letters from girls than the whole rest of our platoon put together. He was going to introduce babes to me after the war." This sergeant said to Richard, "Come on, we are going this way."

"The first shell struck that morning knocked me off my feet. My nose was bleeding, and I couldn't hear very well. I turned on my stomach and looked where Richard was and wondered if that shell hit. I looked on the ridge and saw the body of this boy. His head and one arm was gone. The only way that I knew it was Richard was he carried a Browning automatic rifle, a rifle that will fire thirty rounds at a time. There are only three Browning automatic rifles in a squad. There was a Browning rifle there. It was Richard. They dropped shells constantly.

"It was a horrible day. I was scared, and my mouth felt like it was pulled back. I looked scared. This tough sergeant said, 'Chick, it will get better tomorrow,'" said Arlin. "I did not recognize him. Then I noticed everybody looked that way, so I stopped worrying about it.

"We were going to meet up at this pillbox. We got to the bottom of that ridge, and I didn't see another soul. My rifle didn't work, as it was clogged with sand and rust. Neither would the sergeant's rifle. The only weapon of the three of us that was working was a forty-five pistol. We all had hand grenades, but [they were] useless against machine guns. We got up to the bottom of that ridge, and we started getting machine gun fire. We dived in behind the shell hole. We didn't see a soul for an hour or two. Probably the biggest liar in the whole outfit came up with this Browning rifle. We told him to shoot toward the pillbox, and then we were now able to get inside the shell hole, instead of just behind it.

"The only heroic thing that I did on the whole island is we heard this moaning, and we crawled up to the rim of the shell hole. I saw this guy from our outfit pulling himself along. He was shot in the hips and thigh so that he couldn't walk. I said, 'Frost, that guy isn't going to make it.' We ran up with my poncho, rolled him on it, and jerked him down into the shell hole with us.

"I started working on my rifle. They were shelling the pillbox from the other side, and the Japanese were too busy to pay any attention to us anymore. The lieutenant jumped into the shell hole with us and said we are going to move out, as our rifles are not working any longer. So Frost said that somebody is going to have to move Hardin, the injured soldier. Frost said, 'No, you are not big enough. Move out like the lieutenant told you to do.'" So Arlin left. "I never saw Sgt. Frost again."

"K Rations are the nastiest things in the world," said Arlin. "I had trouble eating them. I couldn't stand the layer of grease on top of them. The crackers were old and stale, like they had been around for five or ten years!

"This guy that I was sharing watch with would always take the second watch. Well, the first watch is from ten to twelve. I would wake him up and say, 'Are you awake?' And he would say, 'Yeah, yeah.'" Arlin said, "He would promptly go to sleep. When it's your time to go to sleep on the front line, you are going to go to sleep because you are so exhausted. In the morning I would be ready to kill him, as they often bayoneted people on the front line.

"Going to sleep on the front line is awful, and every night we both went to sleep." They also disagreed about the size of the foxhole. Arlin wanted it deep, long and narrow, so a grenade couldn't be tossed in it. His foxhole buddy "wanted [it] to be comfortable and big." How can a foxhole be comfortable?

"A good friend of mine awakened with a Jap getting ready to kill my foxhole buddy." Arlin's friend jumped up and couldn't get to his rifle, so he knocked the Jap out with his helmet. Then he got to his rifle and killed him.

"This guy jumped down in my foxhole and said, 'My foxhole buddy goes to sleep every night.'" Arlin said his foxhole buddy did too. So they were able to switch foxhole buddies, so their lives were not in more danger.

Arlin and his platoon were foxholed down in a valley of sand. "They first tried to bring supplies over to us by truck," he said. "The Japanese knocked out the trucks. Then they tried to bring them over by jeep, but they knocked them out too. So now they are short on food and ammunition. Now they were trying it by using men, and only one got through—probably twenty to twenty-five men. We were watching them kill those guys." There was a cliff above, and they were firing on them from above. The one who got through asked Arlin if he would pass out the mail to his outfit. Arlin said, "Yes, I will." So the guy said, "I got to get back before dark, or I will get shot by my own men."

"I was sending it up by air mail—tearing off the corner and putting sand in it, and then calling out a name. One guy had three letters. I called and called to no avail. I thought that maybe he was across this ravine on the next ridge. So

I stood up to call him. We were on a ridge where we were shot from the cliff. You left your foxhole by jumping up and rolling past the line of fire. I was stupid. I was passing it out by air mail. Arlin called, 'Poppin.' Poppin was a soldier who had a letter.

Were you ever injured?

About this time I felt this thing on my jaw. When I put my hand up, I was bleeding profusely. This red-complexioned guy turned completely white when he saw me, because he had lost his whole fire team a few days before that. I said, 'I think I have been shot.'

"It didn't hurt except where it burned my neck. The other guy went to find a corpsman. Then I had to get back across that valley. The corpsman wrapped me. They couldn't get tape to stick because of my beard. He had to wrap it first one way, then another. It looked like my head had been half blown off.

"Getting back across this no man's land from the ridge, I would look for shell holes and zigzag across that way. I was looking for a command post so I could get everything taken care of. There was a guy where a shell had torn his chin off, and his face was covered with blood. 'I am heading for the command post,' [I said]. 'Come with me, and I will get you there.' So I led him back to the command station. The next morning the bandages bled, and this side of my head looked like it had been blown off. I saw a guy from my outfit and gave him the three letters. He said, 'I will get those to him. Thank you.'

"About nine o'clock in the morning, they loaded us in a jeep made into [an] ambulance and took us to the beach. We were waiting for someone to take us to the ship. Everyone said, 'We don't have orders to pick up the wounded.' We were there until two o'clock in the afternoon. Nobody would take us to the hospital ship. Finally this corpsman said, 'The next sailor that comes by will take you guys, or he's not leaving this island.' This guy came by, and the corpsman told him to take us to the ship. Again, the sailor says, 'I don't have orders to pick up wounded.'

"He pulled the bolt on his carbine and said, 'You have your orders now. If you don't take these guys back to the hospital ship, you are never leaving this island.' He said, 'OK, I'll take them back.'

"They took the wounded over to the hospital ship on a Higgins boat. A guy with a megaphone dropped a net down in the Higgins boat that we were in. 'All you guys that can climb, go ahead and climb on up and get aboard,' [he said]. They had two corpsmen down in the boat with the wounded. I started climbing the net when the guy with the megaphone said, 'Don't let the guy with the bloody head climb.' They pulled me back down and made me lay down flat. If I don't get to see the horizon line, then I get seasick. I didn't want to get sick and choke. If I start to vomit, I will choke to death.

"When the corpsmen were working with another guy, I started climbing up the netting. Again they were able to reach me, but this time they stuck me with a needle, and I floated back down. When I awoke, I was aboard the ship. This was my exit from Iwo Jima.

"I was here for three weeks. I went to the hospital on Guam. It was monsoon season, and it poured down rain. They delivered my sea bag, and nothing in it was worth keeping except the Bible the Griffin War Mothers had sent to me." Everything else in the bag was trashed—his clothes, the shorthand note from the waitress in the café in Hawaii, his shoes, and other things—except the Bible, which he had read every night since he'd left home. He was indeed a strange marine.

"After I came back from the hospital, everyone was acting strangely. I was sent down to have work done on my jaw." He was mistakenly sent to a psych ward. After he was reassigned to another ward, "the guy next to me was studying to be a Methodist minister. Out of fifty men in his outfit, only three were not wounded or killed.

"After I left the hospital, I returned to my outfit. We were training for the invasion of Japan. We would have invaded Japan on November 1, 1945. We knew where we were going to attack…everything. Instead we went into Japan as occupation troops. I was acting sergeant. We had a new lieutenant in Japan. My guys on guard kept complaining that this lieutenant kept trying to surprise the guys on guard. You have to scare him badly enough that he won't come climbing by. They both had Browning rifles. When they said, 'Halt, halt, halt,' the lieutenant about died, and he could see sixty rounds coming his way. Well, that stopped that. He never came down through the hills again."

Where were you stationed in Japan?

"The southernmost part of Japan, Kyushu. Our marine division was disbanded. The captain came around and said, 'You do some sketching, don't you?' Mostly they were paintings of guys' girlfriends. He asked, 'Could you take an aerial photograph of this section we are in and make a map out of it?'" Arlin thought, *I haven't done maps since the seventh grade.* "So I made a map of that area." The captain also asked, "Could you take this map and an interpreter and go up in the hills and find the caves where things are stored and the building where things are stored? Then turn the map over and survey what is in all these things."

Arlin said, "We did this. They had lots left to fight with. The interpreter asked, 'Want to ride back to camp?'" They found this little train or tractor. He drove it back to camp for all the guys to see. "It was used to haul torpedoes down to the submarines during the war."

My Only Regret

"This captain who did legal things in the military wanted me to go with him to collect war crimes materials. 'I think you would be handy to have along,' [he said]. 'Do you drive?' Yes, I drive. 'I would like to bring you along with me. You have enough points to go home. It might extend the time you might be overseas. Undoubtedly six months, and maybe as much as a year. Well, we will be in Formosa and Korea and down in the islands. The orders for you to go home will come here, and we may not be here.' Oh, I wanted to go home. I always thought since what is a year in this ninety-year period? What a fool I was." Instead he went to Nagasaki for three months.

Do you think we should have dropped the bomb on Japan?

"It was necessary to stop the war. They were well prepared to fight. Oh my, yes. We had prepared to invade Japan before the bombs were dropped."

Wilbur Meyer – US Navy
"Two days later, this same Jap sub sunk the USS *Indianapolis*."

Wilbur was eating lunch at Edwards Drive-In on Indianapolis's south side. He was wearing his hat with the USS *Catfish* on the front—a sure indicator that he was a WWII veteran. An interview was scheduled for the next day, September 11—it seemed like a fitting day. Wilbur was born on January 20, 1924, so he is ninety-three years old and very sharp about details.

What do you remember about Pearl Harbor?

He related a story in which he was working at a filling station on that Sunday morning. A fellow came in and said, "The Japanese bombed Pearl Harbor. Wilbur said, "Where in the hell is Pearl Harbor?" He went on to say, "It was coming…Germany and Japan were sneaky. I don't trust the Japanese. They are like a pit bull—they will turn on you without you knowing it."

Wilbur was in the Navy for forty-two months, from December 23, 1942, to February 15, 1946. He was eighteen when he went into the navy and went to Great Lakes for boot camp. He went to service school as a machinist. His first ship was the USS *Protector ARS-14*. He was assigned to the engine room and went to Alaska. It was a repair and salvage ship that picked up sunken landing craft and anything that was underwater.

In February 1944 he volunteered for submarine duty. Wilbur went to sub school in New London, Connecticut. He asked for new construction, so he got the *Catfish* around February 1945. Construction started on the *Catfish* on January 6, 1944. It was launched on November 16, 1944. The men slept on barges while it was being built. They practiced on simulators so they would be ready when it was completed. He was a "plankie"—that is, when you commission a boat, you put the boat in commission.

He played a lot of basketball for the sub basketball team. In January 1945 their team was ranked thirteenth. He played a lot of ball waiting for the *Catfish* to be commissioned.

Japan

Wilbur said, "We went to the South Pacific, 4 May 1945, Key West, Panama, Pearl Harbor, and [I] was assigned to Guam. On August 8 the first war patrol of the *Catfish*, and it was sent on a special mission to locate a minefield off Kyushu, Japan."

Wilbur went on to say, "We had the new special underwater equipment, plotting mine fields—sound gear or mine plotting sound gear. Mines were put in a pattern. They [the Japanese] knew where they were, but we didn't. It worked fine straight ahead but didn't work so well off to the peripheral. The mine cables would scrape against the side of the hull. The cables were attached to the mine and went down three or four feet."

In one story he told, Wilbur and his crew were trapped for three or four hours about fifty miles from Nagasaki, near the southern end of Japan, where the atomic bomb was dropped. They couldn't find their way out of the minefield. Wilbur said, "The auxiliary officer thought he might have to relieve Captain Overton because he was getting antsy." Finally, they worked their way out and found an opening to escape the minefield.

Guam

In another incident they left Guam about July 28 for station. Two days after that, the USS *Indianapolis* was sunk. "A Japanese sub fired two torpedoes at us. They had to go to a hard right to split them. The order was 'all ahead flank, hard right rudder' toward the torpedoes. The captain came running into the control room. We knew what was happening. The torpedoes were coming toward the starboard bow." Wilbur explained, "When a torpedo is coming toward a sub, you need to turn and split them. They missed us by about twenty-five feet." The Japanese sub commander was interviewed about the sinking of the USS *Indianapolis*, and he said they had missed a sub two earlier, which was the *Catfish*. Wilbur said, "Two days later this same Jap sub sunk the USS *Indianapolis*."

Wilbur was called Red in the navy, since he had red hair. His job on the sub was to blow the water out of the hole. He was the high-pressure man. If you blow negative—blow water out to go up. Always repeat what they said to make sure of the commands.

The captain of the *Catfish*, Captain Bill Overton, was called in the inquest about the USS *Indianapolis*. He was asked, "Why didn't you report the near miss of the Japanese sub?"

Captain Overton replied, "I am here, aren't I?" The captain was very conservative. He had sealed orders—they tell what to do, and the orders didn't say to engage the sub. "He felt it was more important to plot minefields instead of [playing] cops and robbers," said Wilbur.

After reading *In Harm's Way,* by Doug Stanton, one question stands out: could things have ended differently for the *Indianapolis* if the captain of the *Catfish* had reported their encounter with the Japanese sub?

On July 1, 1971, the *Catfish* was transferred to Argentina. It was renamed the *Santa Fe*. Wilbur said it was involved in the British action about Argentina and sunk at dockage during the short Falkland Islands war. Wilbur said, "I wore a black armband to school for three days." It was towed to deep water and sunk. That was the end of the *Catfish*!

As a sidebar, Wilbur said, "The *Catfish* was out of radio contact for a week while on the way to Argentina." They went into some place and partied for a week, then went on to deliver the sub to Argentina. Wilbur said, "It [the *Catfish*] was the flagship of the Argentina navy. They had one sub and one cruiser. I knew they were in trouble!"

What do you think about dropping the bomb on Japan?

"Truman made a wise decision. We would have killed a lot of Japanese and our soldiers. They would never have surrendered. They were superstitious and thought the world was coming to an end when the bomb was dropped."

When Wilbur came back home, he continued his college education at Indiana State. He'd had one quarter done in 1942 when he'd joined the navy. He got a year and a half credit from the navy, for sub construction and diesel electric. He changed his major to industrial arts and PE. He became a secondary school teacher at the smallest school in Indiana, near Greensburg. There were fifty-nine students in the whole school. Then he taught at schools in Sunman and Plymouth, Indiana. Finally he taught industrial arts at Franklin Township from December 1956 to 1986, when he retired from teaching.

Wilbur is involved in the US Submarine Veterans of WWII, of which there are only fifteen left in Indy, as of this writing. He is the past president of the organization. Many of the remaining artifacts are at the Indiana Military Museum in Vincennes, Indiana, which is located in southwestern Indiana.

John Miller—US Army
"At ninety-three, all my friends are dead now."

When John was sixteen, he quit high school to farm. "They were talking about war, so I joined the home guard at sixteen." The home guard commander was Jack Biggers, a WWI veteran. On June 2, 1941, at age eighteen, John joined the army and did basic training at Camp Wallace, Texas. He was in Midland, Texas, training for war when Japan bombed Pearl Harbor. John was assigned to the 197 Coast Guard artillery. After the news of the attack on Pearl Harbor, "[we] loaded everything on a train and went to New York City to protect the harbor."

After six weeks in New York, he was assigned to the 237th Anti-Aircraft Artillery Regiment and sent to California. He left for the South Pacific aboard the USS *Monterey*, a luxury ship. There were five thousand troops on the ship. They started toward the Philippines. Japan had taken the Philippines, so the ship was sent to Western Australia. After forty days on the ship, they arrived in Townsville, Australia.

"Most of the island around Australia had been taken by the Japanese. They sent General Douglas MacArthur there to build the Sixth Army to fight their way back to the Philippines. The Japs were bombing Townsville. They loaded the unit on an LST ship, and they took Port Moresby, New Guinea. It was about two hundred miles from Townsville, Australia.

"After that was secured, we were sent to Lae, New Guinea, with the Sixth Army. When Lae was secured, the 237th, with the Sixth Army, was sent thirty miles inland, to where the Japs had a good airstrip. The 237th, along with the 513 Paratroop unit, took the airstrip from the Japs. When that was secured, the Sixth Army and the 237th unit was sent to Wadke Island. They were getting close to the Philippines and were sent to Dutch New Guinea to get ready to take back the Philippines. October 20, 1944, the Sixth Army invaded Leyte, Philippines.

"On December 13, 1944, one of our LST ships was hit by a kamikaze Jap plane, and they were sunk. Our unit got an another LST and went with the invasion December 15, 1944. On Christmas Eve, December 24, 1944, the Japs tried to take the island of Mindoro, Philippines, back from the Sixth Army. They fought all night, and the US Navy came back and helped them. So, with the help from the good Lord and the US Navy, they kept the island!"

"After the invasion of Leyte, Philippines, General Douglas MacArthur came wading ashore. He made the statement, 'I have returned.' The 237th unit, along with the Sixth Army, on December 15, invaded Mindoro, Philippines. It was only about three hundred miles from Manila, Philippines. There was a good Jap airstrip on Mindoro, so they took that. We did a lot of praying.

About this time John contracted dengue fever, malaria, and jungle rot on his hands and feet. He was sent home on temporary duty, as he was supposed to return to the Philippines. In thirty days, on May 12, he returned to the United States.

"The war was over in Europe, and I was sent to Camp Atterbury. The army had started the point system to discharge the soldiers. If you had eighty-five points, you could get out of the army. I had been overseas for forty-two months and in the army for four years. I had a hundred and twenty-eight points, and I was the third man out of Camp Atterbury on the point system. I caught a bus to Cave City, Kentucky, and hired a taxi to take me home to Temple Hill. I thanked the good Lord for being home." In 1957 he earned his high school diploma.

While doing some shopping in Glasgow, Kentucky, he met his future wife. "She winked at me, and I got a date that day. I thought she was the prettiest thing I had ever seen. I hadn't seen anybody but New Guinea natives for nearly four years!" They dated for four months; then he and Christine were married. They were married for nearly sixty-seven years, until Christine's death in 2013.

John and one other soldier are the only two still living out of 236 soldiers in the 237th unit.

Dick Negus—US Navy
"Even though I wasn't in combat, I saw men die."

What were your feelings about Pearl Harbor?

"I was thirteen years old at the time of the bombing of Pearl Harbor. That evening my dad was called up to go to the coast to look for Japanese ships. They didn't see any enemy ships or subs." In the 1940s, before or around the time of the Pearl Harbor bombing, the area where he lived was a ranch, but now it's Vandenberg Air Force Base, located nine miles northwest of Lompoc, California.

Two weeks after Pearl Harbor, some soldiers went down to San Luis Obispo to mount thirty-caliber machine guns on the coast, near where Dick lived. There was a fear that the United States could be attacked on the West Coast. A classmate of Dick's saw a sub off the coast and came to school the next day to tell everyone.

In April 1945 there was a shipwreck and several of the Sea Scouts, sixteen- to seventeen-year-olds, were called to help. Dick was a member of the Sea Scouts. They were called out of high school to help with the shipwreck because all the soldiers from Camp Cook were gone fighting the war. Apparently this LCT, or landing craft tank, hadn't negotiated a landing and had come up to the sand dune and landed on the rocks. An LCT is a smaller LST; this one was commanded by a young ensign and his crew.

"It was up on the rocks, and you could see under it," said Dick. They had misjudged where they were. No one was hurt in the incident, but they needed help unloading the LCT. The Sea Scouts helped by taking things off the ship.

Someone handed Dick a box to carry. He slipped on seaweed or something and dropped the box. Everyone became quiet, and someone told him not to do that, as the box contained ammunition—live twenty-millimeter shells. He could have blown up!

Military Service

In 1946, at age eighteen, Dick enlisted in the navy. He had wanted to join at seventeen, but his mom wouldn't let him and refused to sign the papers. He went to boot camp at San Diego and served aboard the USS *Benner DD-807* destroyer. His ship started to head to Hawaii but was called back. The military had a shortage of fuel, so they had to return to San Diego.

"We were targeting at San Clemente, near San Diego, California. Even though I wasn't in combat, I saw men die." He went on to explain about a plane incident. A group of dive bombers were there when one bomb hit an airplane. Due to friendly fire, he saw people fall from the sky.

Dick received a World War II Victory Medal for participation in service. These were given in the armed forces from December 7, 1941, through December 31, 1946.

Howard Norlin—US Navy
"Don't want to hear it. Heard it too much during the war."

Howard Norlin, born in Duluth, Minnesota, in 1923, graduated from high school in June 1941. On December 7, 1941, he and girlfriend, Connie, was at a toboggan ride; when they returned to the car and turned on the car radio, the announcer said Pearl Harbor had been bombed. For the next six months, he paced the floor. He was working, and all his buddies were in the military already. In the spring of 1942, Howard joined the navy and took the train down to Minneapolis. His military career would span mid-1942 until December 1945.

He took a train to Farragut, Idaho Naval Base, near Spokane, which took four days. Later he went to work in a hospital in Seattle, where he stayed downtown in a rooming house. He went to x-ray school and completed six months' training in Bethesda, Maryland. He mentioned seeing FDR coming out of the elevator at the hospital every other day.

He was assigned to the USS *Goshen*, [Marine Troop Carrier] a ship out of San Francisco, California. Howard saw lots of casualties, as he was one of six medical techs aboard. They went back and forth to and from Hawaii to pick up troops. "Our ship fed them with more men. We were involved in twenty to twenty-five invasions." There were about three hundred marines on a ship, who were unloaded onto landing boats from a front hatch when attacking islands.

Celebrations

Some of the highlights of his career were a deck party where an all-black female group performed and another Southern black group performed *Porgy and Bess*. Some of the soldiers and officers were prejudiced at first but changed their attitude after getting acquainted with the performers. There was also a crossing the equator ceremony where they had to crawl across a deck to get through this thing full of garbage. There was a big party afterward.

An incident that might not be considered a highlight was when Harold and four or five other sailors were drinking rum and Coke at a nightclub, Trader Vic's in Honolulu. Apparently Howard made a comment about marines. They took him outside and beat him up. All he remembered was being put on a bus. He spent a week recovering in the hospital. There was always a lot of teasing among the sailors and the marines, such as, "You wouldn't get there without us."

Bethesda Naval Hospital

Howard described himself as a "greenhorn" technician. During an exam on a WAVE, (Women Accepted for Volunteer Emergency Service) while he was assisting the doctor, an error occurred. The exam was for a lower GI barium enema. Well, it was dark in the room, and Harold was supposed to insert the enema in one orifice and mistakenly got it in the wrong opening! The doctor threw him out of the room.

War Is Over

When the war was over, Howard was assigned to another ship, an LST. They sailed from South China to San Francisco in thirty days, after making a stop in Hawaii. There was a storm that lasted all night. The crew had to tie themselves onboard to keep from falling off the ship. The LST was standing up on end, at a forty-five-degree angle. If he had stayed on his original ship, he would have been on the ship with the Iwo Jima soldiers who hoisted the American flag in the famous picture.

On July Fourth, we don't think about the sounds of the firecrackers and big booms of the fireworks going off outside—but Howard does. He said, "Don't want to hear it. Heard it too much during the war."

Did you meet any famous people?

"Different baseball teams would come to the bases, and I talked to Pee Wee Reese."

After the War

Howard and his wife, Connie, lived in Sioux Falls, South Dakota; Cincinnati, Ohio; Columbus, Ohio; Evansville, Indiana; and several other places during his work for GE. His navy x-ray training and experience, gave him the start to his forty-year career with General Electric.

Connie worked in Washington, DC, for the State Department in 1942 to 1945 while Howard was in the navy. She made $1,400 a year. Howard saw FDR, and Connie used to see Eleanor Roosevelt often going to lunch but never talked to her. Connie used to room with girls from Minnesota and is still friends with the ones who are still living. She said she enjoyed those friendships so much.

Connie and Howard Norlin

When Howard was working at Bethesda Naval Hospital in Maryland and Boston Navy Hospital, they would meet in Boston or New York for the weekend. They were married in the chapel at the hospital in Bethesda, Maryland.

Harold "Pete" Palmer—US Army
"As a general, I thought he was pretty good."

Veterans' Day 2016 - Harold's daughter, Sheryl Palmer, recounted these stories about her father and uncle.

How did Pete get his nickname, since his given name was Harold?

"As a child, he was a rascal! A neighbor called him Snagtooth Pete from Kalamazoo, and everyone started calling him Pete after that."

Early Life in Rushville

Pete lived in Rushville, Indiana, on a farm. At age twelve his father died, and Pete became the head of the family; he got a job and quit school at sixteen. There were six children left to raise when Pete's dad died. Being very poor, his mom had to get by as well as she could. She did not remarry. "She took in washing and ironing to help the family survive," said Sheryl. "Later she worked at the International Furniture Factory. Actually Pete worked at the same factory when he got married and was able to build the bed for he and his wife at the factory.

Military Life

"Dad received his notice to report for his army physical on September 2, 1942," said Sheryl. "My older sister, Sandra, was born on September 11, 1942. He was there for her birth but not for very much longer. He was inducted into the army at Ft. Harrison."

Pete was sent to Oregon for basic training. While in Oregon he was a sharp-shooter trainer before being sent overseas. Someone said, "Why are you so good at shooting?" Pete replied, "Well, I had to feed my family. Bullets cost money, and you had to hit what you were aiming at."

While Pete was in Oregon, his wife, Bessie, took a train out to be with him. She stayed for a month. Before she left, her father pinned a Masonic pin on her and said, "People who are Masons will see that and will watch out for you." She got off the train at one point and went into a restaurant. A man came up to her and asked about the pin, and she said her dad was a Mason. He said, "Well, I am buying your lunch." Paying it forward was happening in the 1940s too!

Pete was assigned to the Army Corps of Engineers. "They would clear the land and use it to build bridges," said Sheryl. "According to my dad, they had to blow up the bridges after the Allies used them, so the enemy couldn't use them." Pete was in the Philippines, working in Manila and on Guadalcanal, doing construction on buildings and bridges. He was not involved in combat, just construction. He was on Bataan and saw the mass graves of the death march. It was hard for him to talk about some things. He didn't talk a lot about the serious things.

Homemade beer in the Philippines

He did talk about the funny things, though. "At one point they were in the Philippines and were making homemade beer," said Sheryl. "They had different tents, and they had made some beer. Suddenly they heard there was going to be an inspection. They threw the evidence under one of the other platoon's or company's barracks. So they didn't get in trouble—the others did!

"He was supply sergeant several times. My dad didn't like to be told what to do, and so he had some problems with some people who told him what to do. So he was demoted several times. However, he was restored to sergeant.

Did Pete ever see his brother who was in the navy?

"One time on Guadalcanal, my dad and some other men were up on a hill cutting trees on a workforce. They looked down toward the road, and there was this sailor walking down the road. So they started harassing this sailor by saying, 'Did you lose your ocean? Or your ship? Or are you lost?'

"Well, this sailor shouted back, 'No, I heard down the road that there was a dumbass Hoosier that I should be talking to. I'm looking for him now.' It was dad's younger brother, Earl Wayne Palmer. They spent several hours or a couple days together on Guadalcanal." Sheryl said, "They also got to drink several beers together during the course of their reunion." She wasn't sure how Wayne knew where Pete was located. Maybe through letters from home. Wayne was six years younger than Pete. Pete's mother had had to sign for him to enlist, since he wasn't eighteen when he became a sailor.

"While [Pete] was in Manila," said Sheryl, "another company found a Japanese soldier holed up in a cave. That Japanese soldier became a prisoner of war, but he didn't make it off the island."

General MacArthur

"He was in Manila when General MacArthur landed, and they were up on a hill when they saw MacArthur get off the little boat he was in and walk onto shore. Suddenly he turned and walked back out into the water. Apparently the cameraman for the army was taking a picture of him."

Pete's youngest daughter, Holly, interviewed her dad for a 1991 term paper. Pete said, "As a general I thought he was pretty good." Pete went on to comment, "MacArthur earned the nickname Dugout Doug, as it was rumored among the troops that he was not a front line soldier."

Pete was very depressed and frustrated after the war's end. He would be assigned a ship to go home, then it would be cancelled from some reason. "They would be told to get everything ready, they would get things ready, and then it would be changed," said Sheryl. After being away from home for so long, he was eager to return to Indiana. By Christmas he was home!

Sheryl said, "Dad was really upset when they were coming home on the ship. One of the other soldiers had smuggled a puppy onboard the ship. Which was not the right thing to do. The captain found the dog and threw it overboard. My dad was so upset!

"Since the war in Europe was over so long after the war in the Pacific, the soldiers who came back from the Philippines felt like it was old hat to people. The soldiers returning from Europe were met with crowds of people and parades. Pete felt like his homecoming was just an afterthought, and there were very few people to greet them. He felt like people just wanted to get on with their lives. So he knew how the Vietnam soldiers felt."

Homecoming

"He hitchhiked home on Christmas Eve, so that he could spend Christmas with his wife, Bessie, and small daughter, Sandra. A friend in Rushville took him back to Camp Atterbury, so that he didn't have to hitchhike back for his discharge. He was discharged December 27, 1945. In 2011 Pete died in Indianapolis, Indiana. Sheryl ended the interview by saying, "I always thought my dad was so good looking, somewhat like a dark-haired Van Johnson." What a compliment for a life well lived!

James Pike—US Marines
"Bob Hope told them to move to the back and let the soldiers up front."

Jim was sitting at a table eating watermelon when I first met him. I sat down and had a slice of delicious red melon with him. After he finished his melon, we went out to the lobby area of his retirement home to talk. After the following interview, we went up to his apartment to see his war picture. Unlike many of the vets I have talked to, he has only one picture of his war days. Riding up one floor in the century-old elevator, I was hoping we wouldn't have to finish our visit stuck in the tiny cell!

Jim, born in Union Town, Kentucky, joined the marines in October of 1942, when he was seventeen years old. He quit high school to join the service with two buddies. He didn't tell his mom or grandmother, whom he was living with at the time.

His job was machine gunner in the South Pacific. He was at Guadalcanal, Guam, Iwo Jima, and some of the smaller Pacific islands. He was across the bay when they were approaching the beachhead at Iwo Jima. Jim said, "We cleaned that up for them."

What were your feelings about the war?

"What the hell am I doing here?"

He had heard about the bombing of Pearl Harbor on the radio. "I just took it as it come," he said. "Roosevelt was making a speech, and he said we will just go over and whoop their ass for them."

Did you think it would last?

"Didn't think about it."

Did you see any famous people?

Jim said he saw Bob Hope and the Andrews Sisters when they went over for a show. "I liked him," Jim said of Hope. "Some of the sergeants and noncoms got in the front row. Bob Hope told them to move to the back and let the soldiers up front. So they did." This was after Guadalcanal had been secured. There was still some fighting on some of the other islands.

Should Truman have dropped the atomic bomb? Where were you at the time?

"I thought he was doing the right thing," replied Jim. "My nerves went bad, and I had to go in the hospital in Portland, Oregon, for about a month and half around that time."

Jim Meets Betty

Jim met Betty when the troop train he was riding to California with about three hundred soldiers pulled onto another track in Eldon, Iowa. "It had pulled off to the side to let the other train pass us," he recalled. In doing this it blocked the crossing where Betty and her friend were standing. So, as things happen, Jim started talking to her and got her name and address. They wrote letters back and forth. After Jim's discharge, he went to Betty's house in Eldon to see her. He was invited over for dinner. Actually he went to see her first, before he went home to see his family.

After his visit with Betty, he went home to talk to his mom and grandmother. He told them he was going to marry Betty. So he went back to Eldon with his mother, and he and Betty were married in a church. Betty and Jim were married for seventeen years. Unfortunately, Betty was homesick for her family. She wanted to go back to Eldon to see her family more often than Jim had the money to send her. Hence an argument arose, and she packed her clothes and went back to Iowa.

Paul Pitcher—US Navy
"I am a loner. I don't make many friends, but when I do make a friend, it's for life."

In February 1942 Paul went into the US Navy, at age seventeen. A woman posing as his mother went with him and stated he was eighteen. Boot camp was in Farragut, Idaho. In Idaho there was no heat. His was the first company that went there. In twelve weeks he learned to swim and shoot.

It was time to change over from civilian to navy life. He went in as a seaman second class and graduated from boot camp as a seaman first class. During boot camp Paul learned to operate a movie projector. After boot camp he was kept for another three months for training purposes, and he ran the movie projector.

San Juan, Puerto Rico

Paul was based at naval VR squadron, then promoted to aviation electrician mate third class. Paul went to school in San Juan for six weeks to become a radioman. He was put in the VR squadron of PBYs, amphibious patrol planes. He flew submarine patrol over the Atlantic Ocean, looking for enemy periscopes. If one was found, the patrol would radio the nearest destroyer to sink it. They would go on patrol and leave San Juan. They would refuel at Trinidad. Next they would go to Brazil and refuel in Milan, Italy, at the base there. After seventy-two hours, they would do it again, sometimes going to the coast of England. After eighteen months, they broke up their squadron.

End of 1943—Beginning of 1944

Paul was transferred to Naval Air Station Patuxent River in Maryland. Paul and his crew flew aircraft engines all over the world. After one year he was headed to Olathe, Kansas. He was a radioman for six weeks then went to aviation electronics technician school. He was in the first graduating class of AET, Aviation Electronic Technician, in the navy. He worked on radar transmitters until 1945. Next he transferred to Kwajalein Atoll Island in the Marshall Island group. They met every airplane to check every transmitter. One plane took one hour to inspect.

Operation Crossroads

Twenty or twenty-five miles from Kwajalein Island, an island called Enewetak Atoll was cleared of all personnel and inhabitants. They did, however, leave a goat. The island was used to test drop atomic bombs after the atomic bombs were dropped on Japan. Paul got to ride in a photographer's plane. At one time he had pictures of the bombs after they had gone off.

At one point a destroyer was brought in, to see what an atomic bomb would do to a ship. The military wanted to see how much damage it would cause.

After that it was just routine navy. In the NATS, or Naval Air Transport Service, Paul flew freight over the Atlantic area. He was in the navy but was never on a ship! He was in planes mostly. He saw enemy subs and was shot at once, but Paul was not in any combat. In 1946 he was discharged in Oakland, California, after four years in the navy.

Patuxent River, Maryland

One interesting story: When Paul was at Patuxent River, Maryland, he had a 1937 Ford and lived in a tar paper shack. While he was at the hangar, someone stole his generator. That night he stole someone else's generator. He couldn't buy one because of the lack of supply. That went on for several days until his friend, Bob Deering, said, "Pitch, let's stop this stuff!" They became best friends for the rest of his naval career and remained friends after they were discharged. They spent every Thanksgiving together for fifteen to eighteen years, meeting in Columbia, Missouri. Bob Deering died in 2010.

As a closing Paul said, "I am a loner. I don't make many friends, but when I do make a friend, it's for life."

Robert Poole—US Army Air Corps

"Truman was smart. Millions of lives were saved that would have been killed."

In May 1943 Bob enlisted in the army air corps at age seventeen. Being underage he had to get his mother's permission. His thoughts seem as clear today as they were all those many years ago. He said he had wanted to join the navy, but they wouldn't take him. He felt like, "Let's get this thing over with so we can get home."

His first stop was Ft. Harrison in Indianapolis. An officer said, "Anybody who drives a car, step forward." Bob was a farm boy and wasn't sure about it, so he didn't step up. The ones who did ended up pushing wheelbarrows.

Next stop, St. Petersburg, Florida. He took a train down there and was living in the best hotels on the beach. However, it was hot, sweaty, buggy, and sandy! The soldiers were doing calisthenics on the beach in their birthday suits when the leader told them to jump into Tampa Bay. When Bob saw a large fish, he got out of the water. He was told to get back into the water. He said he wasn't going to get in the water with that big fish. The leader said, "That's a porpoise, and it's not going to hurt you!"

In Miami he and some other soldiers patrolled the beach with rifles and machine guns. There were reports that a German man and woman were captured in a two-man sub along the beach. He said, "I don't know what happened to them." The soldiers were told to shoot out any lights left on in hotel windows, as the city was under blackout conditions. But he never had to shoot out any windows.

While at Camp Crowder, near Joplin, Missouri, Bob gave a letter to a railroader. His father was a railroad man, so the man said he would send it to his dad for him, even though he wasn't supposed to do it!

There were fifty men in Bob's squad, but they are all gone now. Bob's job in the squad was radio operator, probably because he took radio code at Tech High School in Indianapolis.

Later he was stationed at Camp Stoneman, California, across the mountains from San Francisco. One night he was out with his buddies and missed the bus back to camp. He and the men he was with hitchhiked for a while, but the guy they were riding with was driving too fast. So they go out and walked the rest of the way back to camp, arriving back just as everyone else was getting up in the morning. He said, "We didn't get caught!"

He trained in B-17 planes and rode on a Victory ship under the Golden Gate Bridge. As they were getting closer, it looked like they were not going to fit under the bridge. However, when they went under it, he saw they had plenty of room.

On the way to the Pacific Theater, it took thirty-two days to cross the ocean, unescorted, to their destination. They had one submarine scare but didn't see anything. The first stop was French Haven, New Guinea, during the rainy season.

Philippines

In September 1943 Bob was on a B-25 in Leyte, Philippines, as a radio operator. They landed on a corrugated metal runway. During his tour there, he was on about every Pacific Island, from the Philippines to Borneo. His group had a pet monkey. One day when they were playing cards, a very poisonous and dangerous snake fell out of a tree on them. Another time someone shot and killed a twelve- to fourteen-foot python, which was full of pigs! One of the local farmers had complained about losing his pigs...Well, Bob and his fellow soldiers found them.

Bob said they did not have any food for about a month because ships couldn't get into the Philippines. So they had to eat bananas and coconuts. He said, "Today I can't eat coconuts, now; sometimes I can eat a banana." After some food was brought in, the Japanese snuck down from the mountains at night to steal it. No one came out of their pup tents to stop them. On the lighter side, he saw Bob Hope one time in Leyte.

Okinawa

Bob's troop had a red-haired pilot who flew their B-25. "He could fly anything!" said Bob. They wanted to name the plane "*The Witch*—you know, like a broomstick," but they didn't name it anything.

Bob flew twenty-two bombing missions over the South Pacific, dropping bombs on many locations. They got some of the first photos of Hiroshima after the bomb was dropped. When they showed the pictures to the Japanese POWs, the POWs said they didn't believe it. The POWs said the Japanese had people [spies] in Chicago. Bob said, "They had been brainwashed that much!"

Bob was on an LST that carried troops and cargo during the war. They left Okinawa with sixteen LSTs, but ten were lost at sea due to a hurricane. Thankfully Bob was on one of the six that made it to Osaka, Japan. He said, "The big doors came off the LST, and I spent twelve hours at the abandon ship station."

Osaka, Japan

Bob's group were the first American troops on Japan soil. They arrived in Osaka but didn't see anyone around. People were taking things out of stores, but once the MPs got there, all that stopped. Bob still has a beautiful kimono, belonging to a famous actress, that was in the store front window in Japan. Later, many Japanese people came out of underground tunnels. "It was like ants coming out of an anthill." They had been told the Americans would harm them, so they hid.

Bob took the train to Tokyo and stayed in a hotel where MacArthur had once stayed. From where it was located, he could look into the emperor's palace grounds. After that the first sergeant told him, "The boat in the harbor is ready to take you home!" A soldier could go home with sixty-seven points; Bob had eighty-seven. The first sergeant said if he would re-up for six more months, they could bring his wife over to Japan. He said, "No way. I'm going home." In May 1946 Bob was discharged. After that he was in the National Guard for eight or nine years. He was told if he was called up, he would go back to his same unit.

While in Japan Bob saw some of the country's shrines and thought they were wonderful. He said, "The Japanese people were appreciative of what the American soldiers did for them and treated them well. The emperor didn't want war. The Japanese people are a religious people and wouldn't give up."

Japan 1945

When Bob and his unit arrived there, "There was snow up to my fanny." He had never been skiing and thought it was a great idea to try it. He was with a Japanese interpreter and his buddy. The other guys had been skiing before and took off. Bob walked to the edge of the cliff where they had jumped. When he didn't see them, he fell down. If he hadn't fallen down, he would have been killed probably. He never skied again.

In March 1944, during a delay in route in Indianapolis, Bob married his wife. They were together for sixty-five years. Betty died in 2007.

Should the United States have dropped the atomic bombs on Japan?

"Truman was smart. Millions of lives were saved that would have been killed."

Navajo Windtalkers

Bob said, "I heard them on the radio, copied down the message, and gave it to my commanders." There were twenty-nine original Navajos, but he never met any of them. He felt they played an integral part in winning the war.

Indy Honor Flight

On September 5, 2015, Bob went on the Indy Honor Flight to Washington, DC. His son went as his guardian. The Indy Honor Flight organizers do such a wonderful job honoring the WWII, Korean, and Vietnam veterans in Indianapolis. On the flight Bob said, his mail call had sixty letters from the school where his grandson's wife teaches. He had been a special speaker at the school on Veteran's Day.

On his honor flight, Bob met a ninety-seven-year-old Red Tail fighter pilot. They talked for a while and discussed the war. The Red Tail pilots, 332nd Fighter Group, were known as Tuskegee Airmen. Bob said, "The Red Tail squadron were the only fighter squadron that didn't lose a bomber. The Red Tail escorts were always requested by pilots."

Present Day

Unfortunately, on December 27, 2016, Bob died. Previously Bob had said, "I don't want any military tribute at my funeral—no fuss, just the Masonic things." This was the way many WWII veterans wanted things—"just get the job done and get back home."

Robert Sisk – US Army
"Christmas Eve, 1945. It was the worst Christmas I ever had in my life."

Bob was drafted into the army at age eighteen. He attempted to join the Civil Air Patrol when he was sixteen years old, but he didn't pass the physical because of flat feet. If he hadn't been drafted, he would have joined the air force.

He started his military service at Camp Atterbury on October 28, 1944. He took the train to Ft. Knox, Kentucky. As fate would have it, he contracted the mumps and was in the hospital for two weeks. Bob said, "The only thing that saved me was the mumps." The doctor said, "You may not be able to have children." He went on to have six children after he was discharged and married.

While Bob was recovering from the mumps, the rest of his company were sent to Germany. They were involved in the Battle of the Bulge. Some of his neighbors and friends returned with shell shock, or post-traumatic stress disorder, as we would say today. Bob had to wait for another company to come in, "so I had to wait two weeks and do more training, probably a month's delay." Bob stated, "I don't believe in consequences." He meant that many events in his military career kept him from danger.

The next stop was Ft. Mead, Maryland, around April or May 1945. Forty men were picked to train the Japanese-American guys, and Bob was one of them, so for one month he was a tank driver. These guys were being trained to go to Europe. "I was very fortunate to have weekends off, so I got to see many of the museums in Washington, DC, [as well as] the Washington Memorial, Jefferson monument, and Lincoln Memorial.

"In May 1945 I was sent home for leave. I was driving my dad's car, a 1939 Packard. The streetcar came by and took off the front end of the car! In those days you couldn't find anyone to repair things, however, someone from my church fixed the whole front end for just sixteen dollars." His dad was upset about the accident. "The only thing saved me was being in the service!"

From May to July 1945, Bob was in Ft. Knox for advanced training. From Ft. Knox he was sent to Camp Adair, Oregon, for two weeks. There were forest fires in Oregon that "turned the skyline red, as the camp was in a valley." They needed volunteers to fight the fires, but Bob was shipped out before he could volunteer. At Camp Anza, California, he boarded the USS *Broadwater*, and he was seasick. Japan surrendered on August 15, 1945. By that time, we arrived in Manila the war was over.

Philippines

"September 14, 1945. We were barely off the ship when we heard that MacArthur had signed the armistice with Japan aboard the *Missouri*." Bob and his unit arrived in Manila Harbor, where much of the Japanese fleet was sunk. Their ship had to zigzag around the sunken Japanese ships. He remembered passing Bataan and Corregidor, where many horrific battles had taken place earlier in the war.

Starting on September 17, 1945, they got off the ship about fifty miles north of Manila. We stayed in tent quarters for five days. He had K rations for lunch and dinner. He remembered eating Spam. He still eats it, cutting it up and putting it in his eggs.

Bob and the other soldiers were put on trains, in cattle cars, and then on trucks to their permanent company—the 447th engineer depot company. This was eight miles east of Manila, with Quezon City being the closest big city. Manila was completely wiped out.

Bob said, "Because I could type, the only one that could, I held the inventory control position in the office area. Many of these guys were going home, since they had been here for a while. Some of the men had malaria. One guy in our tent had covers piled on him, and he was still shaking so badly. I hadn't seen anything like that."

Bob kept a journal of his time in the service. He read from his journal, of his war experiences, "Christmas Eve, 1945. It was the worst Christmas I ever had in my life."

There were fourteen Filipino girls working in his office. The Filipinos were paid by the US government to work in the office. Many of them spoke English, and Bob picked up some Filipino words from them. He had about thirty guys on the outside working for him. Every day people picked up supplies, so he had to keep track of everything. "The Filipino people are nice people," Bob said, "and there wasn't anything they wouldn't do for you. The Filipinos hated the Japanese.

"There were Korean POWs in our camp. They were just waiting to go home. The Japanese had forced them to join the Japanese army or be killed. The Korean POWs hated the Japanese." Bob said he couldn't tell the Japanese guys from the Korean ones. If a stray Japanese guy wandered into the mess to get something to eat, the Filipinos would nearly kill him. The Filipino workers could tell them apart and knew the Japanese didn't belong there.

Were there any accidents?

One thing Bob and the other soldiers were told before going to this area was "do not pick up any shells." Well, in the tent next to Bob's, some guy wanted to take home a souvenir...so he was pounding on a shell to get the powder out. It exploded and killed two soldiers and wounded three or four.

Bob was assigned a vehicle, so one day he left his assistant in charge, a young man who had graduated from Manila University. Bob, being twenty years old, wanted to see what Manila looked like. "There were Communists, Huks, who would rob you." So he carried a gun when he went outside the camp.

In September 1946 Bob left Manila on the USS *Young America*. When they arrived in San Francisco on September 29, "it was foggy, and you couldn't see a thing." Suddenly it cleared, and they could see the Golden Gate Bridge. "It was beautiful!" Bob recalled. "The guys were pretty happy to see it."

Home

On October 9, 1946, at 2:30 a.m., Bob returned home to banners and "Welcome Home" signs at his house. His mom, dad, two brothers, and two sisters were up welcoming him back home. Everyone was "all up and at 'em!" Bob said.

What did you think about the United States dropping the atomic bomb?

"Great. It saved my life. People don't realize how many more people would have been killed if we hadn't done that. I was on my way to Okinawa when they dropped those bombs. We were somewhat happy about it—except for all the people in Japan that were killed."

Bob said, "God intervenes in things..." His military service could have turned out differently if he hadn't gotten the mumps, if the United States hadn't dropped the bombs, or if he had been in a different company. Bob was discharged on December 1, 1946.

Honors

> Philippines Independence Liberation Medal
> Asiatic and Pacific Medal
> Good Conduct Medal
> World War II Victory Medal
> American Campaign Medal

Bob W. – US Army
"Lamb stew smelled just like a skunk!"

Do you remember Pearl Harbor?

"Yes. I was sixteen at the time of the Pearl Harbor attack. I thought, *I am going in the service soon!* I got to stay home for a few months, then when I was eighteen, I was gone. When I first went in, we had a little boy. He had an overcoat that came down to his ankles and a duffel bag of clothes. In a couple weeks, he was gone. His momma got him back." Bob laughed. "He was fifteen, and he didn't last long."

Italian and German POWs

"When I was a kid, I worked on a truck farm. They would hire the Italian POWs to come work on the truck farms near Whiteland, Indiana. They grew vegetables and trucked them up to the Indianapolis farm market. The farmers would go to Camp Atterbury and pick up the POWs, along with a guard, to work on the farm."

Did any of them ever try to escape?

"No, they liked working there. They had it better here than they did at home. The German POWs worked at Camp Atterbury without a guard." Both German and Italians POWs were paid a certain amount for their work at Camp Atterbury.

"One of the POWs got out on the railroad track and didn't want to go back, but they were sent back to their own country after the war. There was quite a bit of difference between how the Germans and the Japanese treated their prisoners and how we treated ours."

Military Service

Bob, drafted on January 6, 1946, spent six months at Camp Atterbury. Since the war was over in August 1946, he worked as a medic discharging the troops coming back from the war. Bob's job was as a baker for the army.

How did you get to be a baker?

"They just pointed to you to do the job." He never had any talent for it before entering the military, had never seen a bakery. "It turned out pretty good. We started out baking some cakes, but they cut that out. Then we only baked bread."

From Camp Atterbury he was part of the occupation forces sent to Japan. Bob rode over to Japan on the troop ship USS *Admiralty*. "We had a typhoon on the way over there and on the way back."

Japan

"When we first got there, there were three eight-hour shifts. Bakers work twenty-four hours a day. The ingredients we were given [to bake with] had a little age on it, so it was hard to make good bread.

"We only got fifteen hours' sleep the first week." His other duty, besides baking, was guard duty. After working guard duty, he would go back and start baking.

"We landed in Yokohama, Japan, and we traveled by train through many cities that had been bombed. From there we went down to the lower island, six hundred eighty miles. We were told to cover the windows and not look out at the devastation. Being eighteen-year-old kids, we looked out the windows! The train ride from Yokohama to Fukuoka took three days." This was during the occupation of Japan in 1946. Bill saw destruction in the city of Fukuoka and a Japanese shrine in Kashii.

Did you like K rations?

"After eating those K rations for three days, bread baking smelled pretty good to the troops. Lamb stew smelled just like a skunk! It was horrible. I had sardines and crackers on that day.

"K Rations were not good; the crackers were old. There were cigarettes, canned meat and candy bars. C rations were pretty good." According to Bob, "the biggest problem with the army food was the cooks."

"The Japanese island where we were stationed, was the site the Allies had planned to invade. However, the atomic bomb was dropped, and the Japanese surrendered." The women were scared and fled to the hills. They had been told how horrible the Americans were going to be to them. Some of the others had an attitude with the soldiers. While Bob was in Japan, he met an old Japanese man who lived in Chicago. He had returned to Japan for a visit and was unable to return to the United States once war was declared. He said, "I met a lot of nice people and some that weren't." Bob was in Japan for about one year.

Bob's childhood friend Harold, a bomber pilot, dropped bombs on Japan. Bob said, "There are two places that we were told not to bomb: the tunnel connecting the islands and the emperor's palace." Bob said he was glad they didn't bomb the tunnel, as he had just traveled through it to get to the lower island.

Also Bob experienced an earthquake while in Japan. Well, actually, he slept through it! When he woke up the next morning, some guys were talking about it. He didn't know anything about it.

What did you think about the dropping of the bombs on Nagasaki and Hiroshima?

"It served the purpose of stopping them. There would have been a lot more people killed, American and Japanese, if they had come in on the islands down there. I hope they never use them [atomic bombs] again." Bob has seen the damage such bombs can do to a city and its people.

"A war never accomplished anything. Everything was damaged. American taxpayers paid to have things rebuilt in Japan. Japan didn't pay to have Hawaii rebuilt."

Bob was the third oldest of eleven children. His older brothers were also in WWII, one in China and the other in Italy. They were in different branches of the service, one in the army and one in the navy. "We thought it was an honor to be in the military," said Bob.

Indy Honor Flight

Bob went on the flight with his daughter. He said, "It was very nice."

Harold Weber—US Navy
"The water was full of ships when they pulled up beside the USS *Missouri*."

Harold joined the navy in 1943 and was onboard the USS *Taylor DD-468*. He was in the 7th fleet with General Halsey. "It was the first US Navy ship to anchor in peace in Japanese coastal waters at the end of WWII." Harold served on many of the Pacific islands—Corregidor, Guam and New Guinea.

He was a boatswain mate whose job was to take the small boats over to another ship. They would take on stores (supplies), which is a job in which everyone participated.

Harold shared a story about a Japanese parachute. There was a Japanese airplane that was shot down in the water. He got part of the parachute as a souvenir. Harold saw the Japanese pilot in the water. He still has a piece of the large white square of fabric.

Harold said he saw a Japanese mini sub on the beach and that it looked like a torpedo. "There was also one in the water that tried to ram our ship. The ship circled around and rammed it with the bow of the ship. We went to GQ, and it was in the water."

The USS *Taylor* was one of the ships selected to escort the USS *Missouri*. On September 2, 1945, in Tokyo Bay, the USS *Taylor* hauled correspondence for the surrender ceremony over to the USS *Missouri*. The peace agreement was signed on board the USS *Missouri*. Harold recalled, "The water was full of ships when they pulled up beside the *Missouri*." The USS *Missouri*, currently docked at Pearl Harbor, Hawaii, represented the end of the war for many soldiers and sailors.

The USS *Taylor* was mothballed at the end of the war; however, it was pulled out for the Korean and Vietnam Wars. Later it was sold to the Italian navy.

Harold said he liked the navy. "It was a clean place to sleep and had good food." He later said, "Once there was party on a sandy beach. They took you over in a whale boat to this island where each sailor got two or three beers." He was glad to get back to the ship.

Harold spent three or five years in the navy. He was discharged in California after the war ended.

European Theater

We were following what our government told us to do, and that is what the German boys were doing too.

—Ralph Cooley
US Army, WWII

European Theater Veterans

Max Bates

Vernon Bothwell

Tom Boyd

Albert Clark

Ralph Cooley

Melvin Eakle

William Fischer

Eunice Francis

Frank Francis

John Geilker

William Kincheloe

Evanula Ledbetter

Robert Miller

Jerry Moser

William Muller

Ralph Myers

Robert Pedigo

Harold Pettus

Robert Reed

Richard Robinson

Allen Sanderson

William Schmidt

Robert Swift

Part 3
European Theater

The European Theater was also known as the Second European War because it was fought on European soil. On December 11, 1941, Germany and Italy declared war on the United States of America, then the United States declared war on Germany and Italy. This set the stage for the beginning of a world war in Europe and North Africa. Poland and Czechoslovakia were defeated as the Axis war machine continued across Europe into France. France fell to the Axis powers—Germany, Italy, and Japan—in June 1940. In 1941 the Axis powers were in control of much of Europe and North Africa. The Germans were invading Russia following Hitler's plan for total world domination.

The fighting was very different in Europe compared to the Pacific Theater. Fighting in Europe involved tanks and large artillery while in the Pacific fighting was on the water and in the island jungles. The enemy was also different in that the Germans would surrender when outnumbered whereas the Japanese would fight to the bloody end and rarely surrendered.

The Allies gained an advantage and a major foothold in the war after their victory on D-Day. However, the Battle of Normandy will be remembered as the largest invasion in history, which involved land, air, and sea all coming together to fight the enemy.

Below are major battles of the European Theater that WWII veterans included in this book were involved:

*	First Battle of El Alamein	July 1, 1942
*	Second Battle of El Alamein	October 23, 1942
*	Operation Torch (North Africa)	November 8, 1942
*	Battle of Salerno	September 3, 1943
*	Battle of Sicily	July 9, 1943
*	Battle of Monte Cassino	January 17, 1944
*	Battle of Anzio	January 22, 1944
*	Battle of the Bulge	December 16, 1944
*	D-Day Invasion	June 6, 1944

Other important events:

*	V-E Day—Germany surrenders	May 8, 1945
*	V-J Day – Victory over Japan	September 2, 1945
*	President Franklin D. Roosevelt dies	April 12, 1945

Major Battles of the European Theater

Battle of El Alamein

Alamein, Egypt, is located northwest of Cairo on the Mediterranean Sea. Field Marshal Edwin Rommel, major leader of the German army, led the fighting in North Africa. The First Battle of El Alamein, which took place on July 1–27, 1942, was a victory for the Allies. The Second Battle of El Alamein, on October 23–November 11, 1942, was also an Allied victory won primarily by the British. British troops were led by Montgomery. The Germans surrendered their hold in May 1943 and gave up domination of North Africa.

Operation Torch (North Africa)

On November 8–10, 1942, the American, Free French, and British forces invaded French North Africa. Allied forces captured the ports and airports of Oran, Algiers, Morocco, Casablanca, and Algeria. The famous Major General George Patton was in command of American forces, and Major General Jimmy Doolittle was in command of all American aircraft.

Battle of Sicily (Operation Husky)

Sicily is an island located off the southern coast of mainland Italy. The Battle of Sicily, July 9–August 17, 1943, was the beginning of the Italian Campaign, resulting in an Allied victory. The goal of this operation was to rid Sicily of Axis domination. It was important to open the Mediterranean Sea for merchant ships from the Allies. Mussolini was no longer in power in Italy, so it was the time to invade Italy.

Battle of Anzio, (Operation Shingle)

Anzio is located thirty miles south of Rome, Italy. The battle took place on January 22, 1944. There were large losses of life on both the Allied and Axis sides. This battle is part of what is referred to as the Italian Theater. Allied troops had to contend with the Apennine Mountains, inclement weather, and very rough terrain as well as the vicious German army coming at them.

Battle of Salerno (Operation Avalanche)

This battle, fought on September 3–15, 1943, was also part of what is referred to as the Italian Campaign. The Allies wanted control of Salerno, located in Southern Italy, so they could fly planes in from Sicily. There were roughly 2,000 Allied casualties and 3,500 enemy casualties.

Battle of Monte Cassino (Battle for Rome)

Monte Cassino is located eighty-one miles southeast of Rome. The German army was responsible for preventing the Allies from advancing from Cassino. The goal of this assault, which took place on January 17–May 18, 1944, was to clear the way to Rome and retake it from the Axis powers. This battle resulted in an Allied victory.

Battle of the Bulge

This surprise attack, which occurred on December 16, 1944–January 25, 1945, is one of the more talked about and important battles for the Allied forces in Europe. This major German offensive took place in Ardennes region of Belgium, Luxembourg, and France, which resulted in an Allied victory. The Germans retreated to the Siegfried Line. There were major losses, with nineteen thousand American deaths and two hundred British deaths, and approximately three thousand civilian lives were lost. The Americans were surprised and sustained heavy losses; however, the Germans lost much equipment they would not be able to replenish for further invasions. Dwight Eisenhower, later the US president, was supreme allied commander during this battle.

D-Day Invasion (Operation Overlord)

This invasion, which took place on June 6–August 30, 1944, was famous for surprising the Germans when they attacked Normandy instead of Calais, France. Calais was an area where the Germans had fortified the beaches the heaviest, expecting an attack there. The beaches were code-named *Utah* and *Omaha* for the American troops and *Sword* and *Gold* for the British troops. The Canadians were at *Juno* beach. It was a victory for the Allied forces led by American General Dwight Eisenhower and British General Bernard Montgomery. The Axis leader was Field Marshal Erwin Rommel.

Normandy American Cemetery and Memorial

Colleville-sur-Mer, Normandy, France, is the final resting place for more than nine thousand American WWII troops who were killed in Europe during the war. The cemetery was initially established to honor American soldiers who lost their lives during the invasion at Normandy. It is a beautiful, quiet place with rows and rows of white crosses. It is an incredibly sad place yet a wonderful tribute to all those soldiers who bravely faced the enemy and lost their lives.

Two famous Americans—Theodore Roosevelt Jr., oldest son of President Theodore Roosevelt; and Quentin Roosevelt, President Theodore Roosevelt's youngest son, who died on July 14, 1918, in France—are buried in Colleville-sur-Mer. Quentin was in another part of France, but his body was moved to be buried beside his brother in the 1950s. Brigadier General Theodore Roosevelt Jr. walked with a cane and had a heart condition. He led the attack on Utah Beach and survived. He died a month later at the age of fifty-six of a heart attack.

Grave marker of Theodore Roosevelt Jr.in Colleville-sur-Mer, France

Vernon Bothwell Sr. – US Army Air Corp
"I have seen fear. I have been scared to death."

In June 1941 Vernon enlisted in the US Army Air Corp while still a senior in high school. His only stipulation was that he had to wait, until the Indianapolis 500 was run in May, before he left for duty.

Who won the race that year?

He said automatically, "Mauri Rose."

One of Vernon's best quotes was, "I did everything in the war, but I liked flying airplanes best."

Parma and Vernon Bothwell   *Pearl Harbor, December 7, 1941*

Vernon graduated from mechanics school on December 7, 1941. "We were watching *Sergeant York* at the post theater. It turned off; someone came up on the stage and said the Japs have bombed Pearl Harbor—we are now at war. Everything really changed after that. It used to be that people didn't think much of someone in the military. Well, after war was declared, people respected you. We would get the weekends off, and I would try to thumb a ride and would eventually get a ride. After Pearl Harbor people would give you rides. We all got together behind the people who were in the service. It was one hundred percent backing."

To be able to fly, he had to complete many hours of training at various locations in the United States. First was Maxwell Field in Alabama on December 25, 1941. Vernon said they had a big feast that night, since it was Christmas. "There were things there that I didn't normally eat, like oysters on the half shell. I'm a kid from Indiana, and we were all poor." There was a fifty-caliber machine gun attached to the hangar in case they were attacked.

In March of 1942, he got the call to go to San Antonio to become a pilot. He was sent to San Antonio until June of 1942. He took primary training at Stanford, Texas, flying PT-19s; Brady, Texas, flying BT-13s; Lubbock, Texas, twin engine school, flying AT-9s and AT-17s and completing 200 hours of total time. Vernon got his wings on December 13, 1942, with the class of 42K.

In the meantime, while he was stationed in Texas, Vernon married his first love. He wasn't supposed to, but he married the very beautiful eighteen-year-old Parma Jane (Coleen). They went out two times, and then he married her. Her family was "dirt poor and as poor as church mice. Thirteen people lived in a three-room shack and a lean-to." Her family were sharecroppers and a great family.

North Africa and Sardinia

Vernon flew forty missions from North Africa and Sardinia. Vernon was usually the copilot of the Martin B-26 planes. The B-26, built by the Glenn L. Martin Company, was not a well-liked airplane. Ominously, it had many nicknames, but one particularly painful one, the "widow maker." However, it was a hard-working plane, and changes were made to it, so the B-26 continued in service in North Africa.

Vernon mentioned that "some stupid pilots flew into a thunderstorm." The planes went down, but all the crew were safe. "We never did find the airplanes!"

"Twenty-six of us went to the transition place awaiting assignment," said Vernon. "They didn't know what to do with us, so they sent us home for two weeks. It was the Christmas of '42 when they sent us home. It was going to cost us two hundred forty-five dollars to go home, and I happened to have two hundred forty-five dollars because I played poker. I had a buddy, Perry, who didn't have the money because I had taken all his money playing poker! So I felt sorry for him and wired my folks that I needed two hundred forty-five dollars to come home. They wired the money back, and I loaned it to Perry so he could go see his folks. Perry was killed on his first mission. At least he got to see his folks."

Finally Vernon got his orders to go to Omaha, Nebraska, and then overseas. The crew picked up a new airplane and had a naked woman painted on it. "It was a nice-looking woman anyway. Since the pilot was from Tennessee, they named it the *Tennessee Belle*. We got to Hunter Field, and they took our airplane away from us." They stayed there for two weeks and finally got another airplane. "We didn't put a picture on that one!"

They went overseas on the southern route, going to Natel, Brazil, Gold Coast, Sahara Desert, Tinduerf Oasis, and a French Foreign Legion post. It rained for three days, and it hadn't rained for twelve years. So the wine cellar the French had forgotten when they left collapsed. There was wine in that building, so some of the guys dug through it and drank the wine.

French Morocco and Marrakech

Finally they got out of there and went to Marrakech, which was a staging area for going to war. "They weren't ready for us yet, so they sent us to French Morocco along the coast."

In French Morocco they had nice French barracks for about two weeks. There was a train station where the French were building a train track. Vernon turned twenty-one, and his buddies gave him a fifth of Old Grand-Dad whiskey. They bet him he couldn't drink it all in one sitting. He said, "I bet I can!" He said he was "young, dumb, and lucky." When he came to, "I had my arm around a nurse, and she was crying. Well, since I was drunk, I didn't know why. I said I wouldn't get that drunk again. I felt sorry for the nurse since she was crying.

"Combat outfits would come in, and we would join in. I suddenly found out that my pilot could not fly formation. So we got turned down on the first two times that we came in. Then 17th Bomb Group, 95 Bomb squadron, came in, and we joined them at that time." Vernon took over the aircraft, and they passed because in his previous training all they did was fly formation. "My pilot didn't have this experience, so he didn't know how to fly formation."

They went up to another place in North Africa, eventually moving up to Tunisia. They went into combat, joined an older crew, and were with them for three missions. In the meantime, on June 20, 1943, Vernon flew his first mission. As Vernon went on to explain, "We attacked the airfield on Sardinia. We bombed this airfield. Our unit destroyed six fighters that came in on our formation. We didn't lose an airplane."

Vernon told another story of being "young, dumb, and lucky" when he shot some frogs with a forty-five pistol. He heard these frogs croaking while he was lying in bed beneath some palm trees. "Hey, I'm a kid from Indiana, and I have eaten frog legs all my life!" He had perhaps "a couple dozen frog legs" that he fried and ate. That night, after being asleep for three or four hours, he got cramps. He had dysentery and couldn't leave his bed.

He was put in a plane and taken to a doctor. He was put in a med tent, and a nurse gave him some pineapple juice because he was dehydrated. He spent four days in the med tent until he could walk.

He couldn't fly, so another copilot was sent to take his place on the next mission. On July 17, 1943, "the mission was near the leg of Italy where they had to fly over the Italian fleet. Italy was still at war with us at that time. My crew was on the right-hand side of the leader. He was the CO of the bomb group. He got shot down, and my crew got shot up, but nobody got hurt."

When they got back to Tunis and went to land, the wheels wouldn't come down. So the pilot had to land wheels up. He did a fine job, and no one was injured. The plane had 113 holes in it. Talk about lucky!

In two days Vernon was able to fly on a mission to bomb the airfield north of Rome. They had maximum effort on the mission, and "as they were coming in the Italians made a hit on us, but we had five fifty-caliber machine guns and obliterated the fighters that were making an attack. We went on in and bombed the airfields at Rome. About five hundred feet ahead of me, I saw this airplane flying upside down, in an inverted spin. The Italians had captured a P-38 in the desert, and they used it to attack our bombers."

How many missions did you fly until you could go home?

It took Vernon six months to fly thirty missions. On a mission over Lire River Dam, there was lots of flak in the air. He looked over to his right and saw the turret gunner turn "blood and guts" right there in the air. "When I got back that night, lying in my bed, I thought this thing has been going on long enough. So what I am going to do is I'm going to volunteer for every mission by going in for spares." That meant when someone fell out, another man could volunteer to go in his place. "In seventeen days, I completed ten more missions, which gave me forty. When we got back off that mission that day, they said that they had upped the missions to sixty before you get to go home. But anyone who had their forty missions on that day would get to go home." He said that this was another "young, dumb, and lucky" situation that he was involved in during his military career.

He couldn't fly home, so he went to Casablanca and went home by ship. It took him ten days to get home by ship. He was seasick all the time, but he got in a poker game and won $6,000, "which was a lot of money in those days!" He had been playing poker while he was in the service, and he would send all but twenty dollars home to his wife. He gambled with the twenty dollars he had left. By the time he got home, his wife had saved $9,000. "She was special," said Vernon.

While he was in Florida, he found out his dad, Alfred, age forty-two, had been drafted into the military as an MP while Vernon was gone overseas. Vernon served in Bartow, Florida for the duration of the war training pilots on P-51s. He and his wife rented a beautiful house for seventy-five dollars a month. By November 1945 the war was over, and he had enough points to muster out of the service. He bought a farm in Indiana and got a job making sixty-five cents an hour.

Should the United States have dropped the atomic bombs on Japan?

"Greatest thing that ever happened. If not, then another four hundred thousand of our generation and Japanese lives would have been lost."

Vernon said, "The only thing I didn't like when I was in the service was when they were shooting at me. Nobody enjoyed that! I have seen fear. I have been scared to death." Again, young, dumb, and lucky.

Max A. Bates – US Navy
"What those guys had to go through was terrible!"

In 1943 Max, age seventeen, enlisted in the US Navy after he graduated from Ben Davis High School. On July 18, 1944, he left for the navy at age eighteen. He went to boot camp at Camp Peary, Virginia, near the Chesapeake Bay. It is now a CIA base, as Max found out when he and his wife, Mary Ellen, tried to visit it after the war. He was told, "No deal. Turn around and leave!"

Camp Peary was well known for the German POWs that were housed there during the war. "Some of the German prisoners were from captured German U-boats and ships," said Max. "The Allies didn't want the Axis powers to know that these prisoners were captured, so secret code books wouldn't be compromised."

He went to radio man school in Bainbridge, Maryland, where he learned the universal code and to type, and graduated in five months. He took some advanced radio training in Newport, Rhode Island, and Boston, Massachusetts. He was based out of Boston while waiting for his ship, the USS *Helena CA75*, a heavy cruiser, to be christened. All new ships are sent on "shakedown cruises" before they are accepted by the navy. A shakedown cruise is when a new ship sails for its first time. On this first sailing, the crew looks for potential problems involving the ship. On this cruise Max went to New York City, where there were festivities honoring military personnel; Philadelphia, where they fixed some problems on the ship; and Guantanamo Bay, Cuba, where the soldiers practiced shooting at some drones.

Battling a hurricane

In September 1945 they were in a hurricane for four days while heading back to Boston. "This ship was rolling and pitching, so meals couldn't be prepared," said Max. "Some of the kids were sick, but I never was sick on the ship. Our meals, which were served two times a day, consisted of a tin of beef stew. It was the same for breakfast and dinner—beef stew!"

Do you like beef stew today?

"No. I could tolerate it, but I would prefer something else.

"Next we headed to Europe. This was after the war, when we went on our goodwill cruise. We were making visits to different ports. We went to England, Scotland, around the Mediterranean Sea, and Gibraltar.

"My points were up in March 1946. (Points were given for time spent in the military or flying a set number of missions. When soldiers reached the number necessary for them to be discharged, they could go home.) I left this ship at Exeter, England, where I stayed for three weeks." He headed back to the United States on the SS *Colby Victory*. The SS *Colby Victory,* a Victory ship that was a cargo ship. The SS *Colby Victory* was named after Colby College in Waterville, Maine. We stopped in Bremerhaven, Germany, which is on the coast of Germany. We picked up some Army soldiers there who had been in the fighting in Europe. It took us nine days to get home."

There were poker games that went on aboard the ship. "Some guys had saved their money, since there wasn't anything to spend their money on," Max said. "There was this big poker game that went on in the mess hall. When the two meals a day were served, the men went up on deck and played craps."

Did you play in the poker game?

"I didn't play, just one of the many spectators." The pay was twenty dollars every two weeks, and he spent most of his money on shore leave. So he didn't have any money to play poker.

Did anyone ever win a lot of money?

"This one guy had a big pile of bills. As guys would lose their money and go broke, they would drop out and become spectators. Then other guys would take their place."

Was it good luck?

In Newport, Rhode Island, Max was selected to be a radio man on the USS *Indianapolis*. He was to report to the West Coast, where the ship was docked following the run delivering the atomic weapons parts. He thought, *This is great. I am from Indianapolis, and I am going to serve on the Indianapolis.*

However, he contracted what the navy called "cat fever." Max said, "It was really just the flu." In any case, the navy assigned another sailor to the *Indianapolis*, and Max didn't serve on that ship. Knowing what happened to the USS *Indianapolis*, it was good luck for Max. He said, "What those guys had to go through was terrible!"

Marriage and Children

Max and Mary Ellen met at a friend's wedding in Washington, Indiana. Six months later, in 1948, they were married. They were married for sixty-four years before Mary Ellen's death. They had three children—two girls and one boy. Unfortunately, one of his daughters died from pneumonia following a bout of leukemia, and his son was killed in motorcycle accident. Max worked for Eli Lilly for twenty-five years, working with computers. He retired from Lilly in 1989.

Ninetieth Birthday Present

Max made the local news in July 2016 by announcing he wanted to jump out of an airplane for his ninetieth birthday. He skydived from the Frankfort Airport on his birthday, July 18. He said, "I have thought about it for several years." When his honor flight guardian, Jill Fewell, asked him what he wanted to do for his ninetieth birthday, he said, "Let's do it." She set it up for him.

Indy Honor Flight

Max went on the Indy Honor Flight to Washington, DC. The local Indiana military and supporters put together special flights for vets to visit memorials in the Washington DC. He said he enjoyed it very much. It makes the vets feel special, and it is a way to repay them for the sacrifices they made for our country. He has a very nice keepsake book showing what went on while he was on the flight and during the events in Washington, DC.

Tom Boyd—US Army Infantry
"You always wanted to be behind the tanks."

In 1942 Tom, twenty-four years old, lived in Evansville, Indiana, when he was drafted into the service. Tom's son, Jerry, was just walking when Tom left for the service. He spent two years, seven months, and eight days as a serviceman. He was assigned to the 14th Armored Division, 19th Infantry. He went in at Camp Chaffee, Arkansas. An officer came around after a week and pinned a corporal band on Tom. In another two or three weeks, he was given his corporal stripes. He had been in the CCC, Maritime Service, and ROTC before going into the service, and these previous experiences helped him to be promoted quickly. "Three of the guys from Evansville all went in together" he said. "Two of them went into the infantry, and one guy was sent to Florida to take care of soldiers returning with injuries and never left the States."

During cold Tennessee maneuvers, he found out some things about keeping his boots warm. "The winter in Tennessee, we found out, when you go to sleep, you want to keep them warm, or you aren't going to get them on in the morning. You have to either sleep with them on or sleep with them beside you." Tom said, "We stayed out in the weather. We were an angry and mean bunch of guys. We were ready. Actually, the army couldn't have had better training for us. We were scheduled to go to desert training when they were fighting in North Africa; however, the tide turned, and they run the Germans out of there. Rommel was the German general there."

Marseille, France

When Tom found out he was going to be in the infantry, he and another guy went in to see if they could transfer to another outfit. The only thing open was to be a paratrooper. "Well, I [was] not going to jump out of a plane," he said. So he stayed in the infantry. However, his buddy joined the paratroopers. "When I got over to Marseille, France, I started to get off, and who do I see? This guy that transferred to the paratroopers. He said, 'I knew you were coming.' Now, how the heck did he know I was coming? He was right there to greet me when I got off the ship."

Tom told a story of a tank man from St. Louis. "There were a lot of sinkholes where we were staying. He got in one of the sinkholes to stay out of the weather. Well, that night it poured down rain. The next morning the sinkhole was just filling up with water. He and his assistant, Corporal Davis, both got out all right."

Tom didn't know where he was going to be. In fact, "I was sick all the way over. We landed in Marseille, France, which is in southern France. Which is very fortunate, because we didn't have to land on the beaches.

"When we landed, one group of men went one way and another group of men went the other. We went up to the Maritime Alps and the Mediterranean. They had pretty women. We stayed up for a while. We had a lot of canon fire and heavy fire. It kept us busy up in the mountains, which I didn't like at all.

"Nice was nice!" he said with a laugh. Tom's job was squadron leader. "I was a staff sergeant, that was twelve people, counting myself." Tom went on to explain, "There was a half track and a fifty-millimeter gun and eleven guys. They kept me busy, and we had some problems…Everybody did, that's for sure."

Tom said, "We were out, and when I came back they told me that my youngest son was born when I was in Schaumburg, France. We had to drive the Germans back across the Lauter River. We had a lot of battles, and we lost a lot of men. From there we went to a rest area, to Alsace-Lorraine, France. We lost several men.

Did you see General Patton?

"We saw Patton, and he came over and checked our tankers. We had sandbags on the tanks for extra protection. Well, he got all over them and called them everything but good guys. I mean he got on them. After that, that's when the trouble started, and they called him up to where they broke through at Bastogne. They called Patton up with his Third Army, and when they did that it stretched us out real thin. What we had down here was what they had up there [in Bastogne]. The same kind of tanks and everything, but you never heard anything about it. Well, it wasn't advertised or talked about like Bastogne was. We didn't get surrounded; we held them. We did have to back up. Well, it was quite a place, but we got through it. Then we were in Germany for a while."

Tom explained, "I was over there about nine months. When I got into Germany, I kind of lost it, and they brought me back." He was in Southhampton, England, for two or three months. The ship he was supposed to come back on was torpedoed but not sunk. "I left there and was in the middle of the ocean when Franklin D. died. I came back when the war in Europe was over." He was in the hospital in Indianapolis for quite a while. He regretted leaving his dog tags on the head of the bed while he was in the hospital. He never got them back.

"We were in twin towns," Tom said, "and the Germans were going to close the road on us. This is the road where we got supplies. We had to keep that road open, so we went in and attacked them and pushed them back. Which we did. Back out of the way so we could keep our road open. Then it was beginning to get dark, and we were digging our foxholes, and here are three Germans walking in uniforms and rifles and everything...just walking in.

"The guy below me was fixing his foxhole and not paying any attention. He had one of those small shovels that we used to dig our foxholes with, and the Germans just walked up to him. He looked up and pointed his shovel at them, and they laid down their rifles—all three of them. And he captured them with a shovel. I'm standing there with my rifle, not knowing what to do or what was going to happen. Just watching them. They didn't look like they wanted to fight, so I am glad that I held off and didn't do any firing." He took all three of them to headquarters.

Schambach, Germany

Tom told a story about cake and German soldiers. The American troops were driving the Germans out of Schambach, which is located right next to a river. "We went into this lady's house in Schambach, and on the table was a big-size cake, with three nice slices cut out of it. This lady was in the house all by herself, and three slices cut out of it meant somebody else was there somewhere. It might have been two or three or four Germans. Anyhow, we ended up finding one guy in the house. But she was real nice. Needless to say, I had some cake too.

"We had to fight our way out to the river and stayed out there that night. We threw up a lot of smoke to cover ourselves, and it was cold. The Germans kept firing artillery at us. I remember a big tree had fallen down, and there was enough room that I could get underneath it. It was the safest place I could find. It was a good place. The next morning we went across the river and captured a few Germans and brought them back.

"We came back, and I got a letter. We had letters waiting for us there. I found out my son was born, little Tom, and they brought us our beer. The officers got a bottle of booze. Our officer sat down with us when he found out about my son being born. We all sat down there and had a party with beer and whiskey." He laughed. "It was something!"

Alsace-Lorraine

Tom talked about a time in Alsace-Lorraine when their men were under attack, after Patton had taken his men and gone up to Bastogne. "We fall back and hold, fall back and hold. Instead of retreating we were going forward. First the tanks went in, and boy, they really hit them! You always wanted to be behind the tanks. We went up to where there was a line of trees. I knew that line of trees wasn't any good. When a line of trees is hit, the trees scatter all over—shrapnel all over. It is called point detonated. In other words it blows the shrapnel over a wide range.

"Of course my men went up there. They wouldn't stay back, and I found a foxhole and got in it. Well, it was a sad story from there on out. I came out of it with some scratches and nicks but not really wounded. I was bleeding once, but it was only a small place. They bandaged it up, and I went back up there. While I was in the first aid station, there was one man with his arm off and one man with his foot off. Well, you just don't stand around and look around there. You just came on back." That was at Hatten.

As of this writing, Tom is ninety-eight years old. In April 2015 he went on the Indy Honor Flight to Washington, DC. He had never flown in an airplane before this flight. He was reluctant to go at first, but his daughter-in-law, Kathy, urged him to take the trip. He enjoyed it—and the flight!

What did you think of Truman dropping the atomic bomb on Japan?

"Well, it saved a lot of lives, but it took a lot of lives too. It shortened the war, but it is hard for me to say. I am glad he did, but I regret that it killed all those people. I wasn't glad that I went over there, and I wasn't glad that I was shooting at them either. What could you do? What could you think? You either do it to help or not do it and cause a lot more casualties. I guess you could say I am in between. It is no fun."

Albert Raymond Clark – US Army Air Corps
by Shirley Clark Buttler
"It would have cut him in half if he had been sitting in his seat."

On January 28, 1924, Albert was born in Newman, Illinois. His family always called him Ray. There were twelve children in the family—five boys and six girls; one child died in infancy. He enlisted in the US Air Corps during WWII and assigned to Squadron C 2512th AAF Base Unit. He was a tail gunner and flew thirty-five bombing missions over Germany. He flew in a B-17G Flying Fortress. The Flying Fortress, a famous bomber during the war, was responsible for the successful bombing of various enemy sites. From April 1944 - June 1944, Ray attended Gunnery School in Kingman, Arizona.

Ray tried to enlist in another branch of the military, but they wouldn't take him. He wanted to be a pilot, but that didn't happen either.

One incident his daughter, Shirley, recalled was when Ray was sitting in the back of a plane, where the tail gunner was located. He had gotten up from his spot to get more ammo, and a piece of shrapnel came up through the plane. It would have cut him in half if he had been sitting in his seat.

Shirley said her dad talked about the men in his group often and told the family many stories of his military experiences. Ray said, "The Germans in Dresden put American soldiers on the railroad tracks to keep US planes from bombing certain targets." He was given three Bronze Stars; the Good Conduct Medal; the Victory Medal; and the Air Medal with five Oak Leaf Clusters. He was honorably discharged November 5, 1945 at Chanute Field, Illinois with the rank of staff sergeant.

Ray wrote letters to his girlfriend, Juanita Josephine Duncan, during the war. In 1945, after WWII ended, he returned home. He and Juanita were married in 1946. After returning from the war, Ray farmed in Illinois for a while. Later he moved to Indianapolis and began working at Eli Lilly and Company. Eight years later Ray died from colon cancer, on February 16, 2003.

Ralph Cooley – US Army
"In WWII we fought during the day and stayed put at night."

Ralph was a private in the US Army, in the 78th, from 1943 to 1945. Ralph was sent to Ft. Oglethorpe in Jacksonville, Florida. He said, "I was in basic training for thirteen weeks then was sent to Germany on a ship that took ten days to get there." Ralph, eighteen years old, had lived all his life in Dyersburg, Tennessee. His commander was also from Dyersburg.

On the home front, he saw German prisoners who were in the United States working, cooking, and doing other work in Tullahoma, Tennessee. Ralph's mother, Emma Clara Hendrix, was German. She said that German farmers could do as good with fifty acres of farmland as Americans could do with one hundred acres. She also said, "Germans were just like you, except they fought for their flag like we did." Ralph felt like his mom had distant cousins in Germany who were fighting against the United States. Ralph said, "We were following what our government told us to do, and that was what the German boys were doing too."

Military life

He was stationed along the Rhine River. He was in Berlin, Hamburg, Cologne, and other parts of Germany. "I was trained to fire a rifle, bazooka, machine gun, mortars, and grenades." Also, he guarded German prisoners and visited the place where Hitler gave his speeches. Ralph said, "I have been to the Eagle's Nest, where Hitler lived."

Ralph's cousin, Duff, was hit at the Remagen Bridge. Ralph had a gold ring with the bridge on it but gave it to his cousin to wear, since his cousin had been wounded there. The ring had the Remagen Bridge on the top and "Remagen Bridge" on the sides of it. Duff told Ralph his unit was in a wide space near the bridge, and the Germans started shooting at them. They had to fall back, and when they returned to the bridge the Germans had blown it up. So they took platoons across the Rhine River.

One of Ralph's buddies, Cleo Reeves, was a POW for two years. Cleo said, "Field Marshal Rommel wanted to kill Hitler." Reeves told Ralph, "Rommel stood on a stump and told the POWs, 'You will get one meal a day and water to drink. You will not be mistreated.'" Hitler called Field Marshal Rommel to Berlin. Ralph said, "Hitler told Rommel to take his life, or he would take it for him."

Ralph had five buddies who lived on his road in Tennessee who were killed in the war. He said, "I was just lucky to come back alive."

How was the fighting different in WWII than in Vietnam?

In Ralph's opinion WWII was a war of always "pushing, pushing" whereas in Vietnam there was a different way of fighting. In WWII the troops pushed forward the enemy using mortars. They would shoot over the heads of their troops. There were planes behind them, keeping the enemy from attacking from the rear. In Vietnam, it was a "camp"—ten marines and two medics— where they ran patrols at night. "In WWII," said Ralph "we fought during the day and stayed put at night."

Those boys [enemy soldiers] are just like us—just doing their job.

—Melvin Eakle
US Army, Prisoner of War

Melvin Eakle— US Army
"German women were the prettiest women in the world."

Melvin was drafted into the military on April 2, 1942, at age twenty-nine. An article in the *Tompkinsville Times* listed Melvin as missing in action in December 1944. His father, Clayton Eakle, tried to console him when he'd left for the military. He'd told him he would get a pension when he got out.

Military service

Melvin was stationed at Ft. Benning,

Georgia, where, he jokingly said, they had "mosquitoes as big as buzzards." He made corporal, then sergeant; however, he didn't like to give people orders. He gave up his sergeant stripes and returned to the rank of corporal.

During the Battle of the Bulge, Melvin's unit lost 182 men. He was one of the eight remaining men. The regiments formed the southern shoulder of the Bulge. This was a time of fierce fighting, with heavy casualties.

German Prisoner of War

Melvin was taken prisoner sometime during December 16–18, 1944. According to Melvin's Prisoner of War Record, he was in Stalag 12D near Waldreitbach, Prussia where 109 other American POWs were held. Although he was taken prisoner earlier, Melvin's capture was first reported to the International Committee of the Red Cross on February 14, 1945. The last report was made on July 21, 1945.

Prior to his capture, he had been shot in the hand. The bullet hit his rifle and travelled up the gun barrel, then through his hand. Melvin was captured in Luxembourg and sent to a German POW camp. Melvin was imprisoned for at least 157 days.

On one occasion the prisoners were walking a long distance. Being an old country boy, he was used to walking, and it didn't bother him so much. However, some of the city boys had some problems with walking so far. They told the guards they were tired and didn't want to go on. The guards shot them along the road. Glen, Melvin's younger brother, said, "They were on a death march, like the ones in the Philippines."

Melvin was released from the army on September 7, 1945. He had contracted tuberculosis while being a prisoner of war. He went home, and then to a hospital in Western Kentucky for two years to recover from the tuberculosis. After his stay in the TB hospital, he returned to Tompkinsville and worked picking up milk from farmers.

Iree Eakle Francis, Melvin's Sister

"I was a young girl, about eleven or twelve years old, and didn't know much about what was going on with my brothers. At one time there were four of my brothers in the war. Henry, Melvin, and Elmer were in the army. Glen was in the navy."

Iree said, "A mailman brought a telegram to the house. He told Papa that he wanted to read it to him. I was at school when they brought the telegram." She went on to say, "Mama's hair was black when the week started and was gray at the end of the week [when] they found out about Melvin being missing. They didn't know whether he was dead or alive. About this time Mama had a strip of material tied around her head because she had migraines; I guess this made her feel better."

After the war was over, Melvin returned home. He bought a Harley motorcycle, which he stored at Jackson's store. Later he traded it for some land in front of the store. After surviving combat, injury, and capture during the war, ironically, Melvin was killed by a falling tree limb at age sixty-nine.

The Parachute Quilt, by Carol Eakle Smith, Melvin's Niece

Melvin parachuted during his time in the service and brought home the parachute. His mother made a quilt out of it. She (Vada) was a very resourceful woman who used whatever material was available in her quilts. Also there was another quilt that is set together with pieces from that parachute.

Saving Money for a Rainy Day

When Melvin left for the war, he sewed a ten-dollar bill in the lining of his coat. He carried it with him the entire time he was in the military. According to family members, he brought it home with him when he returned.

Trudy Ann Eakle Lillard, Melvin's Daughter

Trudy said, "My dad never talked about the war with me. I remember him saying that the German women were the prettiest women in the world." Also he said, "The soldiers used gasoline to clean their clothes."

After her father died, Trudy contacted the War Department to get his medals for her mother. He was awarded a Purple Heart, a Good Conduct Medal, medals for rifle and sharpshooting, campaign ribbons, a Bronze Star, and many others. Trudy said, "One time I asked him if he was angry toward the enemy soldiers. He stated, 'Those boys are just like us—just doing their job.'"

William Fischer—US Army, Combat Engineer
"While we there, we went into Buchenwald, [a] German concentration camp, and it was a horrible place."

"July of 1943, I went to Ft. Leonard Wood for basic training. From there I went to New York City, Broadway! I stayed in a hotel and went to trade school. Later I went to Camp Kilmer, New Jersey, then overseas and landed in Glasgow, Scotland. I was a replacement and ended up with 294th Combat Engineer Battalion Company D. From there we were onboard the ship USS *Susan B. Anthony*, going for the D-Day invasion. We hit a mine, and the ship sunk." Fortunately, "all the people on the ship were rescued and taken off before the ship sank."

Bill continued, "We waded ashore on Utah Beach and started working on the damaged roads and sweeping for mines. We repaired the roads so the transportation could go back and forward.

"We built bridges for the army. For example, we rebuilt two bridges across the Seine River that the Germans blew up. One of them was dedicated to 1940s singer Dinah Shore. She came to the dedication of the bridge."

Bill and his unit were close to St. Lo, Melun, near Paris. They built Bailey bridges, steel Treadway bridges, and timber trestle bridges. They also made pontoon bridges. Some of them were constructed on land and rolled out to the other bank. Sometimes smoke would be spread across the Rhine River as cover to protect the workers during combat.

"We helped build two bridges across the Rhine River," said Bill. "They were wooden pontoon, and it is flexible, so you could drive a tank across it. After the bridge was built, they would run a tank across it to test it out. The Remagen Bridge fell and was made of wood on the treads. The wood was floating down the river. Our guys had to get out in the water and push the floating wood away from what we were building.

"The code name for the outfit was the Jack Snipe. It was like the signs along the road with verses. Jack Snipe did this or did that. We left a sign on the bridges we built. There were three companies in the battalion, and I was in Company B.

"We ended up in Berlin, guarding German prisoners at this area where the Allied headquarters was going to be. We had the German prisoners refurbish the buildings, so the Allies could move into the headquarters.

"While we were there, we went into Buchenwald, [a] German concentration camp, and it was a horrible place. We saw the ovens, and it wasn't a pretty sight at all. The camp was empty by this time.

During his time overseas, starting in Normandy and ending in Berlin, Bill participated in five campaigns. One time, in the Hertgen Forest, fifty miles east of the Belgian-German border, they found out there was a gap in the line. "We were put in as front line soldiers," he said.

Another time they were working on a bridge when Germans began shelling. They had to get into a bunker. Finally they got to the spotter that was shelling them, and they could complete the bridge.

Berlin, Germany

In 1945 Bill saw Bob Hope when he performed for the troops in Berlin. Bill left Germany on Christmas Day, 1945, on the USS *Lejeune*, a troop ship, to come back home. The USS *Lejeune* was originally built as a passenger liner in Hamburg, Germany. He was released from the US Army in January 1946.

What did you think of the atomic bombing of Japan?

"I think it was the best thing to do to get it over with. It killed a lot of people."

In June 2014 Bill flew to Washington, DC, on the Indy Honor Flight. He has a wonderful pictorial book of his experience. He especially enjoyed the mail call on the way home.

Eunice Walter Francis – US Army
"Little did they know, twenty-one years later, December 7 would be a dreadful day!"

Eunice Walter Francis was born on December 7, 1920, the oldest son of George and Grace Francis. Little did anyone know that this day twenty-one years later would be a dreadful day for America.

Early years

Eunice worked in the Civilian Conservation Corps (CCC) camps circa 1939–1940. The workers during that time did many jobs for the United States, after the Depression and prior to WWII. Many parks still have buildings that were erected by the CCC workers.

Military service

Eunice went into the army on June 11, 1942, in Louisville, Kentucky. He was an antiaircraft gunner and was drafted after WWII started. He brought home some pictures of people who had died during the war, as it was his job to either bury the dead or get someone to bury them.

Family

Eunice had two younger brothers, Richard and Harold. Eunice's other brother, Frank, also served in the army during the war. When Eunice was discharged from the army after the war, he and his wife worked on a farm in Illinois for a while. Later he got a job at Insley, a company that manufactured heavy equipment such as cranes. Eunice and Sandell moved to Indianapolis and lived on North LaSalle Street for many years.

Eunice and Sandell Francis

Eunice was married to Hazel Sandell Stockton. She was fifteen years old when they got married. They didn't have any children. There was always a picture of Eunice in his army uniform sitting on the nightstand by their bed.

Both Eunice and Sandell are buried at Washington Park Cemetery on East Washington Street in Indianapolis, Indiana.

Information: Harold Randall Francis, Eunice's younger brother; and Iree Francis and Edith Francis, Eunice's sisters-in-law.

Frank Milton Francis—US Army

"A WWII grenade always hung on the living room wall at my grandparents' home."

Frank Milton Francis was born August 3, 1922. He enlisted in the army on June 24, 1940, and was discharged on September 23, 1945. Frank was in the Battle of the Bulge where he developed frostbite on his toes. He earned a Purple Heart for his bravery in the war, but his family did not know the details surrounding the award of the medal. Frank kept a trunk of his war things. His daughter, Betty, took the medal and the trunk with her when she returned to Mississippi after Frank's death.

Bill, Frank's youngest brother, thought Frank was a tank driver in the war. Frank was stationed at Ft. Knox, Kentucky, and Ft. Knox had a tank division. Frank was my uncle, and I remember a grenade hanging on the wall of my grandparents' living room. It had been brought back from the war. One thing Bill recalled was that Frank was in a motorcycle accident in Ft. Knox, Kentucky. Frank was riding a motorcycle between two cars and had a wreck. He was the motorcycle escort for some of the generals.

The family went to Ft. Knox to see Frank in the hospital. The family lived in Kentucky. George Francis, patriarch of the Francis family, worked on building the airport at Ft. Knox. So the family lived near Elizabethtown, Kentucky. Bill thought the name of the small town was Vine Grove. This would be about one or two miles north of Elizabethtown.

Frank married Margine Ruth Jeffries in 1942, while he was in the service. She lived with her mother while he was gone. They had two children, Robert and Betty. Margine died from cancer while she was pregnant with their third child, on September 9, 1948; the child, Ruth Anne, also passed. Frank moved to Indianapolis and worked for American Can Company.

Information: Frank's brother, Harold R. Francis.

John Raymond Geilker—US Army
By Judy Geilker Beeson
"My dad was in charge of heavy artillery in Germany."

Both Ray and his wife, Margaret L. Geilker, went to Tech High School in Indianapolis, Indiana. Ray was four years older than Margaret. Ray and Margaret were married in 1943. Ray enjoyed playing golf in his later years.

John (Ray) Geilker was in the US Army infantry. According to Ray's army discharge papers, he was assigned to the 893rd Tank Destroyer Battalion and given a medal for "meritorious service in connection with military operations against the enemy during the period from 23 November 1944 to 8 May 1945 in Germany."

"My dad was in charge of heavy artillery in Germany," said his daughter, Judy. Ray took part in the liberation of Paris in August 1944. The Allies arrived in Paris in mid-August to free the city from the Germans. It had been under Nazi domination since June 14, 1940. Ray's job in the military was to go and ask people to give up their homes so the officers could use them as bases. "He always felt bad about it," Judy said.

His army records note, "First Lieutenant John R. Geilker rendered consistently outstanding service in billeting, supervising the rear echelon installations, and maintaining adequate guard." It went on to mention his excellent character and qualifications to be a great soldier. "His loyalty, initiative, and untiring devotion to duty are in accordance with the highest military traditions."

First Lieutenant Geilker received a Bronze Star for his service in Germany during WWII.

Korea

When the Korean War broke out, many WWII veterans were willing to defend America again. Ray was called up and was sent to Korea. While he was in Korea, his son Jack was born. Another veteran in this book, Richard Greenfield of Indianapolis, also served in Korea as well as WWII.

William Kincheloe—US Army, Tank Division
"I was starting to get in the tank when I was hit."

In January 1943 Bill was drafted into the army. "There were nine of us from Posey County, Indiana, that stayed together and eight hundred in the tank battalion." He spent a year training in Texas and completed additional training in Louisiana. Bill went to New York the following year. Later he sailed to England, where he stayed until June, when the invasion of Europe began. "Then we sailed to France on an LST. The LST held fifteen tanks—that is one company." He didn't think this particular one was made in Evansville.

Bill drove a Sherman tank in Europe. "The Sherman tanks weighed thirty tons, and we fought against the German Tiger tanks. There were five men in a tank," said Bill. "The Tiger tanks weighed sixty tons. They had big guns on them. Our tanks were more reliable—their tanks broke down a lot. We had one boy who was killed in the tank when he got his head behind the gun. When it recoiled, it killed him."

Bill went on to say, "Our outfit missed the Battle of the Bulge. That was some tough fighting in there. There were eight hundred in my outfit, and seventy-nine got killed. That was about ten percent, which was real low. The marines—they took a beating."

Did you like being in the tank?

"Yes, it was better than being in the infantry. You got to ride instead of walk. A lot of times, especially when we were with Patton, we would load our tanks with the infantry. We would tell them to hold on, and we would take them on top across country."

On a map he indicated where he landed on Utah Beach in Normandy. The LST did not sail very fast, and it took all night to get there. They landed at Saint-Mere-Eglise and went through LeMans and Laval. "The day we landed in France was the day they liberated Cherbourg—I think it was the twenty-seventh of June. We stayed with the first army, which made the invasion, until Patton came over. That's when he made his breakthrough at St. Lo, France. We joined his Third Army. We chased them all the way to the Belgium border. Then we just transferred to the Seventh Army, who had made the invasion into Marseille from Italy. They crossed the Seine River fifteen miles from Paris." The bridges were pontoon bridges, or temporary bridges.

"We took this one town three different times," said Bill. "We would take it, and the Germans would run us out at night. Then we would retake it. We finally took it and kept it."

"On the first day of action, we were called up because the infantry was pinned down, and they couldn't move, so we went up there. The lieutenant was leading us, and they showed the lieutenant about where the Germans were located, and he started down there, and then he backed up." Bill's tank had to take the lead and go first. "I was the machine gunner that day, and I was spraying banks and hedgerows and got down there about a hundred yards when two guys said, 'I see them over there.' Well, we backed up the tank and ran over a mine and blew our tank up. We had to get out and get back to our lines. When we started back, these two Germans came out and stared back at us."

Were you ever wounded?

Bill was wounded at Manorfield by a piece of shrapnel. This was quite a piece of shrapnel; it cut through his arm. His group was pulled off the road doing repairs when he was hit. "I was sitting on top of the tank getting ready to go to supper when a shell hit a house nearby, blowing the roof off. I was starting to get in the tank when I was hit." He was flown to Southern France and then to Italy, where he stayed one month. Then, he was put on a ship to return to the States on Thanksgiving 1944.

Upon reaching the States, he was sent to Ft. Sam Houston Hospital in San Antonio, Texas. He spent Christmas Day there. Three doctors conferred at the hospital. Two doctors wanted to take off his arm, but one of the doctors said, "I think we can save it." Bill was glad that doctor was there! Bill received a Purple Heart for his injury. After spending a total of eight months in the hospital, Bill was discharged in June 1945.

Harold Pettus, another WWII vet, and Bill worked together at Bucyrus-Erie, located in Evansville, Indiana. Bucyrus-Erie made armored bulldozers during the war. After the war Bill Kincheloe worked as a machinist at the factory.

Bill's wife, Florence, met Bill "right in the middle of the street" after the war was over, in Mt. Vernon, Indiana. They went to a show on a date—"probably a war movie," said Florence.

The Indiana Military Museum in Vincennes, Indiana, has a tank like the one Bill used during the war. He was able to see it when he went to visit the museum.

As I left their house, Florence said, "When you get as old as we are, when someone comes, it's a treat." They are truly lovely people.

Evanula Ledbetter—US Army
By Jim Ledbetter

"My father never discussed the war with any of his family and got very belligerent if asked about it."

Evanula, called Van by his family, was born on May 18, 1925, in Weir, Mississippi, to sharecroppers Webster and Mariah Ledbetter. Van's father, a very mean man, made his children work hard at a very early age. Van, a large man weighing about three hundred pounds, was about six feet tall. In January 1989 he died of kidney and liver failure. Van was an African American WWII veteran.

Military life

Van was drafted into the army in 1944 at age nineteen. He served two years in an all-black unit. During the latter stages of the war in Germany, he and his fellow soldiers were confronted with enemy fire. As they took cover in foxholes, one of his comrades was killed. For fear of being killed himself, Van hid with the dead soldier for three to four days.

Effects of Posttraumatic Stress Disorder [PTSD]

Upon returning to the United States, he married Mary Seward. At that time there were not many diagnoses of PTSD and little therapy, especially for black soldiers.

Jim said, "My father never discussed the war with any of his family and got very belligerent if asked about it. I don't know what encompassing effects the war had on my dad, but I do know that he was a very bitter and mean man. He seemed to hate his children and beat on my mother and his kids as well. During our life with my dad, we never even held a substantive conversation with him. He generally responded to us with curse words and name-calling. I personally believe World War II had a profound effect on my dad. He was also a chronic alcoholic." Jim has no pictures of his dad.

What was your family home like?

Jim shared, "My family home in Mississippi was uninhabitable." Jim's mother was one of nineteen kids. He saw his dad smile only one time in his life. There was no talking at the supper table.

In 1951 or 1952, the family moved to East St. Louis, Illinois, into a house that was condemned and had large river rats. The house was four and half blocks from the Mississippi River. The house was not as important as the unhappiness that lived inside it.

Jim's brothers and sisters were involved in crimes and are dead as a result. The effects of poor parenting and PTSD; adult children involved in drugs, alcohol, and prostitution. Jim summed it up, "Without a doubt, the effects of poor parenting reaches far and wide!"

How did Jim survive the results of a terrible childhood?

"God saved me from what happened to the rest of my family." He is a retired schoolteacher and coach and a family man who attends church regularly. Jim is married to Debbie Hlavacek Ledbetter. Their fathers were both WWII soldiers. However, their fathers couldn't be further apart in how they treated their families.

Debbie and Jim Ledbetter

I have been deeply moved by many of the stories of the veterans I have interviewed; however, Jim's past is hard to write and difficult to imagine. We don't know what WWII veterans have given to our country—of themselves or their offspring.

Robert W. Miller—US Army

A letter containing sweet, loving comments, from a lonely husband to his wife and baby, at home:

"Honey, the censorship is lifted now. We seal our own letters now and can write anything we please. We can't talk to Russians, Poles or Germans."

—Germany, May 24, 1945

"We were leaving New York City from the harbor at Forty-Second and Broadway!" said Bob. The ship was docked there. "I got up in the morning and looked up and down the river. The guys wanted to go into town but were told they couldn't go into the city. The next morning I looked up the river; all the boats were pulling out. Our ship was pulling out too. We came to the submarine nets then went on through. Seeing a little land, I asked a maritime man, 'Where are we?' And he said, 'Sandy Hook, New Jersey.' As we went out into the ocean, we formed a big convoy. Three days out, we were six hundred miles off from Norfolk, Virginia.

"We went south—why, I don't know. A half day out, we joined up with another convoy coming from New York. It had baby flat tops with it. It pulled up beside us, and we were so excited! They left us on the way to England. We were heading toward Gibraltar. We saw the Rock of Gibraltar and Portugal. Next was Spain and Africa. Every three or four miles, there was a house or building but mostly desert. Sometime during the night, we turned north and went to Sicily, Sardinia, and Corsica. Then the convoy stopped.

"There were seven or eight of us talking down below in the hull. Half of the guys went to breakfast. I didn't go with them, but when they came back they said there are a lot of red cliffs out there. I said which side of the boat are they on? They said on the left side. Oh, thank goodness, because Italy is on the right side.

"No one walks in the armored division! We didn't want to go to Italy in these tanks. Of course we didn't know where we were going. It was

Marseilles harbor." They were told they were going to walk twelve miles up the mountain. "My buddies and I had a plan. We would wait for everyone else to get their bags, and ours wouldn't be so hard to find. However, our bags froze solid that night.

"There was a wine shop next door. Some of the guys drank wine all day. That night they got in a big fight, and they killed four of their own guys."

Bob's job was in a medium tank, without a turret. It had a 105-millimeter gun on it. Their superiors said, "You guys are going to fight." Bob recalled, "It took us a week to pass inspection. We finally passed. We went over to France to practice shooting at a target. The artillery mechanics set the guns close, so they wouldn't hit the target. They were supposed to get close but not hit it.

"GI are crazy. They don't have a lick of sense!

"They asked, 'Which way to combat?' They were told, 'Oh, the regular old way.' The guys answered with, 'We don't want to go that way. We want to go the way Hannibal crossed with forty elephants.' Then the response was, 'Well, you aren't going that way because we have to take the train. What's wrong with you?'"

France

They went to Lyons and Alsace in France. "We got there and camped. While camping there, the Germans had two-hundred-millimeter guns all up and down the line. They would pull them out on railroad flatcars, fire three rounds at three o'clock and six o'clock in the morning. In the afternoon, three or four o'clock, they would pull them back out and shoot three rounds again.

"The 14th Armored Division took over this big laundry out in the middle of this area. They put their ordnance in there. The Germans shot those big guns, hit the laundry, killing twenty-two of the twenty-four mechanics in the building. They shot another round that hit a big cemetery. The cemetery had both American and German alternating crosses. The crosses didn't look alike, and you could tell they were different. They blew those bones everywhere!"

The invasion of Germany began. "Mostly we went at night, with lots of shooting. General Smith said, 'I've got to fire that M7 over there.' We asked

why. He said, 'When an outfit fires their millionth round, I have to fire it.'
So he fired our millionth round.

Meeting General Patton

"We kept on going and went to another town on the Danube in Bavaria. We
are in the third vehicle back when guess who is standing there? Patton!"
General Patton was standing at the river. He said, "Just what are you afraid
of, Sergeant?" to the soldier in the first tank. The sergeant said, "Nothing,
sir." General Patton said, "Get those sandbags off those tanks!"

"General Patch commanded the third division. General Patton, commander
of the Seventh Army, jerked the whole division out—12,500 men—to get the
sandbags off the tanks. General Patton's son-in-law was in Moosburg,
Germany's largest prisoner-of-war camp, so he took a company of tanks,
seventeen tanks, to free his son-in-law. The Germans knocked out all but
five tanks, killing lots of people. Three or four weeks later, Patton admitted
that this was a mistake. It was too late. The whole army was coming, the
Third Army and the Seventh Army combined at this point. Many of the men
did not like Patton.

"We had five-man tents and two-man tents. We would pitch a five-man tent,
staking down the corners, and left the other part open. We would dig a three-
or four-foot trench around the outside, so if needed we could roll out into the
trench. They took the barn doors off the barns, put them inside the tent, and
rolled out our bedrolls to sleep on instead of the snow. Sometimes we had to
roll out into the trench and sleep where it was wet and snowy."

On one occasion "a shell fell outside the five-man tent and killed the
sergeant; the rest of us rolled out of the tent. It blew a great big hole in the
tent! The first aid man came by and picked him [the wounded sergeant] up.
They never brought him back, so I guess it killed him.

"We got one star for the battle of Germany, which lasted about two months
and consisted mostly of chasing after the Germans and not shooting much.
But in Alsace we fought all winter in the snow and fought two real big
battles where the 14th Division lost heavily. We haven't gotten a star for
this, which is the one really should have," Bob said.

Battle of Philippsburg

Bob was in active combat during the Battle of Philippsburg. "The battle took
place in a small town where the buildings were strong, built of stone and

brick." From their arrival in Marseilles until the Germans surrendered, the 14th Armored Division fought in France. After Germany surrendered, Bob was sent to Germany.

Battle of Hatten-Rittershoffen

The second battle, the Battle of Hatten-Rittershoffen, was fought in France during January 10–20, 1945. "Rittershoffen and Hatten were surrounded and cut off from the rest. There were about six hundred men [American] in our 14th Armored Division. We were hit by the 21st German Panzer Division. The snow was about a foot deep, and all the tanks and vehicles were painted white."

"When the second lieutenant came back, he was out of his head, with too much fighting. So they took him to the hospital." They fought for twelve days, and there were houses next to each other where the Americans and Germans would fight each other. One house would be occupied by the Americans, the next house by the Germans. The first lieutenant called for shells on their own building. So they could get shells in there.

"This little town was blown to pieces! This was the most defensive battle of the war. The 14th Armored Division received the French Legion of Honor Medal for their part in the battle. It was the last battle of the war until they went into Germany and occupied the country."

Bob's unit liberated some of the prisoner of war camps in Germany. This is an excerpt from a letter he wrote to his wife:

> Then we liberated the big camp of prisoners and moved on a few days til it ended before we got to Austria. Was I glad. We liberated camp Hammelburg when we first got in Germany, and our section took a Scotchman who was a prisoner for five and a half years. He went through Germany with us and is still with us. This makes his eighth week with us. Our officers used him for an interperater [sic], as he speaks perfect German and French, good Polish, and some Spanish and Egyptian.

Bob went on to elaborate about the Scotsman: "Nice fellow. He had a choice of going to America or going back to Scotland. He chose Scotland."

Riedenburg, Germany

"Bob's unit went into Germany and opened prison of war camps in Germany, 14th Armored Division was called Liberators. In 1944, after Germany surrendered, Bob's unit guarded German prisoners at Riedenburg Castle, in Riedenburg, Germany. When war criminals went down for their trials, they did not come back. This included Goering and other well-known German officers. It was a very large place.

"Every morning our officer of the day would go through the castle. There were one hundred twenty-seven prisoners, officers, helpers, and workers. Their job was to clean the castle. The officer of the day looked up over to another area and saw the prisoners signaling the other side. The officer of the day picked up a machine gun, fired at the guys who were doing it, but no one was hit.

Austria

"A week after the war ended, we went into these big woods in Austria. We went through this large underground room that the Germans had built. There were sacks of ammunition, with occasional rooms where they were two sacks high. The GIs were crazy! One of them said, 'Let's throw it down the street and light it.' Another one said, 'Yeah, let's do it.' Well, it's going up the street, and we are going down the street. It's flaming up about six inches high.

"We saw a big concrete two-story building, and we went in. You could not go downstairs; you had to go upstairs when you went in. About seven of us went up the steps, where there was a big metal door and a big safe. We had this GI with a German Luger. Any chance he had to fire it, he would pull it out and fire it. So he fired about seven shells into that metal door. He never got in, but he got every man that was standing there mad! Because these bullets are all flying around in the room. The bullets didn't hit us.

"I was the only one watching out the window at the flames outside. I saw the fire turn and go into the room with the double sacks of ammo downstairs of the building we were in. I told the guys, 'We better get out of here!'" Everyone ran out of the building.

"There was a big bang! This other guy and I ran into the next building. The rest of the guys took off running, and it [the explosion] pushed them down in the mud. I looked back; the building wasn't there. It blew away!" Bob was discharged in August or September 1945.

Jerry Moser—US Navy
"D-Day—we escorted a convoy to Normandy."

Jerry was on a US naval destroyer during the invasion of Sicily. First he was on the USS *Duran DD-634*. The second ship he served on, was the USS *Orleck DD-886* during WWII. The USS *Orleck* was also used in Korea, Vietnam, and Desert Storm. Currently the *Orleck* is in a museum at Lake Charles, Louisiana.

Jerry was at Operation Husky, which was the code name for the invasion of Sicily. This was an important operation for the Allied forces. This took place during July and August 1943. Jerry's job was a sound operator, which meant he hunted German submarines. The destroyers went in close to the beach to clear a path for the army. Their guns had an eight-mile range. He recalled the town of Gela, on the south coast of Sicily, and Scoglitti.

Jerry was eighteen when he went into the service. In 1942 he graduated from Central High School, Evansville, Indiana, and enlisted in the US Navy. "If I had waited to be drafted, I could have been sent to another branch of the service."

The invasion of North Africa

The destroyer to which Jerry was assigned was a ship that collected intelligence at various times. In 1942 there was an invasion of North Africa. His ship went alone and was not part of a fleet or convoy. There was a cove where they stopped their engines. They stopped and then put six or eight men on a whale boat. All of the men spoke three or four languages— German, French, and Arabic. The men went to find out what was beyond the rugged cliffs. They were out to find out what they could about the area. They found a German airfield and gathered intelligence. While there was some light left, they returned to the ship. They got this intel so we would know where the German air power was located. The invasion started shortly after that. Casablanca was also invaded.

"In Italy the *Duran* DD634 went to gather intelligence of Italy's firepower from the beach. They started firing on us, and we could see how much range they had from the beach. This was after dark, and the German air force spotted us. We shut down all our engines because of the wake. The wake was like phosphorus on the water at night. We did this all night. The enemy couldn't see us, so when we left we could pick up speed again. By daybreak the enemy had turned back."

France

"There was a group convoy in the English Channel with orders to head to Normandy. It was D-Day—we escorted a convoy to Normandy. It was the largest convoy of ships in the war. When we arrived, the convoy began to split up. Some ships went one way, some went another way. We started to turn at a ninety-degree turn down the English Channel. We were the decoy ship. We sailed down the Mediterranean Sea to Oran, Africa. The purpose was to send a signal to Germany that there may be another invasion south of France.

Was your ship ever hit?

"There was a near hit. A torpedo came within fifty feet of hitting the destroyer. Their ship was reported sunk after the run-in with the Germans. Jerry said, "People said, 'We thought you were sunk.'" This was after they returned to their home port at Oran, North Africa. The *Cowan*, another destroyer, was sunk.

Jerry said he saw a lot of people killed on beaches. He received two Bronze Stars for the Battles of North Africa and Sicily. Jerry said, "The LST 325, which is docked in Evansville, was at the invasion of Sicily while he was there." We discussed the LSTs, since some of them were built in Evansville.

Where were you when the war was over?

Jerry was on the USS *Orleck*. "Some were glad to go home. I came home after that." He was discharged in October 1945.

What did you think about the bombing of Japan?

"I think it saved lives. I think it was the right decision, or the war would still be going on!"

William (Bill) Muller—Army Air Corps
A sign at the entrance of the POW camp read, "For you the war is over."

Bill was drafted in July 1941, when he was twenty-four years old. Bill would have been considered an old man, compared to many of the seventeen- and eighteen-year-olds drafted into service in 1941. He was born in Louisville, Kentucky. Bill is an amazing person who is in a wheelchair now.

Bill grew up during the Depression and had a paper route. He graduated from Manual High School in Louisville and even took a few classes at University of Louisville. He had two sisters and a brother. He also worked at the Census Bureau in Washington, DC, for two years.

The War

Since Bill didn't like fourteen-mile hikes so much, he took an exam to get into pilot training. However, he washed out of that and took a job as a bombardier. His first sergeant said he could file paperwork, but he took cadet training to become an officer. He taught training at the bomb site school in Texas. Early in 1943, Pilot Captain Robert Bigelow, Bill's friend, was getting a crew together, and he wanted Bill to be on his crew. Bill would be the bombardier in a B-24 H plane. He was in the 461st Bomb Group, 766th Crew 54, Aircraft B-24 Liberator.

Next Bill's group went to California to get their B-24 bomber plane. They flew all across the country and to Brazil. Bill said the Amazon River was so wide, he couldn't see across it. They flew to Africa and then to Italy, where they were based. In Brazil his group had one of the monkeys there as a mascot. "The superiors finally said to get rid of the monkey. So someone shot him with a forty-five pistol and threw him in the crapper. The monkey came up out of the crapper all full of crap! They shot him again and threw him back in the crapper.

"The morning of a mission, you would go to meetings and have an early breakfast at four a.m. If you were going to fly that day, there would be a big board with red string showing where you were going. The bombers would bomb railroad crossings and do bombing runs." He remembered that "the longer the string, the more nervous you would get."

Shot Down in Austria

On May 24, 1944, after more than twenty-three missions, Bill's plane was shot down. The mission started in Torretta, Italy, on the way to Austria. They were getting flak that took out the number three engine. He knew he had to jump, or the plane was going down. Bill jumped out of the front wheel well when the plane caught fire. He tried to contact the pilot, but was unable to do so.

He recalled how he felt when he jumped: "The plane was noisy, and when I was floating, it was quiet." He said when he pulled the cord, it jerked him, but he was impressed with how quiet it was. When he got closer to the ground, he could hear dogs barking, and church spires appeared. He remembered thinking, *I hope I don't land on a church spire.*

Bill's B-24 Liberator bomber contained ten crewmen. They were flying over Wiener Neustadt, Austria. Bill was wounded in the leg by shrapnel from the damage on the plane. The nose gunner, Sgt. Frank Caron, was the last one to leave the plane before it blew up, killing the remaining soldiers on the B-24.

Bill was captured by the Germans as he landed in a field near a village. He had a medical kit and gave himself a shot of morphine. His leg was bleeding and painful from the shrapnel injury. The Germans took him to the German military hospital. Another guy they picked up had a leg wound. That guy had a bad infection, and they had to remove his leg. Bill's leg healed. A side note to this story is that the original copilot was scheduled to make the flight that day but didn't for some reason, so another copilot was on the ill-fated mission.

Did the Germans treat you well?

"Yes, they did, because I was an officer." If he had landed in Berlin, they would have shot him. He spent six weeks in a German military hospital.

During this time Bill's family didn't know whether he was alive or dead. He was listed as MIA for four or five months. Finally, in February 1945, his family received a postcard from a soldier who had been released in a soldier exchange. He let Bill's family know he was alive and in good health.

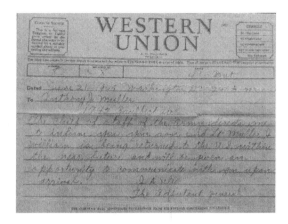

POW Camp

Bill was sent to Stalag Luft I, north of Berlin on the Baltic Sea, from July 1944 until the end of the war. A sign at the entrance of the POW camp stated, "For you the war is over."

The Red Cross sent food such as Spam and crackers to the camp, but the Germans stole it. The POWs planted turnips and rutabagas, which they had for breakfast, lunch, and dinner. They also had some German bread that "looked like it had little chips of wood in it." Bill said he got to like the bread, though. When he went into the POW camp, he weighed 160 pounds; he weighed 130 pounds when he came out. He was under German control for over a year.

Normally, regular soldiers would work, not the officers. During Bill's time in the camp, he said, a Russian colonel was assigned to empty the bathroom box. The soldiers had to use the box at night, since they were not allowed out of the barracks after the doors were locked. The Russians and Germans hated each other. So the American soldiers asked the Russian colonel how he felt about cleaning out the boxes. "If I wasn't cleaning up your mess, it would be someone else's," he replied. The POWs were allowed to go swimming in the Baltic Sea.

Once, when Allied planes were flying over the camp, one guy stepped outside, and the guards shot him. The prisoners would look up when the B-17s from England turned in over the prison camp and say, "Go get 'em! Yay!" But the prisoners were sent back to their barracks. Bill stated, "The guards were rough." Just like in some WWII movies, if the prisoners got too close to the warning wire or the barbed wire fences, the guards would shoot at them. At night the guards let out police dogs.

Liberation of the Camp

The Russians liberated the camp in May 1945. Bill went down to get his medical records. He had to stay in the camp for a couple of weeks after the liberation, since it was not safe to leave. In July 1945 he took a B-17 to Camp Lucky Strike in France, then a ship to Boston. On August 4, 1945, two days before the atomic bomb was dropped on Hiroshima, Bill married Betty Murphy.

Should the United States have dropped the bomb on Japan?

"That ended it."

After the War

After the war Bill wanted to put it behind him. His daughter said she didn't know he had been in WWII until she was in the fifth grade. He never talked about it, just wanted to put it behind him.

In the 1990s Bill's family wanted him to receive a Purple Heart. He applied for it and finally was awarded the medal in 2001. There was some problem because there were no witnesses to Bill's injuries. The other serviceman, Sgt. Frank Caron, was sent to another German POW camp.

Bill's daughter said, "My wedding day was May 24, and as we were walking down the aisle, Dad said, 'This was the date I was shot down.'" That will make you cry every time!

On a lighter note, Bill said he still likes Spam today.

Ralph Myers—US Army Infantry
"In Yokohama, there was a lot of damage—building after building was waylaid."

On Ralph's eighteenth birthday, December 16, 1944, the Battle of the Bulge began. He received his draft paper on December 29, 1944. After being processed, he was sworn in at one of the military sites in Indianapolis. He was to have seventeen weeks of training, but he had only six weeks. One of his brothers was a medic during the Battle of the Bulge, and Bob remembered his brother talking about how he saw his commander killed. The replacement commander ordered them to "Move back. We can't dodge bullets and do any good." So they moved back, or Ralph feels his brother would have been killed as well.

Did you have other family in the military?

Another brother, also took part in the Battle of the Bulge. His brother was in the tank division. One night four of the United States tanks were surrounded by the Germans. They called the American Air Force for help. Their air strikes the next morning, enabled them to escape. The Germans probably didn't know how few of them there were or they would have been killed. A third brother, also in the army, didn't serve overseas because he had a disability. He worked in a military warehouse in Maryland.

Japan

Ralph was home on delay in route, Camp Croft to home to Camp Livingston, Louisiana, when the bomb was dropped. He spent a year in occupation in Japan, from October 1945 to October 1946. He remembered spending time in several cities but remembered Yokohama the best. He and some other soldiers tried to climb Mt. Fuji in April 1946, but when they got about three fourths of the way up, it started snowing. It was cold and they hadn't taken warm coats. So they all went back down without reaching the top.

His job in Japan was in the motor pool. First he was in charge of straightening up the filing system. So he made files and organized it. While he was in Japan, he met a lieutenant from Boonville, Indiana, a neighboring community. He was sent to another place to work. His next job was to do some schooling on motors. He was raised one rank, from a private to a T5. He was in charge of one of the landing boats.

Ralph lived in a Japanese barrack and they said: "If it ever catches fire, you better be out in five minutes. Well, one of them did catch on fire. It took longer than five minutes, but not much. One reason was when they cleaned the floors, they used diesel fuel. It was all soaked in there."

The next project lasted three or four months, and was along the Adzuki River. "Our job consisted of loading gravel into railroad cars to be used for the building of an airstrip in Tokyo Bay. I operated draglines, bulldozers, and backhoes. I could load seven of the cars in thirty minutes. I know this because, we got our first radio when I was ten years old. I developed a love for country music. There was going to be a country music program on the radio, and I wanted to listen to it. I knew how much time I had to finish the job."

Did you ever go to Nagasaki or Hiroshima?

"No, but I saw pictures, and all there was a chimney here or a chimney there. And why would I want to see that?"

When you were in Japan, did you talk to any of the Japanese people?

"The Japanese told me that it was not them that wanted to fight, it was our leaders. We had two girls there, and they were as nice as any girls as you would want to meet. They did our laundry for us for a little money. One day they came and picked up our laundry, which was in two big bags. I thought I would help them out and carry the bags for them. Well, they put the bags on their shoulders, and they were on their way. I had to stop, even though I thought I was in pretty good shape! Before we left they went to a school teacher, who helped them write us a letter. I don't remember all it said, but it was real nice."

"I went to Tokyo and took a ride in a rickshaw, just to say that I had done it. I had read where Tokyo had been bombed, but where I was at, I didn't see it. Now, in Yokohama there was a lot of damage—building after building was waylaid."

"I was sent to Yokohama to work in a warehouse. Because of my experience in operating heavy equipment at Adzuki River, experience that the others hadn't had, I was put in charge of the operation of heavy equipment. One of our guys asked me if he could go to town. I told him I didn't care, but he better ask the company commander. He didn't and went to town with the postman. He was court marshalled. In September, it was hot in the warehouse where we were working. So some of the men took off their shirts. Well, they were told to put their shirts back on. A colonel came in to listen to all the gripes and the next day, we could take our shirts off again."

Shortly, Ralph was told he was shipping out tomorrow. "They put me on a ship going to New Jersey and some camp in Illinois. I had an order to go to St. Louis and another order to go to New Jersey for discharge. Each set of orders had me assigned for KP duty. When I got on that boat, I had them scratch my name off night duty. I went to KP duty for the day, but they didn't call my name. I saw that my name was scratched off. I hid in my bunk each day until KP duty time was over, then I got up and roamed the ship like all the other soldiers. After being discharged from Camp Beale, California, he went by Trailways bus to Salt Lake City, Cheyenne, Omaha, St. Louis, and then home."

Do you think the United States should have dropped the bomb on Japan?

"Well, if they hadn't, then I wouldn't be here today. Like I say, I was set for training in Louisiana to go into Japan. When they dropped the bomb, then I didn't have to go."

Ralph closed by saying, "I have asked the good Lord to keep me going until he wanted me, and He has been doing a good job. I thank Him all the time."

Robert Pedigo – US Army Air Corp

"My big experience in WWII was close encounters with dictator, Adolph Hitler, anti-aircraft cannon fire, and the German Air Force."

Bob was the special speaker for Veterans Day 2015. He is a very colorful man who enjoys telling stories about the war and the men who meant a lot to him. Bob, who was ninety-three years old as of this writing, is very well spoken and eager to tell the younger generation about WWII. He was dressed in a US Army Air Corp A2 brown leather flying jacket and an army tie. On the day of this interview, Bob spoke to a sixth-grade class and a fourth and fifth-grade Gifted and Talented class, which was about forty-five children. This took place on December 8, 2015, and Bob tied in the seventy-fourth anniversary of Pearl Harbor.

After talking for about thirty minutes about his thirty bombing missions and experiences in England, the group asked questions about the war. Their questions were very thoughtful and relevant to the discussion. During the presentation the children were very attentive, and evidently many were listening closely.

Were you wounded?

Bob said, "a piece of flak came through the waist window of the airplane and hit me in the forehead." He pointed out a scar on his forehead.

Did you fly any more flights after the thirty that were listed?

Bob explained his group was supposed to do only twenty-five missions, and then they could go home, but they were asked to do five more. Bob flew thirty missions during the war, from May 22, 1944, to September 8, 1944. It was amazing that they could accomplish this and not be shot down. The children were not aware how dangerous it was to fly thirty bombing missions over France and Germany. There were ten or eleven men who flew in the B-24 Liberator. Bob was positioned in the nose of the plane. He said, "I was

My best wishes to Marilyn.
Bob Pedigo

the first one to the target and the first one home" (quoted in the *Indianapolis Star*, September 3, 2009).

One of the missions starred on his list of thirty missions was number thirteen. When asked why it was starred, he said, "It was to Berlin, and we did a lot of damage in Berlin. It was the most heavily defended city in WWII. It was important to us and the war effort."

What were your feelings about dropping the bombs?

Bob said, "After the third mission, I was numb." He said he went into a hospital after being discharged for combat fatigue. Being children, the audience couldn't understand what an accomplishment flying thirty missions meant to the war effort and at what cost it was for the men in the war.

During his talk at the school, there were several other questions about the Nazis and Hitler. On the last question, a sixth-grade student asked, "Should Hitler have been killed another way instead of shooting himself?" Bob said, "I would have cut him to pieces, because he was a terrible man who was filled with hate!"

How old were you when you volunteered for the army?

"I was nineteen years old and volunteered with my brother." His brother washed out, but Bob had to serve for over three years. He said he often thought about his brother sitting at the kitchen table at home while Bob was bombing the enemy!

Military Service

Bob was a master bomber and flew in a B-24 plane called *Silent Yokum*. The plane was named for a character in the comic strip *Li'l Abner*. Bob was nicknamed Red due to the color of his hair. He was the youngest of the ten-man crew.

Bob was awarded four Air Medals, a Distinguished Flying Cross, four Bronze Campaign Battle Stars for the battle and four campaigns [Normandy, D-Day, Northern France, Rhineland, Air Offense of Europe] the American

European ribbon, and the Good Conduct Medal. He did his basic training at Bowman Field in Louisville, Kentucky; pursuit fighter plane armament in Denver, Colorado; and aerial gunnery training in Ft. Myers, Florida. Bob graduated and was given his wings and promoted to a sergeant. Then he was assigned to a A-24 dive bomber group at Meridian, Mississippi. It was a two-man dive bomber. Bob was the gunner and co-pilot.

Jimmy Stewart

One of Bob's favorite topics is that Jimmy Stewart, the actor, was his briefing officer. Colonel Jimmy Stewart said, when they were readying for a mission that would take them over Sweden, "Anybody caught with skis and yodeling will be frowned on!" (*Stevens Point Journal*, Friday, August 10, 1990). Stewart made brigadier general by the time he retired from the air force.

In 1987 Bob met Jimmy and Gloria Stewart in Palm Springs, California, for a reunion. Bob also said, "Jimmy Stewart is just as nice as everyone thinks he is!" When Bob told Jimmy this, he was visibly touched by the comment. Bob said that Stewart went home on the *Queen Mary* while the rest of them flew back.

Stewart took the men in small groups out into a wheat field on the day before the D-Day invasion. He told them, "We got a big mission in the morning. You guys get your rest!"

Bombing the Messerschmitt factory

Bob spoke about the bombing of the airplane factory that built Messerschmitt Me 262 planes. Thirty-eight new German planes were all lined up outside the factory, and Bob and the other pilots bombed them. "These jets needed to be taken out because of the great damage they were doing to our bomber formations." The next day Operation Valkyrie occurred. A German officer, played by Tom Cruise in the movie, *Valkyrie*, tried to kill Hitler by placing a briefcase containing a bomb near him. The assassination attempt failed.

Harold Pettus—US Army, 788th Field Artillery
"You see 'em, we hit 'em."

Harold, who was ninety-one years old as of this writing, works with bees and gives his honey away mostly. He said his son was interested in beekeeping and was mainly helping him now.

Harold, born in Slaughters, Kentucky, left Evansville, Indiana, to enter the US Army, arriving in Indianapolis for a week. Later he took a train to Ft. Hood, Texas, then Ft. Lewis, Washington, for another training. Next he rode a troop train to Ft. Bragg, North Carolina, where he took heavy artillery training and learned how to use the equipment. There was also training in Camp Shanks, New York, and then he was sent overseas. He went to Congleton, Cheshire, England; La Havre, France; and then Belgium and Holland after the Battle of the Bulge, on the HMS *Pasteur*. He was involved in heavy artillery until the war ended.

The only thing that scared him was bombing from the planes. He was shelled by the 88s many times, but that didn't bother him too much. He was most fearful late in the afternoon, when the B-17s and B-24s would bomb Germany. He was leery of being outside without a helmet because of falling iron (shells). He said they were shelled and strafed, and "what goes up must come down." If you were under it, then there was danger. It had to come down somewhere.

Harold's job was as a powder man. He loaded the powder in the canons—eight-inch howitzers and two-hundred-pound missiles. They could shoot a short range or several miles. There are pictures of the guns he shot.

On Sunday, January 21, 1945, he was on an LST 317, leaving England and going to France. Harold's job was to destroy "a portable bridge and knock out any places the Germans could hide and shoot at us." That might include a chimney, barge, church steeple, or smokestack or any place the enemy could use as an observation point along the Rhine River. His unit stayed behind the infantry, as the large gun was cumbersome to move, so it stayed in position for a day or so before moving. He said the recoil would dig a hole in the ground when the gun was shooting.

The motto of his battalion was "you see 'em, we hit 'em." They cleared out twenty 88s at Brunninghausen and bombed some of the Heinie rail-mounted 88s. The Germans would mount their guns on railroad cars.

Many of the soldiers "found" things they brought back or mailed back home. Harold carried around a saxophone for a while. He said, "It was beautiful." He used to wake up his buddies with it. He got "a cussing too, every morning." He left it there; however, he did bring back some binoculars from the war. He slept in barns in the Ruhr valley.

How did you feel about the dropping of the atomic bomb on Japan?

"How soon we forget. Now we welcome [them] with open arms and buy [Japanese] autos. Lots of innocent lives were lost, but we saved our American lives too."

Harold said his brother-in-law was found in a coal mine in Japan when the war was over. His brother-in-law hated the Japanese, because he was in the Bataan Death March.

Harold has many pictures from the war. This is a picture of his unit with the words "Here we are, Hitler." It's so amazing that even in the midst of danger, these guys could have a sense of humor.

Robert Reed—US Army
"There were a lot of brave men over there. There were a lot of brave men that lost their lives."

What did you think about Pearl Harbor?

"In 1941 I was twenty-one years old. It was a surprise, and lots of guys were killed." He went to Pearl Harbor in 1988. "I think if you were there when it happened, you would remember it all your life."

Did you have other family members in the military?

"My brother, Walter, was an MP in the army. Most of Walter's tour of duty was in Europe and Africa."

On November 10, 1942, Bob was drafted into the army at Ft. Harrison, where he remained for ten days. Then he took a train to White Sulphur Springs, West Virginia. He and his unit were stationed at the Greenbrier Hotel, a very fancy hotel in its time. "The US Army had converted it into a military hospital known as Ashford General Hospital. Soldiers were treated and recovered from surgery at this facility," according to Greenbrier.com. "Wounded GIs were sent there if they were being rehabilitated from their injuries." He worked in an office in the hospital/hotel because he was on limited duty due to a bad eye.

"When we arrived the waiters from the Greenbrier served us our meals. The Greenbrier, at that time, would cost you twenty dollars a day. Before the war twenty dollars a day was a lot of money. We thought, *Wow, we are living high on the hog, and we are getting all this for free*. It was good. I was in the receiving office when I came in. I interviewed the guys when they came in about where they had been and where they were wounded." Bob went on to say, "I was down there for about two years." He had a good time while in White Sulphur Springs.

When did you go overseas?

"When I got married, well, I was sent overseas." He was married to his wife, Dot, on January 9, 1945. Shortly after their honeymoon, he was transferred to Indian Gap, Pennsylvania, to get ready to go overseas. "We left from New York on the *Queen Elizabeth*, which was one of the biggest ships afloat at that time." He thought there were about twenty thousand troops on the British ship, which was converted into a troopship and ferried Allied soldiers for the duration of the war. Bob said, "I remember passing the Statue of Liberty on the way to Firth of Clyde, Scotland, as we zigzagged all the way, because there was a danger of enemy submarines in the area. It was a fast ship, and faster than anything that Hitler had."

Firth of Clyde, Scotland

From Firth of Clyde, Scotland, Bob and his unit boarded a train to go to a town in England and across the channel. "At that time London was still being bombed, and they had to stop the train two or three times to turn the lights out. There were warnings of enemy planes in the area. It made you feel a little funny or weird. We were only in England a night and a day before we got on the ship and went across the channel. The Germans sent buzz bombs across the channel at the Allies.

Normandy

"We landed in Normandy [in] about 1945. The war was still going on, and they sent guys to fight in Japan." Hitler was close to winning the war at the Battle of the Bulge. Many of the guys who worked in the office were put on the front line because they needed guys to fight in the war. "Overseas, I worked in the office for the medical corps. Then I was assigned to ordnance. I was shipping supplies to the front. Semis would come in at night, and we would ship them back. It was a pretty good job. The German people were working for us at the depot. We paid them, so they liked the job. It was the same in Belgium."

Belgium and Bremerhaven, Germany

Bob was overseas about fifteen months. He was in Belgium for about seven months and then went to Bremerhaven, Germany, for five months. "The war was over, and everything was pretty safe then," said Bob. "On Sunday a group of GIs got a six-by-six truck and went out to look over the country. We would go different places over the weekend. It's beautiful country. All the countries had a lot of damage.

"Most of the German people spoke English, and the people didn't want this war any more than we did. They were glad when it was over.

What did you think about dropping the atomic bomb?

"I think it was the thing to do. I'm glad he did it. It saved a lot of lives." Bob was in Germany when the bombs were dropped on Hiroshima and Nagasaki. It was at the end of the war. "Some people said it wasn't the right thing to do, but they weren't in it. There were going to be a lot of people killed, regardless of what happened. It killed a lot of Japanese people. In a flash it was over."

"There were a lot of brave men over there. There were a lot of brave men that lost their lives. When you went into the service, they gave you what you needed. Since I wasn't on the front line, it wasn't a bad life." Bob was discharged from the army on April 13, 1946.

Dick Robinson—US Army
"Italian POWS helped me load bombs that might be used to kill some of their own people."

Dick was an MP at Istres air base in France, in the US Army during WWII. He wanted to be a pilot, but he was an MP instead. He grew up in the Finger Lakes area of New York. He had never been farther away than fifty miles from his home until he joined the military. He joined at age seventeen, and was able to go to college on the GI Bill after the war.

"It was a blessing to be in the service," he said. "We didn't feel special or [like] heroes because everyone joined the military after school."

When the war broke out on December 7, 1941, Dick was trying to play chess with some friends. He thought we would knock the war out in a couple of years, but it took four. He recalled the scrap metal drives to help the war effort.

"Everybody had something to do with helping with the war," he said. "Women worked in the factories. Ice cream was five cents, and candy bars were five cents. The whole country went to war by helping with the war effort."

Indy Honor Flight

"They made you feel so special!" said Dick. "It was a great memory. They take you to the Washington Memorial and to Arlington Cemetery. I came home feeling grateful."

War Memories

Dick said he never got shot at and that he was just one of the guys. He felt that the Europeans suffered because of the bombing. It was terrible. He joined the army air force, and "you didn't have a choice—you enlisted or were drafted."

"The B-17 Flying Fortress was in our unit," he stated. "I didn't fly any bombing raids. There were four hundred thousand US people killed during the war. No one wants to kill, but it is necessary."

The USO was their entertainment, featuring Bob Hope and young ladies to dance with. "The Red Cross brought coffee and donuts," said Dick. "They took their chances with their lives for us. This was the fun part of war. You could get a break from the war for a while."

What was the food like in the military?

"You had to stand in line for an hour to get your food. The best job was peeling potatoes. KP was from four a.m. to ten p.m. You could sit down and talk while you were working. There were K rations in the air force, and every fourth day there was a hot meal." After eating dried eggs, it was a long time before he could eat regular eggs again.

In late 1946 Dick got out of the service at age nineteen. "I had seen the world!" he said. After the war he went to Sampson College and later transferred to Syracuse. In 1952 he graduated with a mechanical engineering degree. In 1954 he started working for Allis-Chalmers. "The war was over, and we were all so positive," he said. "We would be getting married, have kids, and get jobs—happy times!"

Patriotism

"Nothing is free in this country. Things have a cost. This is the greatest country in the world! It cost the lives of a brother, son, father, or those who didn't come back." Dick further said, "It is kind of humbling. Everybody did it [joined in the war effort]. It was our country. A free country!" Dick said, "Italian POWS helped me load bombs that might be used to kill some of their own people."

Footnote

Dick was a panelist at the Indiana State Museum in Indianapolis. He said he was not afraid of dying. His father had been over one hundred when he died. There was a discussion of why people live a long time. Perhaps a positive attitude toward life had something to do with it. Dick has buried two wives and is happy living alone with his dog, even though he misses his wives very much. It seemed very important that the twenty-five or so young people in the audience understood about the war.

Allen Sanderson—US Army Air Corp

"When we returned from the war, we got a job and didn't talk about the war."

Allen Sanderson, a P-47 pilot during WWII, flew 118 missions. He enlisted in the air force at age eighteen. Allen, age ninety-five at the time of this interview, doesn't look like a man of that age—he is short in statue but very straight and very involved in the Evansville Wartime Museum in Evansville, Indiana. Allen is involved with getting a P-47 airplane back in Evansville. The Air Force Museum at Wright Patterson Air Force Base in Dayton, Ohio, has a wonderful P-47. There are only five such operational planes in the United States. Some were given to Mexico, and the others' whereabouts are unknown; it is also unknown how many exist today. Allen flew P-47s from 1943 to 1947 and felt they were among the finest aircrafts around.

Have you gone on the Honor Flight?

"I have seen it already and would not want to take a seat away from someone who hasn't seen it." Allen, a very soft-spoken, humble gentleman, went on to say, "When we returned from the war, we got a job and didn't talk about the war."

The P-47s were used in England first, mainly as escorts for bombers. His group was the first to introduce them to the Mediterranean area and Italy. One of the highlights of his time in the service was flying in Northern Italy. He wanted to take out an enemy gun placement. He was told, "Don't take it out—it's the Leaning Tower of Pisa! Allen said, "Three days later the same gun placement at the Leaning Tower of Pisa put a big hole in my wing and knocked out my instruments. My wingman helped me back to Corsica." The Germans hid in some of the cathedrals and monuments. Also they hid out at Monte Cassino, which is where Ernie Pyle was located.

"In Italy there was this beautiful horse farm. There were probably fifteen to twenty horses there. Each night we helped him out by taking materials off his barn—ten by tens, etc. Since he was a fascist, we used the building materials from his barn to build an officers' club."

How did the war change your life?

"It was good for anybody. I was right out of high school when I joined the military. These great experiences made you grow up in a hurry. Nothing but a benefit from it."

Do you fly today?

No, he doesn't fly today and didn't after the war, since his company moved him from the Roanoke, Virginia, area to the Midwest. He currently lives in Evansville, Indiana.

After I visited Allen at his home in Evansville, Indiana, he continued his story from the Indianapolis Regional Airport pilots' panel. Allen went back to Rome fifteen years ago. In Naples he told a young driver that during the war he had bombed the area around where they were. The driver couldn't believe it.

Did you meet any famous people?

In January 1943 he was at Maxwell Air Force Base in Montgomery, Alabama. While he was training, he went to dances where Capt. Glen Miller and his orchestra were playing. At the time Allen was a cadet. He said Glen Miller's theme song, "Moonlight Serenade," was his favorite song.

Allen reflected on his time when he had just entered the military. He did his basic training in Nashville, Tennessee, but didn't have to report until October 1942, so he played in Virginia Beach for five months. He remembered going to the Cavalier Hotel, a historic hotel built in 1927, to hear Jimmy Dorsey play and Helen O'Connor perform. The hotel was taken over by the US Navy in 1942 and used as a training facility. Financially the hotel was never the same again.

Allen was in Nashville until early January and then was sent to Decatur, Alabama, where he learned to fly. He had always wanted to be a pilot. He soloed there on the PT-13 biplane. He has flown many different kinds of planes. In July 1943 he graduated and got his wings. He went to Chattanooga and married his high school sweetheart, Jane.

 His P-47 airplane was named *Lady Jane*. His first impression of the plane was "about the air scoop—I could slide all the way through that!" He had twenty-five to thirty hours' training on it. Allen states, "The P-47 is a great airplane, one of the best." The motto of his group was "1st in the blue."

Next he was shipped to Africa on a liberty ship. There were six hundred infantry men and twenty-four air force people. The air force was in the bottom of the ship. Their bunks were right next to where they thawed the meat. Needless to say, they didn't spend a lot time there. Then there was a three-day trip by rail to Tunis.

They shipped the P-47s by boat. "We picked them up in Iran. The rest of the group moved on to Italy in December '43." During that time Mt. Vesuvius erupted. Lava came down, and some of the guys lost clothes and their belongings. They got out in time, though.

In January and February 1944, said Allen, "Goering was moving north, and we chased them to the border." The war in Europe was about over by that time. Allen's group blew up trains carrying supplies and dive-bombed the German sub base and airfield in the area.

What were your thoughts on dropping the atomic bomb on Japan?

"Happy. The war had been going on for a long time. No respect for Japan. Mr. Truman made the right decision."

In December 1944 he left Corsica and went home. Allen was in Las Vegas, at Nellis Air Force Base, for a while. He left the air force in 1947.

Dr. Bill Schmidt—US Army

"So here I am with the amphibious corps with the marines, and I swim like a rock!"

Pearl Harbor

"My mother remarried and we moved to Hailey, Idaho. It was on December 7th after Sunday Mass, and I went to a local ice cream parlor. There was an announcement that Pearl Harbor had been bombed. The main line railroad was where we watched the many troops being carried to the West Coast. On Monday morning the entire student body listened to Franklin Roosevelt declare war.

"Patriotism was at an all-time high fever pitch. Two high school seniors and I traveled to the Twin Falls recruiting station to sign up for the Marine band. We felt it was our duty to sign up. All of us were underage, so parental permission was necessary. Only one of us gained permission to join. He was a farmer, so they allowed him to harvest the crops; he was inducted into active military service. The only music I heard was leaving our shores. My friend was killed on the day he was to be relieved from his post in Mindanao.

Military life

"Even though I was still underage, I wanted to get into the war effort. "I applied at the Bremerton Navy Yard. My first duty was a sweeper of the deck of ships in dry dock. From here I was made a timekeeper in the office with extraordinary officials. Truly this was dream come true with a permanent deferment, advancements under civil service regulations. This was not sufficient to quench my thirst for military service, so I quit what was a dream job. I applied for involvement in the V12 Navy program, but color blindness quenched this option. I enlisted at Ft. Bannock in Boise, Idaho. The recruiter said he could find placement in virtually any area. The choice that time was the Canine Corps, which was being activated. So I was sent to Ft. Warren, Wyoming. This was the dead of winter." When this didn't work out for Bill he applied to the Rangers, OCS and ASTP [Army Specialized Training Program].

"I was accepted into both programs. The company commander suggested ASTP, as it required a higher IQ. I was accepted as a cadet and sent to the University of Wyoming for basic training. Each cadet was given ten choices as to his academic choice. I chose linguistics as the first choice and Engineering as the last choice. A group was assigned to the University of South Dakota, in Vermillion. My number ten choice was engineering...I got engineering! As we arrived three months ahead of time, the school was still in session, so the cadets slept in the gym and made do for other necessities."

"At the conclusion of basic engineering, the latrine rumor was that we would go to the University of Wisconsin for electrical engineering, we left Vermillion with some regret, but with great enthusiasm to receive a coveted degree. The enthusiasm was at a very high pitch when the train stopped, and were greeted with military music and military brass. The whole atmosphere changed when the top dog announced 'Welcome you fighters as you now are part of the 97th Infantry.' There certainly was no exuberance as the train began to pull out."

"I was assigned to the 303rd regiment and our first two staff sergeants could not read or write, so the future was bleak for college charges. One day I checked the company bulletin board, there was my name telling me I had an appointment at headquarters. I appeared and was given a battery of questions to which I replied, "No." Just a few weeks later, I was told to once again apply, but this time I was informed that I was now part of Regimental Headquarters I & R platoon—that is intelligence and reconnaissance under the direction of the commanding officer.

"From Fort Leonard Wood our division went to the West Coast to begin amphibious training with Marines from Camp Pendleton. For those involved this is a most rigorous adventure and a contingent of cavalry trained with at Pismo Beach and San Clemente Island. So here I am with the amphibious corps with the marines, and I swim like a rock! Completing this phase of training, the division embarked on vessels at San Diego where we languished for two days.

"We debarked and went by rail to Ft. Lewis in Washington. We shed our tropical gear and were issued artic gear and all new shots. Next we were transported by rail to Camp Gold, New Jersey where we were double loaded on one of the largest task forces. This was the dead of winter and the North Atlantic was not at all hospitable. From the harbor of La Havre, the troops boarded rail cars and went on active military with the Battle of the Bulge. It was winter and history has recorded the elements of the action."

"At times we were in both the First and the Third Army. In Patton's outfit you better have a tie on. Very few had one in their possession; so we tore the bottom of our shirt off and made a tie out of it, in case Patton came along. He put the fear of God in the Germans. They really respected him. We went through Aachen, and the devastation was unbelievable!"

"One Easter Sunday, on the Rhine River, ahead of the advancing troops, we were told to find billets. I remember going down the street, knocking on doors and telling these people that they had two hours to get out because soldiers were going to occupy your house. I think back, and what if plans were reversed, and that happened to us?

Europe

"The 97th traveled across Europe with the supplies and equipment that our motherland prepared for troops in such a short time; while the Germans had begun preparing a long time ago. We found, for the most part, their equipment was superior to ours. During the latter part of our trek, two jeeps and members were assigned to deliver a diplomatic pouch to the approaching Russian troops. We billeted near the designated area and during the night a knock on the door revealed a German general who wanted to surrender a division of troops. We could only direct them to our headquarters.

"The next day we motored north and encountered the Russian troops who were all Mongols. They were totally horse drawn. It was as if we turned back history and were in a different era. The documents were delivered, and we witnessed some of the ill treatment to the German stragglers by the Russians.

"We returned to headquarters and learned the division was returning to La Havre, but along the way we liberated two concentration camps, which words can't describe. When we arrived at the port we were greeted by the original destruction.

"The return trip was far different than the trip over. The troops were given furloughs and time to consider the liberated items. Since the 97th was one of the first to leave Europe, regulations had not been placed. When I arrived home in Hailey, the cordial driver offered to get my duffel bag. He did not anticipate the weight of the bag. He said, 'have you got Hitler in there?' All veterans enjoyed being relieved of military regulations. After the furloughs ended, the division re-assembled in Ft. Leonard Wood. We got back on the train again. There were marine guards were stationed on either end of the car to prevent any guys from going AWOL. When the train passed near a town, a concerned soldier heaved his duffel bag out the window and went AWOL.

We were told, 'Where we are going, you would not need any money.' The suggestion was not heeded as our ship developed engine problems, so we had an emergency stop in Hawaii. We were given leave to wander on the island, but we had no money. One enterprising youth activated Western Union and we had a small amount of change. Everywhere we went there were vendors selling fresh pineapple, like ice cream cones in the states. Everyone partook of what little we could afford. Back on the ship, in a very hot and humid heat, we left the island. Our memory of our stop was in sharp contrast to the average tourist. Everyone who ate the pineapple suffered great gastronomical consequences as the latrine became the 'necessary place.'"

Japan

"Early one morning the ship stopped, the veterans were able not only to see the array of other ships, but also check the landscape. We had seen many other active military scenes and this had to be Iwo Jima with Mt. Suribachi looming in the distance. The most traveled division was not part of the clean-up operation for claiming this forward base for the occupation of Japan.

"There were no harbor facilities, so lighters were used from the ship to the volcanic shore. When we first hit the beach, there were hundreds of white bags, all casualties. This initial personal impact was like the very early death of the soldier killed by a booby trap. The Japanese were dug in an almost impenetrable chain of underground bastions. The final source on containment was using bulldozers to cover the entrances. All action was from ship to shore, which was terminated when a huge typhoon was sighted to hit the island. So with no means to stay on the island the entire military boarded ships and headed out to sea. While on European soil there was an adage 'there are no atheists in foxholes; but here we resorted to praying the Rosary.'

After the War, in 1945

"Our ship docked in Yokohama where we billeted for a few days. We were lodged in quarters there, but in Japan there were a series of earthquakes. From there they went to Sendai and Hiroshima. "Sendai was really a nice place up in the mountains. There was no reason for occupation anymore, so we were all made military police."

Robert Swift—US Army
"Guys were just doing their jobs. We were busy with our job!"

Robert, a combat medic during WWII, was in Company C, 371st Medical Battalion, 71st Infantry Division, and George Patton's Third Army. With the Rhine River crossing, they joined the Third Army for crossing Germany and Austria. The 71st Infantry was activated on July 15, 1943, in Camp Carson, Colorado. In June 1944 it was reorganized as a mechanized triangular infantry division. They were part of the Light Infantry. They were told to move their patches from the right shoulder to the left.

Robert was involved in the liberation of concentration camps. Eva Kor, well-known Holocaust survivor, was liberated by the 71st Infantry Division. Some of the camps he mentioned were Staubing, Gunskirchen, and many smaller Austrian concentration camps. Bob's Commanding Office, Major General W.G. Wyman stated, "his unit was involved in capturing over 80,000 German prisoners; the bulk of them being captured the hard way." Bob was captured by the Germans near the end of the war for three days. The Sunday Star newspaper quote: "He described being locked away without food or water in an old barracks at one of the camps; and smelling the stench of rotting bodies for three days until his unit found him."

He was involved in helping the wounded during and after the battle with the Reich's 6th SS Mountain Division in Central Germany. This was one of the final military battles of the Nazis and was a very fierce battle for both sides.

Hitler's Eagle's Nest

Bob has pictures of himself seated in front of Hitler's mountain retreat, the Eagle's Nest. Much of the complex surrounding it was destroyed by the Allied bombing of the area. The Eagle's Nest was located in Berchtesgaden, Germany, in the Bavarian Alps. It was built on the top of a massive stone mountain for Adolph Hitler's fiftieth birthday.

There were some Nazi items that Bob "liberated" during his time in Germany. He has on display on his back porch a large red flag with a swastika on it. Bob said, "It makes my neighbors nervous." He "liberated" it from a flagpole in Austria.

Bob also has some other interesting items that he "found in this building that had been bombed. We had orders to destroy things." However, when he found a picture of Hitler, covered in plastic, he cut off the frame, rolled it up, and shipped it home.

Bob Hope

Bob is one of the fortunate WWII service personnel who got to enjoy a performance by Bob Hope. He stated, "Bob Hope had a USO show in Austria shortly after the end of World War II. I was a medic. At that time we had turned the concentration camps over to hospital units, and we were trying to help with forced labor camps. One of the camps was primarily men that had been in the Hungarian army. Several had been professional musicians, and some had played in the Budapest Symphony. We had a very large mess hall serving several units. We found musical instruments for them. There was wonderful music while we ate in our mess hall. The musicians were happy to work for leftovers. For some reason, Bob Hope ate in our mess hall. Bob Hope was so impressed that he took our band with him for a week."

In 2011 Bob Swift was honored to meet Linda Hope, Bob Hope's daughter, in Carmel, Indiana, at a ribbon cutting at the Palladium for the Great American Song Book performance.

Should the United States have dropped nuclear bombs on Hiroshima and Nagasaki?

Bob replied, "Great! Guys were just doing their jobs. We were busy with our job! There were so many things we didn't know in Europe."

Dragon Parade — Taku, China

China, Burma, India Theater

As a boy I wanted to be a Flying Tiger. I stayed in the same barracks as the Flying Tigers. While I was there, I met Chenault and Chiang's wife twice and him once. Madame Chiang Kai-Shek gave us candy and ignored the Chinese kids that were there.

—Herman McGregor
WWII Army Air Force

Burma, China, India Theater

Gilbert Coleman	India
Gene Leffler	India
Herman McGregor	China
Albert Oliver	India and China

Veterans Who Served but Not Overseas

Elmer Eakle
Henry Eakle
Richard Greenfield
Donald Kuhlenschmidt
Harry Lyons

WWII Stories from Germany and Ukraine

Ivan Andrijiwskyj
Elisabeth (Liz) Ford
Maria Lewcun
Phillip J. Scaffidi
Peter Szahaj

Part 4
China, Burma, India Theater (CBI)

China, Burma, and India were considered the three Asian countries that made up the China, Burma, India Theater, or CBI, during the fighting in WWII. Fighting took place in this area from 1942 to 1943.

China is the largest country in Asia. In June 1941 US Colonel Chennault and the Flying Tigers were sent on missions to fight the Japanese forces. The Flying Tigers were in a P-40 aircraft carrying sorely needed supplies to the Allies in the region. In April 1942 civilians and British troops were surrounded by the Japanese army. The Chinese forces saved them during the Battle of Yenangyaung on April 19, 1942. The commander of the Chinese forces was Chiang Kai-Shek; Lieutenant General Stilwell led the US forces.

Burma, located in Southeast Asia, lies between India and China. In the spring of 1942, Japanese forces took over Burma. By blocking the Burma Road, they essentially cut off a way for supplies to reach Chiang Kai-Shek in China. Allied forces were led by Gen. Harold Alexander. In April 1942 troops were sent to India.

India, located in Asia, was a British colony at the time. Troops were sent to India from China and Burma. India was mostly a staging area. Indian soldiers also volunteered and fought in North Africa, Italy, and Germany. The Indian army was instrumental in helping Britain by providing weapons, food, and natural resources.

Flying the Hump

Missions started in April 1942 and ended in August 1945, when the war was over. Pilots of C-46 and C-47 who had to fly over the Himalayas were said to be "flying the hump" from India to China. It was a risky mission for the Allied pilots and crews. The passage over the hump was 530 miles, and often air crews faced Japanese Zeros, difficult weather conditions, and high mountain peaks. A notable hump airlift participant was Lieutenant Colonel Robert McNamara, former secretary of defense.

Lt. Gilbert Coleman—US Army
By Rosemary Coleman

"Back in those days, most people were pretty gung-ho about serving their country. It was just something we thought we should do."

"Gib" was from Mount Carmel, Illinois, across the Wabash River from Princeton, Indiana. In 1943 Gib was a senior at Indiana State Teachers College, known today as Indiana State University. Gib was quoted in the *Indiana State* magazine: "In 1942, as a junior, I was subject to the draft," and "I was on the draft list like everyone. My number was called, which meant I would be going to the service in three or four months." In the spring of 1943, he enlisted in the army, and the college mailed him his bachelor's degree diploma. He received it six weeks before graduation, so he didn't go through the graduation celebration.

In the magazine he said, "Back in those days, most people were pretty gung-ho about serving their country. It was just something we thought we should do. At the time I was getting ready to graduate. I called the reserve people and told them I was ready to be drafted."

Gib went to basic training at Kearns, Utah, and Camp Koehler in California. He ultimately was sent to India. On the ship to India, Gib's job was policing the bottom of the ship, where it was hot. In Bombay he was a cryptographic technician. He coded and decoded messages between areas of the armed services and the Pentagon. He became a corporal in the army and was stationed in India for a year.

After Gib and his wife, Rosie, were married, he came home and went to officers training school in Pittsburgh. Four months later he graduated as a second lieutenant and was sent to Galesburg Hospital, an extension of the Mayo Clinic. Gib went to training in Atlanta,

Georgia, to work with paraplegic soldiers returning from the war. Rosie went with him for a visit; then she went home on the train.

Later they both went to Washington and Lee University in Lexington, Virginia. Gib had a four-month stay and training there. Rosie said, "The soldiers had marching exercises every Saturday." Rosie went with him to Lexington. They walked across the street to a sorority house, where they took their meals. She especially remembered the hot bread they served and how good it tasted to her.

Rosie quit after two years at Indiana State University to go with Gib. She took classes at Washington and Lee University. Laughing, she remembered, "I beat Gib at bowling—he never bowled again!"

In August 1946 Gib was discharged from the service as a lieutenant. He taught school at Oblong High School in Illinois for one year and at Washington High School in Washington, Indiana, for nine years. Then Gib went into banking and back to school again. This time it was banking school at the University of Wisconsin. In 1962 he graduated from the school of banking. Later he became the president of Chillicothe State Bank in Chillicothe, Missouri.

Gib always wanted to walk across a stage to receive his college diploma. So, at age eighty, he walked across the platform, shook the college president's hand, and received his diploma from Indiana State University. It took a lot of years to finally finish what he had started and WWII had interrupted.

Gene Leffler
Letter home to Indiana, July 30, 1944

Dearest Martha,

Today was Sunday and my day of rest, but instead of taking things easy, I worked on the back porch of our basha. It was really a hard, hot job, but now that it is completed, I am glad that I did it. I am sending you a picture of my basha, or should I say our basha, in which ten of us live. You probably would think it a little crowded, but we are used to it; besides, there are many more inhabitants occupying our home besides us. We also cater to a dozen or so toads and probably a few dozen mice. The toads are welcome guests, as they help eliminate some of our bugs, but the mice are very unwelcome. Of course I mustn't forget the few million ants and various forms of spiders that also share our household. Boy, the other night I saw the biggest spider I ever saw in my life. The body of the spider was about the size of a half dollar. Our mosquito nets serve a double purpose at night, as we tuck the net in tight around our bedding, and it not only keeps out the mosquitoes, but it keeps the mice from playing tag on PU [stinky] bodies at night. One night I had my foot against my net, and a mouse bit through my net and nipped my big toe, and it scared me to death. That's enough, I expect, on the horrors of life in India.

Last night, we had a little party for the lab men. We had a number of men working with us from another unit, and as they were leaving we thought it appropriate to have a little farewell party. We really had a good time. We had sandwiches and punch; the punch was very good, as it contained a little brandy and a little gin. The liquor over here isn't fit to drink unless you mix it with something. We also had, as the treat of the evening, a drink of Mexican whiskey. Our music was furnished by Victrola.

All my love,
Your husband,
Gene

Gene Leffler-US Army
By Linda Harshman Leffler

Gene Leffler was born in Greensburg, Indiana, in 1915. After an unstable childhood of living with grandparents, aunts, uncles, mother, and sometimes father, he and his two brothers managed to graduate from Washington High School in Indianapolis. He married Martha Ellen Morgan on July 15, 1940. Martha, born in 1921, was an excellent student living in Mattoon, Illinois. She too had moved from home to home, working for relatives and friends. They became the parents of their first of five sons, Robert G. Leffler, in 1941.

Gene was drafted in 1941. After basic training in Louisiana, he was assigned to the India-Burma Theater with the 20th General Hospital. Because of having had chemistry in high school, he was assigned to work testing blood samples for malaria and other tropical diseases. Malaria was a bigger threat to soldiers and civilians in the area than the Japanese.

The 20th General Hospital was given citations for its remarkable record of keeping malaria deaths to a low rate. The hospital was located very near the Burma Road. The Americans were building the Ledo Road, which was used to get food and supplies to the Chinese people. Nearby, British and American troops were fighting against the Japanese.

Gene received a Bronze Star during his service, while still stateside. He had always been an excellent diver and swimmer. He retrieved a body from a river, at great risk to himself.

While Gene served overseas, Martha worked for two years at the Naval Avionics plant in Indianapolis, along with many other women, making parts for the Norden bombsight. The intricate work was very secretive, and no one person knew what another was doing. The Norden bombsight was used to make the dropping of bombs more accurate. In 1945 it was used to drop the atomic bombs on Japan.

Herman McGregor—US Army Air Corps
"As a boy, I wanted to be a Flying Tiger."

Herman "Mac" McGregor was born in Hazelton, Indiana, in 1924, at the family farmhouse. Mac was talking about the war: "in 1944 the US lowered the draft age to eighteen. If I had waited to be drafted, I would have gone into the navy instead of the army air corps." At that time the air force was not separate from the army. His discharge was from the army. Uncle Mac likened his experience in the military to the book *Of Mice and Men*, by John Steinbeck.

On December 7, 1941, the day Pearl Harbor was bombed, "I was seventeen years old and was bowling. I wanted to enlist, but my mom said no. In November 1942 I enlisted in the Signal Corp Reserves. There was training at Owensboro Technical High School. After three months I would be in active service.

"August 1943, I went to Camp Atterbury to sign in. I studied transmitter and radar in Lexington, Kentucky. Then to Miami Beach, Florida, army air corps basic training. I learned to fire three different guns—M1 rifle, Tommy gun, and a forty-five handgun." Herman did a lot of traveling before he left for foreign lands. Next it was Camp Murphy, near Palm Beach, Florida. "In Boca Raton, Florida, I learned to swim. I studied airborne radar and air-to-air radar while there.

"The military thought I might need an operation on my legs for varicose veins. So I didn't get shipped out. There were all kinds of people there, from college students to pilots and navigators."

Next, he was sent to Boston, Massachusetts. In 1944 Mac went to MIT to learn long-range navigation systems and water ports held by the Japanese in China. During that time the Allies couldn't get supplies into China. Also he spent three months in Wichita Falls, Texas, waiting for equipment to arrive.

Hollywood celebrities were willing to entertain the troops. Mac saw great performances at the Hollywood Canteen, Hollywood, Florida. "Actress Bette Davis and bandleader Kay Kyser were there to entertain the troops."

Australia

Mac traveled the south of Australia, Melbourne to Perth. "I couldn't get off the ship. It was the first time I had gone thirty days without seeing a movie. We went from the Indian Ocean to the Ganges River."

India

"We left on a ship with five-inch guns to India. It took the *Horace Greeley*, with Red Cross nurses aboard, about thirty-seven days to make the crossing." The *Horace Greeley*, a Liberty ship, was named after a famous American. Mac didn't get seasick, but lots of others did. He had MP duty, and "we read books and played bridge." He saw the Southern Cross, and "when we crossed the equator, there was a naval ceremony.

"We went to Camp Cantrapara for two to three weeks. We stayed in hot white tents with beer and other rations. We took the train north to Ganges and Bangladesh [as it is known today]. I flew the hump, which was my first flight. I had a small carbine rifle and was told, 'If the light goes on, you will have to jump.' Our plane landed where the Flying Tigers had been stationed prior to the war." The Flying Tigers, a voluntary group of pilots, flew for the Chinese Air Force. They were commanded by Capt. Claire Chennault. Mac said, "As a boy I wanted to be a Flying Tiger. While I was there, I met Chennault once.

"In India there were two cooks, MPs, four technicians [Mac was a technician], and four operators. They would work for twenty-four hours a day and wait for orders to leave for China."

China

Mac was ordered to fly to Chang Tou to set up. "Upon arriving at Chang Tou, we were called back. From that we knew something was in the works. The atomic bomb was dropped August 1945, and we all felt like it saved more lives than were lost. He spent all this time working on a long-range navigation system. "They dropped the bomb, and it was over," Mac said.

"With the end of the war, many of the groups became air controllers. The commies were in the northern part of China. The United States wanted to make sure that Chiang, not Mao, got the equipment. Next we went to Chun King, on the shore of the Yangtze River, where we had a small transmitting station. It was there that I heard the Cubs playing the Tigers at three a.m."

Exciting things were going on: "A Chinese boy was accidentally shot, and a guy detonated a piece of a bomb. Then we were sent back to the Flying Tiger area, where I teletyped for two months. From there we flew to Shanghai, where I saw the movie *State Fair*. We were excited to see hamburgers being fried, dog racing, and a Japanese war trial.

"I stayed too long listening to Russian refugee musicians and missed the last bus. I was afraid I was going to be stuck in Shanghai! However, I got a ride to where we were going to be shipped out."

Kumming, China

He was stationed at Kumming, China, and stayed in the same barracks as the Flying Tigers. "The cooks would make chicken and mushrooms, and it was delicious. I still remember it today."

"I met Chiang's wife twice." Mac said, "Madame Chiang Kai-Shek gave us candy and ignored the Chinese kids that were there." Mac mentioned that he received the WWII award Battle Star for the Chinese Offensive.

"After leaving China, we shipped out to Korea's Golden Bay. Then on to Okinawa, and from there to Seattle, Washington. The voyage took seven days. From there I went to Camp Atterbury by train, being discharged April 16, 1946."

After the War

"Four or five really close friends were killed on Iwo Jima. A good friend I worked with at the bakery before the war was one of those killed.

"I worked at Western Electric after the war. Then I went to Evansville College, now University of Evansville, to get my teaching degree. There was a reunion in New Orleans twenty or twenty-two years later; my best war buddy and one operator were there. The girls who were onboard the ship made a booklet about the crew's experiences for us."

C Ray Minton Jr. (nephew) and Herman McGregor

Albert Thornton Oliver—US Army
By Sandy Ferguson Oliver
"What would happen to my country and my wife at home?"

Albert Thornton Oliver, called Bud, grew up in the west of Indianapolis, an area called Haughville, which was home to many Slavic immigrants. He enlisted at thirty-two—much older than most servicemen in 1942. The doctor told him he had a heart murmur and a wife and didn't have to serve. Bud said, "What would happen to my country and my wife if I don't?"

Bud's wife, Norma, said, "I didn't know what kind of shape he would be in, but I always knew he would come back home." Norma had brothers in the service too and thought they might not come back.

Bud worked at Eli Lilly & Company in Indianapolis before entering the US Army. With some medical background, he was sent to India and China as a medic. His job was to guard the medicine. Shipments would come in, and he managed them. People with minor injuries would come in, and he took care of them. He did just simple medical things.

On the way over to India, the food was so bad on the ship, he took up smoking and eating candy. As a result his teeth developed cavities. Bud took the cellophane from the cigarette packs and filled his teeth with the wrappers. When he came home after the war was over, the dentist said, "You need to go to school for dentistry. You did a heck of a job of dental work on your teeth." Those things were still in his teeth. "You had to keep it from hurting." replied Bud.

Sandy recalled her dad flying the hump and saying he had to sign a waiver. However, that paper would make his insurance invalid. So Bud folded the paper and put it in his jacket. He just went along with all the other guys, without signing the paper. She thought he flew from India to Kunming, China. As with other vets, Bud didn't talk about his experiences very much.

Fired on by Japanese

One time Bud and his unit were in a convoy, and they took fire. They jumped out of the truck and laid in the rice paddies, pretending to be dead. Bud said, "This was the closest I came to thinking I was going to die." The enemy came by and kicked them to see if they were dead, then went on. Sandy said, "The Japanese had no respect for human life."

They were given descriptions of how the Japanese and the Chinese looked. One was taller and thinner, and the other was shorter and stockier. Bud said, "That wasn't necessarily so, because the ones from the mountain weren't tall and thin, they were short and stocky. Nobody had a label; you couldn't look at their forehead and see 'enemy!'"

"One time I fired my gun, and they found blood trace but didn't find anybody. I have always prayed to God that whomever it was got away." He thought somebody, perhaps a villager, not the enemy, was after medicine.

Hungry Indian Woman

He told his family a story about how hungry the Indian people were during that time. All the food he had with him was K rations. Bud offered a hungry Indian woman carrying a deceased child the food. She was holding on to the hand of a naked child with paper-thin arms. This K ration contained beef, and cows are sacred in India; she threw it down and refused to eat it or give it to her child. "We all went hungry that night!" said Bud. He said, "You have no idea how poor those people were. All you saw was hopelessness. There was no hope there."

Toward the end of Bud's life, he had flashbacks of the Japanese attacks and combat during the war. The war affected him in ways his family could not understand.

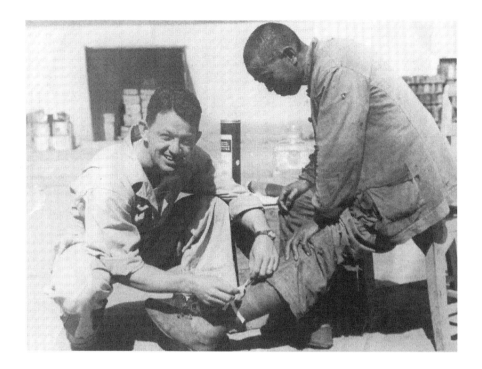

Bud was photographed helping a man who was in the area.

WWII Veterans Who Did Not Serve Overseas

Our military was needed at home as well as in foreign countries during WWII. When soldiers were injured or needed medical attention, servicemen were available on American soil to care for them. As more recruits were drafted, military instructors were used to train new soldiers for combat and flying missions to defend our country.

Many of them had jobs such as mechanics repairing aircraft; driving heavy artillery and tanks; hospital corpsman and x-ray technicians. Other jobs included office work; processing out soldiers discharged military personnel and other medical staffing needs. All these veterans helped to aid the men fighting on the front lines.

The following stories are about men who served in the military stateside during WWII:

> Elmer Eakle
> Henry Eakle
> Robert Eberhart
> Richard Greenfield (served in the Korean War)
> Donald Kuhlenschmidt
> Harry Lyons
> Raymond S.

Elmer Eakle—US Army
"It was the talk of the town, with all the guns and tanks going through the town."

Elmer was born to Clayton and Vada Eakle; eventually he would have nine siblings. During WWII there would be four brothers involved in the war effort.

In the 1930s Elmer started working in the CCC. Elmer's brothers Melvin and Henry were working in the camps to earn money as well. All three brothers, along with brother Glen, later entered the war effort when the war began.

During the war Elmer was a mechanic and driver. He was not sent overseas.

About 1942, one event left an impression on Elmer's niece and nephew, Edith Francis and Edward Eakle. Elmer was on a convoy driving through Monroe County, Kentucky. He was on maneuvers along with another GI from the area, and he dropped by the family home to say hello. It was the middle of the night, and "we all got out of bed and sat up the rest of the night talking. It was the talk of the town, with all the guns and tanks that went through the town," said Edith, who was about nine years old at the time.

Edward said, "Elmer was driving an army jeep with a big machine gun in the back." This was big news for a small, rural Kentucky town not used to that much excitement!

After the conclusion of the war, Elmer attended Campbellsville College with his WWII veteran brother Glen. While attending school Elmer met his future wife, Elizabeth. During his time at college, there was a fire on campus. Both Glen and Elmer lost all their possessions. However, some people helped them out with donations to replace their lost items.

Elmer taught school near Stanley, Kentucky, for a while. Later he and his wife moved to Indianapolis, where he worked at Allison. He and Elizabeth, had three children. Elmer died of colon cancer in January 2001.

Information: Iree Francis, Harold Francis, Edith Francis, and Edward Eakle

Henry Eakle—US Army
"My dad never talked about the war."

Henry, the fourth oldest child of the ten children of Clayton and Vada Slate Eakle, lived on a rural farm near Tompkinsville, Kentucky. Since times were hard in the '30s, with the Depression and few jobs, three of the Eakle brothers—Henry, Melvin, and Elmer—worked in the CCC camps. Melvin was discharged from the Civilian Conservation Corps at Mammoth Cave, Kentucky, in 1937. The CCC, a public work relief program, was developed by the federal government. It was a way to help young unmarried men make a living during difficult times in our nation. Henry's sister, Iree, said, "They made one dollar a day and sent part of it home to the family." According to Darryl, Henry's son, his dad worked on the roads surrounding the Hoover Dam around 1939.

Henry's brother and WWII veteran Glen Eakle said, "None of them [his brothers] were happy with it [the CCC], and all of them got out early. They went halfway to Indianapolis to pick strawberries and tomatoes, but that didn't work out either."

Eventually four Eakle brothers—Henry, Melvin, Elmer, and Glen— would be in the military. Henry enlisted in the US Army after WWII had begun. He worked with tanks and artillery. During this time, he seriously injured his back and received a medical discharge from the military. Henry never had an oversea assignment.

Henry went to Louisville, Kentucky to get a job. While in Louisville, he met Oma Keith. Oma was from the Tompkinsville area also. They married and had one son, Darryl. Darryl said, "My dad never talked about the war." Information: Iree Eakle Francis, Glen Eakle, and Darryl Eakle.

Dick Greenfield—US Navy
"War is a living mess!"

Dick and Carmen Greenfield of Beech Grove, Indiana, spoke to a fifth-grade parochial school class. The following information was shared with the class.

Dick enlisted in the navy in Indianapolis, Indiana. In 1945 he was still in high school. "They asked me where I worked. I said, 'I don't work. I'm still in high school!' So they asked, 'Where does your father work?'" Dick replied, "My father was a pharmacist." He continued, "So they said that I would be a hospital corpsman." He did his training at West Coast Amputee Hospital in San Diego, California.

What was the hardest part of the war for you?

"Being away from home." His work was easy at the amputation hospital, where he was the military's version of a nurse.

"War is a living mess!" said Dick.

Are you still in touch with any of your friends from the military?

"Yes, Glen Truex from North Dakota."

Also, he said, there was a nurse from Indiana at the Great Lakes hospital who gave him a small blanket to keep his feet warm. He still has it in a cedar chest.

The Korean War

In 1950 or 1951, Dick was called up again to serve as a corpsman. He reported to Great Lakes and was stationed there for thirty days. Then he was sent to Japan to take care of the marines. "There were three hundred marines in an eighty-bed area." He was in Japan for ten or eleven months.

What would your day have been like?

"First, check with the nurses, and then I took care of the men." One time he stitched up a man's hand after he had injured it on some barbed wire.

Indy Honor Flight

Dick was one of seventy veterans on the Indy Honor Flight to Washington, DC, on Saturday, October 18, 2014. He visited the Arlington National Cemetery and viewed the changing of the guard. He was greatly moved by the activities and events, and he wore the T-shirt he was given during the trip. Dick's son made shirts with Dick's military picture on it for the family; Carmen was wearing one of the shirts when she was talking to a school class in Indianapolis, IN.

Dick and Carmen Greenfield

Dick and Carmen's wedding day
Carmen Greenfield—Navy Wife

The children asked Carmen some questions, and her answers are below.

"In 1941 I was eleven years old. When I came home from the movies on Sunday, December 7, we listened to the radio. Roosevelt declared war on Japan. We didn't have a television, so you had to get your news on the radio.

"We used stamps to buy sugar and meat. Many things were rationed, like coffee, sugar, shoes, and tires. We would have meatless Tuesdays. Mom bought an eggplant, cut it up, and breaded it to fry. It tasted so good that I didn't care about not having meat!

"We had victory gardens, where we grew tomatoes and other vegetables. It helped you remember the soldiers and the fact that they had very little.

"Another thing we did on Friday afternoon was sell war bonds. Children would bring in pennies; when the book was filled up, you would be given a war bond."

Donald Kuhlenschmidt
"I have remorse for all the boys that were killed."

Don was a mechanical draftsman. As a child he'd had an interest in planes and made model planes. Before the war he had thought about what would interest him.

Don enlisted in September 1942. A government program, the civil pilot training program, was developed in anticipation of needing pilots for the war. "I went down, and they strangely accepted me into this program. The first three months were just plain flying and doing maneuvers. I went through primary and secondary, which was mainly acrobatics. I enjoyed that immensely. Then there was cross country, which was boring but a process of learning. How to navigate across country and how to land a larger airplane. Instrument training was next. This program was later taken over by army air force.

Summer 1943 - Mississippi, North Carolina, Ohio

In the summer of 1943, the army took over. Don was sent to Mississippi, then North Carolina where he retook secondary flight training. Then he was sent to Ohio for instrument training. The army stopped all flight training for the group of 5,000 pilots. Don was in the original Civilian Pilot Training Course pilots.

North Carolina and Wisconsin

Don was sent to North Carolina for electronic training, then to Wisconsin for additional training. Don was made an electronics instructor.

Women pilots

"They gave me a two-week furlough. Then I went back up to the barracks." They told him he was getting discharged. "'You are not supposed to understand. Go to that barracks over there.' He was told he and the rest of the 5,000 pilots in his program were discharged. He would be drafted back into the infantry in ninety days. General Arnold needed the 5,000 commissions for the 5,000 women, later called the WACS or Women's Army Corps.

"A senator from Indiana, who knew about Arnold's plan for the 5,000 male pilots, introduced a bill which passed congress, probably aided by a write-in campaign by family members of the 5,000 men, that the military could not redraft discharged servicemen. This prevented General Arnold from redrafting Don and the other pilots in his group. So General Arnold had gone out and enlisted five thousand women to be made pilots.

"We knew we weren't going to be flying anymore. We had the choice of either accepting a discharge or stay with no flying rights. Well, that went over with me like a lead brick! He had to put us back on flying duty. He could not flunk us on a military flight test. It had to be done by a civilian flight test. So what happened was he didn't get his girls. He discharged us—every one of us! So I came back home and worked at the Chrysler plant." He thought he was going to be working there for ninety days then go into the infantry.

One day he received a letter stating he was discharged and couldn't be drafted. So he was a free man. This was about 1944, during the Battle of the Bulge.

The group Don was in had some men who couldn't get into the regular army. In Don's case he had an astigmatism. There were some attorneys in this group too. Everyone had some little something wrong with them. So they joined the reserves, and they were going to ferry their planes around.

As explanation, General Hap Arnold, one of the few five-star generals in the army, supported the WASPs—Women Airforce

Service Pilots—and wanted to commission them directly as service pilots. Male civilian pilots were normally used for this job. "On 12 January 1944, the Comptroller General of the Army Air Forces ruled against these practices." According to statistics, there were only a little over one thousand women who were able to complete the program.

"General Hap Arnold, top general in the Air Force, was the one dealing with Congress," said Don's wife, Margaret. "When Congress read all these letters, they said, 'You can't do this,' and they wouldn't let him have the women. He was furious at that time. He wanted these women pilots!"

The men were mad because they wanted to ferry planes and because the way it was written, they couldn't be drafted. So then Don had a civilian job. "As far as I was concerned, they could have put Arnold in jail!" said Margaret. "It has made me feel sick at my stomach by some of the poor decisions made by our generals."

After the war

Don worked at Servel after the war too. "The only problems we had during the war was rationing, especially for gas," said Margaret. "You couldn't go anyplace, just back and forth to work. There was very little left over for the weekend or to take any trips. You almost always had to go by bus. The buses were always crowded. There were no telephones, really; you had to rely on pay phones."

Don continued to fly after the war. During his training he would send home most of his money, keeping only a small amount. He would use that money to rent a plane to go flying. At age 68 he stated building a wooden airplane. He completed it at age 75. "The unique thing about it was it was all wood and fast. It was a beautiful little plane," said Don. "The first plane I bought, I paid a hundred and twenty-five dollars for it! The only reason that I don't fly now is that I can't," said Don.

Margaret said, "They had a grass landing strip, but now it has been put back into crops."

Do you still have your plane?

"No. He donated his last plane to the Evansville Wartime Museum in Evansville, Indiana," said Margaret.

Should we have dropped the bomb on Japan?

"Some people said we shouldn't have done it, but I think we did the right thing. We lost many men. That would have been a mess. Strange, we people, strange," said Don. "I have remorse for all the boys that were killed."

Harry Lyons—US Army Air Force
"I trained a lot of men who never came back. That's what hurts so bad."

Harry was born on September 8, 1918, in Freedom, Kentucky, near Glasgow. Although he was ninety-six years old at the time of this interview, he was very clear and distinct about his memories of WWII. Harry was wheeling down the hallway of a Kentucky nursing home in his wheelchair, wearing a WWII veteran's hat. Harry agreed to chat on the outdoor porch about his WWII memories. He said he was not shipped overseas but would talk about what he did during the war.

Military Training

Harry was drafted into the Army Air Force on January 27, 1941, and served for four years, nine months, and twelve days. He was drafted at twenty years old while working at the Wheeler Catering Company in downtown Indiana, on the Circle. He later said he didn't like Indianapolis very much.

He was stationed at several air force bases in California. He got his physical at Ft. Harrison in Indianapolis. Also he had training in Louisiana for three months and in South Carolina for six months. He thought he got some good jobs out of it all. He trained rookies when they came into the service. "I trained a lot of men who never came back. That's what hurts so bad."

He recalled, "This little corporal said, 'Fall in,' and he was a hateful guy. We lined up, and he said, 'You damned dog faces,' while this big guy said to the corporal, 'Don't call me a dog face, or I'll bury you in this mud.'" Harry said, "He couldn't get along with the Yankees. They had people from all over that he had to train. There was a guy from Hazard, Kentucky, that they couldn't do a thing with. They are not raised the way they should be. This boy was sent back to Indianapolis."

Pearl Harbor

On December 7, 1941, "things were popping! Another guy and I were going to San Francisco to ride the cable car. When we got to the gate, we didn't know the Japs had hit them [Hawaii]. They stopped us, and we returned to the barracks. There was a fellow who had just returned from Pearl. We were listening to a little radio telling about the bombing while it was happening. He named off the ships that were sinking." When asked how he felt at that time, he said, "Very sad feeling."

Harry continued, "I saw the man that didn't heed the warning at Drew Field near Tampa, Florida. I saw him face to face. He was on our base on his way to Washington, DC. This was the guy who was watching the radar screen. I am guessing he was released from the service." The soldier Harry was referring to was Kermit Tyler, who was on duty on the day of the Pearl Harbor bombing. Mr. Wood, the only surviving man from Pearl Harbor in the Glasgow area was from Barren County, Kentucky. Harry said he had not met Mr. Wood, but there was a write-up in the local newspaper about him.

Harry was in Battle Creek, Michigan, when the war was over. Harry was promoted from private to three-stripe sergeant and was a motor sergeant at Drew Field.

What did you think about the Allies dropping the atomic bomb on Japan?

"That's what ended the war. They thought we had more bombs, but we just had one more left."

He had a friend who was a POW. His friend wouldn't talk to anyone else but Harry about his experiences in the war. However, his friend has passed away.

Harry ended the conversation with this story. "I was at Hamilton base in California on guard duty one night. I was cold, so I got up in the bomber to get warm." He said it was the only time he was in an airplane while he was in the air force.

Did you get in trouble?

He said, "No, no one knew about it!"

What type of plane do you think it was?

He thought it was an XB-19. The plane seemed to be an experimental bomber, of which only one was produced during the war. As Harry said, it was "too heavy to take off" and couldn't be used for fighting. It was probably a Douglas XB-19 (SBLR-2) experimental heavy bomber, made in 1941.

Sadly, Harry died on November 29, 2016, at age ninety-eight.

Raymond and Berniece S.—US Army and army wife
"I remember about General Patton and all that he was doing. He had quite a colorful life, I think."

Berniece graduated from Broad Ripple High School, Indianapolis, Indiana, in 1938. She had five sisters and a brother, Robert. Robert went into the navy but didn't see combat. She is the only surviving sister now.

She went to work at the American Legion Auxiliary while Raymond was gone. "My aunt was the national treasurer there, and she wanted me to work for them doing secretarial work." The American Legion Auxiliary is a women's patriotic service organization. According to their website, "It has been serving, helping, and meeting the needs of our nation's veterans, military, and their families—both here and abroad."

What was life like for you when the war started?

"I was married and nineteen years old. I remember when it first came over the radio, with President Roosevelt saying, 'It was a day of infamy' and declaring war."

What did you think about Pearl Harbor?

"Shock. We just couldn't believe that could happen. We were living in a little apartment in somebody's home at that time. We had the radio on that Sunday morning, and we just didn't know what to think. It really was shocking."

Berniece was introduced to her husband, Raymond, by her sister Joanne. Raymond drove her sister to a special school because she had a disability. Joanne said, "You should see my sister." Well, they met and dated. Berniece married Raymond in 1941, and they were married for sixty-one years before his death.

Raymond was not immediately in the war because his company kept getting deferments for him, since he was a truck driver. His job hauling supplies was helping the war effort. "'Finally,'" he said, "'no more deferments' when his twin brother, Kenneth, went into the army. Raymond felt that he should be serving in the military too. I think this was about a year or year and a half before the war ended. In a short time, they were serving in the tank division together."

What was his job in the army?

"He was in tank destroyers with his brother and in the military police. He did not see combat because the war was over before they shipped out."

Family Life

"While he was in the army, I got pregnant with the only child we had. Thankfully the army helped us with the hospital and everything." The child was injured at birth and had special needs all her life. Raymond and Berniece took her to a school in Owensboro, Kentucky, that specialized in children with her type of injury. It was a very difficult thing for Berniece and Raymond to do. They hoped the school could help her.

What about the rationing during that time?

"We got coupons, and you could only get so much. At first we didn't even have a car. We were struggling young kids. The first one we bought was from a neighbor. It was a Chevrolet coupe. Later we graduated to one from my aunt Minnie. It was a little better and bigger car. Gradually we got so we could buy our own—nice ones. We had to be on our own because my folks couldn't help us. They had all these other ones. In fact we were taught that we had to do things on our own, to be responsible, in other words."

Do you think the United States did the right thing when they dropped the atomic bombs on Japan?

"Yes, I think so. Because they wanted to end that war, and we had lost so many boys with that surprise attack. We were still at war and getting our people killed and all. I'm sorry that it killed a lot of civilians, but that's war. What could we have done? Just waited, and got more and more of our people killed. They were all over those islands. I remember James Doolittle when they dropped that bomb on Tokyo.

"I remember about General Patton and all that he was doing. He had quite a colorful life, I think."

Berniece looked much younger than her ninety-four years at the time of this interview. She was very active and still drove her Cadillac. Her cars have become much better!

Part 5
Evansville, Indiana

Evansville is located in Southwestern Indiana, and the Ohio River borders its downtown riverfront. Evansville converted its peacetime industry into making war materials and supplies for the military in the 1940s. These Evansville veterans and residents had some part in winning World War II:

* Anna Johnson—Servel factory worker
* Bill Kincheloe—US Army, tank division
* Don Kuhlenschmidt—CPT pilot
* Charles McDonald—US Army infantry
* Arthur McGregor— Civil Air Patrol, Republic Aviation Inspector
* Herman McGregor— US Navy, communications
* Arlin McRae—US Marines, infantry
* Jerry Moser—US Navy, sound operator
* Bill Muller—US Army Air Corps, bombardier
* Connie Norlin—State Department worker in Washington, DC
* Howard Norlin—US Navy, medical technician
* Harold Pettus—US Army, powder man
* James Pike—US Marines, machine gunner
* Allen Sanderson—US Army Air Corps, P-47 Pilot
* Dorothy Wahnsiedler—LST factory worker
* Lucy Wahnsiedler—factory worker
* Emma Weber—Faultless Caster supervisor and Briggs factory
* Harold Weber—US Navy, boatswain mate

All these brave men and women risked their lives daily to do their jobs. At the time of this writing, their ages ranged from ninety to ninety-nine years old. All of them had unique stories to tell about the war. All of them were welcoming and glad to tell their stories.

Women in the Factories

The original Rosie the Riveter, Rose Will Monroe worked in a Ford plant in Michigan building B-24 and B-29 bombers and died in 1997. She was a famous symbol of women who did their part to help the war effort working in the defense plants around the country. There were around eighteen million women involved in making war materials in the United States after war was declared in 1941. With all the plants in Evansville making parts and war armaments, there were many stories of women who worked in these factories and women who worked helping the injured soldiers when they returned from the war as well.

LST—Landing Ship Tank were built in Evansville during the period of 1942-1945. These ships were not expected to last beyond WWII and were not given names, but were numbered. They have been nicknamed, Long Slow Targets as they did not move very quickly. LSTs carried tanks, truck, troops, and jeeps to and from battle sites. LSTs were built in other locations, but the ones that were built in Evansville were built at the Naval Shipyard near the Ohio River. Then they floated them down the Ohio to New Orleans. Workers would climb aboard the ship and finish working on them on the trip to New Orleans. The Evansville Shipyard made 167 ships until the conclusion of the war.

LST 325 is docked in Evansville, Indiana. During her WWII service, she won two battle stars. LST 325 was involved in the Battle of the Bulge unloading ships and soldiers on Omaha Beach.

Evansville —WWII War producing city

The following stories are about some of the men and women who worked in factories during WWII. These factories retooled when war was declared and produced war materials after 1941. Evansville was an important supplier of war supplies for the war effort.

P-47 Air craft

The P-47 Thunderbolt, one of the main American fighters, was made in Evansville by Republic Aviation. It was a fighter bomber made from 1941-1945. It was one of the heaviest planes in the war when fully loaded. It was one of the best at diving, but no so good at climbing until paddle blade propellers were installed on the P-47 in early 1944.

One of its best features was it could withstand significant damage and get its crew back to safety. It was nicknamed the "Jug", a shortened version of juggernaut and "T Bolt". The top speed of the P-47 was 440 mph. P-47 pilot, Allen Sanderson, said, "The P-47 is a great airplane, one of the best."

There is a P-47D Thunderbolt on display at Wright Patterson, United States Air Museum in Dayton, Ohio. The bright yellow and silver P-47 Thunderbolt, Five by Five, sports an elephant on its nose. There are several P-47s around the world.

Evansville Maritime Museum

The Evansville Maritime Museum is located in Hangar One at Evansville Regional Airport, Highway 41 in Evansville. According to it website, "Its mission is to collect and preserve accounts and objects to educate future generations about the sacrifices of the men and women of those who protected our freedom." The museum contains many items that were produced in the Evansville factories as well as aviation memorabilia. It is their hope to one day have a P-47 airplane donated to the museum.

The Evansville Story

The following men and women were highlighted as working for the war effort during WWII in Evansville, Indiana. They include: a nurse; airplane factory workers; army wife; airplane inspectors and civil air patrol member. There stories show the pride and dedication of the citizens of a small town on the Ohio River in the 1940s.

Evansville worker stories:

Jane Eberhart
Mildred Ginger
Kew Bee McDonald
Arthur McGregor
Anna Johnson
Florence Miller
Dorothy Wahnsiedler
Lucy Wahnsiedler
Emma Weber

Certainly there are many more people who worked in the war producing factories who are not mentioned in this book. These are only the ones I was fortunate enough to interview and record their personal story. When most of the able-bodied men were drafted, or enlisted, the women and remaining men had to fill in where needed.

Jane Eberhart—Nurse

"It took about three years before I could get a car after the war was over."

Jane graduated from high school in 1943. "I had a scholarship for nursing school. I started nursing school at Deaconess Hospital in Evansville. In 1943 they were recruiting student nurses to move nurses into any branch of the service they needed them. At that time they didn't know how long the war was going to go on, but they were preparing, and of course they were recruiting graduate nurses too. Graduate nurses went on and joined whatever branch of the service that they wanted, but no guarantee."

Jane went on to say, "Many of us in the class, there were thirty-six of us in the class to start with, about half of us joined the Nurse Cadet Corps. We were told at that time when we finished our schooling that they would give us an opportunity to ask for a service that we wanted to join. Well, as it turned out, the war ended in 1945. So at the end of my schooling, they assigned me to one of their veterans' hospitals in Dayton, Ohio. I went there for six months. We were outfitted with both summer and winter uniforms. Unfortunately I don't have any part of the uniform left."

Jane does have a picture of herself wearing the uniform. "When we were off duty, we would wear it [to] downtown Evansville or downtown Dayton." By that time Jane was twenty-one years old.

"I was paid eighty dollars a month. I don't know what the soldiers got, but that was very good pay," said Jane. "They were also paying for my schooling. Nursing schooling was not that expensive at that time. I think it was two hundred a year. We went year-round, without vacations. We lived at the hospital where rules were strict, and we followed them."

Jane's husband, Robert, was in the army air force, but he was color blind, so he couldn't fly. He did basic training in Utah. He spent his career working in an army hospital in Montgomery, Alabama. He worked as an X-ray technician. He later went back to school and eventually became a teacher.

Did you have any interaction with any WWII soldiers at the VA hospital?

"When I was at the VA hospital, on the unit that I worked on, we may have had three or four WWII veterans. All the rest were old, and they were WWI and may have had some Spanish American War vets. This was a big hospital, with about four thousand patients." Jane said, "This was after the war, about 1946, and they were just getting the transfers from the war. Penicillin was discovered in 1939, and came into more common usage during the war. It was just being used, so people with infections were helped by an antibiotic and never went to the hospital. Many medical advances are made in war time."

"During the war years, 1943 to 1946, I corresponded with several soldiers. There were five or six from Camp Breckenridge, Kentucky. Every weekend they came by buses. The USO was a great place for dancing and meeting people. All my correspondents came home safely from the war. Only one married an Evansville girl. I have no recollection of the other soldiers."

How did you meet your husband?

"I met him through a friend in Evansville. Indirectly we met "dragging Main Street," a common activity for young people of the 1940s. We were engaged for eighteen months before we got married. By that time we got to know each other pretty well."

He had come from a family where he was an only child, and she had come from a family of five children. They had to compromise some. They had four children—three daughters and one son. "I enjoyed having the kids. They were fun for me." At the time of this interview, she had just received word that she had a new great-grandchild. Her husband, Robert, died in 1976.

Do you recall how things were as a nursing student and during the war?

"Everybody was doing the same things, so you didn't think too much about it. I found out about things that were going on at the time, that I didn't have any idea that were happening. Simply because I didn't learn how to drive a car until I was twenty-one, because you didn't have gasoline and didn't have tires if they wore out. That was it, unless you could find some used ones somewhere. We only had one vehicle in the family at that time. People didn't make cars until the war was over. You had to put your name on a list to get a car. I was saving my money to get a car. My dad knew somebody who had a dealership, and he moved me up on the list so that I could get a car. It took about three years before I could get a car after the war was over.

Was there rationing of food and supplies?

"There was rationing, like sugar. I barely remember the ration books because I didn't have to deal with them. People had to stand in line to buy cigarettes, but that wasn't a problem for me because I didn't smoke. For instance, you had to stand in line at the movies, and you did. It was not uncommon to come into the movies in the middle of the show and watch the end of the movie, and then stay to watch the beginning. We thought nothing of it!

"The bus back and forth to the hospital was always crowded, often it was easier to walk. That was all the transportation people had to get around. Every six months I would take the bus home from Dayton, Ohio, and then walk about a mile to my house. Many times friends or neighbors would stop and give me a lift part of the way. There was usually one vehicle to a family. Even when I got married, we only had one vehicle for a long time."

She babysat for one of the doctors at the veterans' hospital in Dayton. "It paid fifty cents an hour, big money for that job." Jane recalled, "The doctors hired by the VA had been drafted, so they had to assign army doctors to the VA hospital. The doctor that I worked with at the VA hospital was an obstetrician. To me it was kind of funny that they had taken away a doctor that would have normally been there and assigned somebody who the men didn't need."

Mildred Ginger—Female Republic Air Worker
Told by Robert Ginger
"She quit nursing school to build airplanes for the war effort."

Robert Ginger's mother, Mildred, worked in the Republic airplane plant building P-47 planes. While he was growing up, Bob never knew his mother had worked in the Evansville Republic plant during the war. Wright Patterson Air Force Museum in Dayton, Ohio, has a wonderful P-47 Thunderbolt on display.

Mildred quit nursing school to build airplanes for the war effort. She thought Bob would be disappointed in her if he knew. Bob said, "Quite the opposite was true. I was proud of her." Some women in Evansville were working in the factories, since many men were drafted into military service.

With the money she made from working at the plant and what his dad made, they bought their home in Lakewood Hill, Evansville, Indiana.

Bob was born on August 6, 1945, the day that the United States dropped the first atomic bomb on Nagasaki, Japan. The next day he was adopted by his new family—Mildred and Andrew Ginger.

Kew Bee Mc Donald—Army Wife and WWII Schoolgirl
"I was in Sunday School. When we came home, we heard it on the radio."

"There were no tires, silk hose, makeup, or coffee. The high school band couldn't travel because there were no tires." Kew Bee was active in the war effort on the home front, as she sold war bonds. She said, "You got a Stamp and Bond Representative book that cost $18.50 when it was completely full. After a time, you would redeem it for $25. The stamp cost twenty-five cents." It was a poor man's saving account. Before the United States was in the war, "we collected chewing gum foil and lard to send to Great Britain."

Kew Bee explained how difficult times were during the war years in Evansville and what the community did to help.

"Workers who made arms came here to work from Illinois and Kentucky, then they stayed," Kew Bee said. During WWII in Evansville, it was a family effort to support the war. Kew Bee's brother-in-law, C Ray Minton Sr. was a LST shipbuilding inspector at The Evansville Naval Shipyard; her husband, Charlie McDonald, US Army, served in the Pacific; her brother, Arthur McGregor, was in the Civil Air Patrol and an inspector at Republic Air in Evansville; and her brother, Herman McGregor, US Army Air Corp in China.

What did you think about dropping the atomic bombs on Japan?

"It was terrible what they did at Pearl Harbor. It was terrible what they did to the Japanese children. The Japanese would not have given up without the bomb being dropped on them."

Arthur McGregor—Civil Air Patrol, Second Lieutenant
"As close as any brother can be."
By Herman McGregor

Herman McGregor, nicknamed Mac, remembered his brother Art being "as close as any brother can be." Art was eleven years old when Mac was born. He said, "Art took me to Walsh's Kew Bee Bakery." Kew Bee was a brand of bread sold during this time. His sister, Kew Bee, is named after the bread.

Art had many jobs—at Walsh's Kew Bee Bakery; Ideal Dairy, where he delivered milk by wagon and often took Herman with him; Republic Aviation; and Kraft Foods. Art took over supporting the family when he was sixteen, after his dad couldn't work any longer. Mac and Art went to the movies after Art's work was over.

Art always wanted to fly, so he took flying lessons, often taking Mac with him, and received his pilot's license. When Republic Aviation began making planes for the war effort in 1942, Art got a job there and later became the chief of final inspection at the modifications center. Republic, in Evansville, built the Thunderbolt P-47 aircraft. They were sent to other parts of the country and to the battle sites overseas.

Art was always looking after his younger brother, and he told Mac, "Maybe I could get you transferred to Evansville." However, during that time, in November 1942, Mac was in the Army Signal Corps Reserve and was at school in Owensboro and then Lexington, Kentucky. This would have been about August 1943.

Art wore the CAP (Civil Air Patrol) uniform and was a second lieutenant. He had an important job to do on the home front to aid the war effort. The CAP was created in 1941 to provide civilian air support to border patrols, military training, and courier services. The CAP was originally part of the army but was moved to the air force after the war.

Anna Johnson—War Materials Worker
"I had my parents, then I had five brothers for parents."

Anna grew up on a farm in Breckenridge County, Kentucky, during the Depression, and her family did not have any modern conveniences. "We were not the only ones that lived like this. Our neighbors lived the same as we did. No one had electricity. This place was a very primitive area. We canned everything, so we had plenty to eat," said Anna. "We were richer than most because we had two wells of water on our property."

Why did you work at Servel?

One of her brothers convinced her to come to Evansville to get a job. Anna got a job at Servel and stayed in Indiana. "Gasoline was rationed, and I lived with my brother who lived between Evansville and Rockport. I was in a carpool to get back and forth to work." Her brother, Shellie Lloyd, worked on the LSTs [Landing Ship Tank] in Evansville. She learned the basics of riveting at North High School. Her job was to work on the ammunition boxes in the wings of the plane. Later she worked on the gun cover that went around the guns in the wing. She worked on P-4 wings doing the riveting. "People think rivets are rivets, but the big thing that was assembled was called a spar. The rivets that went through a spar are different. They have to be frozen. They were too hard to drive if they weren't frozen."

Describe what you did at the factory?

"If your drill bit became dull, you sent it to the shop, and they sharpened it. You hoped that they got it good and round. If they didn't, your drill might go scooting across the wing. I was introduced to this little fairing tool and a bottle of oil. You would have to rub out the crack you made, so you were very careful with that drill. You didn't want to stand there with that oil and rub it until it looked shiny."

Next, "the people who worked on the wings after we did, got inside the wing with a vacuum cleaner and got all the shavings out. Then they would clean it out with rags and wash it down again. They didn't just say, it's done! Each part or job would be checked by a Servel inspector. They would use a long stick with an attached mirror to check the work. If an inspector saw a rivet that was crooked, then you had to take it out and repair it. She would look at it again; then she would turn it over to the army inspector who would inspect it. It didn't just go out of there." The wing was transferred to the paint shop.

"It gave you a good feeling to finish up that wing. The finished wings were on a dolly, and they were sent to Republic Aviation to be assembled into P-47 airplanes." Republic Aviation had a government contract to produce planes.

How were the working conditions at the factory?

For our security there weren't any windows in the factory. The factory owners and the government didn't want the enemy to see the light from the building, if enemy planes would fly over. I worked from seven p.m. to seven a.m. Also we worked seven days a week." She didn't remember how much she was paid, because she didn't keep any of the pay stubs.

Anna sold war bonds for the war effort at the factory. "They had war bonds that were sold during this time, Series E savings bonds. There were stamps that you bought. When you collected $18.75, you could exchange it for a twenty-five-dollar bond." She explained, "I didn't do well talking to people back then. So they decided that I would sell war bonds. I went up to this supervisor, who I was frightened of, and got up the nerve to ask him to buy a bond. He bought a fifty-dollar bond from me, and that was the biggest one sold that night."

Another security event was when President Franklin D. Roosevelt's train went through Evansville. They wouldn't let us get within a block of that railroad crossing. They stopped us at least a block away from the railroad tracks. Security was very tight."

What did the men think of the women working in the factory?

"They were mighty glad for you to help them. Everyone was grateful to do something for the war. Every able-bodied man was drafted, so they had to rely on the women."

She worked at Servel until the war was over. "I went to work that night [the night the war was over] and they met us at the gate and said 'you don't have to work.' We all went down to Calvary Baptist Church to give thanks the war was over. It was a good memory."

Do you think they should have dropped the atomic bomb on Japan?

"Yes, I do. Can you imagine a group of people standing in church or sitting in church trying to give prayers to God and them [the Japanese] come over and bomb them and bomb those boys and bury them so deep that they are still down there? I think it's an eye for an eye. I used to dream that I was in the army for many years."

The war affected her and her family with the loss of her brother. "My brother, Hugh Lloyd, was in the navy and serving on a light destroyer. I was at home on vacation, when I heard them say 'missing in action,' and it was my brother. He was married and had a little girl. It was years before we discovered he was killed when a torpedo hit his ship." A sailor wrote to Hugh's wife and explained how Hugh had died. Another family member, Ann's first husband, Paul Wilson, was a WWII serviceman who received a Bronze Star for capturing an enemy division.

In 2011, Allen Sanderson and Anna met at the Evansville airplane hangar where a local maritime museum meeting was being held. Allen Sanderson, a former WWII P-47 pilot, said to Anna, "I want to thank you for having my back." It meant a lot to Anna for him to say that to her.

Florence Miller—WWII Worker
"I was too little and too green to go inside the ships."

Florence was a shy woman who worked at Bristol-Myers and the Evansville naval yard during WWII. Her job was to carry messages. She was not on the ships or inside the ships. "I was too little and too green to go inside the ships," she said.

The naval yard built LSTs during the war. The plant employed many people in the area; many women were working at the facility since the men were in the military.

Florence was not a woman without loss, as her son was killed in Vietnam.

Florence thought the naval yard was an interesting place to work and remembered when the last ship was made. She saw it, as it was christened.

One funny story: Florence was pregnant, and her plant supervisor asked her to name the child after him. In exchange he would make her child an heir to his estate, since he didn't have any heirs. Florence declined, as her husband, Bob, still in the military, had already named the unborn child.

Florence said she received a censored letter from Bob about once a week while he was in the service. She recalled the following items being rationed during this team: meat, sugar, shortening, and shoes. After the baby was born, she had a ration book for both herself and the baby, Pamela Elaine. The baby needed more things than she did and had a separate ration book.

Lucy Wahnsiedler—WWII Factory Worker
"It's the plane that won the war!"

Lucy graduated from Ridgeway High School in Ridgeway, Illinois, at age eighteen and began working in Evansville riveting P-47s. At the time of this interview, she was ninety-one years old. Her sister, Margaret, also worked where Lucy did, as an inspector. Lucy and Dorothy, Lucy's sister-in-law, live next door to each other in Evansville, Indiana. Her job involved working on the elevator or tail assembly of the P-47 aircraft. She also worked at Shane Manufacturing, which made carbine cases and uniforms for the war.

"Everybody came to Evansville to work, and I lived at my aunt's house. Some worked at the shipyards, and some were at Mead Johnson." She worked using an air gun. She worked at Hoosier Cardinal, then the parts were transported over to Republic Aviation, where the airplanes were assembled. She said, "It's the plane that won the war!"

At work, Lucy recalled, "We had inspectors that looked over our work, then the army inspectors would inspect our work."

She said, "When I was growing up, my dad wouldn't let me wear pants; we wore dresses." Lucy had a book showing a woman wearing pants while using an air gun. "Then, when the war came, everyone wore slacks."

She had a cousin who was killed in Okinawa and another relative who was injured in New Guinea.

Where did you meet your husband?

"I was working here [in Evansville] when I was in a wedding." Her future husband, John, also went to the wedding, and they met. She trained at Mechanic Arts School in Evansville. She and John had seven children. They were married for sixty-three years; John died in 2009.

What did you do for entertainment?

"Well, it was big band era. They had dances down there [in Evansville]. Glenn Miller's band came here too. There were movies, and the soldiers from Camp Breckinridge, Morganfield, Kentucky, south of Evansville, were here too. They had a USO here. I didn't go to those dances, because I was dating John."

Dorothy Wahnsiedler—WWII Factory Worker
"There were soldiers everywhere!"

In 1943 Dorothy graduated from Reitz Memorial at age eighteen. She worked for one year at the Evansville shipyard, where LSTs were built for one year. She worked in the welding department and the field hospital insurance department. "Sometimes I would see launchings and such, but that's about as close as I got," she said. "The workers would come into the field hospital with flash burns from welding and smashed fingers.

"Sometimes I helped at the field hospital getting people in to see the doctors. We had a first aid station down on the docks. They would launch the ships then would finish the interior to get it ready to ship out. If the secretary was gone, then I would go down and help the nurse. In November 1944 I walked across the street to Mead Johnson and worked there for forty-five years. Some of us went over to the Red Cross, learned to roll bandages, make beds, and things like that.

"We just got along the best we could. We couldn't buy things. Your gas, sugar, and meat were rationed. We got two pair of shoes a year or had them resoled. We couldn't buy hose, so we used leg makeup. It was similar to what we use on our faces now." Dorothy said she went "to some of the dances at the USO downtown and to Breckinridge one time. There were soldiers everywhere in Evansville!" Dorothy, Lucy's sister-in-law, did not marry, because she wanted a career; she has continued to live next door to Lucy.

Were there any deaths where you worked?

"Not where I worked, but there were lots of accidents. Of course there were beds in the field hospital. There were many injuries like burns from the welding, falls, and hands and fingers. Deaths from falls on the cranes. They worked twenty-four hours a day at the shipyards. Lights were on at night."

Dorothy said, "There is one thing that I won't forget seeing as an eighteen-year-old girl. There was a woman who worked at the factory, had a miscarriage. I can still see that little baby on the table back there."

Dorothy recalled a supervisor she had at that time: "He just loved to say things that would make me blush. He told me, 'I just love to see you blush, Dorothy.' He may have been the reason she moved on to Mead Johnson!

Emma Weber—Evansville Factory Worker
"I heard a girl scream!"

In 1941 Evansville converted many of its industries to war-product-producing factories. Emma's first job was at Faultless Caster, a company that built rifle grenade parts. Her part of the job was the "half block," which entailed getting the burrs off it. She was the timekeeper and supervisor, with ten girls working under her.

Once, Emma said, "I heard a girl scream!" Emma went to check on her and found a girl was working on a machine. "Her long hair was going around the wheel. I looked at her, turned the wheel backward, and got her out of it." Emma's quick thinking saved the girl's life, or at least her hair.

Emma was in charge of the time the girls started, how much work they did, and the time they quit, using time cards. She stated that "everybody got along."

Eventually she was laid off at Faultless and had to find a new job. Her next job was also in the war-product industry of Evansville, at a company called Briggs, located at Columbia and Evans Street. Briggs had a contract for parts for the F-4U Corsair plane. Emma worked on the wings. Three girls would take turns drilling and bucking the rivets. She worked up the next wing for the next girl to work on. Every two hours the girls would switch jobs, so they got the wings done. She thought they were parts for the P-47, but research seems to show they were for the F-4U Corsair or F-4F Wildcat.

She said the fuselage was built on the other side of the plant. Emma didn't like the idea of building war materials, but made the best of it. Later she had a job at Deaconess Hospital for eighteen years, as a housekeeper. She loved spending time with the patients. Her other jobs were at Swift packing house and a local restaurant.

Did you have any other family in the war?

Emma had several family members who helped with the war effort as well. Her dad, Ed Owen, worked at the shipyard as a pipe fitter. He wouldn't talk about it at home. She had an uncle who was in the marines. He said he walked over many dead bodies. He was at Iwo Jima, and her uncle was next in line to go if the soldiers raising the flag were shot. He was glad they made it!

Her brother, Estil Owen, was an aerial photographer. He rode in planes to get pictures and even crawled out on the wings to get better pictures. One time he even opened the hatch below the plane to take a photo. The pictures indicated when bombs were dropped from the plane, where the bombs hit, and when they blew up. Other pictures showed where the bombs were supposed to go before they went down. The picture would be enlarged to show where to drop the bombs.

In 1951 Emma met a man named Harold on a blind date. A friend she worked with at Swift wanted her to meet him. Their first date was at the VFW. They have been married for fifty-four years as of this writing. Emma and WWII veteran Harold Weber live in Evansville.

Part 6
USS *Indianapolis*

USS Indianapolis *Reunion, 2016*

The seventy-first USS *Indianapolis* reunion was held at the Hyatt Regency Hotel in Indianapolis, Indiana, on July 9, 2016. Edgar Harrell, a USS *Indianapolis* survivor, spoke about his experiences after the ship sunk. He has written a book, *Out of the Depths*, describing the events that unfolded after the ship went down.

Ed outlined the events of the four days he spent in the Pacific. He said, "There are times when you pray. I poured my heart out to the Lord. I don't want to die. I am seeing what I think is eternity out there." Many years after his survival, he reflected on this nightmarish time spent in dangerous shark-infested water: "I don't know what all I promised Him, but probably much more than I have lived up to."

Another survivor, Cleatus Lebow, was at this reunion. There were fourteen fewer survivors in 2016 than were at the previous year's reunion, age and disease being the killers this time. As Cleatus was on his way to get a milkshake at the reunion, I asked what was his favorite flavor was. He said, "All of them."

How many sailors did not survive?

There were 1,196 aboard the USS *Indianapolis*. About nine hundred made it into the cold Pacific water. Of them, only 317 survived.

Although there are many stories and lots of heartbroken families, there are two sailors who are highlighted here. One, Paul Ross Feeney, was remembered at the USS *Indianapolis* Memorial on the canal in downtown Indianapolis in 2015. Paul's grandson, Mike, brought his wife, Kim, and baby daughter, Kayla, to honor the grandfather he had never seen. Mike's grandmother had been pregnant with Mike's father while Paul was in the navy. When the USS *Indianapolis* was dry docked for repairs, he saw his son only once.

The second seaman lost on the USS *Indianapolis* was John (Johnnie) Rozzano Jr. His body was never recovered, and his family had no idea if he was killed on the ship or vanished in the water after the attack. Johnnie was a very handsome eighteen-year-old man. His family made a very poignant documentary of his life. They have since had a funeral, and they have erected a monument in his honor in his hometown of Lorain, Ohio. It is very distressing to have lost such a bright young life and not have a body or any information about what happened that fateful night.

The best way to tell the story of the sinking of the USS *Indianapolis* is by letting one of the survivors, Edgar Harrell, explain what happened each day. The USS *Indianapolis* had just delivered to Tinian Island the components of the atomic bomb that would end the war. His account of what happened after being hit by the German sub is in the next section.

USS *Indianapolis Memorial*

Since the USS *Indianapolis* was named for the city of Indianapolis, the people of Indianapolis feel a fondness for the survivors and the lost sailors of the ship. The memorial was erected in 1995. Reunions are held on a weekend in July near the date of the sinking. There is a black and gray granite memorial on the canal in downtown Indianapolis. It lists all the men who served on the ship as well as some history of what happened to it. There is usually a wreath ceremony held at this site as well as speakers and luncheons at a nearby hotel. The survivors are treated with the honor they deserve and are featured in the local newspaper and on local TV stations. The highway that circles around Indianapolis, I-465, is named the USS *Indianapolis* Memorial Highway.

Edgar Harrell and Cleatus Lebow were interviewed in August 2016.

Indy Honor Flights

According to the Indy Honor Flight website, "Indy Honor Flight is a nonprofit organization created solely to honor Indiana's veterans for all their sacrifices." Their mission is to fly veterans to Washington, DC, to see the memorials and Arlington National Cemetery at no cost. Each veteran is assigned a guardian and a wheelchair, if needed. They have mail call on the return flight home. The returning vets are greeted by lovely ladies dressed in 1940s era attire who plant a kiss on each veteran's cheek.

.

One of the veterans who has been on the Indy Honor Flights expressed his feelings about the trip to Washington DC.

Max Bates: "It makes the vets feel special, and it is a way to repay them for the sacrifices that they gave for our country."

Part 7
Indianapolis

WWII Sites in Indianapolis

Like many cities in the United States, Indianapolis converted or adjusted its prewar products to wartime materials once the Japanese bombed Pearl Harbor and war was declared in December 1941. The following companies were involved in the war effort in the 1940s in Indianapolis.

Eli Lilly and Company

The company was founded by Colonel Eli Lilly in 1876. The company is still an important part of Indianapolis today and employs and gives back to people in the area regularly. During WWII Eli Lilly produced blood plasma, typhus and flu vaccines, and penicillin.

Naval Ordnance Plant

It has had several name changes during its history. Many people in Indianapolis still refer to it as Naval Avionics or NAFI. Whatever you call it, it was an important part of the war effort.

According to the Armed Forces Museum website, "The secret was that the Norden Bombsight was being developed and constructed for naval use by NOP [naval ordnance plant]. Indianapolis company received the Navy's "E" flags for excellence in service in 1943, 1944 and 1945." It was important to keep this new development from the enemy. Germany and Japan did not have this technology, which enabled pilots to more accurately locate exactly where the bomb should be dropped.

Veteran Bob Pedigo worked at the Naval Ordnance Plant on the Norden bombsight before going into the air force when the war started. Bob was a bombardier and flew thirty missions over France and Germany in 1944. The Norton was on the plane to which he was assigned—*Silent Yokum*. In the movie *Thirty Seconds over Tokyo*, Jimmie Doolittle told his men to drop their Norden bombsight before they arrived in Tokyo. They did not want it to fall into the hands of the enemy if their planes were captured during or after the bombing of the city.

Ft. Atterbury

Ft. Atterbury, also known as Camp Atterbury, which is just south of Indianapolis, was built in 1941 after the bombing in Hawaii. It was the home to German and Italian POWS during WWII. An article in the *Indianapolis Star* newspaper featured the artwork or murals that were painted by the POWS during their internment at Camp Atterbury. A small Catholic chapel was built by the Italian prisoners.

The Atterbury Bakalar Air Museum website states, "The Camp Atterbury stone was carved by Libero Puccino. He returned to the US after the war and became a US citizen." Many of the veterans from Indiana were sent there for training or to be discharged from the military.

The Camp Atterbury Stone

Ft. Benjamin Harrison

Ft. Harrison, named for President Benjamin Harrison, is located on E. Fifty-Sixth Street, northeast of Indianapolis. It was built in 1908 by the Army Quartermaster Corps. As stated in the Indiana Military website, "The Fort Benjamin Harrison Reception Center opened in 1941 and was the largest reception center in the United States by 1943." Within Ft. Harrison was Camp Glenn, in which there was an MP school by early 1942. There were Italian and German prisoners housed there from 1944 through 1945. The base has been officially inactivated. However, it has now been redeveloped and is a state park. "In 1995, it was added to the National Register of Historic Places." (Indiana history.org)

Indiana World War Memorial

This beautiful limestone building of the Greek classical style is located in downtown Indianapolis and is a national historic landmark. "A museum on the lower levels portrays Hoosier involvement in every military conflict from revolutionary times to current Middle East actions." Outside the building, "a black granite cenotaph, or 'empty tomb,' is located in the center of the sunken garden. Cenotaphs were built in ancient times to commemorate leaders." The director of the memorial is Brigadier General Steward Goodwin.

The museum was built to honor the men who were killed in World War I but lists all soldiers from Indiana who were killed or missing in action through the Vietnam War. There are programs and special speakers, like WWII veteran Bob Pedigo, to honor special days throughout the year.

"Indianapolis devotes more acreage than any other U.S. city to honoring our nation's fallen, and is second only to Washington, DC, in the number of war memorials" (visitindy.com).

Veteran's Memorial Plaza

Located in the war memorial district of downtown Indianapolis, it has an obelisk that reaches one hundred feet, which was constructed of black granite in 1930. A hundred-foot-diameter fountain made from pink Georgia marble and terrazzo surrounds the obelisk. Its purpose is to honor all of Indiana's veterans.

Paul Ross Feeney—US Navy
By Mike Feeney

Paul Feeney entered the Navy on April 6, 1944. He had received his training at Great Lakes training station. He achieved the rank of Seaman Second Class. His wife, (Mary) Katherine, was pregnant. After Mike was born, Paul saw his son only once when the ship, which had been hit by a kamikaze attack, was in dock for repairs. After delivering the atomic bomb parts to Tinian Island, Paul's ship, the USS *Indianapolis* came under attack and sank. Paul was reported missing in action in the South Pacific since the time of the I-58 German submarine attack on the USS *Indianapolis*. Later it was established that he was one of the sailors killed in action when the battle cruiser USS *Indianapolis* was hit by enemy fire.

Seventy years later -

Paul's grandson, Mike; Mike's wife, Kim; and Paul's great-granddaughter, Kayla, from Pittsburgh, Pennsylvania were in Indianapolis for the seventieth USS *Indianapolis* reunion honoring the men who were lost at sea and those soldiers who survived the terrible ordeal. Mike carried a picture of his grandfather, who died before

Mike was born, in his uniform and took pictures of his grandfather's name engraved on the wall of the USS *Indianapolis* Memorial. Mike said his grandmother has some letters from Paul. These are some of the ways Mike can keep the memory of a lost great-grandfather alive for his daughter.

Edgar Harrell—US Marines, USS *Indianapolis* Survivor
"He saw more sharks than he saw boys."

At the seventy-first USS *Indianapolis* reunion, Edgar Harrell was a speaker at the Saturday program. I was fortunate to be able to attend the program and chat with him before and after he spoke. He didn't like the fact that he didn't have an hour to talk. He said, "It's like a sermon that you don't get to finish." His talk to the audience was very much like a sermon, and he mentioned God many times. As I have heard, there are no atheists in foxholes—apparently not in the Pacific Ocean either.

He started off saying, "If you have heard me before, then we will only charge you half price, and the rest of you can get in for free." He wrote the book *Out of the Depths*; he gives 50 percent of the proceeds to an *Indianapolis* survivors organization.

As an eighteen-year-old boy from Kentucky, Edgar volunteered for the Marine Corps. He went to Indianapolis to be sworn in. He went to San Diego for Sea School, so he knew he would be seagoing. He left from San Francisco, California. This was his first look at the big USS *Indianapolis*. He said, "You can imagine what this country boy thought when he saw this big ship." It was his home for the duration of the war.

"We were delivering the components of the atomic bomb to Tinian Island." In Okinawa they were hit by a kamikaze plane and had to make a trip back to the States to get the ship repaired. "On July 16, 1945, we look out on the deck, and we saw all kinds of navy brass that were excited about something. We saw this big crane reach over and set a box on the quarterdeck. 'Edgar stay with that crane, and don't allow anyone to loiter around that.' Some men came aboard. He was told to follow them upstairs. Harold asked, 'Who are they?' He was told that they didn't know. It was spot welded to the floor. It wasn't going to get away!" Edgar said, "They weren't air force officers; they were scientists from Los Alamos, New Mexico!"

The USS *Indianapolis* arrived on Tinian Island ten days later. Next was Guam. Captain McVay was told to go to the Philippines to prepare for the invasion of the Philippines. He asked for an escort, but he was told he didn't need one. Four days earlier a destroyer had been sunk in the area. "They sent us out in harm's way, and we set sail on July 26. On the night of the twenty-ninth, we encountered the Japanese sub I-58, and it sent two torpedoes into the USS *Indianapolis*. A Japanese sub who had not sunk any enemy ships during the war. They spotted the *Indianapolis*, and it was not zigzagging. It was a good target for the sub.

That night Edgar was just coming off duty and made a bed all the way forward to sleep on the open deck, because it was so hot below. He took off his shoes and was just relaxing when a massive explosion occurred. He said, "This ship was doomed. There was twenty-five feet of the ship was cut off, not there anymore."

The ship was still moving at seventeen knots and taking on water. The propellers were still moving and pushing the ship forward. His emergency station was midship, so he started to make his way there. He didn't have a life jacket. Some of the men were flash burned. They were asking for help, but there wasn't anything Edgar could do about it.

"As I got closer to the quarterdeck, I tried to cut down some of the new kapok life preservers, but the officers said, 'Not until we get word to abandon ship.'" Ed said, "If you don't know what a kapok life preserver looks like, you know what a horse collar looks like…" He put it on because he knew he would be leaving this ship, "or the ship would be leaving me." Ed also said, "The water was rushing in, and we became a funnel."

He was waiting desperately, because there was water on the quarter deck. The ship was listing. They were waiting for word to come back from the top. Captain McVay had sent someone below to see if the ship was salvageable, but that person did not come back up. There wasn't any electricity. The only light was from the inferno below decks. They continued to wait but faintly heard "abandon ship." At the reunion Edgar tried on the kapok life jacket for the audience, so they could see what he'd had to wear while he was in the water.

Everyone rushed to the port side. They climbed over one another. Edgar grabbed ahold of the rail and looked out at all the oil that was on the water. He said no one measured it, but it looked like a half inch of oil. "I am hoping that I am not going to go headfirst into it. There are times when you pray. I poured my heart out to the Lord. I don't want to die. I am seeing what I think is eternity out there." Ed had his mom and dad, six brothers, and two sisters back home. He said, "I don't know what all I promised Him, but probably much more than I have lived up to.

"I also told him that there is a certain brunette that said she would wait for me. And may I say, she is still waiting. We were married July 25, 1947."

Edgar jumped into the water feet first and swam away from the ship. He had been told never to stay near a sinking ship. He saw the screws still turning. The ship sank in twelve minutes. He didn't feel any pull. The ship was sinking, and the air was pushing the foam and water out of it. He swam for about seventy-five yards, and he and the men started to take inventory of who was out there. There were many severely injured who didn't make it, and several were without lifejackets. They formed circles to keep his buddies together.

Edgar mentioned Miles Spooner, another marine, and Leland Hubbard, who didn't make it. They spotted some sharks. There were eight- to ten-foot swells. The men started to drift apart, but they tried to stay together.

First Day

When morning came they could take inventory. When someone with a temperature started to hallucinate, they took off on their own. They didn't make it. "You hear a scream, and the kapok jacket goes down and springs back up. Fins and blood."

They were desperate and losing boys. They were having trouble staying together. It was 110 degrees at times, and they were desperate and struggling. They were so thirsty and tempted to drink seawater. One sailor drank some. Within an hour he started to hallucinate and thought his buddy was a Jap. He tried to kill the person who assisted him. They may have had to drown their own buddy.

Second Night

"It is about eighty-five degrees, but you are soaking wet, and the body temperature drops too far, hypothermia set in. Especially those guys that only had on skivvies." Edgar was lucky to have had on his work clothes, which helped to hold in his body heat.

Many were desperate for water. "You have to swim all the time to make it. The more you swim, the thirstier you get. You are tempted to drink the seawater. Their lips are chapped and bleeding, and they get oil and salt on them…they are parched. It's raining—thank the Lord! Well, if you open your mouth, the oil is all over you. You take those greasy hands and get a tablespoon full."

Third Day

"Eighty men are now to seventeen. There are lots of guys praying. By now, what are you doing? The kapok jackets are not holding our heads out of the water. We are seated in them now."

"They came up on a swell, and they could see in the distance a little raft made of crates that were lashed together. There were five sailors, but no one was on the raft. They had kapok jackets they had taken from some men who had expired. They were drying out the jackets. They were trying to paddle to the Philippines. The men didn't know the Philippines were five hundred miles away!" They joined the other five sailors heading west.

On another swell they saw something out there. Edgar found a crate of potatoes. Again he said, "Thank the Lord." The first one was rotten, but he grabbed another one and peeled it with his teeth. Then he put some in his pockets. His buddies came on out, and they had a picnic of sorts eating the potatoes."

"It's dark when someone comes to the raft. It's McKissick, another member of the USS *Indianapolis* crew."

Fourth Day

"Where's Spooner? We turned loose of the raft during the night." There were three left in his group now. One of the sailors gave up and died. They saw a plane, a B-25, Edgar thought, coming in low, two thousand or three thousand feet. They had been spotted by the aircraft. The pilot saw something from above and went down to see the debris, sharks, and men in the water. He radioed back and said, "Ducks on the pond"—code for men in the water.

Another pilot came on the scene and said he saw more sharks than he saw boys. They were going to do something even though they were not supposed to land in the water. "It was a no-no. They can't leave these guys here to wait for help. They picked up fifty-six survivors."

Cleatus Lebow—US Navy, USS *Indianapolis* Survivor

"I watched the raising of the first flag raising on Iwo Jima from the deck of the USS *Indianapolis*."

Cleatus Lebow of Memphis, Texas, was in Indianapolis for the weekend activities honoring the survivors of the USS *Indianapolis*. This was the seventieth reunion honoring the survivors. There were thirty-five survivors left; one had died only the previous day. His family was there in his place—that's how much the reunion means to these families.

Cleatus entered the navy on his nineteenth birthday. He has attended all but one of these reunions, which gather all the remaining men from the USS *Indianapolis* and give them the honor they deserve. Paul Feeney's grandson placed his daughter, Kayla, in Cleatus's lap and took a picture. Cleatus was amused that Paul's great-granddaughter had the same name as his own great-granddaughter. It's a small world.

Cleatus was a range finder operator. It was like radar, and he said, "Yes, but you use your eyeball." He looked through eight-foot gun turrets that were twenty feet long, to see what was happening on the sea and on the islands they were bombing.

He was the only man who had his name misspelled on the USS *Indianapolis* Memorial. The memorial has all the names of the men who served on the ship engraved in granite. The lettering has his name with a capital *B*; however, he spells it with a small *b*—Lebow instead of the incorrect LeBow. He said, "It really doesn't matter."

It was a very warm, humid day, but Cleatus was eager to talk about what happened to the USS *Indianapolis*. He has been on the honor flights to Washington, DC that left from Amarillo, Texas. They go for three days instead of the one day Indiana WWII veterans are allowed.

Cleatus has spoken to school groups and said, "I told them I don't take many showers or go swimming, but if you offer me water, I'll drink it." It was a warm day at the reunion, and he was glad to have a bottle of water.

"I watched the raising of the first flag raising on Iwo Jima from the deck of the USS *Indianapolis*," said Cleatus. He talked some about Okinawa when informed about another veteran, Les Brown, who was a survivor from the Battle of Okinawa. On Cleatus's hat were eight stars, one for each of the eight campaigns in which the USS *Indianapolis* was involved. He was involved in all the campaigns, from the Gilbert Island on down. These campaigns are listed on the memorial. When asked where he was for the other campaigns, he laughed and said, "I was in high school."

Cleatus Lebow was a gentle, unassuming man who said, "Thanks for caring" when thanked for his service. He was in a wheelchair and wore a hearing aid, but his mind was very sharp. He remembered that day in July and the men who were on the ship.

He told a story about shooting at a tin building on an island. "There were about one hundred Japanese who went out the door. One man jumped on a bicycle and went up the hill." When asked if the one on the bicycle was killed, he said, "I don't know. Many of them went to caves to hide." There was so much bombardment that the ground was leveled off in places.

Cleatus said he was fifteen feet away when the bomb went into the ship. He was in his bunk when the attack took place because he had late watch that night.

The rest of the story is chronicled in the previous section. Cleatus was rescued from the water after the Japanese sub attack on his ship.

After a wreath was placed on the memorial, Cleatus sat reverently in his wheelchair, perhaps remembering those men in the shark-filled water or those sailors who went down with the ship. Cleatus was twenty-one years old when the ship sank.

LaPorte, Indiana

Kingsbury Ordnance Plant

"The Kingsbury plant was built on a twenty-square-mile plot between 1940 and 1941 to be one of the largest shell-loading plants in the nation." The plant was built in rural LaPorte County in Northern Indiana. The thinking at the time was that this location was in the middle of the country and away from major populations. "The War Department constructed a new town right outside the factory gates. Kingsford Heights consisted of more than 2,600 dormitories, trailers, and prefabricated homes." (indianapublicmedia.org)

As with other war-material plants in Indiana and other parts of America, there was a need for workers. Since the majority of young men who were physically able were fighting in Europe or Japan, it fell to women to fill these jobs. "Work at Kingsbury was dirty, difficult, and dangerous, and African American employees were consistently assigned to the most hazardous tasks."

As with the airplane factories that were camouflaged, Kingsbury was making materials for the war effort, thus security was a consideration. "The plant's design reflected the potential for disaster—four separate buildings were partially underground, so if one exploded, the structural integrity of the others would not be compromised." The pressure of producing for the war only compounded the physical dangers that were common to ordnance work. (Indiana Magazine of History)

The Kingsbury factory was made up of employees who were "measuring and pouring explosives into artillery shells, bombs, land mines and grenades of all shapes and sizes." Certainly sounds like a recipe for disaster. However, no accidents in the factory have been noted. Instead of a "Rosie the Riveter", the women in the plant had their own mascot, "Tillie the TNT Girl". This was dangerous work for women who made up half the factory, at this time. "Pouring TNT, and other explosives, was a common job at the plant for WOWs, or Women Ordnance Workers." (Indiana Magazine of History)

Estel L. Harshman—Ordnance Plant Worker
By Linda Harshman Leffler
"Everyone is celebrating your birthday."

Being almost thirty years old when the draft for WWII began, and being married and having one child, Estel was not drafted into the military. He relocated from the small town of Stinesville, Indiana, to join hundreds of others working at the Kingsbury Ordnance Plant near La Porte, Indiana. He was employed immediately and worked at the dangerous job of building shells for large weapons. The plant employed so many workers, there was not enough housing for all who came, so the government built barracks-type housing for the workers. Parkview Heights near Knox, Indiana, was where Estel; his wife, Ila; and their baby daughter, Linda, lived. All the housing looked exactly alike and was within walking distance to stores and the plant.

Gas, eggs, shoes, and many other products were rationed, and citizens received rationing books, which had stamps with which to purchase items. When the stamps were gone, one had to wait until it was time for new ones to be issued. Many women also worked at other employment. The children living in these housing units were cared for by mothers who stayed home. All of them became friends. The neighbors were friendly and took care of one another.

The daughter of Estel and Ila has only faint memories of this time, as she was born in 1941, before the bombing of Pearl Harbor. One memory was her father taking her to LaPorte to get a dog. The dog and girl were very attached to each other, but one day Brownie disappeared, and Estel went door to door asking about him. Her dad whistled at one door, and the dog immediately came running to his true owners.

Another memory was walking to the grocery store, and on the way home Estel carried a sack of groceries in one arm and young Linda in the other. He tripped on a railroad track, and both sack and Linda went flying. The story was always told that he was much more concerned about his rationed eggs than his daughter!

The last memory Linda had was of V-J day, August 14, 1945. Many people traveled to Knox and surrounded the courthouse, shouting and cheering. Horns were blowing, and people were dancing and singing. Four-year-old Linda, who had been born on August 14, 1941, asked her father what was going on. She very clearly remembered him telling her, "Everyone is celebrating your birthday." Linda said, "This is a great memory to this day."

The KOP, Kingsbury Ordnance Plant, closed shortly after the war, and the Harshman family moved to Greencastle, Indiana, where both Estel and Ila found work in a grocery store.

Part 8
Famous People

Franklin Delano Roosevelt

FDR, the thirty-second president of the United States, served from 1933 to April 1945. FDR was well known for his famous quote concerning the Japanese attack on Pearl Harbor; on December 8, 1941, he called it "a date which will live in infamy." Anna Johnson remembered when Roosevelt visited Evansville when she worked at Servel. President Roosevelt came to town on the train. "They wouldn't let us get within a block of that railroad crossing," said Anna. Another Evansville resident, Harold Norlin, who worked at Bethesda Naval Hospital, said, "I saw FDR come out of the elevator at Bethesda Naval Hospital."

Eleanor Roosevelt

Anna Eleanor Roosevelt was first lady from March 1933 to April 1945, when her husband, Franklin Delano Roosevelt, died in office. During World War II, she "divided her wartime work in to three categories: refugee issues, home front issues, and soldiers' concerns." Connie Norlin, who worked at the State Department in Washington, DC, said, "I used to see Eleanor Roosevelt often going to lunch but never talked to her." A veteran, Bob Pedigo, told a story of seeing Eleanor early in the morning, about 2:00 or 3:00 a.m., near a subway station. She asked him, "What are you doing here at this time in the morning?" He thought, *What are* you *doing here at this time of the morning?*

James Stewart

Jimmy Stewart was a well-known movie star and military officer. He was born in 1908 in Indiana, Pennsylvania, and died in 1997. He enlisted in the US Army. Since he had flying experience and an interest in aviation, he rose to the rank of two-star general in the Army Air Corps. Later Stewart was in the Air Force Reserves.

"In November 1943, he flew 20 missions over Europe as a captain of a B-24 Liberator in the 703rd squadron, 445th Bomb Group."

Stewart told his men when they were readying for a mission that would take them over Sweden, "Anybody caught with skis and yodeling will be frowned on."

WWII veteran Bob Pedigo, master bomber, knew Jimmy Stewart, as he was Bob's briefing officer. Bob said, "Jimmy Stewart was just as nice as everyone thought he was."

In 1987 Bob Pedigo met Jimmy and Gloria Stewart in Palm Springs, California, for a reunion.

Bob Hope

Bob Hope was an American actor and entertainer of troops in WWII and many other wars as well. "He provided a welcome respite for the U.S. forces, a reminder, in Hope's words of what they were fighting for." The US troops looked forward to being entertained by Hope and the beautiful ladies who accompanied him on tour to remote locations where soldiers were stationed. "In 1997, Bob Hope was named an honorary veteran by the United States Armed Forces." He wrote a book about his experiences entertaining WWII troops, entitled *I Never Left Home.*

James Pike, a WWII veteran from Evansville, said of Hope, "I liked him. Some of the sergeants and noncoms got in the front row. Bob Hope told them to move to the back and let the soldiers up front. So they did."

Bob Poole, a WWII veteran from Indianapolis, said he saw Bob Hope in Leyte, Philippines. Bob Hope sure got around the world!

Dick Robinson, a WWII veteran from Indianapolis, summed it up well: "The USO was their entertainment—Bob Hope and the young ladies to dance with. The Red Cross brought coffee and donuts. They took their chance with their lives for us. This was the fun part of war. You could get a break from the war for a while."

Orchestra Leaders and Singers

Probably the most well-known orchestra leader was Captain Glenn Miller, whose plane was lost over the English Channel in December 1944, on the way to France to play for American troops who helped to liberate Paris. The plane and Miller's body were never recovered. His signature song, "Moonlight Serenade," was a favorite of WWII P-47 pilot Allen Sanderson, who saw Glenn Miller at Maxwell Air Force Base in Montgomery, Alabama, in January 1943.

Sanderson said, "I remember going to the Cavalier Hotel to hear Jimmy Dorsey play and Helen O'Connor perform." The historic hotel was built in 1927.

Lucy Wahnsiedler, a WWII Evansville factory worker, said, "Well, it was big band era. They had dances down there [in Evansville]. Glenn Miller's band came here too."

USO Canteens

There was an USO canteen on Eighth Street in Evansville because there were so many soldiers from Breckinridge, a US Army base south of Evansville. The building is torn down now, but the four large pillars that were on the front of the building are now positioned on the riverfront in downtown Evansville, honoring veterans of war. WWII vet Dick Robinson said, "The USO was their entertainment." Many soldiers were happy to have some respite from the rigors of the war. The 1940s movie *Hollywood Canteen* portrayed actresses and actors entertaining the troops.

Lucy Wahnsiedler, a WWII factory worker, said, "They had a USO here [in Evansville] and dances." Lucy didn't attend the dances, since she was dating a soldier, but her sister-in-law, Dorothy, went to the dances at the USO in downtown Evansville and to Breckinridge army base one time. "There were soldiers everywhere in Evansville!"

The Andrews Sisters

The Andrews Sisters—Patty, LaVerne, and Maxene—entertained the troops and were very popular in the 1940s swing era. One of their albums showed the sisters in uniform. One of their most popular songs was "Boogie Woogie Bugle Boy," about a swinging soldier playing reveille in Company B. They were nearly as committed to entertaining the troops as Bob Hope. They toured and sang all around the world for the military and did some movie work. A couple of films featured the Andrews Sisters and the USO canteens of WWII. One of their more successful military films was *Hollywood Canteen.*

Harry S. Truman

Truman, the thirty-sixth president of the United States, succeeded Franklin Delano Roosevelt. FDR died in office on April 12, 1945, when the Second World War was near its end. The United States had been involved in the war since December 7, 1941, and the nation was ready for it to be over.

Truman ordered the atomic bombs to be dropped on Japan after millions of leaflets were dropped on Japan, warning them of the devastation that would follow. Harry Truman visited and conducted military business from the Little White House in Key West, Florida.

WWII United States Allies

Australia

Australia was not prepared to fight a world war and was grateful to the United States for their help keeping the Japanese from attacking Australian shores. Many American soldiers were stationed in large cities in Australia. As the war continued, Aussie soldiers fought alongside British troops at the Battle of Britain. Australian troops were sent to the Burma and India Theater.

England

Britain and Germany were engaged in an air battle involving the German Luftwaffe and the British RAF (Royal Air Force). Germany bombed the city of London and surrounding areas for weeks. Many British parents elected to move their children out of the large cities into the countryside for their protection. Prime Minister Winston Churchill refused to negotiate with the German Fuhrer Adolf Hitler. Following the bombing of Pearl Harbor, the United States entered the war against Germany and Japan.

Russia

Joseph Stalin was the leader of Russia during this time. On June 22, 1941, Germany invaded Russia, and by September 22, 1941, the Germans had taken Leningrad. However, the Russian winter stopped the German advance short of Moscow. The Big Three—Stalin, Churchill, and Roosevelt—worked together to defeat Nazi Germany. During the Yalta Conference, the world leaders worked out a plan for the postwar reorganization of Germany.

France

France was occupied by the German army from 1940-1944 when the United States freed the capital city during the Liberation of Paris. Troops landed on the shores of Normandy during the invasion on June 6, 1944. The French underground worked with the Allies to sabotage German war efforts during the occupation of their country.

China

China, led by Chiang Kai-Shek, helped to keep the Japanese from advancing on land. September 3 is Victory Day in China, when the Chinese celebrate the end of WWII. Ret. Capt. Chennault and the Flying Tigers, a group of volunteer pilots, helped fight the Japanese invasion of China.

Stories from Allied countries

The next two stories are about English and Australian women who married American servicemen. After the war they moved to the United States to live with their American husbands. The women outlined their hardships and victories as they adapted to a new country.

Beryl Chatterton
"Everyone had to do their duty for the war."

WWII began in the United Kingdom in September 1939. Beryl Stacey, born on November 25, 1932, was six years old. Her first memories are of being evacuated from her home in Birmingham, England, and sent to Ludlow to spend some time away from the nightly bombing. Her mother, Winifred May, went to school and took her and her younger sister away. Beryl said, "Kids had tags on them at the train station. Some of them were being sent to family members and others to people who were required to take in the children. Everyone had to do their duty for the war."

Beryl spent about two years in Ludlow, from 1939 to 1941. It was about three hours away, with bus and train connections. Beryl's dad would visit on the weekends and do some fishing in the river nearby. Beryl's mom also came with Beryl and her sister to Ludlow. She liked the farms and the country. They stayed in different places; one was an ordinary row house, and another was a really old house, with a thatched roof and no electricity. They had to use candles to see at night. They went to school in Ludlow, where Beryl learned to knit.

When Beryl returned to Birmingham, she went to a new school. She remembered riding her bike to school, which was quite a long way. She didn't have enough money to ride the bus. She attended Erdington Grammar School for Girls, wore a uniform, and studied French and Latin.

In Birmingham Beryl and her family lived across the street from the Wolsey-Morris Motor Company. Before the war the company produced the Austin and Morris cars. After the war started, they converted to wartime goods, such as tanks and gun casings. She said,

"When they were finished with the tanks, they would bring them out a huge gate and roll them down the street. It was a huge rumble on the street. The factory was a target by the Germans. They had smoke screens, ugly cylinders that burned fuel, that produced smoke in front of the factory during air raids. They were set at intervals and were smelly and messy, but they blurred things in front of the factory. The smoke screens were used for quite a few years.

Barrage balloons were also used in many of the large cities in England. They were used in Birmingham and London to prevent aircraft from hitting targets on the ground. There were lots of them in Birmingham, perhaps one hundred. They were tethered to the ground, fifty to sixty feet long, and shaped like fish or whales.

Beryl's mom worked part time in the factory, on the assembly line. She wore a turban or colorful scarf to work. It was important to keep her hair out of the way. Her dad worked for GEC (General Electric Company). He had a very important job as a tool and die maker. He made prototype models of whatever they were doing.

What were the bombings like for you?

The bombings went on a good part of the night. There were no bombings on their house, but the block behind them was hit by a bomb. Unfortunately the whole block was taken out. When the air raid signal sounded, they went to the shelter. Each home had an Anderson shelter in the backyard. A kit was provided of corrugated steel. They had four bunk beds and a table in the shelter. It was approximately six feet by six feet. One year, Father Christmas came while they were in the shelter. Beryl's father put sod over the top of their shelter. She remembered hearing the sounds of the enemy planes. She said, "I was too young to realize the danger."

Explain how rationing was used in England?

Rationing books were used in England, just like in the United States, and each person could have one egg, two ounces of sugar, two ounces of butter, and milk each week. Oranges and bananas were unheard of during that time. There were long lines to wait for meat, bread, and fish. When it was gone, it was gone and no restocking. At

Christmas they would save up dried fruit to make a fruit cake. Shoes, candy, and gasoline were rationed. Rationing went on for three or four years after the war was over. Beryl remembered going to Clark shoe store, which is now over one hundred years old.

Her family had a friend who worked at the Cadbury chocolate factory. This friend would visit Beryl with substandard candies, or seconds, that they could buy, or maybe she gave them some. Beryl wasn't sure.

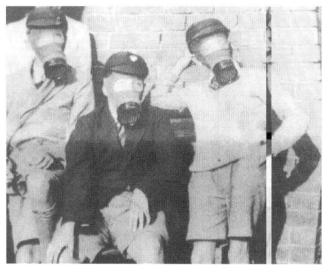

They had to carry their gas masks with them all the time.

They smelled very bad! They would have gas masks at drills at school. Beryl's dad was an air raid warden and wore a tin helmet.

A couple of things she remembered about the blackouts were that the windows had to be taped crisscrossed to keep the glass from shattering. Also, they had blackout curtains to keep the light from shining outside. There were buckets of sand outside the door to put out fires if there was a fire caused by the bombing.

The Women's Institute, or WI, was active during that time. Many women would drive ambulances and roll bandages. They helped with nursing in the hospitals. There were food trucks that served tea and donuts to both American and British servicemen.

Black marketing was common during that time. Beryl's uncle owned a news agent shop. Because he was merchant, he could exchange some tobacco for other scarce items. "Dad came home with a pound of bacon," said Beryl.

"In 1939 they said the war would be over by Christmas," said Beryl. "It lasted for six years." When she was twelve or thirteen years old, there was an announcement at school that they should go to the assembly hall. The war was over! Many people held block parties, and there were flags, buntings, and big parties.

At age twenty-three Beryl married Matthew John Chatterton, on September 22, 1956, and they moved to the United States that November. They sailed on the *Queen Mary* to New York City. Ellis Island was closed by that time. They had four children—Karen, Paul, Laura, and Kevin. Beryl's husband was a pattern maker. The Ford Motor Company sponsored John to come to the United States; however, he never worked for Ford. He ended up working for Chrysler and GM. Beryl and John were divorced in 1978.

Back in England John had delivered newspapers early in the morning, being careful not to fall in the bomb craters from the previous night's bombing. No streetlights were allowed, and he had to be careful of unexploded bombs too. He also had the job of knocking on doors and waking people up in the morning. So later, when he worked at Fisher Body in Marion, Indiana, he said he "knocked up ladies in the morning." He got kidded about that remark! Some things changed in the American English translation.

What did the English people think about the Americans in England?

She quoted a well-known phrase—"overpaid, oversexed, over here"—but said "the feeling was about fifty-fifty about the US involvement in the war. The further away you were from the big cities, the stronger the anti-US feeling, and the less sophisticated the people." Since England was a conservative people, they felt that the Americans were brash. The British men resented the Americans when it came to women. Many British women liked American men.

AUSTRALIA

The Sydney Harbor Bridge, located in Sydney Harbor, is nicknamed the Coathanger because of its arch design.

Part 9
Australia

Sydney

One of the most striking features of Sydney Harbor is the Sydney Harbour Bridge, which opened March 19, 1932. The bridge is nicknamed the Coathanger because of its arch design. It is open to foot traffic today as well as vehicles. It is the world's tallest steel arch bridge. During WWII there were parapets and antiaircraft guns installed on the pylons of the bridge. There is a marvelous view of the city of Sydney and the harbor from the bridge.

Since there was fear of invasion by the Japanese, America helped to protect Australia and set up a base there for fighting in the Pacific area. It was also used as a place for American servicemen and servicewomen to use for rest and recreation. Many American service personnel were stationed in the cities of Townsville, Cairns, and Brisbane.

In March 1942 MacArthur, supreme commander of the Allied forces, arrived in Australia from the Philippines. He travelled by train to Melbourne, a city to the south of Sydney.

The only fatalities that occurred in Sydney during WWII were in 1942, when the USS *Chicago* was docked in the harbor. A Japanese midget sub came into Sydney Harbor and fired at the heavy cruiser; however, it missed the *Chicago* and hit a ferryboat, killing twenty people.

Grace Hotel, Sydney

The Grace Building was headquarters for Gen. Douglas MacArthur from 1942 to 1945, when the war ended. He stayed here after Pearl Harbor. It is a very ornate art deco hotel in downtown Sydney. General MacArthur travelled from the Philippines, after the fall of the island to the Japanese, to Australia in a PT boat. There were believed to be underground tunnels in the Grace Hotel so MacArthur could be evacuated if need be.

MacArthur made his famous speech, "I came through, and I shall return," at Terowie railway station in South Australia.

War Brides

After World War II, there were "over 8,000 war brides from Australia and New Zealand." During the trip from Australia, the women, many of them with infants or small children, were assisted by the Red Cross, the US military, and the US State Department. The amount of "total war brides was 65,000 women who married American soldiers." Many of these women came to America to join their GI husbands, whom they married during the war.

The SS *Mariposa* was a luxury liner built in 1931. In March 1946 the *Mariposa* carried war brides to the United States after making stops in New Zealand and Hawaii.

Patricia Hawn, Australian war bride, said, "Many of the war brides returned to their original homes. They could not adapt to living in another country. They missed their family and went back home." Pat returned to her first home, Australia, only one time after she left in 1946. She visited for two months after her children were old enough to take care of themselves without her.

Canberra

Aussies are a very patriotic people and are still thankful to America for its support during World War II. One of Canberra's wonderful military museums is the Australian War Memorial. It is a beautiful memorial to those deceased during all wars involving Australia.

Canberra, Australia

Patricia Marcelle Hawn—WWII War Bride
"The Japanese were going to invade Australia with a ship and troops. The United States sunk the ship."

Pat Hawn, from Queensland, Australia, was born on March 9, 1924 on a country farm in Coulson. She had two sisters, one six years older and one six years younger. She grew up during the Depression and early war days of WWII.

Pat's best friend growing up was a young Aboriginal girl. Pat cannot remember her name after all these years, but she said she was tall and a good runner. Her best friend lived in the rental house on the family farm. "In the evening the Aborigines would sing to my mother from the edge of the property, not getting too close to the house." Pat's mother, whose maiden name was Parker, immigrated to Australia from England. Pat said, "Mother moved to Australia to get away from the cold weather in England."

Pat remembered times were difficult for many people during the war because of rationing and restricted items. She said she and her family used ration coupons for food, but not for new clothes. Her family was lucky because they had cream, butter, and vegetables, since they lived on a farm. She rode a black pony, Melba, around the farm and to school. Her home did not have air-conditioning or phones. Her family didn't own a car either.

Pat recalled a visit from the archbishop of Canterbury, who came to visit Queensland from England. She remembered his beautiful robes and that he visited Boonah, a province of Queensland about an hour from Brisbane.

Pat was cleaning houses in Brisbane for a living, and one evening she went to a dance that would change her life and her country! It was the custom of Australia to host dances in either a school, if you lived out in the country, or in the hotels in the city. Girls went to these dances for entertainment, to listen to American music and to dance on a Saturday night.

Patricia mentioned some of the dances of the time. There was the waltz. Lancers was a military line dance from India. In England it was danced at the Lancers Ball. It featured lines of men and women. The Chartize was also a dance she mentioned. The last dance would be to "God Save the Queen." The soldiers would salute and honor their country. "The Australians were loyal to the British throne because they were good to us," she said.

Since it was 1943 or 1944, there were many American soldiers at the dance. Pat noticed there was a "good-looking guy standing beside me." They started talking, and he asked, "Do you like the music?" They went out in the hall and had refreshments. She didn't think she would ever see him again. He said he couldn't dance, but he got her name and called her. His name was Nelson Hawn; he was an MP and was at the dance patrolling the other soldiers to make sure they were behaving. Nelson had his captain introduce him to Pat, so everything would be proper.

Nelson and Patricia dated for about six months, and then they were married. Nelson was shipped out to the Philippines the day before their first child, Nelson Jr., was born.

In the Philippines Nelson was shot by a sniper, and the bullet lodged near his heart. He received a Purple Heart. Nelson was sent home to America, and Patricia took Nelson Jr. and lived with her parents. She needed permission to come to America.

How did Nelson and the Americans happened to be in Australia?

"The Japanese were going to invade Australia with a ship and troops. The US sunk the ship. The Japanese bombed Darwin, Australia, in the Northern Territory, near the top of Australia. Australia's military was weak in arms and not prepared for war. They bombed England and decided to clean us out too."

It would be two years before Patricia would board the SS *Mariposa* to make the two-week trip across the Pacific Ocean to America. Pat remembered the hula dancers in Hawaii and how much she enjoyed seeing Hawaii for a few hours. Baby Nelson was about two years old and had dual citizenship.

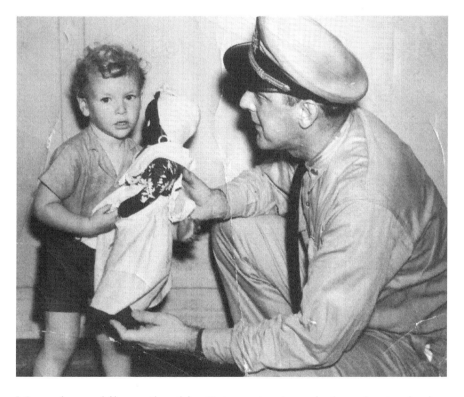

Many days while on the ship, Pat went out on deck and sat enjoying the beautiful Pacific Ocean. This sailing was very peaceful and calm. She watched the sun come up and go down on the ocean. Beautiful! One day Nelson Jr. got away from her and was later found eating bread and jelly with some American girls. He had jelly all over his face! During the trip, Pat heard music but didn't get to do any dancing. There was an American group onboard that sang and danced for the women.

There were three ladies in Pat's cabin on the ship. She did not stay in contact with any of them. The meals on the ship were very tasty. After being restricted in what she could get in Australia, American food was very good!

Arriving in the United States

The *Mariposa* arrived in San Francisco, California, and Pat was "overwhelmed with this country." She said, "We went under the Golden Gate Bridge and docked in San Francisco. It took all day to get everyone off the ship and through immigration. They divided us up by trains and by where we needed to go. So I went from San Francisco to Chicago, Illinois. It was about four days on the train to get to Chicago. The next day we went on to Clarksville, Indiana." Finally she was back together with Nelson.

Married life

There were hard times, but Nelson got a job. It was not a good one because he didn't have a lot of education. Pat and Nelson had three children—Nelson, Jim, and Marcelle. She was very proud of her children after her days during the Depression in Australia. Pat worked in a drugstore then the Clark County Bank. Once the bank was robbed of $4,000. She was terrorized. "I will never forget that as long as I live."

In conclusion Pat stated, "No more wonderful thing than people who live in this country [the United States]." She became a US citizen as soon as she could on her arrival from Australia.

Part 10
Faith in the Foxhole

Many soldiers felt God was there or had a hand in protecting them from harm. Many of the WWII servicemen thanked God as their strength during dangerous times—when bombs were falling, in a foxhole, when times were bleak. Bob Sisk, a WWII vet, said, "God was looking out for me."

No one can truly know why God allows wars. Why did babies and women die? Melvin Eakle, a POW in Europe, told his sister, Iree Eakle Francis, about the conditions at the POW camp: "Every morning they would take out the dead babies and women."

How do you forget about what you have seen? One method was to rarely or never talk about it to your family. Perhaps soldiers would talk only to other GIs, knowing only they could understand the circumstances or why it happened to them. Unfortunately some GIs turned to alcohol as a way to forget the nightmares.

Many WWII veterans did not talk about what they saw and heard until now, as the end of the trail is near. As they are approaching the ends of their lives, many veterans are telling the rest of us how it was for them during the war. They are talking to newspaper reporters, to outsiders, and to another generation, talking even to a woman author. This is deeply humbling!

Former US Marine and WWII veteran Arlin McRae didn't feel it was just unusual; the only thing that survived from his sea bag was the Bible that he read every night since he left home. The Griffin War Mothers gave it to him when he left for the military.

Former WWII soldier Scott Brown mentioned his faith several times. He became a minister when the war was over. When the Japanese surrendered, Scott was stationed at Pearl Harbor; as others were celebrating, he went to the chapel.

Ralph Myers said, "I have asked the good Lord to keep me going until He wanted me, and He has been doing a good job. I thank Him all the time."

Richard Kolodey, US Navy, a WWII veteran, hasn't missed going to Sunday school in sixty-eight years. His goal is to get his seventy-year pin of no misses. God bless!

Stories from Germany, Italy, and Ukraine

This book includes the stories of English and Australian women and what they endured during WWII. Other countries that were involved in the war, also suffered from the effects of the war. American soldiers and the American people sacrificed their young men, and the home front did without certain foods and supplies. It is interesting to know how people from the Allies and the Axis countries dealt with the war. The people in the following stories, eventually, became American citizens when WWII was over.

The next stories are not from countries that were our Allies; they are from countries that were our enemies during the war. The people and the situations are uniquely different. Their sacrifices were great, and sometimes beyond their control. Not only are their stories interesting, but give a view from the other side of the war. The German people had to ration food as well as the American people. Children during the WWII war time experienced many of the same difficulties whether they were in Italy or Ukraine.

The American people experienced bombing at Pearl Harbor. The German, Japanese, and English people were bombed in their cities, sometimes nightly. Ukrainian men and women were not allowed to make their own choices of how they would live. They were forced to work for the Germans, even though they did not share the same beliefs. These stories of hardship show the mental toughness of all the men, women, and children in this book.

Ivan Andrijiwskyj, Maria Lewcun, Stephanja Szahaj, Peter Szahaj
"The only way for them to survive the war was to follow orders."
By Lesia Lampton

In June 1942 the Germans went to the village (*cello*) of Mukhaniv in Northwestern Ukraine. Stephanja was twenty years old, and Ivan was seventeen years old. They were the oldest of six children. Their father was a master tailor and the village arbiter of good taste. Stephanja, not wanting to do any housework, chose to work as her father's apprentice, helping with the daily chores in his shop. Ivan also trained to be a tailor under his father. (Ivan "Dido" is pictured.)

As the Germans were advancing on their village, Stephanja and Ivan were sent to the nearby town of Radekhiv to work and hide. This proved to be unsuccessful, and soon they were both taken by the Germans to Lviv. They were bathed, had their hair cut, were changed into different clothing, and were sent to Germany. This is where their stories separate.

After his capture Ivan was conscripted to fight with the Germans against the Russians. He fled, hiding in a wheat field until he was recaptured. When the Germans learned he was a tailor, they sold him to work as such, fixing the German uniforms. When he was freed, the person he worked for wanted to hire him outright, but Ivan refused and went to the displaced persons camp in Regensburg. It was there that he met Maria Lewcun while attending church services.

Maria worked as a baker and a brickmaker in Germany. She and Ivan soon married, and their priest sponsored them to go to the United States. They settled in Salem, Massachusetts, and then moved to Philadelphia after learning that a large Ukrainian population had settled there. They lived together in Northeast Philadelphia until Ivan's death in 2006. Maria still resides in Philadelphia.

Stephanja was taken to Passau, Germany, where she was lined up with other people, similar to a slave auction, and chosen according to her work abilities. She was taken to a dairy farm where she and a Polish man who had preceded her arrival worked for a family. She acted as a maid and milked the cows while the Pole worked the farm. Given the circumstances, Stephanja said, she was treated very well by this family and even ate dinner with them. Many other Ukrainians were in the area, and she met with them in the evenings during her three years of servitude. It was through this new community that stories of the war were spread, and they learned of the war's end.

Like Ivan, Stephanja found her way to the displaced persons camp in Regensburg. Life at the camp was not easy. They were fed, but with so many people needing to be served they had very few other commodities. A black market thrived at the camp. Stephanja met Petro Szahaj at Regensburg. Petro had been conscripted to the 2nd Division German Army with the purpose of fighting the Russians. He and Stephanja were wed in June 1946 in a nearby town. Shortly thereafter Belgium announced a program where displaced persons could immigrate there. If they found work within three months, their families would be permitted to join them. Petro went to Belgium and found work in the coal mines. Stephanja joined him there, and their first child, Myrosia, was born in 1949.

In 1950, with the help of Ivan and Catholic Services, Stephanja and her family joined Ivan and Maria in Salem. They later moved to Hartford, Connecticut, and lived there until Petro passed away in 2012. Stephanja now lives with her daughter in Virginia.

Stephanja did not like to talk about her experiences until recently. There was a certain shame she felt for their involuntary participation in the war. Although she and Ivan were forced laborers, they felt as though they were helping the Germans through their servitude. The only way for them to survive the war was to follow orders. In all the time they were in Germany, their family did not know what had happened to them. Stephanja and Ivan were the only members of their family who came to the United States following the war.

Elisabeth Ford—German Child
"All the Americans were good to us, especially to the kids. When you see the movies, you think, shoot, I was one of them!"

Liz, a little curly haired girl of five years old, was born in 1939, just as World War II was starting in parts of Europe. Hitler had invaded Poland on September 1. Much of the world was wondering what was happening to their lives. Her family lived in Augsburg, Germany. She said, "I surprise myself that I remember some of these things. I can see myself just like it was yesterday. I don't know why. Honestly, I remember everything that happened during that time."

Allied bombing in Augsburg, Germany

"I remember my mom in February 1944, sitting in a chair at night, half-dressed because when the siren went off, we only had so many minutes to pack up and rush off." The siren went off, and Liz's mother, Theresa, had to put her clothes on and pack up. One time when the town was bombed, the kids were taken from school straight to the train and out to the countryside. "The children didn't even come home," said Liz. "My mom only had my sister and me with her. My sister was smaller than me, so she must have been two or three years old. My sister lives in San Francisco today.

"We went to the bomb shelter, and the old people were crying and carrying on. Then they made an announcement that the top of the building was on fire. So they gave us so much time to get out. They started with the women with children first, then the older people, and then the rest of them. I remember that it was snowing like crazy."

Liz recalled, "It was cold, and Mom was pushing the old-fashioned baby buggy with both of us in it. She pushed it many miles as the planes were flying over us. I saw one woman, still in her nightgown, going crazy. She just lost it! I don't know if she made it out or not."

This vision is in her mind even today. Her dad, August, worked in the city. He wasn't with them at the time. Liz doesn't know exactly what he did, but he was in the German reserves not active duty.

"She [Liz's mother] walked and walked to a big church. There was straw on the floor, so people could lay down and sleep." Later they left the church. Then a bus came, and they counted off, and it took them out into the country. "We were taken to Baumgarten, which was sixty or seventy miles from my hometown."

Baumgarten, Germany

Liz went on to explain that "each farmer had to take someone in. They hated it, but they had to take us in. We were lucky that we had a place where a lady lived in the house by herself. She locked everything up but two rooms. Then the lady went to stay with her son. She liked my mom, and she said I know you won't mess up her home. Here you are, bringing in people you don't even know. We had a kitchen and a bedroom we were allowed to use. It was only my mom and the two kids, as my dad had to stay in the city. The other children, we didn't know where they were." Liz had two brothers and two sisters who had been taken by the Germans on a train elsewhere when the bombing started in Augsburg. "They didn't come home that day, since they left from the school for the country."

"They announced on the radio that from two to four, they would give out names of the kids—where they are at," stated Liz. "We found my sister and my two brothers, but we couldn't find my sister Anna. Mom was crying every night. My dad would ride around on his bicycle for hours looking for her. We didn't have a car or anything. He would knock on every door and show her picture. At that time you didn't have much as far as pictures. My mom said she wasn't giving up." So finally someone said, "The old couple up the road has a little girl up there." They went up to the farmhouse and found her. "We were all happy to see her."

Liz explained, "They didn't want to give her up. I mean, she had it made—she had everything, but she wanted to go home." Anna was about eight years old at the time. The couple had no kids, so she had everything. "They didn't mean no harm. We went visiting them later, as though they were relation, but they weren't.

"The farmers at the time, at five o'clock, had to donate so much milk. It depended on how many were in your family, so we had this good milk, better than what you get in the city. It wasn't watered down. So we loved it out there, at least the kids did.

"The mayor lived right below us, and he had nine kids. He loved us kids. I mean, he was really good to us." Liz continued, "A funny story was we were all running around barefoot because the shoes we had, we had to save them. We played with the mayor's kids. In Germany the chickens ran everywhere. Mom said that the mayor told her to come down to his house around noon. She wondered what had happened. The mayor said, 'I want you to watch what Liz does.'"

Liz laughed. "Well, the chicken would go into the outhouse every day around noon and lay an egg." The mayor explained he saw Liz go into the outhouse every day at noon. He found out Liz would go in after the chicken laid the egg and take it home to her mom to cook. The mayor said not to mention it to Liz, because he got such a kick out of watching her coming out of the outhouse with the egg.

After the war, in 1945, "when we still lived out in the country, the Americans came with their tanks. They came through the middle of the village to search the houses. They stayed there overnight. They came in and had the things to see if anything was buried. It was the first time I had ever seen a black person, other than the chimney guy who cleaned the chimneys. It was cold and raining outside when they came in. My mom asked, 'Are you hungry?' So she made a Bavarian dish made with eggs—*pfannkuchen* and fruit, which was all they had." Pfannkuchen was similar to a pancake, but not as sweet.

"All the other rooms were locked up, and the house had really nice, shiny white doors. So we are not speaking English, and they are not speaking German, and it is hard to communicate with them. There were five guys staying with us, and they asked her what is here and here, and my mom said, 'Nix, nix,' which they knew meant no. My mom didn't want to get in trouble with the woman who owned the house."

The soldiers didn't like the fact that there were all these rooms and her mom and the kids were only in two rooms. "We were all sleeping in one bedroom. The soldiers were all staying all night too." The soldiers may have also wondered if there were other people hidden in the other rooms.

"The soldiers were not being mean to us or anything. They were really nice to us. It was more like, 'Why are you all living like this when there are all these rooms?' Mom dried their clothes." Her mom said, "I have two boys, and you never know where they may be someday. I hope someone takes them in."

The American soldiers kicked the shiny white doors open and went into the other rooms. They found jars of food that the farm woman had canned. Liz said, "They said, 'Come on, babies, look at this food,' and they made us eat it." Liz laughed. "My mom was about to have a heart attack, as she never wanted to take advantage of anybody. So we sat down and ate, and they [the soldiers] ate with us. They stayed all night, and when they left the next morning they waved and hugged us. They also said, 'Go, go upstairs.'" *Maybe they left us something*, five-year-old Elisabeth thought. When they went upstairs, under the pillows were Hershey bars and other things. "They were nice guys; they really were.

Back home in Augsburg

"We walked on the autobahn with a wagon of our things—dishes and things. We didn't have much to take back home." When they returned to their home in the city, all the windows were blown out, and they had to replace them. Liz remembered, "My dad had been in and out of the house, trying to repair the damage from the bombing." The town of Augsburg had been bombed because there were many factories there, including a U-boat engine factory. Augsburg was a very old city located in Bavaria, sixty miles northwest of Munich, Germany.

Liz said there was rationing in place too. Because there were six kids in the family, they didn't have the money to get some of the stuff. Her mom would trade with other families to get a little bit of food. "My mom would just walk away and say she wasn't hungry. I know she was hungry, but there wasn't enough to go around. And my dad wasn't the kind to say, 'I'll give you some of mine.' He just wasn't that type." Liz's parents were Theresa and August. They were orphans. By the age of six or seven, they had been by themselves, given away to farmers to work.

After the war Liz's mom found her sister and brother. Her mom's sister lived in the mountains. Some of the kids went to visit her. Her brother lived in East Germany. With a visa secured by Liz's mom, he came for a visit to Liz's family and never returned to East Germany. "He had money in the soles of his shoe, since he was only supposed to bring a certain amount of money with him to West Germany," said Liz.

Her German friend Gerda married an American soldier during WWII. When Gerda first came to America, she couldn't believe all the food at Kroger. She was afraid something would go wrong or something might happen to her family in Germany while she was in America. Liz and Gerda's children grew up together.

Many years later Liz married an American soldier and moved to America. "My husband would say, 'Thanks for the good meal.'" She said, "You are working and putting the food on the table. I never heard my dad say anything like that to my mom."

Food from the American soldiers

The Americans used the Drei Mohren Hotel since the German barracks were damaged by bombing. Liz said, "That's when the fun started. At four o'clock, when the soldiers got done eating, what they had left they threw out. The German people would go in and get what was left." Liz said, "My mom said, 'I would like to try that sometime.'" Liz said she would go with her mom to try it. She recalled, "I didn't have a chance. People were just running over me, I remember that.

"This one guy, I assume that he was a cook, as he had an all-white uniform on, he saw me not getting anything. I saw these donuts, and I wanted to get one. I remember today when my kids would ask me what kind of doughnut I want, it flashes back to that time when it didn't matter what kind it was. I just wanted one.

"So he took me out of the mess, where everyone was fighting. My mom was a little lady too." Liz's mom said, "I don't think this is a good idea for us—we are going to get killed here."

Liz continued, "She had a bag that she was going to put the food we were going to get in, but we didn't get anything. So the guy picked me up and put me over to the side, as he said, 'No good for baby.' In other words, you have no business over there! So he said, 'One minute. Wait here.' He came out with a big brown bag. There were all kinds of foods in there. It was the first time I had ever seen a banana. I didn't even know what it was."

There was Spam and all kinds of food. The cook said, "Tomorrow, don't go over there. You come here." Finally there was food for the family. "We did that for a couple days, and Mom said, 'I feel bad taking it all the time. What can we do for him?' So she asked him if he needed his washing done. The cook said, 'Yeah.' So her mother took his clothes and washed them for him as payment for the food he was giving the family. Mom would scrub his clothes on the table and hang them in the kitchen to dry and try to press them. She and Liz would return the clothes when they went to get more food. "Then one day we found a little gold chain in his uniform, and we opened it up and found a little girl with curly hair about my age. We thought that was why he gave us the food. He was thinking of his little girl.

"We did that for quite a while. Then one time he said, 'No more. I go to America,' and he had tears in his eyes. He will always be in my mind, because he nearly saved us! All the Americans were good to us, especially to the kids. When you see the movies, you think, shoot, I was one of them!

Collecting tobacco

"My dad smoked a pipe, and every other day we kids had to go uptown and pick up the cigarette butts. Then we would go home and open them up. If we had a good day, we had a day off. If we had a bad day, we had to go another day. My sister hated it, because my dad was short tempered if you didn't do what he said to do. So she would say to me, 'I do the dishes all week if you will go with dad.' I didn't care and was ready to go outside."

There was a small PX in the middle of Augsburg. There was a guy smoking a cigar, and he flipped the ring around the cigar onto the ground. "Well," said Liz, "I went after it and put it on my finger. You know kids. He looked at me and said, 'Hey!'" She thought, *Well, you didn't want it...*"He went into the PX and got me a whole carton of Hershey bars—not just one but a whole carton! You never had any toys or anything, so these little things meant a lot to you.

"I almost got hit by car one time when a guy threw out a cigar, and I charged for it." She laughed. Liz was a spunky little girl!

Christmas 1941 – left to right – Anna, Theresa (mom), Wally, Elisabeth (dad's lap), August (dad), Gottfried, August Jr.

For Christmas when Liz was about eight years old, she was chosen to get some gifts from an American soldier. The children went to a large gymnasium where there was a huge Christmas tree, and she received a china tea set. "I'm Dreaming of a White Christmas" was playing. "To this day, when I hear that song, I think of that American soldier," she said.

She went on to explain, "We got hot chocolate to drink, a cookie, and a candy bar. Anything that I could save, I would put in my bag and take home to share with the rest of the family. I couldn't save the hot chocolate; I had to drink it."

There was a playground where Liz played with her best friend, Renate, who also moved to the United States. Renate lives in Arizona now. They always said they would stick together. Their playground was the shells of houses that were bombed out.

Another Christmas memory: "My brother brought home three American soldiers for Christmas. He was supposed to only bring one home, but he said there were three left, and he couldn't choose just one of them. Later the American soldiers returned in a cab and brought gifts for the family. They brought a set of dishes for my mom that she never used. She put them in the cabinet and saved them." The dishes were very special to her mom. The soldiers brought gifts to the rest of the family too. Today Liz never passes up a donation kettle. She recalled being one of those kids who didn't have anything. "We are spoiled and wasteful today," said Liz.

When did you get married?

At the age of twenty-three, Liz married an American soldier and came to America in 1962. She and her husband, Richard, had four children. Her husband is no longer living. She still Facebooks some of her husband's friends who served with him. Ironically, Richard was the last person to see Liz's mother before she passed at age eighty-three. Her husband was in Germany with the air guard during his time. Liz had her ticket to go to Germany but was a couple of weeks late to see her. Her mother was very fond of Liz's husband.

Liz said, "I never dreamed when I was a little girl that when I grew up, I would live in America." In America she worked for Packard Shirt for about twelve years; it was owned by a Jewish man, Ed Wormers from Chicago. Liz thought it was ironic that she, a German, would work for Ed, a Jewish man. "He was the best guy I ever worked for," she said.

Pearl Harbor Seventy-Fifth Anniversary

This interview was conducted on December 7, 2016. "The war was terrible," said Liz. "I think people need care. It doesn't go away. Today, when I see fire, I still remember that woman standing there in front of her home in her nightgown and her hair was loose. All I could think was, she went crazy because she had lost everything. That's what those soldiers go through. Soldiers need help."

Christmas Day 2016

Amazingly, on Christmas Day 2016, the city was evacuated after workers constructing an underground parking garage found a 1.8 ton British aerial bomb. It was defused, and fifty-four thousand people were allowed back in their homes. Much of Augsburg's historic city center had been destroyed on February 25–26, 1944, by Allied bombing. It was determined to be a British-made bomb that had been dropped on Augsburg during the war but hadn't explode.

Philip Joseph Scaffidi
By Eleanor Scaffidi Collcsano

Philip was born on February 5, 1902, in San Piero Patti, Sicily, near Messina, to Carina and Joseph Scaffidi. He was one of nine children. Of his nine siblings, Anthony, Philip, Charles, and Biagio moved to America. His brother Russell immigrated to South America.

"My father said he was in the Italian army," said Eleanor. "I have no data; however, he stood face to face with Mussolini. At that time he admired Mussolini for building schools and making housing available to the common person. All of this was prior to Mussolini becoming friendly with Hitler."

He came to America in early 1920, after being picked in a lottery. He traveled by way of a large ship; his voyage lasted thirteen days and nights. He did not enjoy the trip, as he was seasick the entire time!

"There was an illness onboard that caused the ship to be diverted to Philadelphia rather than Ellis Island, New York," said Eleanor. His aunt (his mother's sister) and uncle (his father's brother) had settled in Buffalo, New York, some years prior, and he went to live with them.

His uncle, a construction laborer, helped him obtain a job within the construction industry. "My father was a bricklayer and stonemason by trade, which he learned growing up in Sicily," said Eleanor. "When he was a young boy, he would skip school to watch the men work, and he picked up the desire and talent for his trade. He was immediately recognized for his work ethic and talent. He built many structures of various sizes and shapes; however, he specialized in building fireplaces, many of which still stand today.

"During his career he worked for many major construction companies as well as handled man side jobs on his own. Even after his retirement from the bricklayers' union, he would still receive and accept calls from the major companies.

"He did not have a formal education as we know it today. He would say he went as high as the third grade in Sicily. However, I am not sure how that compares to our third-grade level or what he meant exactly. He had an amazing ability to understand math and perform complicated math equation in his head, in order to perform his trade.

"January 10, 1927, he married my mother, Ida Incavo. Ida, born in America, to two Italian immigrants, was the youngest of six children." In 1928 they started their family with their first child, Mildred. Their second child, Joseph, was born in 1929. Their third child, Philip, was born in 1938, and their youngest child, Eleanor, was born in 1940. Since I was the youngest child, I cannot talk about the years before my time, other than the discussions at home.

"My mother encouraged my father to go to classes to learn English. She was concerned about stigma the family would get because he was from Sicily. It was very common in those days to carry a negative stigma if you were unable to speak English. [During WWII some Americans may have had a negative feeling about someone from Italy; even though he had not lived in Italy for several years.] He attended some classes and learned enough of the English language to get by but never mastered the language. Many times he would combine English and Italian words, but again was able to get by and communicate effectively with his broken English. My mother never allowed him to speak Italian at home; consequently, none of his children learned the Italian language other than a few words or phrases.

"My father lived the American dream. He became a US citizen; his personality, talent, honesty, ethics, and hard work made him a very proud and successful man! He passed all of that on to his children."

Acknowledgments

Dr. Mark Browning, Evansville Wartime Museum, Evansville, Indiana

The Eakle, Francis, McDonald, Meier, and McGregor families for searching their archives for information and photos.

Former Senator Richard Lugar, The Lugar Center, Washington, DC

C. Ray Minton Jr., husband, chauffeur, and encourager

Diane and Marion Meier, Evansville, bed-and-breakfast accommodations, editing text

Amy Cooley Pitcher, book formatting and editing advice

All my friends, my mom, my sister, my brother, and my children for encouragement and stories

Women factory workers for recalling all the happy and unpleasant times of their lives

WWII veterans—this book would not be possible without your memories

Epilogue

There is no better way to thank a WWII veteran, or any veteran, who has put his or her life on the line for America than to say, "Thank you for your service."

WWII veterans were not the only people who helped win the war for America's freedom. So did the dedicated men and women who were left at home and worked in the factories, ordnance facilities, and shipyards. Soldiers couldn't fight without weapons and supplies that were made on the home front in various cities in our nation; only a few were highlighted in this book.

The WWII families left at home sacrificed luxuries—sugar, coffee, tires, gasoline, and nylons—so our boys would have what they needed to fight our enemies—Germany, Japan, and Italy.

Thank you for reading, *WWII Heroes: They Were Only Doing Their Jobs.* My life has been enriched by listening to and recording these special WWII veterans, both firsthand and posthumously via their families. They are all heroes, and many of them are now my friends!

God bless America
Linda Minton

Dick Beeson, Robert Pedigo and C Ray Minton Jr.

Men Who Worked in Ordnance Plants

Estel L. Harshman—Kingsbury Ordnance Plant, Knox, Indiana
Robert Pedigo—Naval Ordnance Plant, Indianapolis, Indiana

Stories of Men, Women, and Children during WWII

Ivan Andrijiwskyj—Ukrainian citizen forced to fight for
Germany Elisabeth Ford—German child
Maria Lewcun—Ukrainian citizen
Philip Joseph Scaffidi—Italian Army
Stephanja Szahaj—Lived in displaced persons camp
Petro (Peter) Szahaj—Conscripted in the German army

WWII-Era Women Who Contributed to the War Effort

Erelene Brown—American schoolgirl
Beryl Chatterton—British citizen
Bobbie Downey—American schoolgirl
Jane Eberhart—WWII Nurse
Mildred Ginger—WWII factory worker
Dorothy Gillette—Navy wife
Carmen Greenfield—Navy wife
Patricia Marcelle Hawn—Australian War Bride
Anna Johnson-Serval—WWII P47 wings worker
Su Lautzenheiser—Army wife, airplane factory worker
Martha Leffler—Naval Ordnance Plant (Naval Avionics)
Kew Bee McDonald—American schoolgirl
Florence Miller—Evansville Navalyard
Connie Norlin—State Dept. in Washington, DC
Bernice S.—American Legion secretary, army wife
Dorothy Wahnsiedler—LST factory worker
Lucy Wahnsiedler—WWII factory worker
Emma Weber—WWII factory worker

INDEX

F

G

H

I

J

K

L

M

N

O

P

Q

R

S

V

W

X

Y

Z

Soldiers and their cars—

Gib Coleman

A few good cars —

Don Kuhlenschmidt

Many wonderful veterans!

Richard Kolodey

Bibliography

Websites

1. **www.armedforcesmuseum.com/norden/bombsight**. Last modified January 26, 2012.
2. **www.368THfightergroup.com**. Accessed March 25, 2017.
3. **www.alaforveterans.org**. Accessed February 1, 2017.
4. **www.atterburybakalarairmuseum.org**. Accessed January15, 2017.
5. **www.brittannica**. World War II, John Graham Rayde-Smith, Accessed Feb. 12, 2017.
6. **www.defensemedianetwork.com**. Accessed March 26, 2017.
7. **www.evansvillemaritimemuseum.org**. Accessed March 25, 2017.
8. **www.greenbrier.com**. Accessed February 1, 2017.
9. **www.historynet.com**. Accessed March 24, 2017.
10. **www.history.state.gov**. Accessed March 24, 2017.
11. **www.indianahistory.org**. Accessed March 23, 2017.
12. **www.indyhonorflight.org**. Accessed April 16, 2017.
13. **www.indianamilitary.org**. Revised September 8, 2016.
14. **www.indianapublicmedia.org**. Accessed April 16, 2017.
15. **www.loc.gov**. Accessed February 3, 2017.
16. **www.lstmemorial.org**. Accessed June 17, 2016.
17. **www.militaryhistorynow.com**. Accessed March 25, 2017.
18. **www.navsource.org**. USS Lejeune (AP-74), Last modified December 2, 2016.
19. **www.portlandtribune.com/pt/9.news**. December 5, 2016, Lyndsey Hewitt
20. **www.substreet.org/kingsbury-ordnance-works**. Accessed December 19, 2016.
21. **www.ussindianapolis.org**. July 15, 2016.
22. **www.u-s-history.com**. Accessed March 25, 2017.
23. **www.ussmissouri.org**. Accessed March 2, 2016.
24. www.ussvi.org. (for submarine veterans) Accessed September 12, 2015.
25. **www.vfw.org**. Accessed June 15, 2016.
26. **www.visitevansville.com**. Accessed March 27, 2017.

27. **www.visitindy.com**. Accessed March 27, 2017.
28. **www.warbirdalley.com**. Accessed June 18, 2016.
29. **www.womenofwwii.com**. Accessed March 27, 2017.

Magazine and Journals

1. *Binghamton Press*, March 26, 1946.
2. *Indiana History Magazine,* 110 September 2012, Kingsbury Ordnance Plant, Turk, Katherine, "Black Women, War Work, & Rights Claims at the Kingsbury Ordnance Plant."
3. Indiana History Museum, Vincennes, Indiana
4. *Star and Stripes*, July 25, 2014.
5. Stevens Point Journal, August 10, 1990.

Museums

1. Wright Patterson Air Force Museum, Dayton, Ohio
2. Indiana History Museum, Vincennes, Indiana. Visited July 2017.

Made in the USA
Lexington, KY
17 September 2017